GD-10089

hw.d
graphic-design
communication
hw.design gmbh
Türkenstraße 55-57
80799 München

D1617788

RotoVision

The European Design Annual 4

EDA

The European Design Annual 4

A RotoVision Book
Published and Distributed by RotoVision SA
Rue Du Bugnon 7
CH-1299 Crans-Près-Céligny
Switzerland

RotoVision SA, Sales & Production Office
Sheridan House, 112/116A Western Road
Hove, East Sussex BN3 1DD, UK

Tel: +44 (0) 1273 71 60 27
Fax: +44 (0) 1273 72 72 69
e-mail: sales@RotoVision.com

Copyright © RotoVision SA 1999

All rights reserved. No part of this publication
may be reproduced, stored in a retrieval system
or transmitted in any form or by any means,
electronic, mechanical, photocopying, recording
or otherwise, without permission of the
copyright holder.

The photographs used in this book are
copyrighted or otherwise protected by legislation
and cannot be reproduced without the permission
of the holder of the rights.

10 9 8 7 6 5 4 3 2 1

ISBN: 2-88046-395-5

Book design by Navy Blue Design Consultants

Production and separations in Singapore by
ProVision Pte. Ltd.
Tel: +65 334 7720
Fax: +65 334 7721

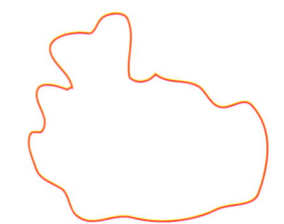

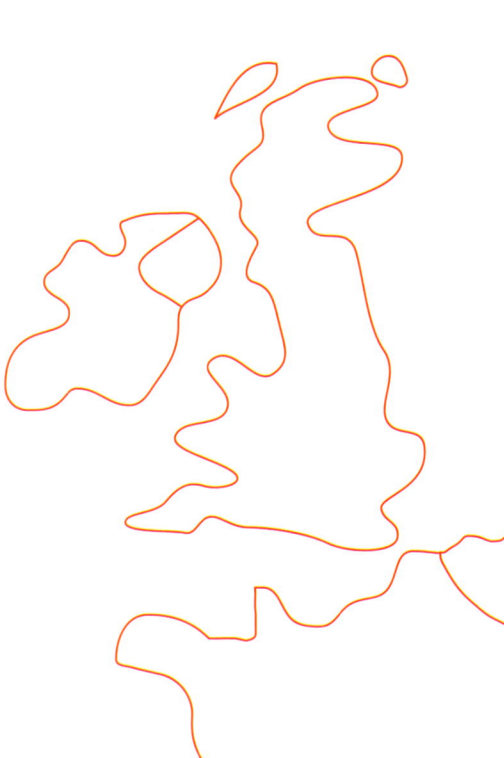

Acknowledgements

A project the size and breadth of the European Design Annual requires assistance from many people and organisations, and RotoVision would like to sincerely thank the following people for making the fourth European Design Annual such a success:

Andy Kner, Carol Stevens, Tim Rich, Kehrt Reyher and Olaf Stein, the five jury members, for their co-operation and enthusiasm in judging thousands of pieces of artwork during one short but very full weekend, and for all their help and advice throughout the year; Sarah Jameson for turning a logistical challenge into a tangible result (promoting the Annual across Europe, liaising with entrants in 24 countries, hosting the judging and archiving the work) and Alex Matwijiszyn who not only put on a marathon show of over 1000 slides for the jury, but has cheerfully assisted with the Annual in innumerable other ways over the last 12 months. Pat and Simon Jameson, Amy Davies and Nick Anderson for helping to make the judging weekend run so smoothly; Simon Hennessey for his tireless help on all manner of production and database matters; Tomasz Sobecki of IDEA98/99 and Jan Grabialo for putting on the first exhibition of winning European Design Annual works at the State Art Gallery of Torun, Poland, in April/May 1999; the team at Print Magazine who have been unerringly helpful throughout the year (we are very pleased to have their continued collaboration and support with the European Design Annual); Clare Lundy at Navy Blue Design Consultants for designing this book and the whole Call for Entries promotion for the fifth Annual.

Finally, we are grateful to the following people, associations and magazines for all their help and advice in promoting the European Design Annual to designers in their countries:

Advertising Association of Sweden
Acta Graphica magazine, Croatia
Allianz Deutscher Designer, Germany
Art Directors Club für Deutschland
ADG/FAD/Art Directors Club of Spain
Art Directors Club Schweiz
Association Design Communication, France
Associação Portuguesa de Designers, Portugal
Barcelona Centre de Disseny, Spain
Beroepsorganisatie Nederlandse Ontwerpers, The Netherlands
British Design & Art Direction, UK
British Design Initiative, UK
Buchhandlung Lia Wolf, Austria
Bureau of European Design Associations
Bruil & van de Staaij, The Netherlands
Creative Club Austria
Centro Portugues de Design, Portugal
Creative Review magazine, UK
Croatian Designers Society
Design Austria
Design and Applied Arts Index (DAAI), UK
Drustvo Oblikovalcev Slovenije, Slovenia
Etapes Graphiques magazine, France
Föreningen Danske Designere, Denmark
Föreningen "O", Sweden
Föreningen Svenska Tecknare, Sweden
Grafill, Norway
Grafia Ry, Finland
Hungarian Advertising Association
IDEA98, Poland

Index Book, Spain
Institute of Creative Advertising & Design, Ireland
Institute of Practitioners in Advertising, UK
João Mario de Silva, Portugal
Jump Magazine, Italy
Kodia Photo & Graphis, Slovenia
Kopp Fachbuch und-Medienversand, Germany
LineaGrafica magazine, Italy
Lithuanian Association of Graphic Design
MM magazine, Slovenia
Media Polska magazine, Poland
Navy Blue Design Consultants, UK
Packaging Design Association, France
Page Magazine, Germany
Platforml Illustratoren, The Netherlands
Rat für Formgebung, Germany
Slovensko Oglasevalsko Zdruzenje, Slovenia
Society of Typographic Designers, UK
Struktur Design, UK
TegneCenter, Denmark
Vormberichten magazine, The Netherlands

RotoVision SA
Publishers
April 1999

The European Design Annual 4

Introduction	04	Creative Futures	133	
Creative Distinction Awards	05	The Almighty Euro	134	
		Distant Relations	138	
Austria	10	Russian Eclectic	142	
Belgium	14	Far From Ephemeral	146	
Croatia	16	Klein Aber Fein	150	
Denmark	18	Icelandic Saga	156	
Finland	22	Spanish High	160	
France	24			
Germany	28	Winners Directory	165	
Hungary	48			
Ireland	50			
Italy	52			
Lithuania	60			
The Netherlands	62			
Norway	70			
Poland	72			
Portugal	80			
Russia	Belarus	86			
Slovenia	88			
Spain	92			
Sweden	98			
Switzerland	106			
Turkey	110			
United Kingdom	112			
Yugoslavia	130			

A note on the Gazetteer: the listings at the front of each country's section are a new departure for the European Design Annual. We have aimed to select the more quirky or unusual places that may be of interest to designers on their travels around Europe. We are very grateful to Pentagram for allowing us to make use of their great little book, Feedback, for some of the entries. If you would like to make any recommendations for next year's Annual, please write to Sarah Jameson at the RotoVision address opposite and we will try and include them.

We are grateful to Print Magazine for allowing us to reprint the articles at the back of this book.

Europe
Population | 1000 **872**.9
Design Population | 1000 **251**.9

The European Design Annual began in 1995 as a joint venture between RotoVision SA and Print Magazine of America. Aiming to bring together the best in contemporary graphic design across Europe, the Annual has steadily grown in size and influence over the last 4 years, and is sister to Print Magazine's own North American Regional Design Annual. Graphic design work is invited from graphic designers all over Europe every year, and an international jury convenes each Autumn to select the best work from each country for inclusion in the Annual. Work is judged country by country, regardless of category, and this is how you will find the work displayed in the following pages. This is the fourth European Design Annual featuring almost 500 pieces of winning graphic work from 24 European countries.

Area 1000 k/m2

Austria	**083**.9	Hungary	**093**.0	Russia	Belarus	**17,075**.0	**207**.6
Belgium	**030**.5	Ireland	**070**.3	Slovenia	**020**.3
Croatia	**056**.5	Italy	**301**.0	Spain	**505**.0
Denmark	**043**.1	Lithuania	**065**.2	Sweden	**450**.0
Finland	**338**.0	The Netherlands	**041**.5	Switzerland	**041**.3
France	**552**.0	Norway	**324**.0	Turkey	**779**.2
Germany	**357**.0	Poland	**313**.0	United Kingdom	**243**.3
		Portugal	**092**.4	Yugoslavia	**103**.2

Introduction | Tim Rich

Tim Rich, a contributing editor of Print and former editor of Graphics International, has been actively involved with the European Design Annual since its inception in 1995, serving as a judge for the competition, an insightful reporter, and a primary editor of the articles section. He is a London-based columnist for Design Week and an editorial and design consultant for British Telecom, Bass breweries, and PhotoDisc.

Welcome to the only Annual devoted entirely to European graphic design.

Many design awards spend years honing their judging criteria to a fine pitch. This is admirable and can help raise important issues. It may even help improve standards. But there is no holy grail of objectivity for an awards scheme. With this in mind, the Print European Annual does not pretend to be a scientific analysis of European graphic design. As we declared in the very first Annual and each year since, our intention is to assess the work submitted to find examples that we consider excellent, unusual, innovative, controversial, entertaining, or just plain brave. To sum it up in one word, we want to discover the "remarkable" from the selection before us.

We do, however, carefully consider ways the judging can be improved. This year, it was strengthened by increasing the number of judges to five. This initiative reflects the growth of the project and helps to bring fresh perspectives to the judging process. The three judges who worked on the annual in 1995, 1996, and 1997—Print's art director, Andrew Kner, Print contributing editor Carol Stevens, and I—were joined by Olaf Stein and Kehrt Reyher. Stein is a founding director of one of Germany's most admired design companies, Factor Design. Based in Hamburg, the consultancy has had many items selected for this Annual in previous years. It has enjoyed great success in international awards schemes and had five pieces selected in the 1998 German Prize for Communications Design competition. Reyher is publisher of the highly influential Media Polska magazine in Poland. He is also one of the owners and organizers of Kreatura, Poland's top advertising creativity awards scheme, and is publisher-in-chief of Marketing Polska and OKO Photo Quarterly. Media Polska is an award-winning publication and has been one of the most successful entrants into this Annual in previous years.

This year's entries came from 24 countries: Austria, Belarus, Belgium, Croatia, Denmark, Finland, France, Germany, Hungary, Ireland, Italy, Lithuania, the Netherlands, Norway, Poland, Portugal, Russia, Slovenia, Spain, Sweden, Switzerland, Turkey, , United Kingdom and Yugoslavia. We viewed the work in a space close to the offices of RotoVision (co-sponsor of the Annual) in Brighton, England. The entries for each country were laid out on tables and the judges toured the tables separately, nominating work for inclusion with markers. We then came together as a group and walked around, discussing nominations and other points or issues that arose. When necessary, staff from RotoVision were on hand to assist with translations and contextual information. Judges were, of course, excluded from voting for their own work.

In previous years, I have offered an impressionistic country-by-country sweep of the collection of entries. The Annual has now reached a size and diversity that precludes such an offering. Suffice to say, we witnessed an extraordinary collection of work, some of it poorly constructed, some simply unimaginative, but the vast majority considered and well-produced. Sitting above this, we found many entries marrying imagination and fine execution. Every country produced a number of excellent items and some—particularly Germany, France, Portugal, and Slovenia—contributed a body of work that was (for me) one level up from their entries in previous years.

What we determined to be the most interesting work is shown on the following pages. I think you'll find some gems there.

One point of interest: Although we did not actively request Web sites or CD-ROMs, we received a significant number of them. We can only imagine how many such projects will be entered if we actively pursue these categories next year. Discussion and debates in the industry about creative standards in digital design, and the judging criteria needed for such work, rage on. We applied our existing judging principles to this area but assessed the work back in our own offices. Away from the intense time pressures of a two-day judging session, we were able to explore fully the architecture and interactivity of the work. Personally, I think the Web is a crucial new agent in the development of contemporary design. Some dismiss it as a faddish toy that promotes superficial design thinking, but I believe that engaging with the three-dimensionality of the medium will expand and increase our understanding of traditional print design media and what it takes to be a meaningful and effective designer. I welcome Web design to the Annual.

On a different note, it is always interesting to see recurring visual motifs in the entire body of work entered. My previous bête noire, images of businesspeople shaking hands, has almost entirely disappeared. Indeed, there were far fewer figurative shots. Instead, I noticed an increasing use of images from the natural world. There were 11 instances of nautilus seashells, numerous water and whirlpool images, and several chickens. Cocks and hens were, however, overrun by pigs, who were definitely the stars of the graphic farmyard. Top marks to the designers who managed to get a pig onto a skateboard with no evidence of Photoshop. I have no problems with images of pigs. They're exceptionally intelligent creatures and considerably more photogenic than some of the boards of directors in Europe's annual reports. Exactly what the beach load of oceanic and aquatic imagery says about the European business environment is unclear; perhaps design output is reflecting a move toward softer values and an increasing propensity toward mild abstraction.

Two days of judging and discussion completed, I asked the panel to nominate their personal "star" of the show. Fuelled by a box of delicious Belgian biscuits, we sat down to clarify our thoughts.

Olaf Stein selected the fashion literature produced for Uns & Outros by Portuguese consultancy Ricardo Mealha Atelier. The work embodied a strong overall showing by Portugal, and, Stein noted, demonstrated fine handling of both retro and contemporary esthetics—a sort of graphic remixing.

Carol Stevens chose a poster by João Machado for Papeis Carreira featuring leaf symbolism—one of a series for the company by this acclaimed Portuguese designer. "Simple, fun, effortless," in Stevens's words.

Kehrt Reyher selected posters by Swiss designer Niklaus Troxler for the Jazz in Willisau festival. "You see a lot of posters for jazz and music, but this is just excellent simplicity," said Reyher.

Andrew Kner chose the series of advertisements for British book chain Waterstone's by TBWA GGT Simons Palmer, London. "They are conceptually very clever," remarked Kner of the attention-grabbing poster ads.

And though I was tempted by the excellent record sleeve work out of Portugal, I plumped instead for an annual report for a German bank, VVBS Vereinigte Volksbanken. Designed by the impressive Maksimovic and Partners in Saarbrücken, the report epitomizes every aspect of annual report excellence. It even achieved the extraordinary feat of making the directors look genuinely happy to be pictured.

What united all of the judges was the enjoyment of seeing such a volume of excellent work. I think you'll find a collection of diverse and dynamic graphic design work on the following pages; I certainly hope you see something remarkable.

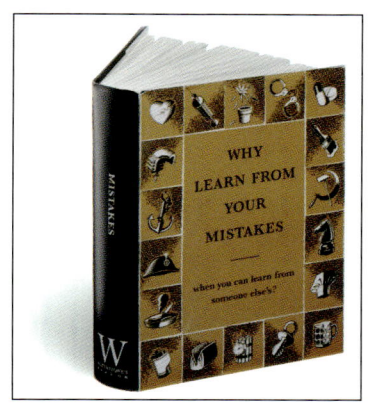

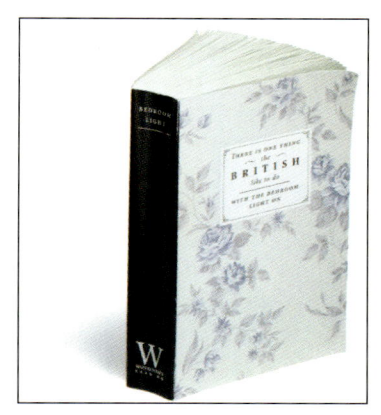

Creative Distinction Award | TBWA GGT Simons Palmer, London, UK

Following the 2-day judging session, each jury member was asked to choose their own personal favourite from the thousands of pieces they had seen. Here you can see what each member of the jury chose; some brief thoughts from each judge on the entry in question; and a short explanation from the people behind the work.

Andrew Kner was born in Hungary, and after moving to the United States became Executive Art Director at the New York Times in the 1970s. He left to join Backer & Spielvogel as Senior Vice President and Creative Director and later joined RC publications as Creative and Art Director of Print Magazine. A winner of over 150 awards for design and art direction, his posters are part of the permanent collections of the Museum of Modern Art, the Smithsonian and the Louvre. He served as President of the New York Art Directors Club from 1983 to 1985.

"I fell in love with this series of posters on reading because they originally fooled me so completely. The book jacket theme is so slyly executed that I originally thought they must be jackets of real books. The humour, both graphic and verbal, is irresistible. I think that any book jacket designer would blush with shame on seeing how completely the genre has been satirized".
Andy Kner

"Our brief was to create a series of advertisements that would differentiate Waterstone's from other book shops and convey the feeling that books are more than a mere commodity to them. We created a campaign that pointed out this passion for books, using insights that might serve as a reminder to those who've forgotten about books and reading, while displaying an empathy for those who haven't. The problem then was to create as distinct a look as possible for the campaign. Designing the ads as book covers achieved this, and obviously could not have been more relevant. It meant that the options for each in terms of typography and illustration or photography were infinite, but it would still be instantly recognised as part of the Waterstone's campaign".
TBWA GGT Simons Palmer

Ad campaign for Waterstone's Booksellers

Agency TBWA GGT Simons Palmer
Art director Paul Belford
Copywriter Nigel Roberts
Typographers Alison Wills, Paul Belford, Nigel Ward, Alan Dempsey
Photographers Laurie Haskell, James Nachtwey, Joel-Peter Witkin, Glen Erler
Illustrator Ian Wright

Creative Distinction Award | João Machado, Porto, Portugal

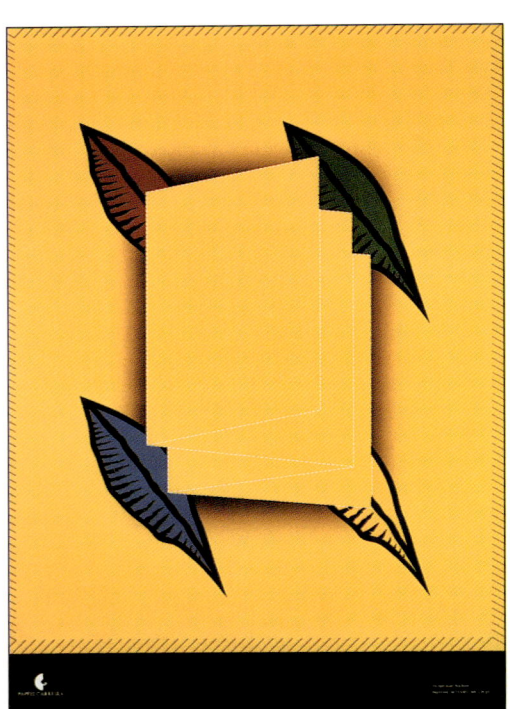

Carol Stevens Studied at the Univeristà degli Studi in Florence, Italy, and graduated from Smith College with a major in Art History. She joined Print Magazine in New York where she served as managing editor and writer. She has written articles for the Encyclopedia of World Art, the French publication, Connaissance des Arts, and several editions of Print casebooks. She is currently a contributing editor to Print.

"João Machado's posters for the Carreira Paper Company are eloquent in their simplicity. Each design, celebrating one of the four seasons, also hints at what's to come. Cold white leaves blowing across autumn's vibrant red; the azure of a Mediterranean winter sky holds in its yellow leafy overlay the sunny promise of spring; spring's green showers predict the red of summer heat; and summer's gold embraces all others. Leaves. Paper. Paper for all seasons".
Carol Stevens

"I always like to use good, bright colours with an airbrush, and pastels for the softer effects. The simple, clearly defined forms are achieved by cutting out bold paper shapes and arranging them again and again until I reach the desired effect. In this instance, the client was a paper company, Papéis Carreira, and I was invited to produce a set of posters that showed how their paper could be used for different purposes (stationery, books, wrapping paper &c). I was given total freedom to design these four posters, and they were also used to illustrate the company's annual report".
João Machado

Promotional posters representing the seasons for Carreira Paper

Design firm João Machado Design LDA, Porto
Designer/illustrator João Machado
Client Papéis Carreira

Creative Distinction Award | Maksimovic & Partners, Saarbrücken, Germany

Tim Rich is a design writer and editorial consultant. He is a contributing editor to Print, a columnist for Design Week and a consultant to a number of companies, including Bass plc, BT, PhotoDisc and ICO. Previously, he was the Editor of Graphics International and Ads International magazines, and the UK correspondent for the Dutch creative arts magazine, Blad.

"Most reports are so dull. Often it's because they've been stifled by the personal and professional limitations of the people–both clients and designers–involved. I suppose 'dull' is the right approach for some organisations, but I'm not interested in investing in or working with unimaginative companies. That's why this annual report, for German bank Vereinigte Volksbanken, epitomises annual report excellence for me.
The designers made me want to read the copy and think about the company. I liked the way it conveyed energy and confidence. The report has stayed in my memory. And it even achieved the extraordinary feat of making the directors look genuinely happy to be photographed".
Tim Rich

"The brief was to design the 1997 Annual Report for Vereinigte Volksbanken (United People's Bank) and it was to celebrate the 125th anniversary of the bank. The client gave us a lot of freedom, which was important for making this project a success. They were not even disturbed by us using punching and embossing techniques on the normally 'serious' financial review facts and figures section!"
Maksimovic & Partners

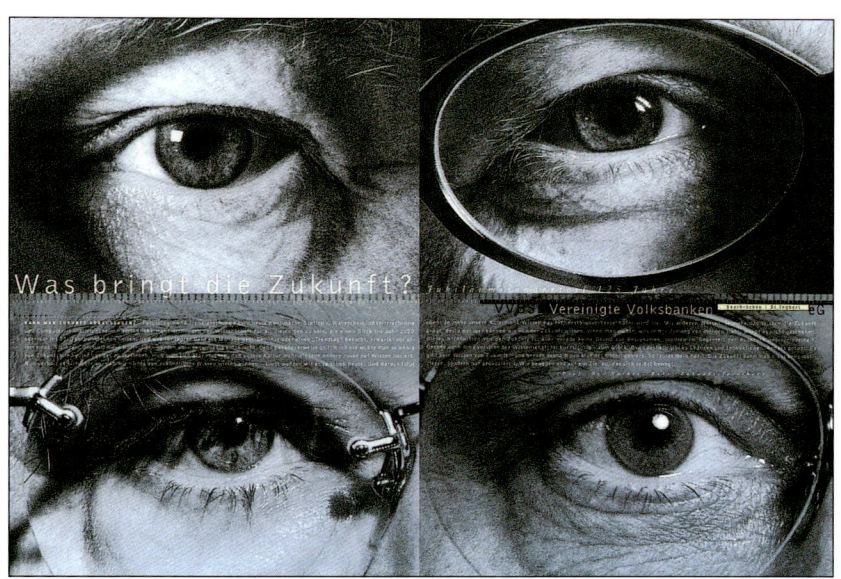

1997 Annual Report for a bank

Design firm Maksimovic & Partners, Saarbrücken
Art directors Ivica Maksimovic, Patrick Bittner
Photographer Gerd Westrich
Client Vereinigte Volksbanken, Saarbrücken

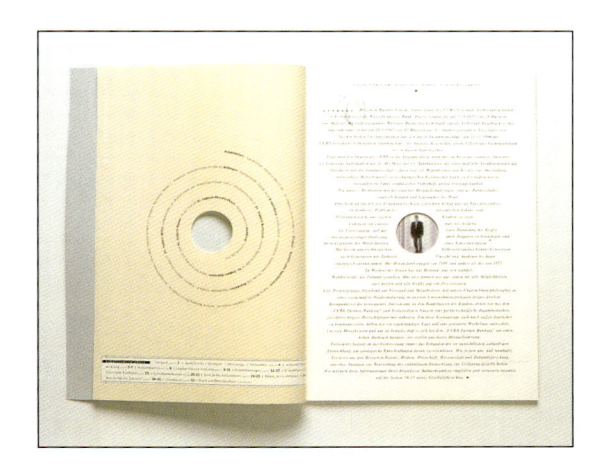

Creative Distinction Award | Ricardo Mealha Atelier, Lisbon, Portugal

Olaf Stein is a founding director of one of Germany's most admired design companies, Factor Design. Based in Hamburg, the consultancy has enjoyed great success in international awards schemes.

"I selected the fashion literature produced for Uns & Outros because the work demonstrated fine handling of both retro and contemporary aesthetics–a sort of graphic remixing. I particularly liked the colour palette of the piece and really enjoyed the Sixties approach. I was astonished that the design firm is from Portugal".
Olaf Stein

"We are a young team and have been involved in many cultural, fashion and product projects. One of the most important things about the Uns & Outros project (for a new male shoes label) was the trust and freedom the client gave us right from the start. The client brought us the product, and, together, we defined the strategy and target. There were very few changes made to the first concept and the effort involved in working on the brief was rewarded with the fun we had doing it. We pictured the hypothetical consumer to be simultaneously elegant and sober and we had to appeal to masculine taste. Usually, these kind of labels have a face, but instead of using the human model, we decided to relate the product to a certain lifestyle and ambience by using graphic elements, forms, colours and words. We chose brown and grey, and stripes (a sign of the male universe) and played around with different fonts and font sizes".
Richardo Mealha

Brochure and stationery for a shoe manufacturer

Design firm Ricardo Mealha–Atelier, Lisbon
Art director Ricardo Mealha
Designer Ana Margarida Cunha
Client Uns & Outros

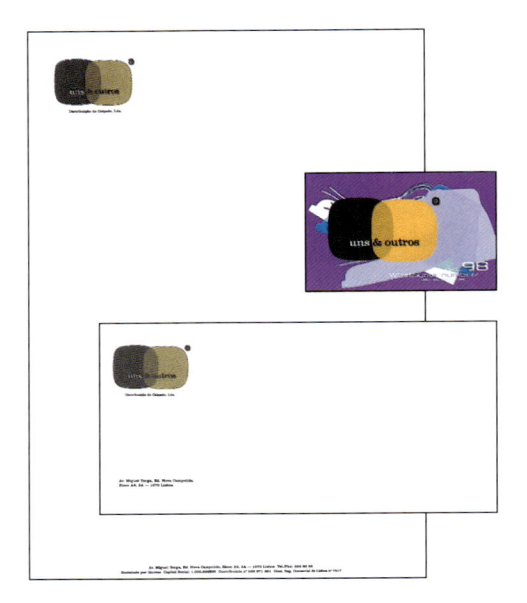

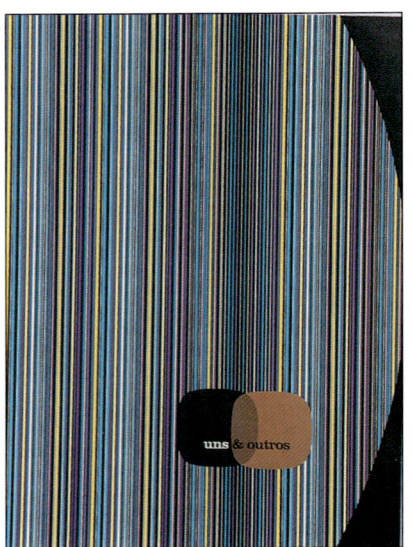

Creative Distinction Award | Niklaus Troxler, Willisau, Switzerland

Kehrt Reyher is the publisher of the highly influential Media Polska magazine in Poland. He is one of the owners and organisers of Kreatura, Poland's top advertising creativity awards scheme, and is publisher-in-chief of OKO Photo Quarterly.

"You see lots of posters for jazz and music, but you can sum these posters up in just two words– excellent simplicity".
Kehrt Reyher

"I feel a poster has to have a personal style and convey an artistic message. Personal interpretation is all important. Moreover the design of a poster has to be true to the medium, and it's essential I create 'a Poster'. The solution, really, is simplicity. The secret is to rely on my own curiosity and let myself be carried away, always trusting that my taste and sensibilities don't allow banality. Message has priority over form, creativeness over aesthetics and expression over perfect design".
Niklaus Troxler

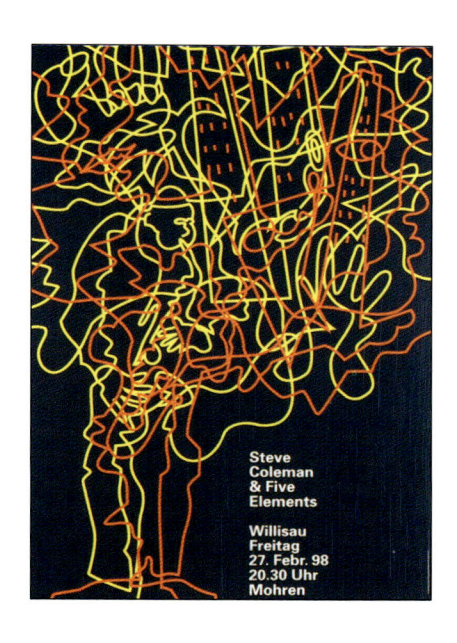

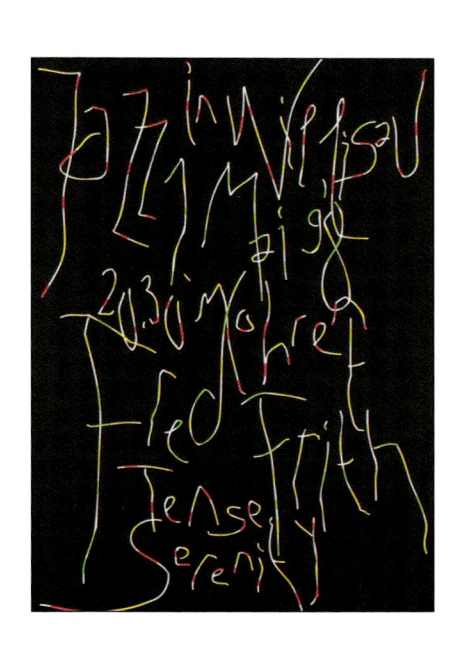

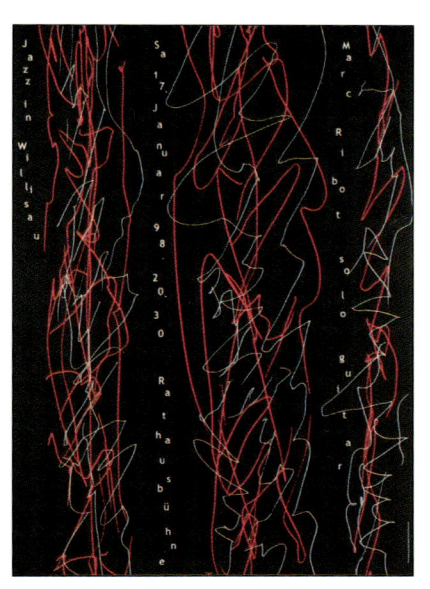

Posters for a jazz festival

Design firm Niklaus Troxler Design, Willisau
Designer Niklaus Troxler
Client Jazz in Willisau

Gazetteer

Hotels

Martinspark Hotel
Mozartstrasse 2
Dornbirn
T +43 5572 3760
F +43 5572 376
A good half way stop-off between Zürich and Munich, in the centre of Dornbirn, on the Swiss / Austrian border is this excellent private hotel, opened in March 1995.

Restaurants & Bars

The American Bar
Kartnerstrasse 4
Vienna
Adolph (ornament is crime) Loos was not only Austro-Hungary's sharpest architectural critic, he was also the first designer to be able to give luxury a modern form.

Tiergarten
Schönbrunn Palace
Schönbrunner Schlosstrasse
Vienna
T +43 1 877 9294
Houses Europe's oldest menagerie, established in 1752 for courtly amusement. An extensive assortment of animals can be viewed from the original Baroque enclosures.

Museums & Galleries

Graphische Sammlung Albertina
Inner City
Augustinerstrasse 1
Vienna
T +43 1 53483
Internet:
http://www.2.telecom.at/albertina
The largest collection of graphic art in the world, the Albertina holds over 44,000 drawings and approx. 1.5 million prints, not to mention maps, posters, playing cards, 15th-century printing blocks and a huge library of books.

Josephinium
Institute for the History of Medicine
University of Vienna
9, Wahringer Strasse 25
Vienna
On the first floor of a grand, late 18th-century house, built by Joseph II, is an astonishing display of life-size wax anatomy specimens.

Uhrenmuseum
Schulhof 2
Vienna
T +43 1 533 2265
A wonderful collection of clocks and watches in a tiny baroque house. Try and be around when they all strike noon. Next door to an interesting toy and puppet museum.

Bookshops

Buchhandlung Lia Wolf
Bäckerstrasse 2
Vienna
T +43 1 512 4094
For graphic design books.

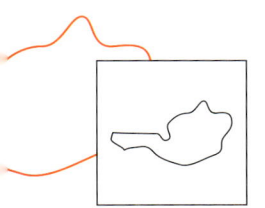

Austria

Austria
Local name   Oesterreich
Coordinates   47 20 N, 13 20 E
Population | 1000   8,134
Design Population | 1000   002.5
Languages   German
Capital   Vienna
Monetary unit   Austrian schilling (AS)

Area 1000 km	2				
Belgium	**030**.5	Hungary	**093**.0	Russia	Belarus	**17,075**.0	**207**.6
Croatia	**056**.5	Ireland	**070**.3	Slovenia	**020**.3
Denmark	**043**.1	Italy	**301**.0	Spain	**505**.0
Finland	**338**.0	Lithuania	**065**.2	Sweden	**450**.0
France	**552**.0	The Netherlands	**041**.5	Switzerland	**041**.3
Germany	**357**.0	Norway	**324**.0	Turkey	**779**.2
		Poland	**313**.0	United Kingdom	**243**.3
		Portugal	**092**.4	Yugoslavia	**103**.2
083.9					

1 Promotional book for Heson
Design firm Createam, Linz
Art director Sabine Scherhaufer
Photographer Thomas Smetana

**2 Identity materials for
Manic Botanic, a florist**
Design firm Heider & Klausner Atelier für Corporate Design, Vienna
Designer Heider Clemens

3 Business cards for Knut Klinger Studio
Designer Richard Bayer, Linz
Photographer Reinhard Mayr

4 Poster for Gruppe 80 Theatre
Designer Markus Göbl, Vienna

5 Invitation to a trade show for Engel, "Future Symposium, '97"
Design firm Projektagentur, Linz
Designer Richard Bayer
Photographer Paul Grebliunas

6 CD cover for Vienna Art Orchestra
Designer Elisabeth Kopf, Vienna

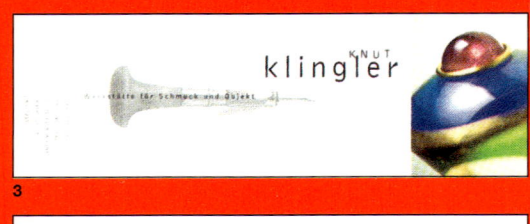

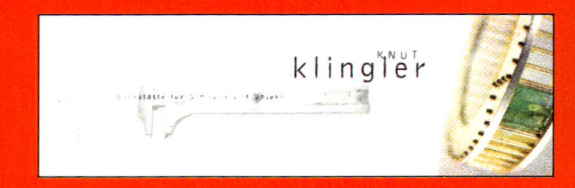

7 Logo for Brigitte Berger-Görlich, an opera singer
Art director/designer Robert Kaitan, Vienna.

8 Symbol for Rudolf Berger, director of the Opera du Rhin
Designer Robert Kaitan, Vienna

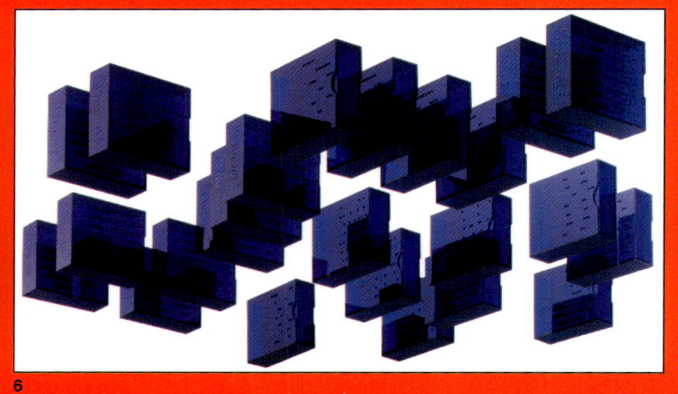

9 Promotional material for DesignerDock, a personnel recruitment agency
Art director/illustrator Stefan Gandl
Designers Stefan Gandl, Antje Booken
Copywriter Johanna Clausen
Photographer/concept Andrew Dewhirst

10 Promotional mailer for Artwork Werbe GmbH
Design firm Art & Joy, Vienna

11 Poster for Druck im 8'ten, a printer
Art director Lothar Ämilian Heinzle, Vienna

12 Cover of brochure for Jugend am Werk
Design firm Faschingbauer & Schaar Werbeagentur, Graz
Art director Roberto Grill
Creative director Siegfried Faschingbauer
Photographer Croce & Wir

13 Party invite for Ismirschlecht Music
Designers Richard Bayer, Astrid Bartsch, Linz
Photographer Thomas Smetana

14 CD cover for Mego Records
Design firm Inwirements, Vienna
Designer Tina Frank

15 Stationery for Norbert Rasp, a textile distributor
Design firm Caldonazzi Grafik Design, Frastanz-Amerlügen
Illustrator Wilma Zündel

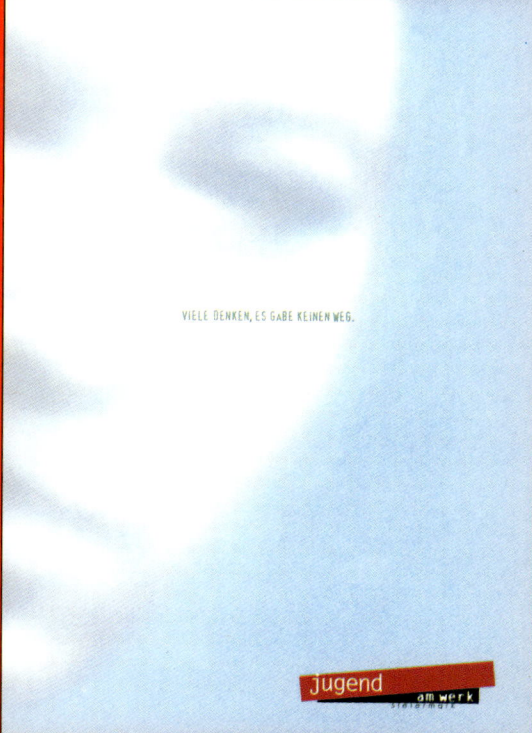

Austria 13

Gazetteer

Restaurants & Bars

Chez Jean
Rue des Chapeliers 6
Brussels
T +32 2 511 9815
Old-timer next to the Grand'Place has been serving good honest Belgian food for 65 years (shrimp croquettes, waterzooi, salmon-and-endives cooked with beer…)

Restaurant Christina
Napoleonkaai 45-47
Antwerp
T +32 3 233 5526
Enjoy a lunch of mussels (cooked in one of a dozen ways) in one of the small dockside restaurants in Antwerp at very modest cost.

Museums & Galleries

Museum Plantin-Moretus
Vrijdagmarkt 22
Antwerp
T +32 3 2330294
Christopher Plantin (1514-1589), was printer to King Philip II of Spain. The museum's rooms are hung with priceless works of art, but also include the original workshops, the type foundry and two of the world's oldest presses still in working order.

Victor Horta House
Amerikastraat 23-25
Saint Gilles
Brussels
T +32 2 537 1692
Victor Horta (1861-1947) the famous Art Nouveau architect designed many of Brussels' most beautiful buildings. This is his house, built in 1898 at the peak of his creative activity. Now a museum, it is one of Europe's best preserved examples of Art Nouveau architecture.

Centre Belge de la Bande Dessinée
(Belgian Comic-Strip Centre)
Rue des Sables, 20
Brussels
T +32 2 219 1980
In a splendid Art Nouveau building, this museum celebrates the comic strip and focuses especially on Hergé, Tintin's creator.

Places of Interest

The Fallen Angel
Jan Breydelstraat 29
Ghent
T + 32 9 23 94 15
A dream shop, selling artists' supplies long out of stock elsewhere.

Auberge du Moulin Hideux
Noirefontaine
Ardennes
T + 32 61 46 70 15
The charm of an old mill nestled away in its valley lost in the Ardennes forest. With private fishing and walks.

Belgium

1 Self-promotional 1998 calendar
Design firm Zizó!, Antwerp
Designer Jan Hendrickx

2 CD cover for Sony Music
Design firm Seven Productions, Wilryk
Designer/illustrator Sven Mastboons

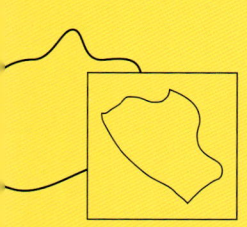

Belgium
Local name **Belgique/Belgie**
Coordinates **50 50 N, 4 00 E**
Population I 1000 **10,174**
Design population I 1000 **001**.0
Languages **Flemish, French, German**
Capital **Brussels**
Monetary unit **Belgian franc (BF)**

Area 1000 k/m2					
		Hungary	**093**.0	Russia I Belarus	**17,075**.0 I **207**.6
		Ireland	**070**.3	Slovenia	**020**.3
Austria	**083**.9	Italy	**301**.0	Spain	**505**.0
Croatia	**056**.5	Lithuania	**065**.2	Sweden	**450**.0
Denmark	**043**.1	The Netherlands	**041**.5	Switzerland	**041**.3
Finland	**338**.0	Norway	**324**.0	Turkey	**779**.2
France	**552**.0	Poland	**313**.0	United Kingdom	**243**.3
Germany	**357**.0	Portugal	**092**.4	Yugoslavia	**103**.2
	030.5				

Croatia Gazetteer

Museums & Galleries

St Mark's Church
Markov trg.
Zagreb
With its colourful painted-tile roof, this church houses the work of Ivan Mestrovic, Croatia's most famous modern sculptor.

Museum Mimara
Rooseveltov trg 5
Zagreb
One of the finest art galleries in Europe housed in a neo-Renaissance former school building. Houses the collection of Ante Topic Mimara, who spent most of his life in Austria, and donated nearly 4000 priceless objects to his native Zagreb. Closed Mondays.

Places of Interest

Mirogoj
20 minute ride on bus no. 106 from the cathedral. One of Europe's most beautiful cemeteries with English-style landscaping enclosed by a long 19th-century neo-Renaissance arcade. Some gorgeous mausoleums.

Euphraisan basilica
Porec
A world heritage site with wonderfully preserved gold Byzantine mosaics. Entry to the church is free, and for a small fee you can visit the 4th-century mosaic floor of the adjacent Early Christian basilica.

Bookshops

Algoritam
Gajeva 1
Zagreb
T +385 1 481 8674
For graphic design books.

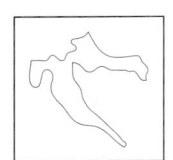

Croatia
Local name	Hrvatska
Coordinates	45 10 N, 15 30 E
Population I 1000	4,672
Design population I 1000	000.2
Languages	Serbo-Croatian, Other
Capital	Zagreb
Monetary unit	Croatian kuna (KN)

Area 1000 k/m2

Austria	083.9	Hungary	093.0	Russia I Belarus	17,075.0 I 207.6
Belgium	030.5	Ireland	070.3	Slovenia	020.3
Denmark	043.1	Italy	301.0	Spain	505.0
Finland	338.0	Lithuania	065.2	Sweden	450.0
France	552.0	The Netherlands	041.5	Switzerland	041.3
Germany	357.0	Norway	324.0	Turkey	779.2
	056.5	Poland	313.0	United Kingdom	243.3
		Portugal	092.4	Yugoslavia	103.2

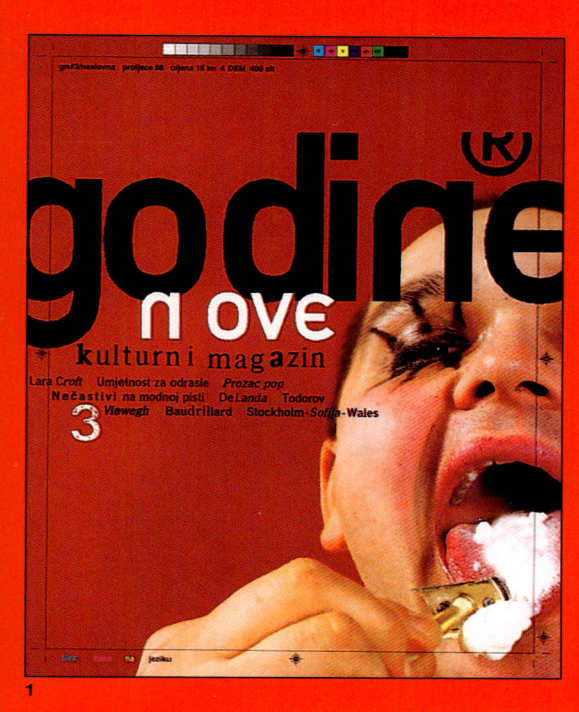

1 Cover of Godine Nove,
a culture/arts magazine
Design firm Sensus Design Factory, Zagreb
Designer Nedjeljko Špoljar
Photographer Renata Skrinar

2 1997 calendar for Croatia Airlines
Designer Ivana Ivanković, Zagreb
Photographer Damir Fabijanić

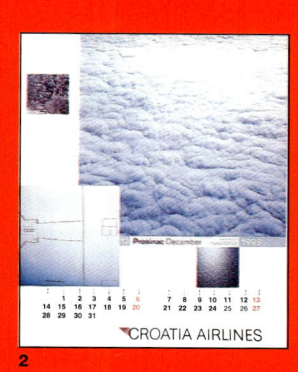

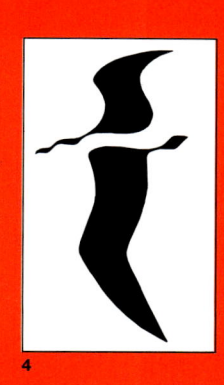

3 Logo for LC, a speech pathologist
Design firm Likovni Studio D.O.O., Sveta Nedelja
Art director Danko Jakšić
Designer Tomislav Mrčic

4 Symbol for Albatros, a travel agency
Design firm Likovni Studio D.O.O., Sveta Nedelja
Art director Danko Jakšić
Designer Tomislav Mrčic

5 Spread from Godine Nove magazine, about toy and model artists
Design firm Sensus Design Factory, Zagreb
Designer Nedjeljko Špoljar

6 Symbol for Varaždinske Toplice, a thermal springs spa
Design firm Likovni Studio D.O.O., Sveta Nedelja
Art director Danko Jakšić
Designer Tomislav Mrčic
Illustrator Takako Adachi

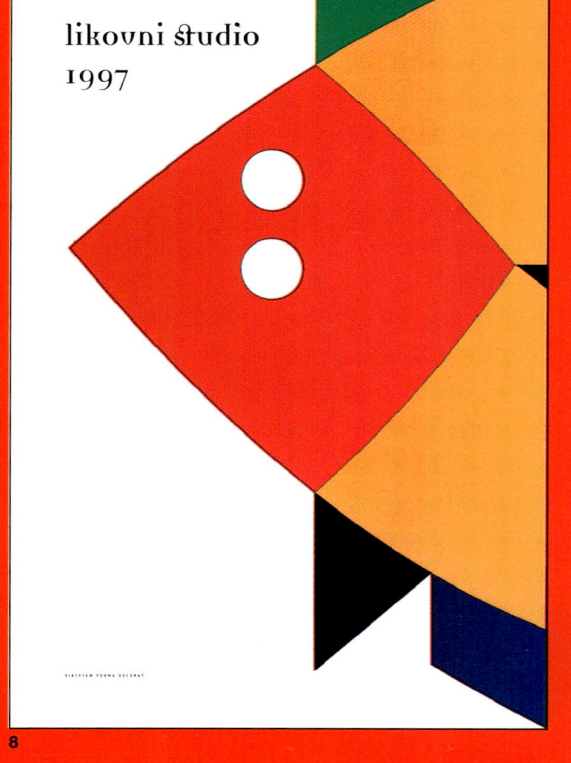

7, 8 Business card (Fig. 7) and annual report (Fig. 8) for Likovni Studio D.O.O., a design office in Sveta Nedelja
Art director Danko Jakšić
Designer Tomislav Mrčic

Croatia 17

Denmark Gazetteer

Hotels

Skovshoved Hotel
Strandvejen 267
Charlottenlund
Copenhagen
T +45 31 64 00 22
Originally a fisherman's pub, this small and unpretentious hotel in Copenhagen's leafy suburbs is near Arne Jacobsen's Klampenborg housing scheme of the early fifties. Eat in the elegant conservatory, or at the tiny thatched Restaurant Den Gule Cottage just a mile up the road (**T** +45 31 64 06 91).

Nyhavn 71
Copenhagen
T +45 33 11 85 85
In a 200 year old warehouse, this quiet hotel overlooks the old ships of Nyhavn. The maritime interiors have been preserved and the tiny rooms with warm woollen bedspreads and leather armchairs make for a cosy stay.

Restaurants & Bars

Lumskebugten
Esplanaden 21
Copenhagen
T +45 33 15 60 29
Pronounced 'Lom-ske-buk-ten', which roughly translated means 'Treacherous Bay', this is a wonderful restaurant near the harbour and old fortress serving marvellous seafood.

Museums & Galleries

The Viking Ship Museum
Strandegen
Roskilde
T +45 42 35 65 55
In the late fifties some amateur divers discovered some fragments which led to a major archaeological find. Five Viking boats were lifted, preserved and re-assembled and this exemplary museum was built to house and show them. A cafeteria overlooks the fjord.

Places Of Interest

Paustian
Kalkbraenderiløbskaj 2
Copenhagen
T +45 33 18 55 01
Denmark's most successful retailer of contemporary furniture has moved to a purpose-built showroom designed by Jorn Utzon in Copenhagen's Docklands. A perfect backdrop to view the best in Scandinavian design in acres of space. Excellent restaurant on the ground floor.

Bookshops

TegneCenter
Store Kongensgade 21
Copenhagen
T +45 33 63 90 33
For graphic design books.

Branners Bibliofil
Aps Bredgate 10
Copenhagen
The place for rare books in Copenhagen.

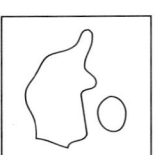

Denmark

Local name	**Danmark**
Coordinates	**56 00 N, 10 00 E**
Population l 1000	**5,334**
Design population l 1000	**000**.6
Languages	**Danish, Faroese, Greenlandic, German**
Capital	**Copenhagen**
Monetary unit	**Danish krone (DKr)**

Area 1000 km l 2

Austria	**083**.9	Hungary	**093**.0	Russia l Belarus	**17,075**.0 l **207**.6
Belgium	**030**.5	Ireland	**070**.3	Slovenia	**020**.3
Croatia	**056**.5	Italy	**301**.0	Spain	**505**.0
Finland	**338**.0	Lithuania	**065**.2	Sweden	**450**.0
France	**552**.0	The Netherlands	**041**.5	Switzerland	**041**.3
Germany	**357**.0	Norway	**324**.0	Turkey	**779**.2
Denmark	**043**.1	Poland	**313**.0	United Kingdom	**243**.3
		Portugal	**092**.4	Yugoslavia	**103**.2

1 Postage stamps for Post Danmark
Design firm Kontrapunkt AS, Copenhagen

2 Cover of Lige:nu, a magazine published by the Danish Equal Status Council
Design firm Hovedkvarteret APS, Copenhagen
Designer Lisbeth Høyer

3 Postage stamps celebrating the anniversary of the founding of the Danish Trade Unions
Design firm Kontrapunkt AS, Copenhagen

4 1997 annual report for the school Egå Ungdoms Højskole
Design firm DataGraf Auning AS, Auning
Designer Sidsel Gaustadnes
Photographer Joachim Ladefoged

5 Book published by Denmark's Royal Library and given to attendees at an International Library Conference held in Copenhagen
Design firm Kontrapunkt AS, Copenhagen

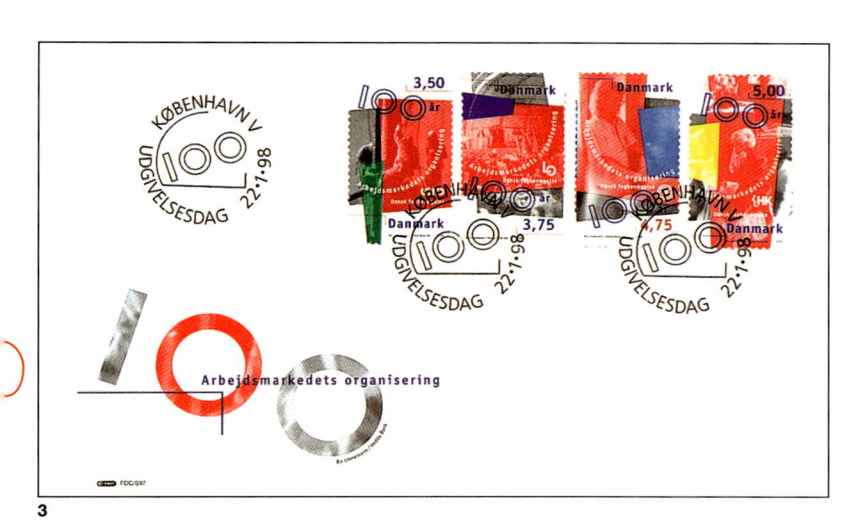

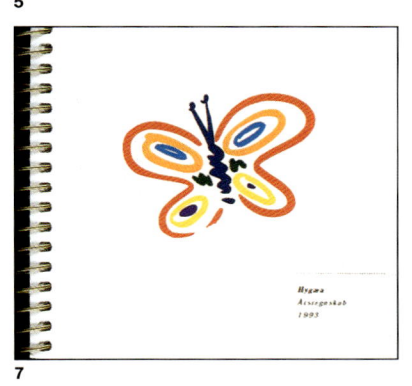

6 Symbol celebrating opening of a new wing of the Nordsømuseet (North Sea Museum), the world's second largest aquarium
Design firm Griffin Grafisk Design, Aalborg
Designer/illustrator Leo Griffin

7 Self-promotional brochure
Design firm Griffin Grafisk Design, Aalborg
Designer/illustrator Leo Griffin

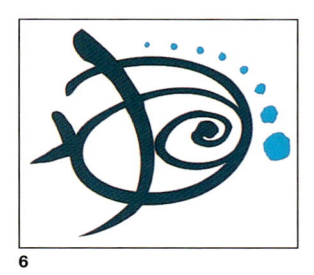

Denmark 19

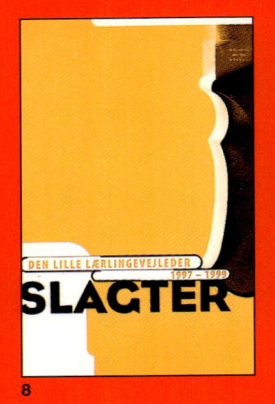

8, 9 Covers of apprentice guides published by the NNF, the Danish Food and Allied Workers Unions
Design firm Hovedkvarteret APS, Copenhagen
Designer Pernille T. Larsen

10 Self-promotional brochure for Kühnel Grafisk Design, Copenhagen
Designer Jakob Kühnel

11 Symbol for Jill Nørgaard, a "zone therapist"
Design firm Griffin Grafisk Design, Aalborg
Designer/illustrator Leo Griffin

12 Identity for the Cutty Sark '99 Tall Ships Races in Aalborg
Design firm Griffin Grafisk Design, Aalborg
Designer/illustrator Leo Griffin
Client Aalborg City Council

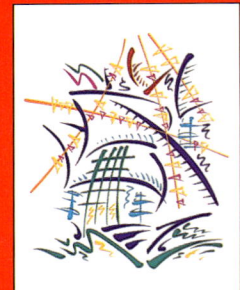

13 1997 annual report for DSB, Danish State Railways
Design firm Hovedkvarteret APS, Copenhagen
Designers Helle J. Eliasson, Maria Elskær

14-16 Identity for DSB, Danish State Railways
Design firm Kontrapunkt AS, Copenhagen

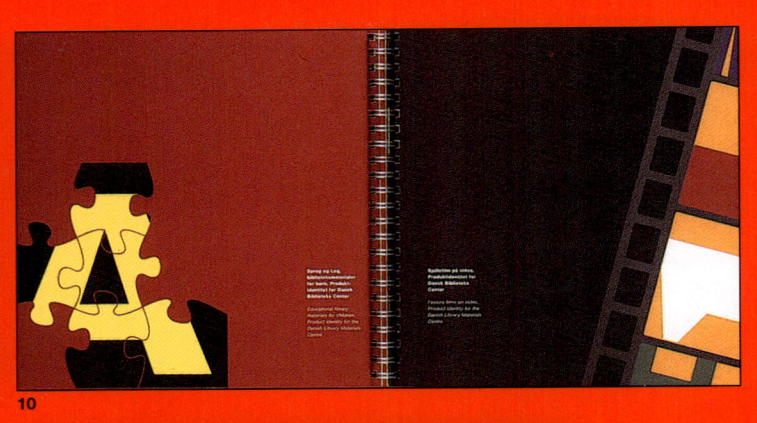

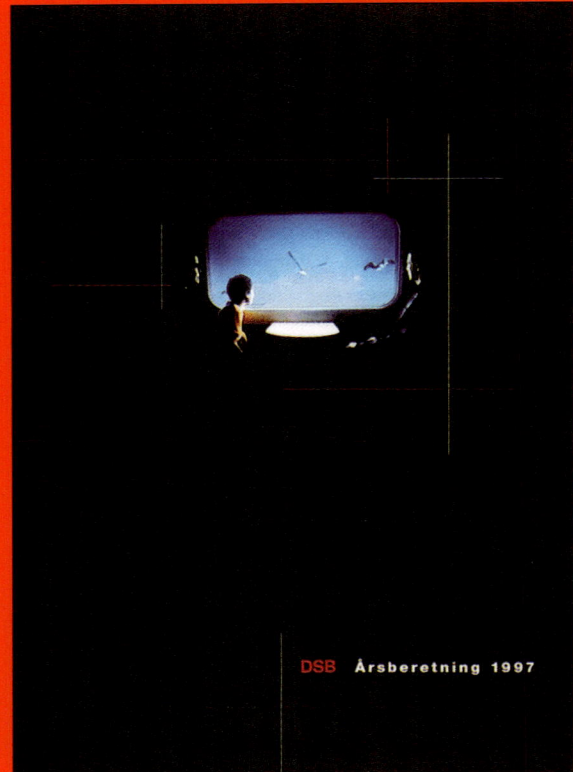

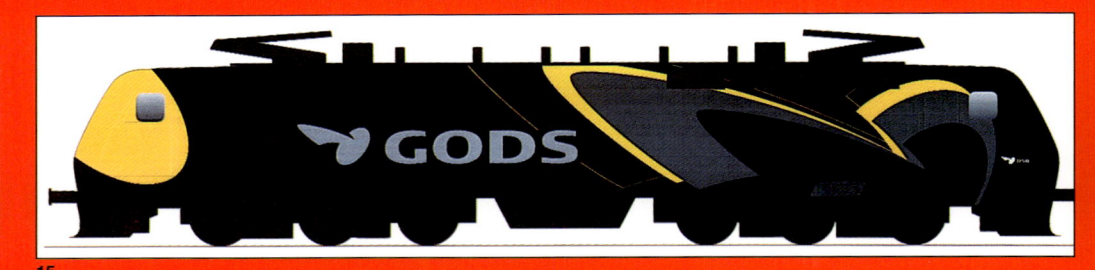

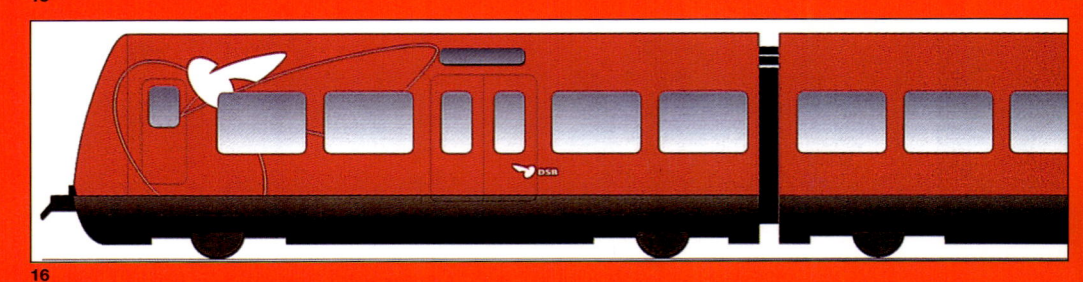

17, 18 Product brochure (Fig. 17) and catalogue (Fig. 18) for Fritz Hansen furniture designers and manufacturers
Design firm Kühnel Grafisk Design, Copenhagen
Designer Jakob Kühnel
Photography Piotr & Co.

19 Brochure showcasing lamp and lighting creations of ten designers
Design firm 2 x Brix Design, Copenhagen
Designers Mette Brix, Peter Brix
Photographer Sofie Helsted
Client Lysfortællinger

20, 21 Ads for José Cuervo Tequila
Agency Umwelt, Copenhagen
Photographer Sandra Greig
Client Better Brands

22, 23 Colour samplers for B.W. Wernerfelt, a textile company
Design firm Special Production, Copenhagen
Designer Flemming Hjartved

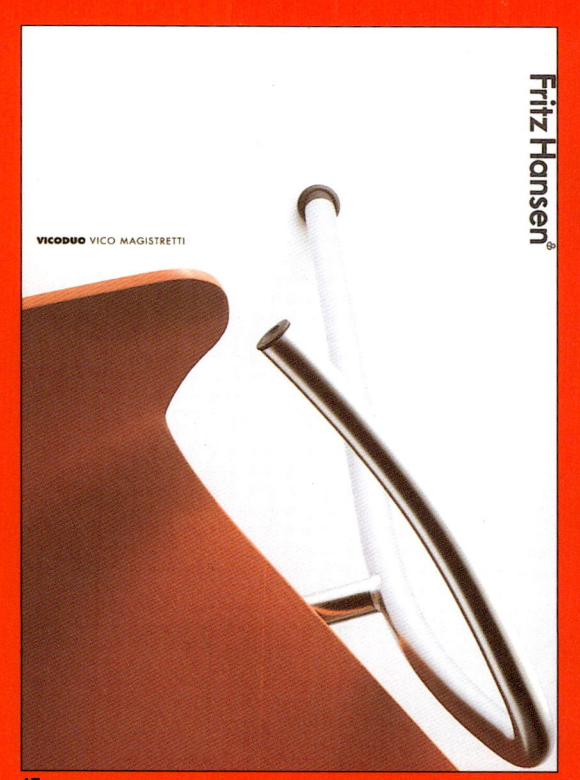

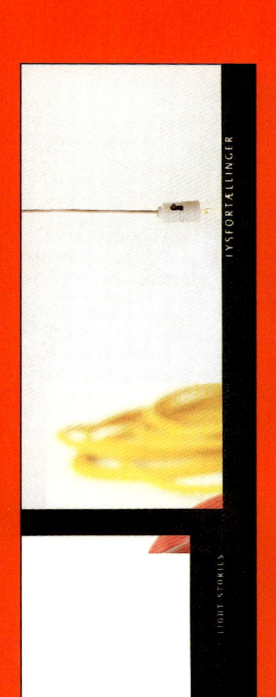

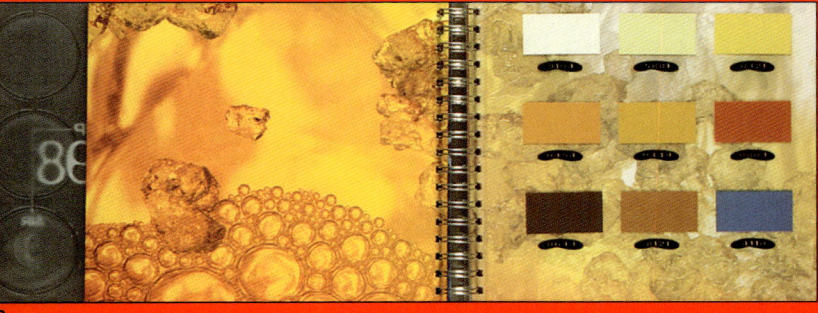

Finland Gazetteer

Restaurants & Bars

Kosmos Restaurant
Kalevankatu 3
Helsinki
T +358 9 647 2555
Without good food and decor, it is a wonder why local artists of all kinds nest and drink here. But they all do. Start your Helsinki orbit into Kosmos.

Kuu
Töölönkatu 27
Helsinki
T +358 9 2709 0973
For the true character of Helsinki, try simple, friendly and atmospheric restaurants like Kuu (moon), which has retained its local character and clientele. Finnish specialities served.

Maxill
Korkeavuorenkatu 4
Helsinki
T +358 9 638 873
Café-bar with a reputation for serving the best omelettes in town, in a lively and colourful street.

Places of Interest

Brando Seglare
Hylje
00570 Helsinki
T +358 9 684 8032
Middle-class yachting club in a middle-class garden suburb, at the water's edge on a rocky jet islet.

Uimahalli Yrjonkatu
Yrjonkatu 21 B
Helsinki
T +358 9 647801
Most visitors to Finland try the Finnish sauna in a hotel. Most Finns enjoy the sauna elsewhere, namely in their homes or in a public sauna. Public sauna number one, ambience-wise, is Yrjonkatu (George Street) Sauna with the beautiful large plunge pool featured in the Gorki Park murder movie.

Hvitträsk
Luoma, Kirkkonummi
T +358 2975 779
Site of a community founded at the turn of the century by Eliel Saarinen and fellow architects Gesellius and Lindgren. Superlative lakeside setting. Climb up to the cliff-top tomb of Saarinen after a good meal at the restaurant. 30km west of Helsinki.

Finland

Local name	**Suomi**
Coordinates	**45 10 N, 15 30 E**
Population | 1000	**857**.9
Design Population | 1000	**000**.9
Languages	**Finish, Swedish, Lapp, Russian**
Capital	**Helsinki**
Monetary unit	**Finnish markka (FMk)**

Area 1000 km | 2

		The Netherlands	**041**.5	Russia | Belarus	**17,075**.0 | **207**.6
		Hungary	**093**.0	Slovenia	**020**.3
Austria	**083**.9	Ireland	**070**.3	Spain	**505**.0
Belgium	**030**.5	Italy	**301**.0	Sweden	**450**.0
Croatia	**056**.5	Lithuania	**065**.2	Switzerland	**041**.3
Denmark	**043**.1	Norway	**324**.0	Turkey	**779**.2
France	**552**.0	Poland	**313**.0	United Kingdom	**243**.3
Germany	**357**.0	Portugal	**092**.4	Yugoslavia	**103**.2
	338.0				

1 Poster for theatre performance of Markiisitar de Sade
Design firm Taivas Oy, Helsinki
Designer Klaus Haapaniemi
Client Espoon Kesäteatteri

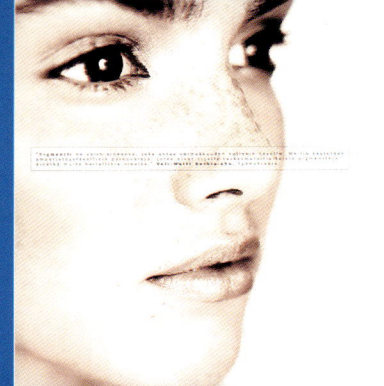

2 Promotional "Summer Book" for printer
Design firm Suunnittelutoimisto Kirnauskis Oy, Helsinki
Art director Jaana Puhakka
Photographer Kari Auvinen
Copywriter Sirkka Knuutila
Client Erweko Painotuote Oy

3 Annual report for printer
Design firm Taivas Oy, Helsinki
Art director Veli-Matti Hilli
Designers Elsa Hakala, Tarja Tervonen
Photographer Arne Pastoor
Client Erweko Painotuote Oy

Finland 23

Gazetteer

Hotels

Hotel Duc de Saint-Simon
14 rue de Saint-Simon
Paris
T +33 1 45 48 35 66
One of the most stylish and discreet hotels in Paris (and probably anywhere in Europe), on a quiet street off the Boulevard St. Germain. Enter through wooden gates into a cobbled forecourt and find a 17th-century mansion full of antiques. Unpretentious, but quite small and often booked up. A short walk away from some of the best cafés and jazz clubs in the city.

Restaurants & Bars

Café Charbon
107 rue Oberkampf
Paris
Typical Parisian café, and the perfect place to meet the young generation of artists, designers, photographers and architects who live and work nearby.

Le Petit Saint Benoit
Rue Saint Benoit
Paris
Small restaurant near the book shop La Hune (where you should go for the best books and magazines in town about design, graphic design, architecture and art). Straight, simple French food - and excellent value. Share one of the tables on the pavement outside on a sunny day.

Ice Cream Café
Rue St. Louis en l'Isle
Paris
At the west end of the street and simply the best ice cream in Paris

Auberge du Cep
Place Eglise, Fleurie
T +33 74 04 10 77
This smallish restaurant serves excellent food and, because it is in the middle of France's largest wine-growing area, it also has a remarkable wine list.

Museums & Galleries

Le Musée du Jardin Botanique
Cherbourg
The small 18th-century house standing in the garden contains a miscellaneous collection: butterflies, Chinese polychrome sculpture, Eskimo outfits, photographs of African queens and stuffed animals. Oddities and beautiful things.

Musée Historique des Tissus
34 rue de la Charité
Lyon
T +33 4 78 38 42 00
This Historical Textile Museum is housed in a charming 18th-century building and features two floors of fabulous fabrics–Coptic, Egyptian, Middle Eastern, Oriental as well as Italian, Spanish and the famous Lyon silks. Closed Mondays.

Places of Interest

La Maison de Verre
31 rue Saint-Guillaume
Paris
One of the most beautiful buildings in Paris designed by Pierre Chareau in 1931 and tucked away in a courtyard. Occasionally open to the public, but it is usually possible to sneak into the courtyard to take a look.

The Sunday market
Isle sur la Sorgue
A lovely town built on the river and a marvellous place to be on a warm Sunday morning. Take your pick from the hundreds of stalls selling everything from olive-oil soap to 38 kinds of goat's cheese.

Chateau Vignelaure
Rians
Aix-en-Provence
T + 33 94 80 31 93
Travelling through Provence do not forget to visit the little town of Rians, 39km east of Aix-en-Provence.

Marché Victor Hugo
Toulouse
One of the great covered markets of France still providing an astonishing display of the freshest food. High amongst the steel trusses of the roof structure are hidden the most secret collection of small café restaurants.

Bookshops

Galerie-Librairie Jacques Matarasso
2 rue de Longchamps
Nice
T +33 93 87 74 55
A small shop on a small Nice side street that's a veritable cornucopia of rare and interesting books. Picasso exhibited here in the 50s and there are some interesting prints for sale, some at bargain prices.

Interart
1 rue de l'Est
Paris
T +33 1 43 49 36 60
For graphic design books.

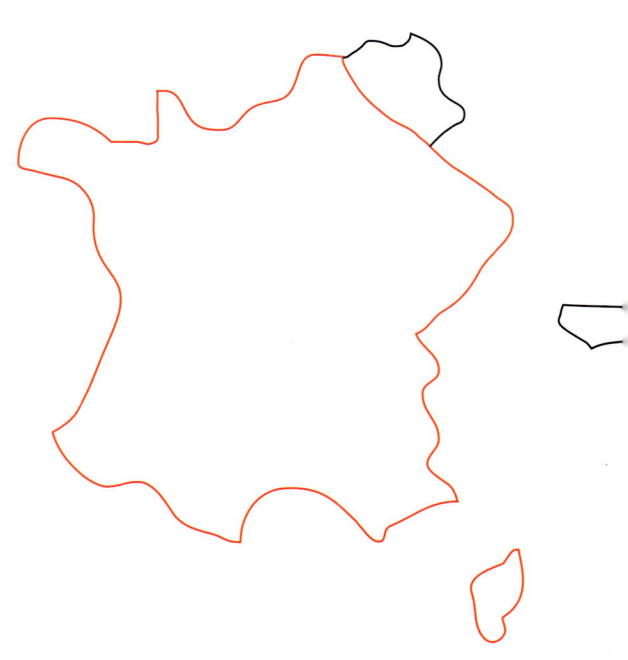

France

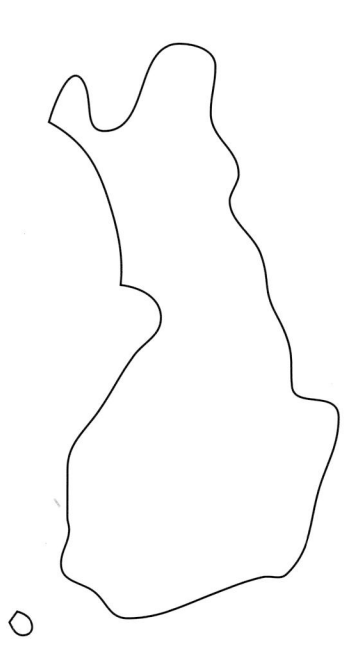

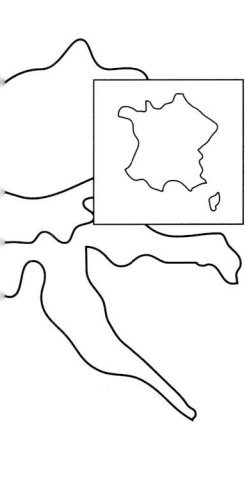

France
Local name | **France**
Coordinates | **46 00 N, 2 00 E**
Population | 1000 | **58,804**
Design Population | 1000 | **002**.0
Languages | **French**
Capital | **Paris**
Monetary unit | **French Franc (FF)**

Area 1000 km | 2

		Hungary	**093**.0	Russia	Belarus	**17,075**.0	**207**.6
		Ireland	**070**.3	Slovenia	**020**.3
Austria	**083**.9	Italy	**301**.0	Spain	**505**.0
Belgium	**030**.5	Lithuania	**065**.2	Sweden	**450**.0
Croatia	**056**.5	The Netherlands	**041**.5	Switzerland	**041**.3
Denmark	**043**.1	Norway	**324**.0	Turkey	**779**.2
Finland	**338**.0	Poland	**313**.0	United Kingdom	**243**.3
Germany	**357**.0	Portugal	**092**.4	Yugoslavia	**103**.2
France	**552**.0				

1 Spread from Iz (Trace), a book featuring the work of illustrator Selçuk Demirel
Designer/illustrator Selçuk Demirel, Paris
Art directors Selçuk Demirel, Pinar Kazma Çinar
Client Editions Yapi Kredi Yayinlari

2 Graphics manual for Berthoud, a plant-spray equipment manufacturer
Design firm O 'De Formes, Lyon
Creative director Thierry Batin
Photographer Philippe Le Du

3 Logo for Bad's restaurant
Design firm O 'De Formes, Lyon
Art director Thierry Batin
Designer Eric Lombard
Client Stemmelen

4 Type specimen of Le Monde type family
Design firm Porchez Typofonderie, Malakoff
Designer Jean-François Porchez
Client Le Monde newspaper

5 Spread from "Sous le Signe de L'Ange," a catalogue for a photography exhibition
Design firm Saluces Design & Communication, Avignon
Designer Jean-Paul Camargo
Photographer Alberto Terrile
Client Musée du Petit Palais

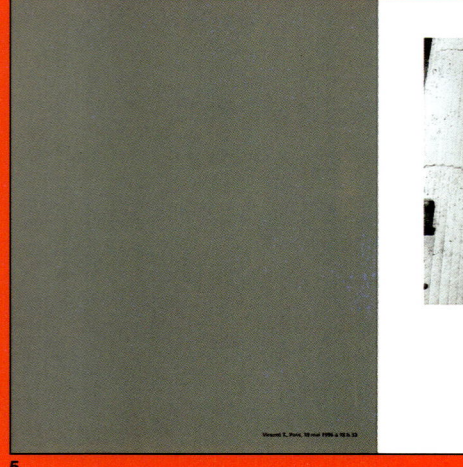

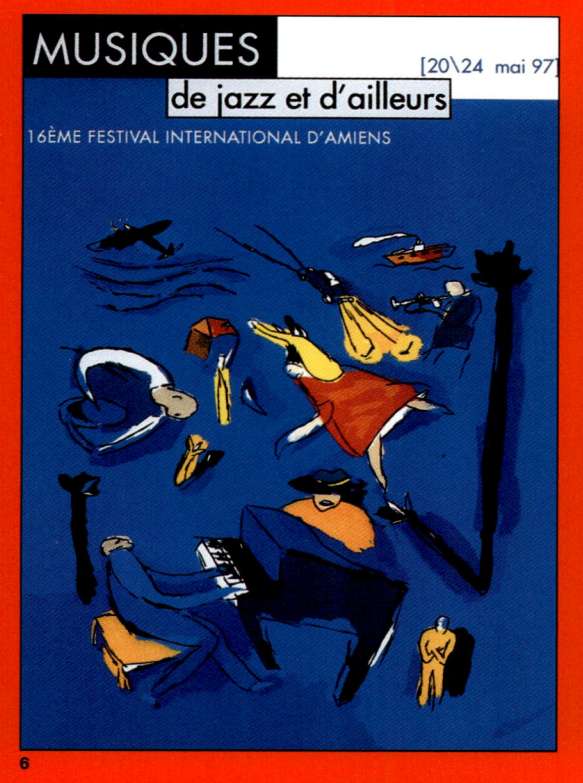

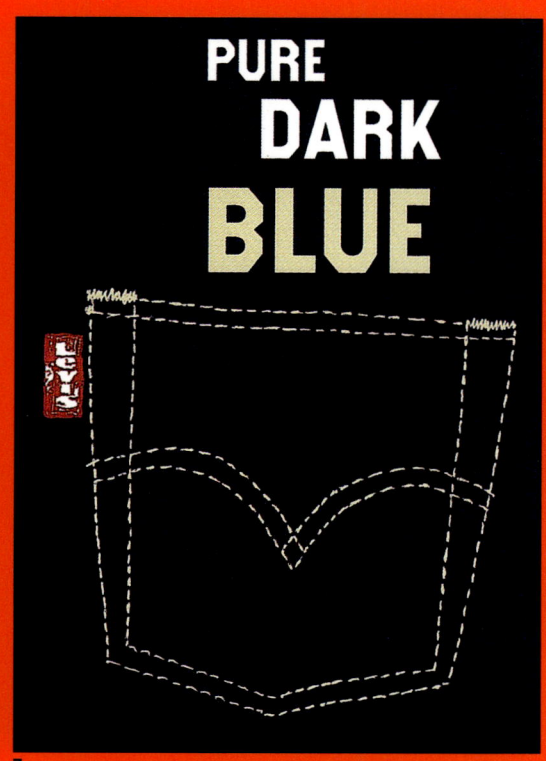

6 Poster for 16th International Amiens Jazz Festival
Illustrator Roger Patrice/De-Vi-Zu, Paris

7 Postcard for Levi's blue jeans.
Design firm Borgers Unlimited, Paris
Art director Marc Borgers
Client Levi-Strauss & Co.

8 Brochure promoting the attractions of the Charente region
Design firm Daedalus Design, Angoulême
Art directors Gérard Billy, Cyrille Bartolini
Designer Pascal Gautier
Photographer Gérard Martron
Copywriter Alain Blasi
Client Conseil Général de la Charente

9 Cover of exhibition catalogue
Design firm Alyen, Marseille
Art directors Didier Mazière, Hubert Campigli
Photographer Jean-Luc Mabit
Client Museon Arlaten/Musée Ethnographique

10 Illustration for Faits de·Sociétés magazine
Illustrator Philippe Mairesse/De-Vi-Zu, Paris
Art director Dominique Brudy

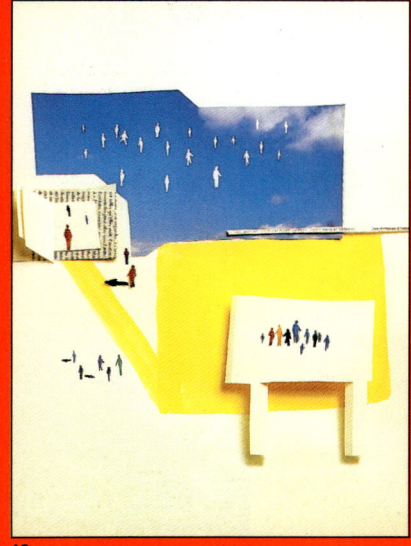

11 Party invitation for artists' agent De-Vi-Zu
Design firm Doctor Design, Paris
Art director Marc Charpentier
Designer/illustrator Daniel Boursin/De-Vi-Zu

12 Logo for Goutte d'Or, a film distributor
Designer Claude-Henri Saunier, Sainville

Gazetteer

Hotels

Hotel Sankt Nepomuk
Bamberg
One of the few towns saved from destruction during the Second World War. Many architectural wonders. A small hotel at the brow of a little island where the waters rush by. Family run. Don't miss it.

The Hotel Savoy
Fasanenstrasse 9-10
Berlin
One of the older hotels in Berlin with a touch of English elegance.

Hotel Robert Mayer
Robert-Mayer-Str. 44
Frankfurt
T +49 69 970 910
A small turn-of-the-century hotel with each room decorated by a different Frankfurt artist. Furniture delights include Rietveld and Frank Lloyd Wright.

Wedina
Gurlittstrasse 23
Hamburg
T +49 40 243 011
A compact hotel with 27 rooms and rustic Italian in style.

Restaurants & Bars

Paris Bar
Kanstrasse 152
Berlin
T +49 30 313 8052
Good food and wines entertain an interesting blend of actors, artists, entrepreneurs and globetrotters. Simple, natural ambience.

Steinerness Haus
Braubachstrasse 35
Frankfurt
A lofty hall with newly-built hammer beam roof provides the perfect ambience for the excellent steaks that are delivered to your table on a preheated piece of lava rock.

Café Schöne Aussichten
Alle Botanischer Garten, 2000
Hamburg
T +49 40 34 01 13
A great secret spot hidden in the botanic garden, serving an excellent varied breakfast.

Museums & Galleries

Museum für Moderne Kunst
Domstrasse 10
Frankfurt
T +49 69 2123 0447
Housed in a distinctive triangle building by Hans Hollein.

Ägyptisches Museum
Schloss-Strasse 70
Berlin
T +49 30 320 911
An outstanding museum containing an elegant portrait sculpture of Nefertiti, and a fascinating collection of Egyptian antiquities.

Kunsthalle
Glockengiesserwall
Hamburg
T +49 40 2486 2612
One of Germany's finest painting collections with work from the 14th through to the 20th centuries.

Places of Interest

Poster Galerie Hamburg
Grosse Bleichenn 31
Hamburg
T +49 40 34 68 50
One of the largest poster shops in Germany.

Bauhaus School
Gropiusallee 38
Dessau
One and a half hours from Berlin by train, in Dessau, you come to the original Bauhaus school, restored and bursting with new activities.

Bookshops

Herr Günther Kopp
Maintal / Bruchköpel
T +49 6181 450 74
For graphic design books.

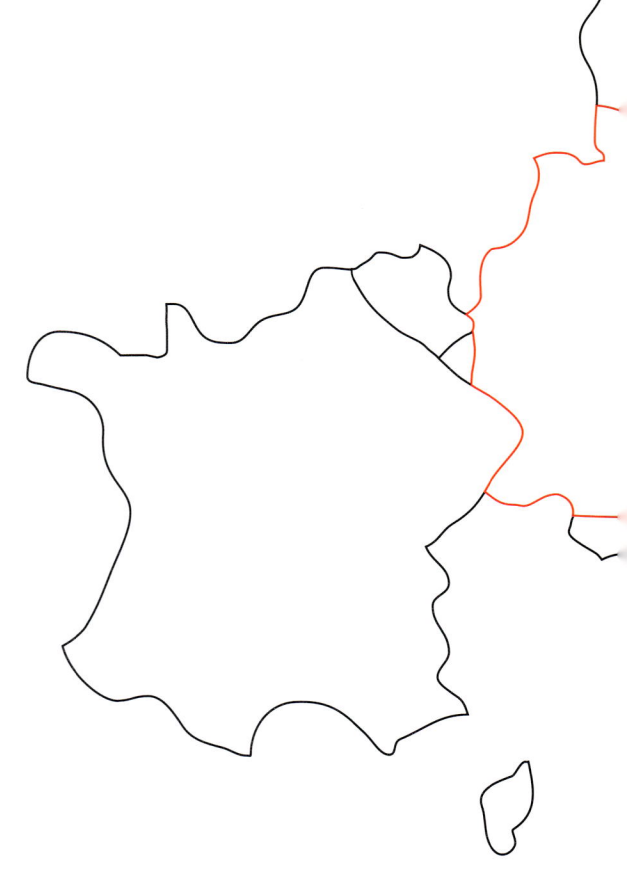

Germany

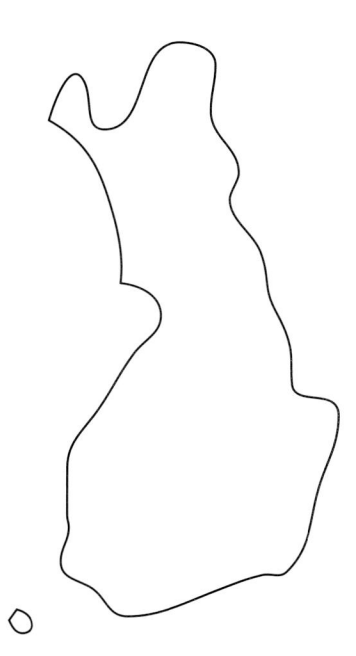

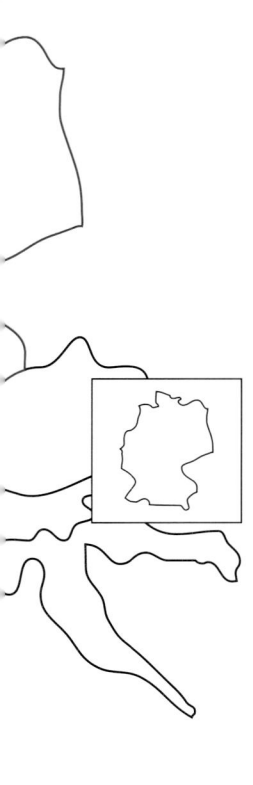

Germany
Local name — **Deutschland**
Coordinates — **51 00 N, 9 00 E**
Population | 1000 — **82,079**
Design Population | 1000 — **15.0**
Languages — **German**
Capital — **Berlin | Bonn**
Monetary unit — **Deutsche mark (DM)**

**Area 1000 km	2**					
		Hungary	**093**.0	Russia	Belarus	**17,075**.0	**207**.6
		Ireland	**070**.3	Slovenia	**020**.3
Austria	**083**.9	Italy	**301**.0	Spain	**505**.0
Belgium	**030**.5	Lithuania	**065**.2	Sweden	**450**.0
Croatia	**056**.5	The Netherlands	**041**.5	Switzerland	**041**.3
Denmark	**043**.1	Norway	**324**.0	Turkey	**779**.2
Finland	**338**.0	Poland	**313**.0	United Kingdom	**243**.3
France	**552**.0	Portugal	**092**.4	Yugoslavia	**103**.2
Germany		**357**.0			

feel good.

Die Menschen sitzen heutzutage viel. In Autos, auf Parkbänken, Sesselliften, Zahnarztstühlen und natürlich im Büro und zu Hause. Und die Menschen sitzen unterschiedlich. Weil sie unterschiedlich gross und schwer und bewegungsfreudig sind. Die Wissenschaft von der Beziehung zwischen Menschen und Geräten, also auch Sitzgeräten, ist die Ergonomie. Wir wenden Erkenntnisse der Ergonomie an, um Stühle zu entwickeln, die dem Körper Komfort, Sicherheit und die notwendige Stützung bieten.

Vitra hat für jeden den richtigen Stuhl. Ergonomisch optimierte Stühle wie unsere stellen sich nämlich auf das Gewicht des Sitzers ein, passen sich den Bewegungen des Körpers an. Manche automatisch, andere per zusätzlicher Feineinstellung. Einige sind mit einer besonderen Technik ausgerüstet, die den Sitz beim tischorientierten Arbeiten nach vorne absenkt und dadurch die Wirbelsäule automatisch aufrichtet. Beschwerden in Rücken, Schultern, Nacken sind nicht nur unangenehm, sondern auch häufig die Folge schlechter Sitzbedingungen. Sitzen Sie bequem.

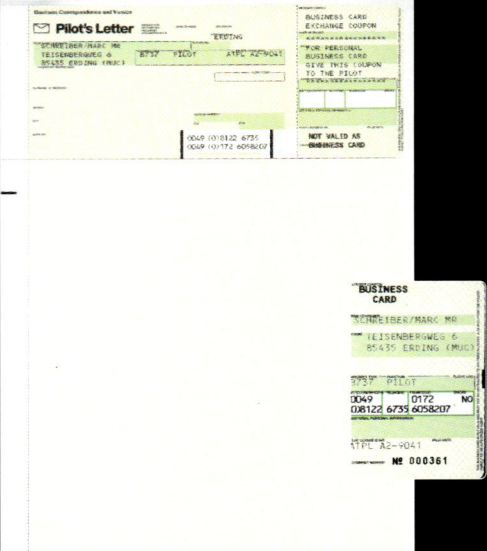

1 Brochure for Vitra, an office furniture manufacturer
Design firm Rempen & Partner: Das Design Büro, Düsseldorf
Designer Stefan Baggen

2 Letterhead and business card for a pilot
Agency Heye & Partner, Munich
Designer Frank Widmann

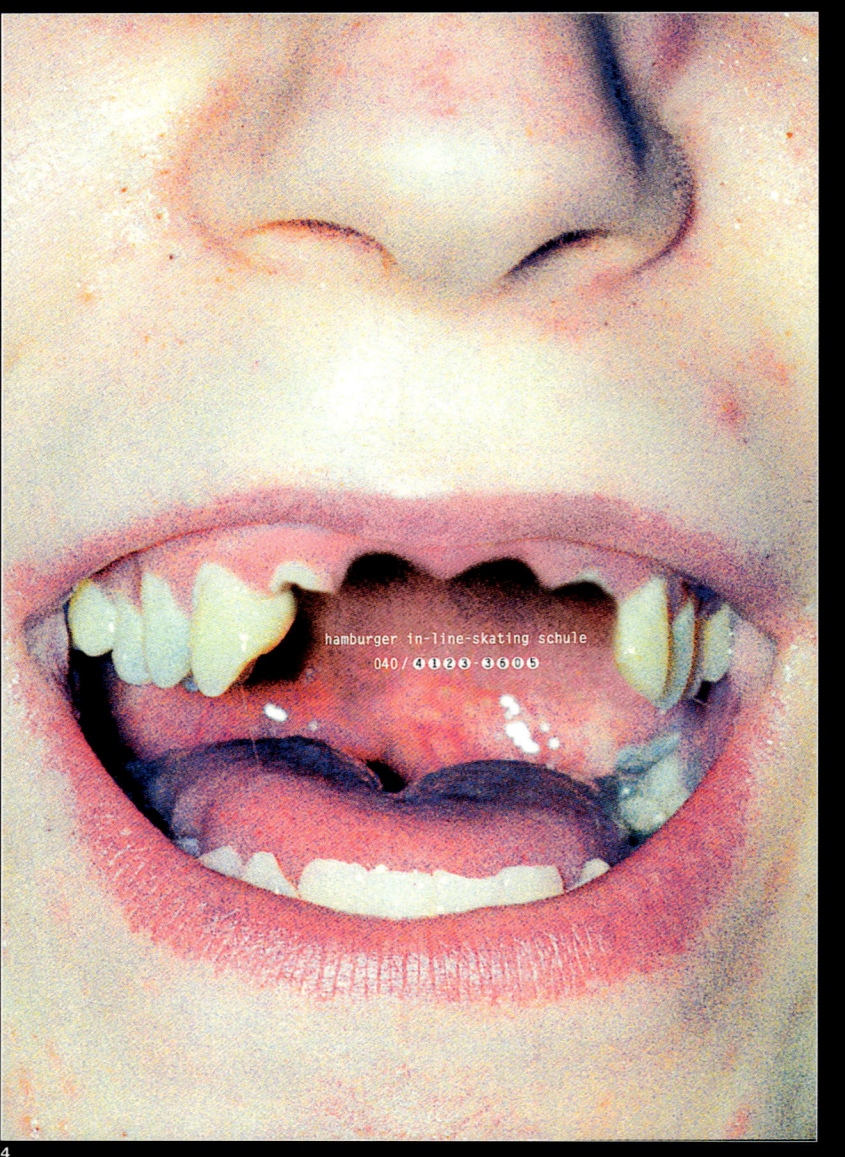

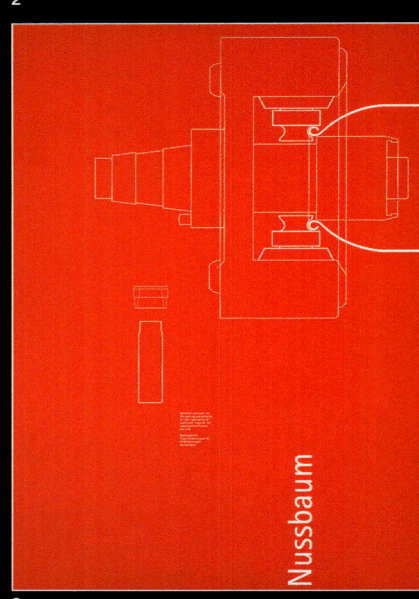

3 Poster for in-house fair and showroom for a mechanical engineering firm
Design firm Sisa & Winkler Büro für Gestaltung, Schwäbisch-Gmünd
Designers Güler Sisa, Eberhart Winkler
Client Nussbaum

4 Corporate ad for in-line skating school
Agency Springer & Jacoby, Hamburg
Art directors Torsten Rieken, Söhnke Busch
Designer Heike Saalfrank
Photographer Gerd George
Client Hamburger In-line Skating Schule

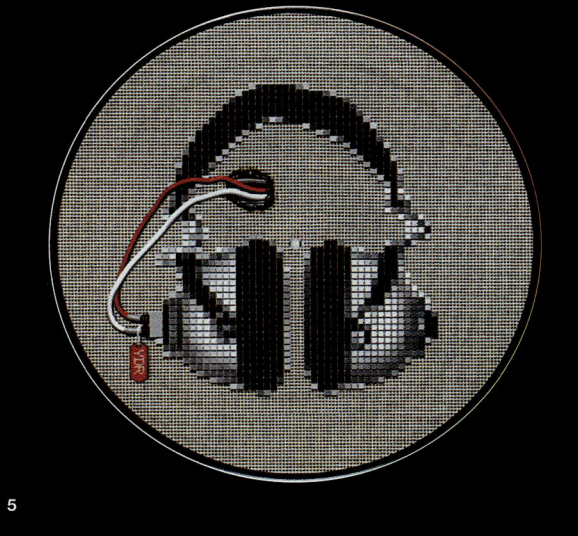

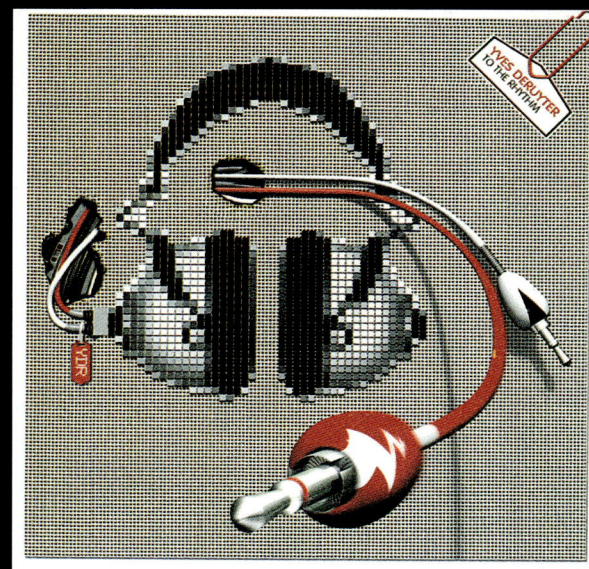

5–7 Vinyl design and album covers for Orbit Records
Design firm Eikes Grafischer Hort, Frankfurt
Art directors/designers Eike König, Ralf Hiemisch
Photographer Bernd Westphal

8, 9 Ads for VideoCON, a video-alarm system
Agency Macron Advertising, Munich
Art director Michael Goerden
Illustrator Gabriele Dünwald

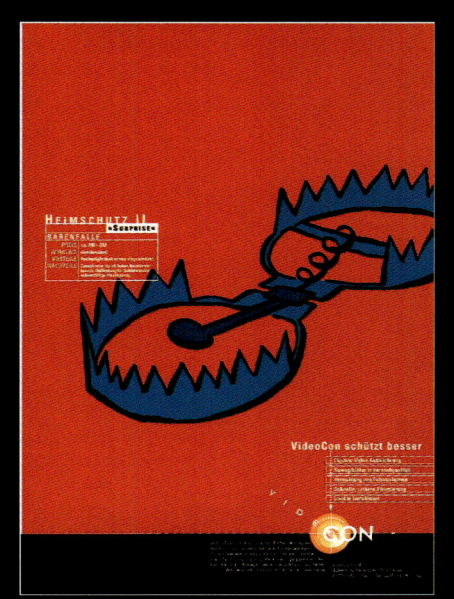

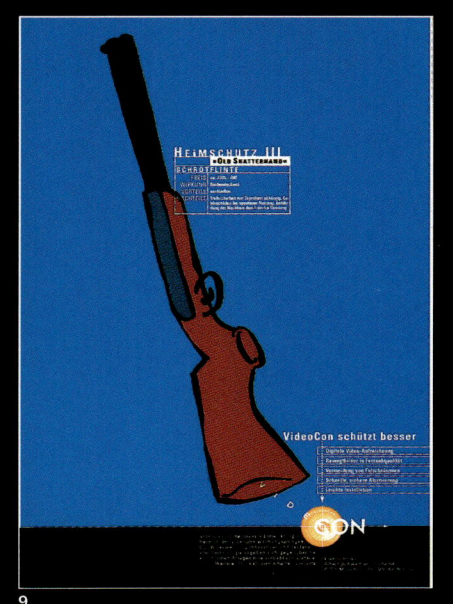

10 Invitation to anniversary party for Deutsche Post AG/Direct Marketing Center
Design firm Fantastic New Designmut GmbH, Wiesbaden
Art directors Thomas Lass, Michael Rasch
Copywriter Melanie Maly

11 Self-promotional "Events of the night" symbols
Design firm Matthias Schäfer Design, Wiesbaden
Designer Matthias Schäfer

12 Cover of [Sic!], the literary supplement of Vista magazine
Design firm Rong Design, Waiblingen
Designer Friederike Gauss
Illustrator Silvia Neuner
Photographer Benjamin Katz

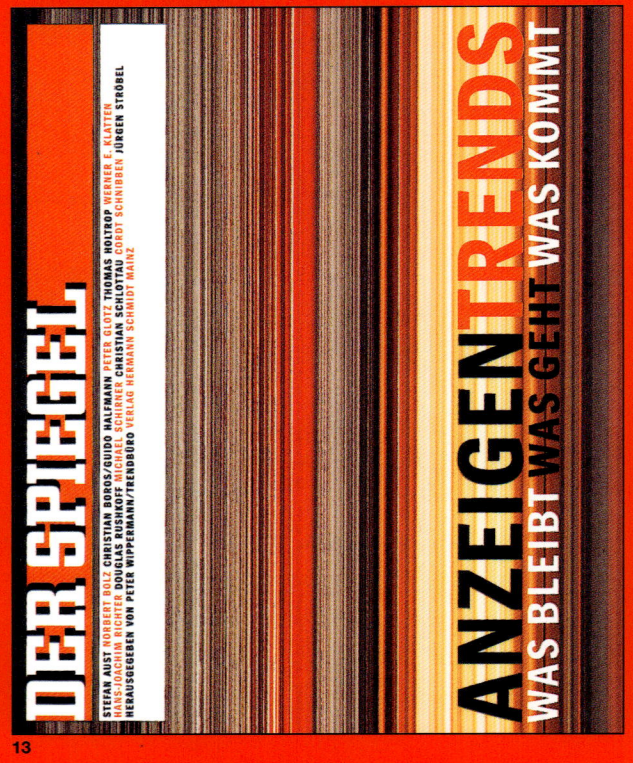

13 Cover of Anzeigentrends, a book chronicling 50 years of advertising in the magazine Der Spiegel
Design firm Büro Hamburg
Designer Régine Thienhaus
Illustrator Birgit Eggers
Clients Der Spiegel, Christian Schlottau/Hermann Schmidt Verlag

14 Brochure promoting Audi TT Coupé
Agency JvM Werbeagentur, Hamburg
Art director Timm Hanebeck
Illustrator Schiffmann
Photographer Christopher Thomas
Client Audi AG

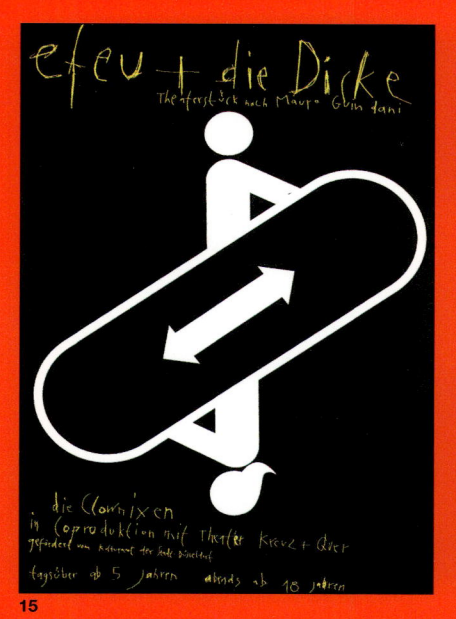

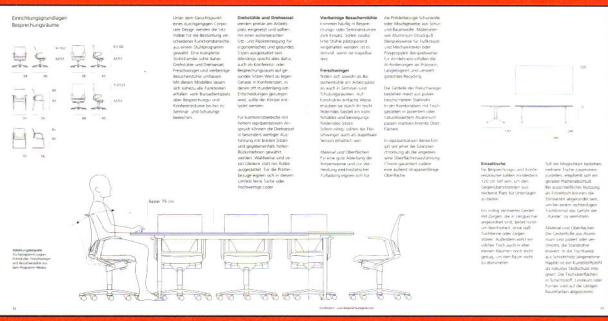

15 Poster for a performance
at the Clownixen Theatre
Design firm Gesine Grotrian-Steinweg
Design, Düsseldorf
Art director/ illustrator
Gesine Grotrian-Steinweg

16 Poster celebrating 50 years
of the German mark.
Design firm Klaus Lemke Team, Melsungen
Art director Klaus Lemke
Client Laks-Hessen

17 Design Plus 1998, a catalogue
featuring winners of a product design
competition
Design firm Heine/Lenz/Zizka, Frankfurt
Art director Sonia Reck
Creative directors Achim Heine, Michael
Lenz, Peter Zizka
Photographer Tom Vack
Client Nils Holger Moormann

18 Tourism brochure
Design firm Scheppe Böhm Associates,
Munich
Designers Florian Böhm, Wolfgang Scheppe
Client Tyrolean Tourist Board

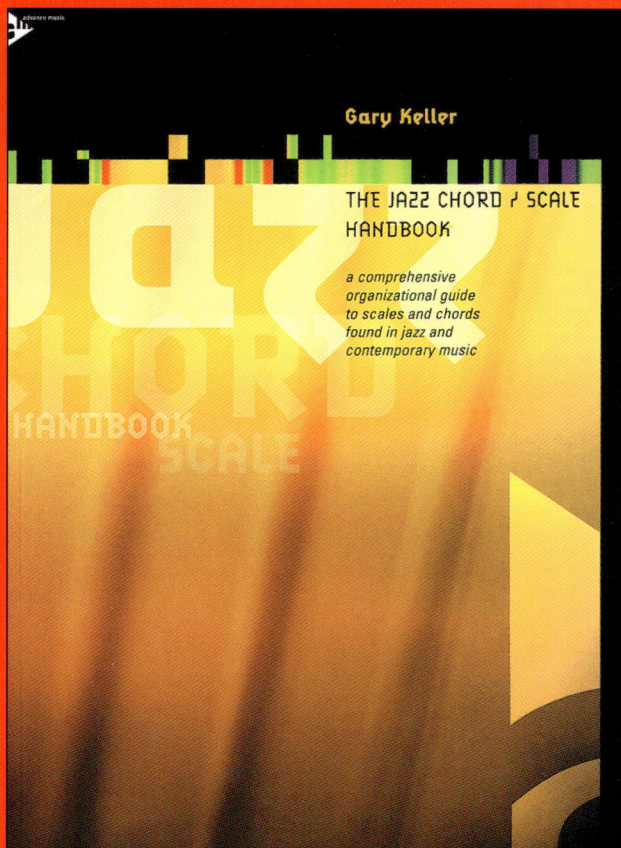

19 Spread from a book
for Wilkhahn, Bad Münder
Design firm Englich+ Wagner, Berlin
Art directors Guido Englich,
Burkhard Remmers
Illustrator Guido Englich

20 Book cover for Advance
Music Publishers
Design firm 10eG Visual, Oberhausen
Art director Peter Howe
Designer Tim Ulrich

Germany 33

21 Poster announcing an exhibition of graduate student artwork at the University of Hildesheim/Holzminden
Designer Prof. Gerd Finkel, Kreiensen

22 Poster promoting the city of Borken
Design firm Klaus Lemke Design Team, Spangenberg
Designer Klaus Lemke

23 Letterhead and business card for a psychologist
Design firm Fleischmann & Kirsch, Stuttgart
Designer Stefanie von Hösslin

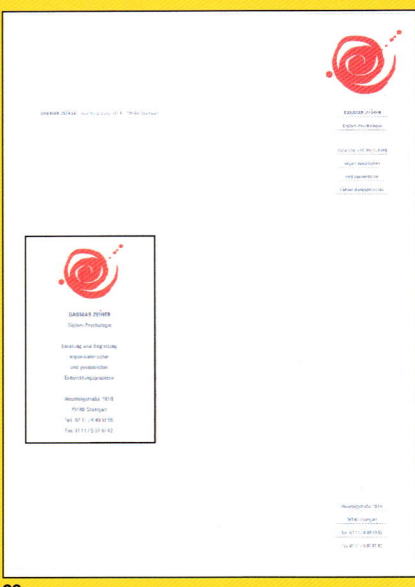

24 Letterhead and business card for a copywriter
Design firm Sabine Bock Grafik, Ketsch
Designer Sabine Bock

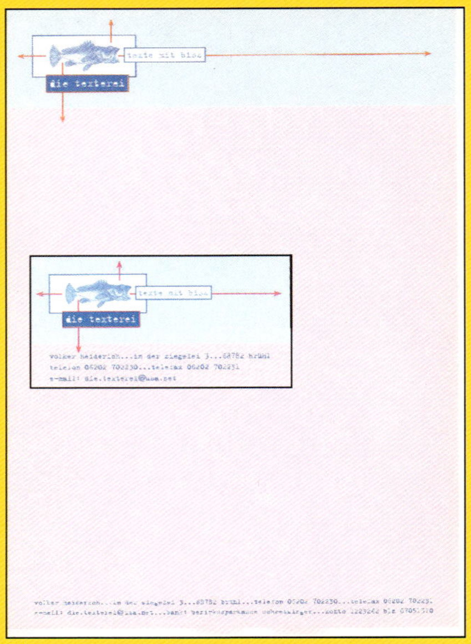

25 Cover of catalogue for "German Art," an exhibition at Singapore Art Museum
Design firm Oktober Kommunikationsdesign, Bochum
Art directors/designers Silke Lühmann, René Wynands

26, 27 Opening and end pages of books for Gustav Lübbe Verlag publishers
Design firm Pencil Corporate Art, Braunschweig
Designer Achim Frederic Kiel

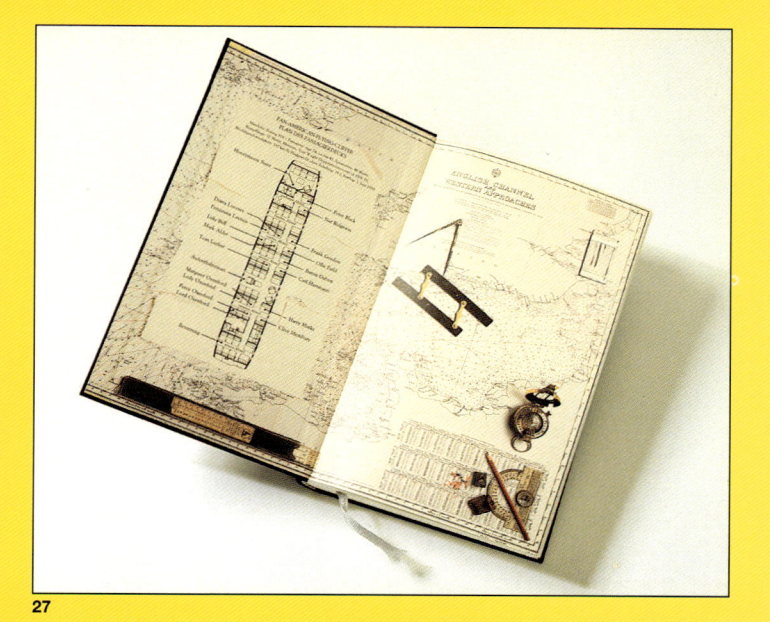

28 Symbol for Theben Gallery
Design firm Matthias Schäfer Design, Wiesbaden
Designer Matthias Schäfer

29 1997 annual report for Deutsche Handelsbank
Design firm W.A.F. Werbegesellschaft, Berlin
Art director Klaus Fehsenfeld
Designer Heike Lichte
Photographers Tom Peschel, Wolfgang Scholvien

30 Self-promotional icons for a box and Web site
Design firm Factor Design, Hamburg
Designer Eva Ralle

31 Letterhead and business card for a tax consultant
Design firm akzent Design, Mühltal
Designer Ralf Geselle
Photographer Tobias Feld

32 Poster for a ride tournament
Designers Stephan Waidmann, Mechthild Post, Heuchlingen
Client Reitverein Heuchlingen

Germany 35

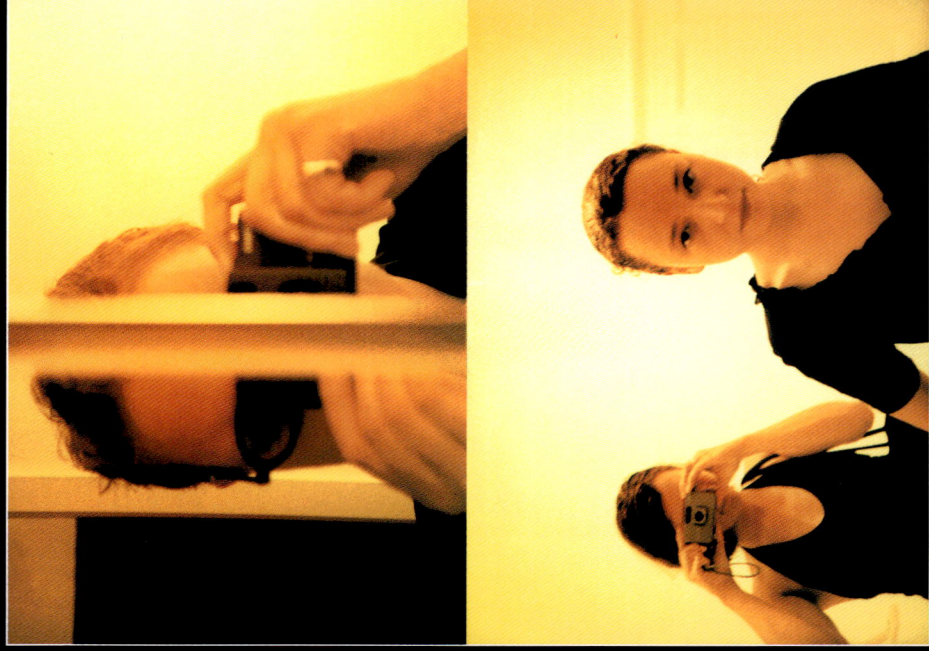

33 Men's fashion catalogue
Design firm Werbewelt, Ludwigsburg
Designers Wolfgang Benz, Tobias Ulmer
Photographer Vlado Golub
Client Holy's Exklusive Herrenmode

34 Self-promotional publication
Design firm Sign Kommunikation, Frankfurt
Designer Antonia Henschel

35, 36 Ads for BMW Hammer
Design firm Barten & Barten: Die Agentur GmbH, Cologne
Art director Constantin Rothenburg
Creative directors Erik Hogrefe, Stefan Oehm
Photographer Mitja Arzensek

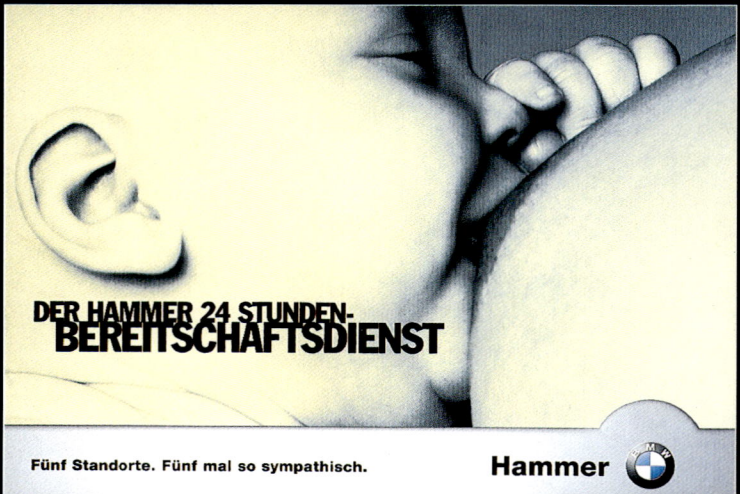

37 Self-promotion mailed to ad agencies in Hamburg
Design firm Neumann Design, Hamburg
Art director Robert Neumann
Photographer Rolf Seiffe

38 1998 calendar
Design firm Scarabaeus Dialogwerbung, Rosenheim
Designer Stephan Guggenbichler
Photographers Klaus Maria Einwanger, Otto Stefan Schindler

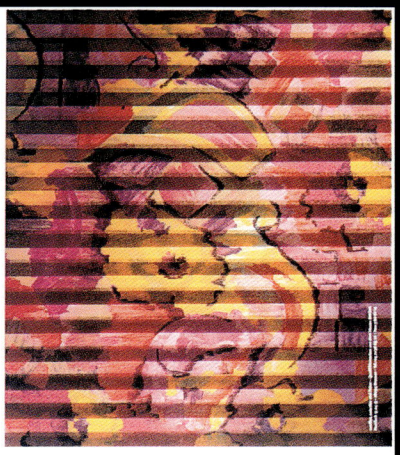

39 Poster promoting the city of Dresden
Design firm Firma Ströer, Dresden
Designer Jürgen Haufe

40, 41 Self-promotional image campaign
Design firm Wächter & Wächter Werbeagentur GmbH, Munich
Art director Axel Buergler
Photographer Thomas Spiessl
Client Bloecker GmbH

42, 43 T-shirt and condom promotion for an AIDS prevention organization
Design firm Schreiter's Ideeanarchiv & Artwork, Frankfurt
Designer Jürgen Schreiter
Photographer Heinz Pflug

44 Poster for a sporting event
Art directors Mechthild Post, Stefan Waidmann, Heuchlingen
Client Sportverein Heuchlingen

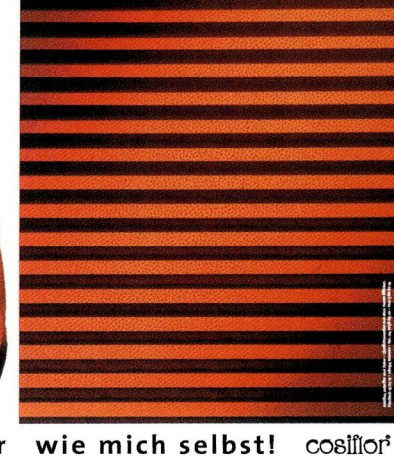

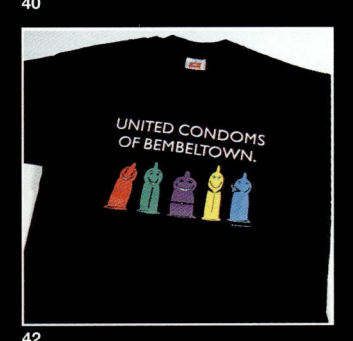

Germany 37

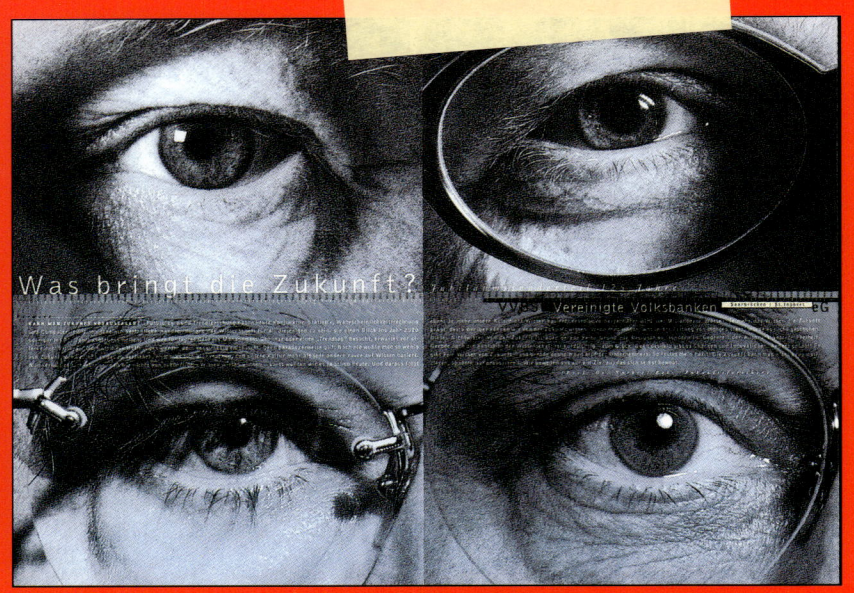

45 1997 corporate report for a bank
Design firm Maksimovic & Partners, Saarbrücken
Art directors Ivica Maksimovic, Patrick Bittner
Photographer Gerd Westrich
Client Vereinigte Volksbanken, Saarbrücken

46 Bottle design for Alpirsbacher beer
Design firm Taste!, Neu-Isenburg
Designer Claudia Fratz

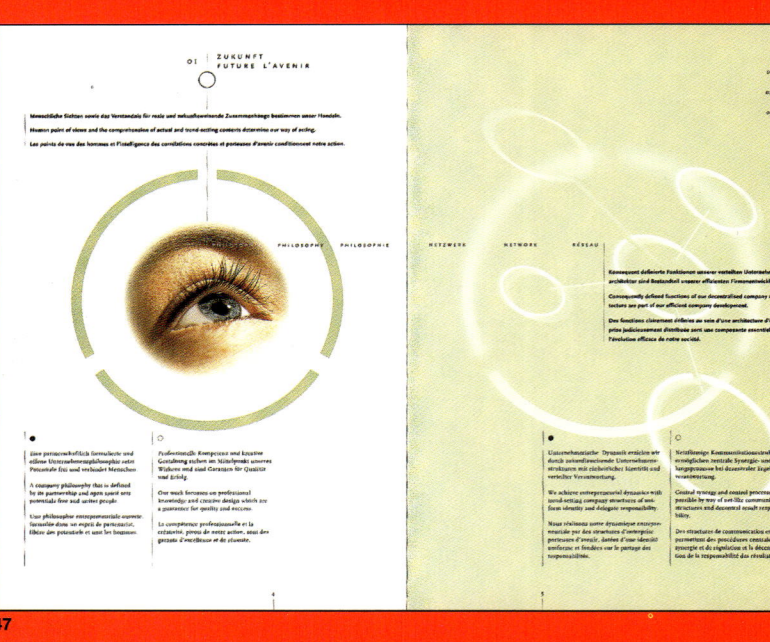

47 Self-promotional brochure for a software developer and consultant
Design firm Factor Design, Hamburg
Art director Johannes Erler
Designer Luisella Ströbele
Illustrators Uwe Melichar, Eva Ralle
Photographer Frank Stöckel
Client Bauer & Partner

48 Poster for the band Nonex
Design firm Fons M. Hickman Design, Düsseldorf
Art director Paul Roberts
Designer/photographer Fons Hickmann

49 Promotional brochure introducing a paper range
Design firm Factor Design, Hamburg
Art director/illustrator Paul Neulinger
Designers Paul Neulinger, Kristina Düllmann
Client Römerturm Feinstpapier

50 Self-promotional Website
Design firm Backe/Meixner/Gross, Frankfurt
Designers Tanja Backe, Alexandra Meixner, Daniel Gross

51, 53 Spreads from Econy, a business magazine
Design firm Meiré & Meiré, Königsdorf
Creative director Mike Meiré
Art directors Monika Schmidt, Alice Weigel
Client Manager Magazin Verlag

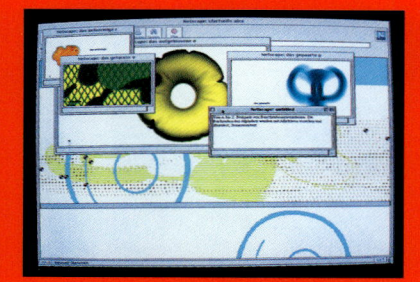

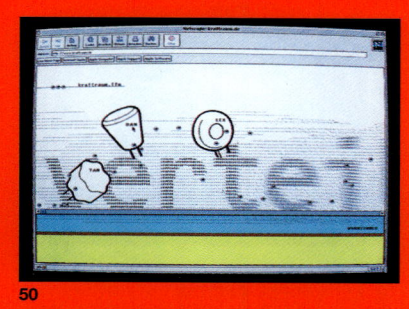

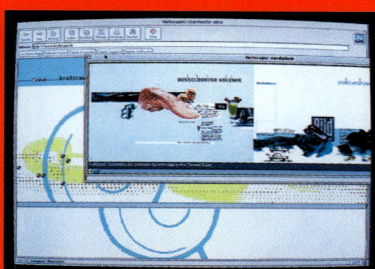

52 Self-promotional brochure for a tool-making company
Design firm Zink & Kraemer, Trier
Art director Evi Lamberty
Designer Matthias Schmitz
Photographer Rainer Langer
Client Tectro Kunststofftechnik

54 Brochure for City Repro-Technik
Design firm Bruchmann, Schneider, Bruchmann, Cologne
Designers Felix Bruchmann, Stefan Schneider, Jörg Bruchmann

55 Letterhead for a dentist
Agency Springer & Jacoby, Hamburg
Art director Söhnke Busch
Designer Heike Saalfrank

Germany 39

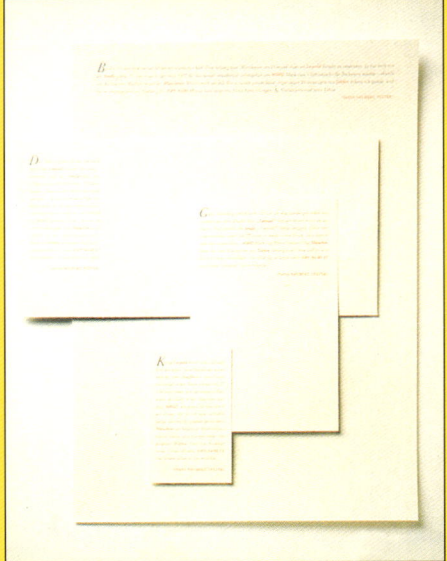

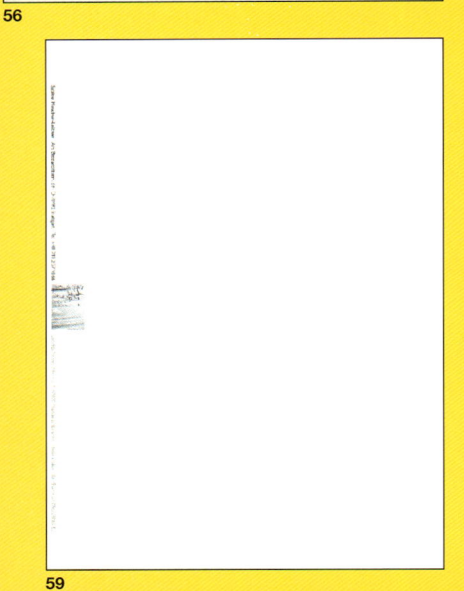

56 Identity package for Hans Neubert
Design firm Wüschner und Rohwer, Munich
Art director Ekkehard Frenkler
Creative director Ekki Frenkle

57 Brochure for a
conference on ornament
Designer Carolyn Steinbeck, Berlin
Client Einstein Forum Potsdam

58 Promotional advent calendar
for paper company and design firm
Design firm Kommunikationsdesign, Kalletal
Designer Andrea Träger
Client Weroca

59 Letterhead for Sabine Mescher-Leitner
Design firm Fleischmann & Kirsch, Stuttgart
Designer André Kirsch

60 Brochure for a photo studio
Design firm Trafo Design, Neuss
Designer Thomas Weltner
Photographers Stephan Romer, Thomas Jape
Client Packshot Boys/Romer/Jape

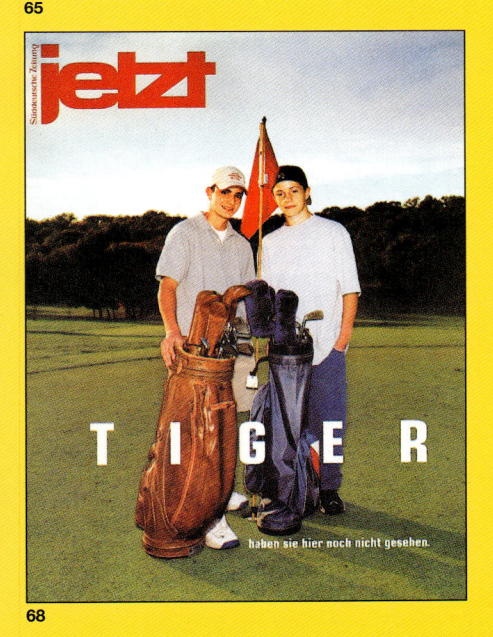

61, 62, 68 Covers of Jetzt, a magazine supplement for the newspaper Süddeutsche Zeitung, Munich
Art director Markus Rindermann
Illustrator (Fig. 61) Tom Ising
Designer (Fig. 62) Tom Ising
Photographer (Figs. 62, 68) Dieter Mayr

63 Stationery and identity
Design firm Milch Design GmbH, Munich
Art directors Michaela Kohlrus, Friedel Patzak, Judith May
Designer Dominik Wullschlege

64 Spread from Shrift und Typografie, a self-published book on type
Designer Stefan Waidmann, Heuchlingen

65 Ad for a recording studio
Agency Wüschner und Rohwer, Munich
Art director Stefan Hempel
Creative directors Ekki Frenkler, Thilo von Büren
Client Giesing Studios

66,67 Posters designed to raise awareness of Munich's homeless
Design firm Wüschner und Rohwer, Munich
Art directors Chris Mayrhofer, Sven Achatz
Creative directors Ekki Frenkler, Thilo von Büren
Client Inner Mission Munich

69 Logotype competition catalogue
Design firm xplicit Ffm, Frankfurt
Art director Thomas Nagel
Designers Thomas Nagel, Marco Dörr
Client Forum Stuttgart 21 e.V.

Germany 41

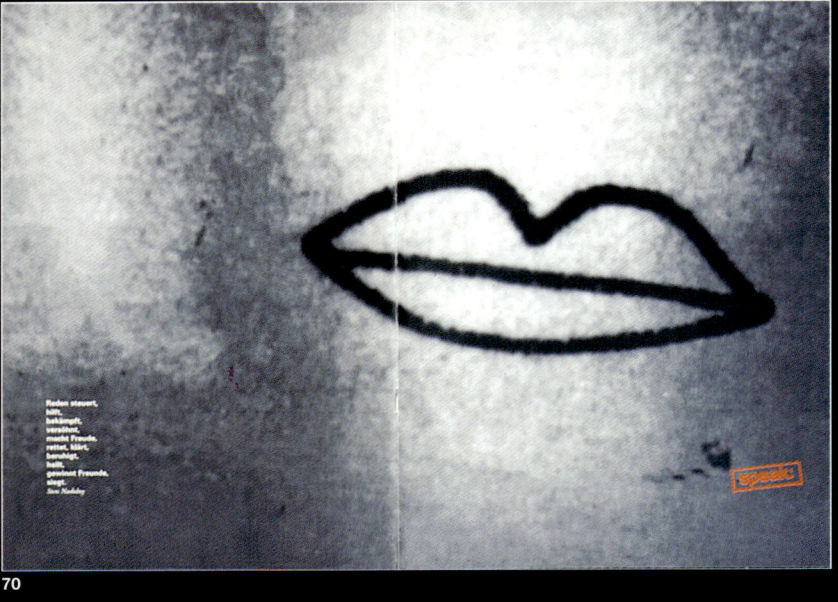

70

70 Spread from Speak, a magazine project by typography students at Universität-GH Essen
Art director Anna Berkenbusch
Designers Gaby Baltha, Beate Diergardt, Lisa Eidt, Roberta Hermanns

71, 72 Illustrations for the magazine Psychologie heute
Design firm Münkillus, Hamburg
Illustrator Siegmar Münk

73 Promotional book for Römerturm Feinstpapier
Design firm Factor Design, Hamburg
Art director Johannes Erler
Designers Johannes Erler, Olaf Stein
Photographer Marek Vogel

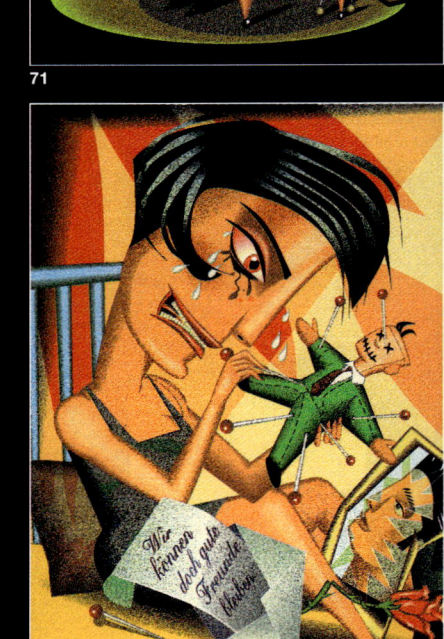

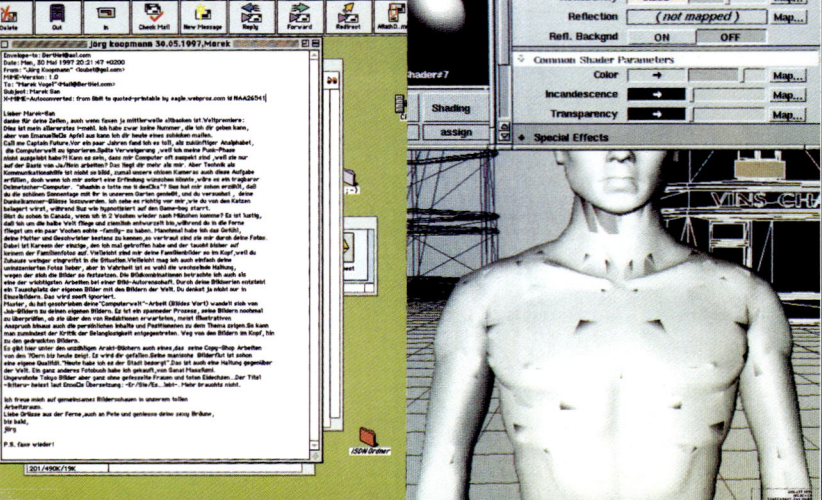

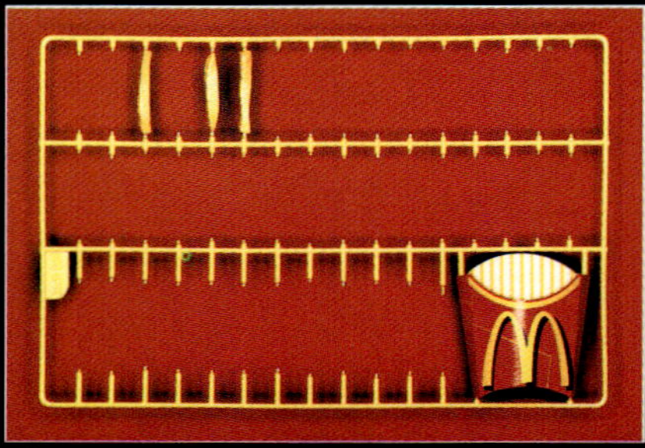

74 Print ad for McDonald's Austria
Agency Heye & Partner, Munich
Art director Frank Widmann
Photographer Niko Schmidt Burgk

75 Promotional material for Audi
Agency JvM Werbeagentur GmbH, Hamburg
Art director Jörg Barre
Photographers Iver Hansen, Sigi Kercher

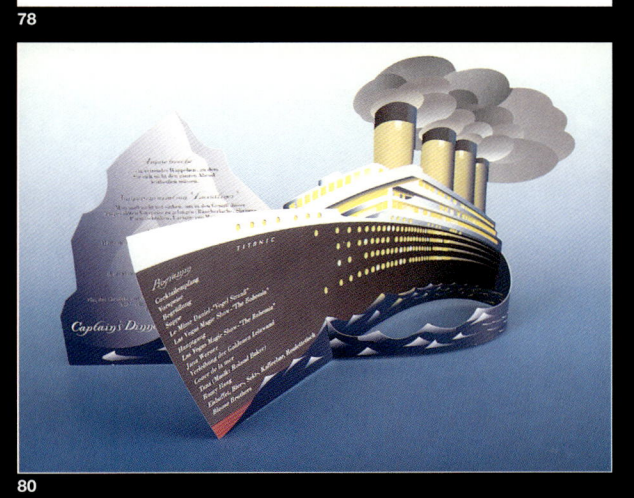

76 Self-promotional design book
Design firm Knopp Werbeagentur, Göppingen
Designer Günther R. Knopp

77 Self-promotional package for Factor Design, a Hamburg design firm
Art director Olaf Stein
Designers Olaf Stein, Eva Ralle
Copywriter Hannah S. Fricke

78 Pages from a self-promotional Website (www.factordesign.com)
Design firm Factor Design, Hamburg
Designer Jeff Zwerner

79 Promotional materials for Face 2 Face, a type foundry
Design firm xplicit Ffm, Frankfurt/Moniteurs, Berlin
Art director Alexander Branczyk
Designers Alexander Branczyk, Thomas Nagel, Stefan Hauser, Heike Nehl, Andrea Herstonski, Annette Waisthoff

80 Programme for a Titanic-themed gala
Design firm Fantastic New Designment, Wiesbaden
Client German Association of Cinema Owners

81 Invitation to trade show for VideoCon
Agency Macron Advertising, Munich
Designer Michael Goerden
Illustrator Gabriele Dünwald

Germany 43

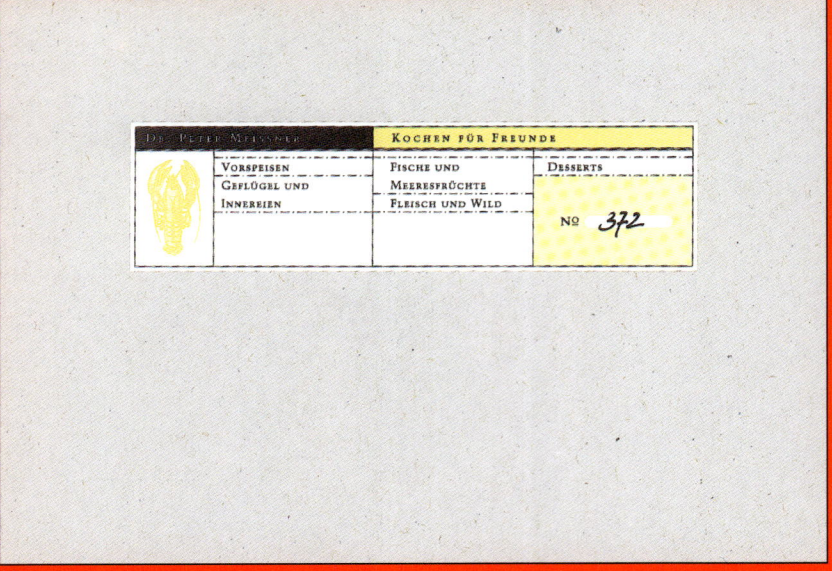

82

82 Self-promotional booklet for
Büroecco! Kommunikationsdesign,
an Augsburg design firm
Designers Stephan Beißer, Roman
Schellmoser, Raffaela Pederiva
Illustrators Reinhard Blumenschein,
Betty Schellmoser
Photographers Brechenmacher & Baumann

83, 86 Self-promotional posters
Design firm Münkillus, Hamburg
Illustrator Siegmar Münk

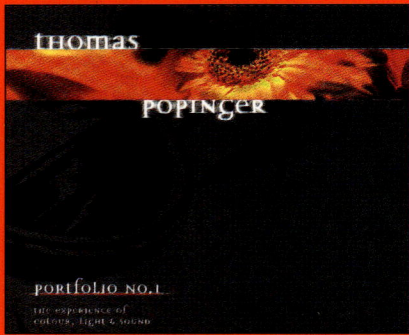

83

84

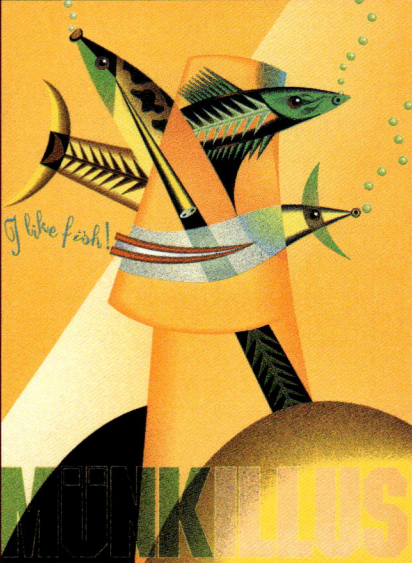

85

86

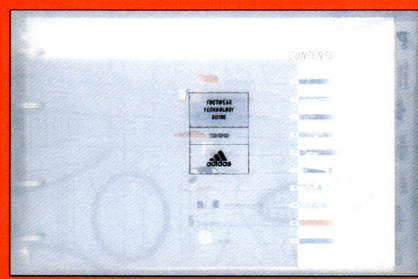

87

84 Cover of promotional
CD-ROM for a photographer
Design firm Scholz & Friends n.a.s.a.,
Hamburg
Art director John Eberstein
Designer/illustrator Oliver Hinrichs
Photographer/client Thomas Popinger

85 Statements, a culture
magazine based on bathing
Design firm Meiré & Meiré, Königsdorf
Art directors Mike Meiré, Birgit Reber

87 Guide to footwear technology
for Adidas International
Design firm Adidas Salomon AG,
Herzogenaurach
Art director Bettina Enenkl
Illustrators Sanmann, Hammer & Roske
Photographer Günther Schmidt

88 Accessories for Leventehaus, a shopping mall
Design firm Bach-Backhaus, Hamburg
Designers S. Bach, C. Backhaus

89 Calendar for Drescher GmbH, a printer
Concept Sibylle Schwarz, Weissach
Illustrators Sibylle Schwarz, Jeff Fisher, Rita Sauerteig, Steffan Sauterteig, Jean-Christian Knaff

90 Catalogue for Dumont Publishing
Design firm Groothuis+Malsy, Bremen
Art directors Victor Malsy, Gilmar Wendt
Designer Gilmar Wendt

91 10-year retrospective self-promotional brochure
Design firm Imago 87 GmbH, Freising
Designer Peter Krüll
Photographer Robin Rehm
Creative director/copy editor Maité Herzog

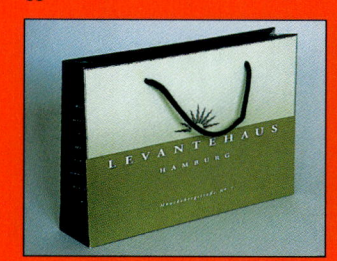

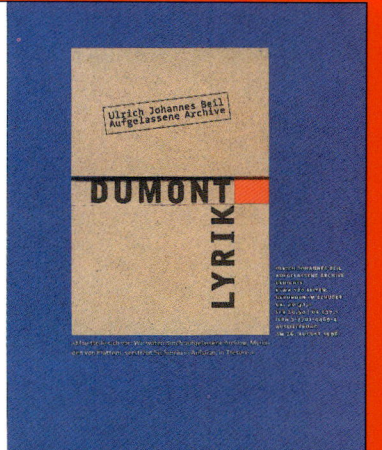

92 Spread from cookbook for Gräfe und Unzer Verlag GmbH, Munich
Photographer Ulrike Holsten

93 Beer packaging
Design firm Taste!, Neu-Isenburg
Art director Günther Burkhard
Creative director Theo Probst-Bartolomee
Client Faust Brauerei

Germany 45

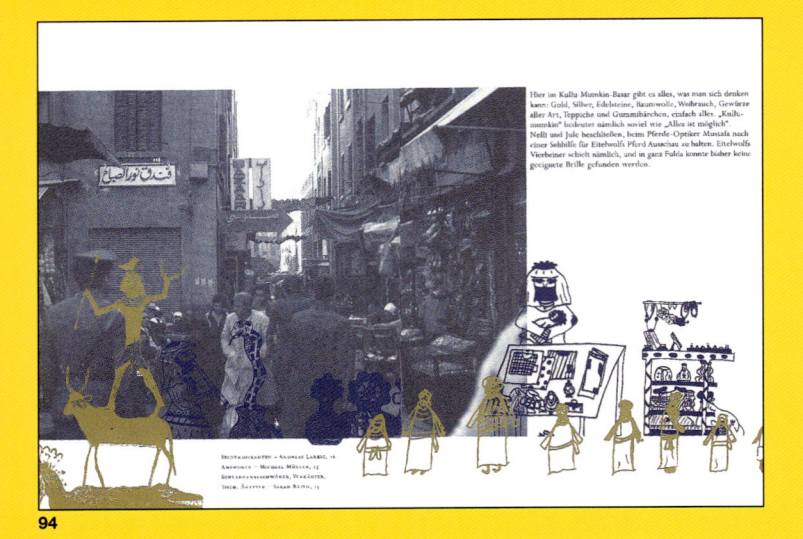

94 Spread from a book of illustrations
Designers Matthias Beyrow, Marion Wagner, Berlin
Illustrators Andreas Larbig, Michael Müller, Sarah Reith
Client/photographer Werner Döppner

95 "Butler School", a promotional book for Römerturm Feinstpapier
Design firm Factor Design, Hamburg
Designer Olaf Stein
Photographer Peter Granser

96 Ad for Süddeutsche Zeitung
Agency Wüschner und Rohwer, Munich
Art directors Stefan Hempel
Creative directors Ekki Frenkler, Thilo von Büren

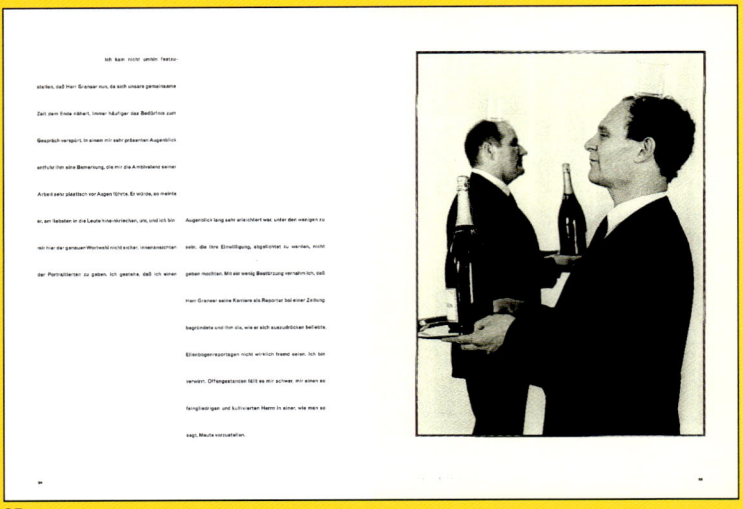

97 Ads for Daimler Benz
Agency Springer & Jacoby, Hamburg
Art director Jürgen Vossen
Designer Simon Schwaighofer
Photographer Brian Baderman

98 Promotional brochure for a printer
Design firm Weigang Marketing Partner, Würzburg
Designers/illustrators Jürgen Hümmer, Susanne Hollmann
Photographers K. Westermann, R. Grunert-Held
Client Stürtz AG

99 Covers of medical textbooks
Design firm Scarabaeus Dialogwerbung, Rosenheim
Designer Stephan Guggenbichler
Client Sanitas

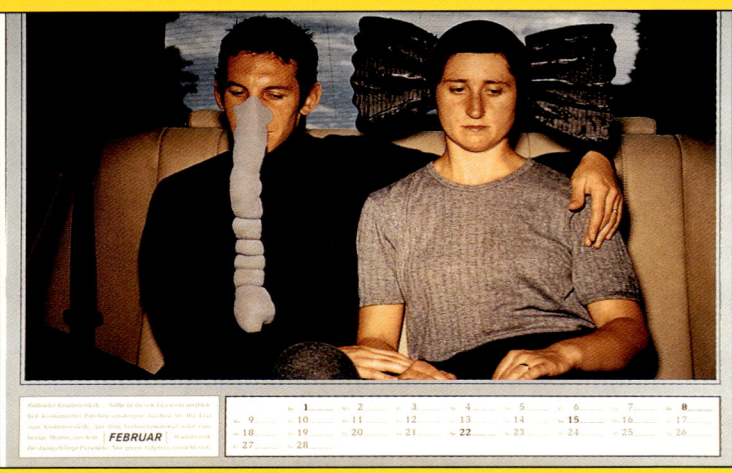

100 Catalogue for Svedex Türenwerke GmbH, a door manufacturer
Design firm Scheppe Böhm Associates, Munich
Art directors/designers Florian Böhm, Wolfgang Scheppe

101 Annual report for Vorwerk & Co
Design firm Vorwerk & Co., Wuppertal
Art directors Hermann Michels, Regina Göllner
Concept Manfred Piwinger

102 Spread from a book of architectural façades for Alsecco
Design firm Simon & Goetz, Frankfurt
Art directors Rüdiger Goetz, Oliver Meyer-Hieronimus
Designer Rüdiger Goetz
Photographers Hans Georg Esch, Thomas Eicken
Illustrators Manuela Schmidt

103 Promotional book for Toucan-T, a carpet manufacturer
Design firm Büro Kottmann, Reutlingen
Designer Petra Kottmann

104 Spread from book Faces of Darmstadt
Design firm akzent design, Mühltal
Art director/illustrator Lothar Rössling
Photographer Woltram Eder
Client akzent Verlag

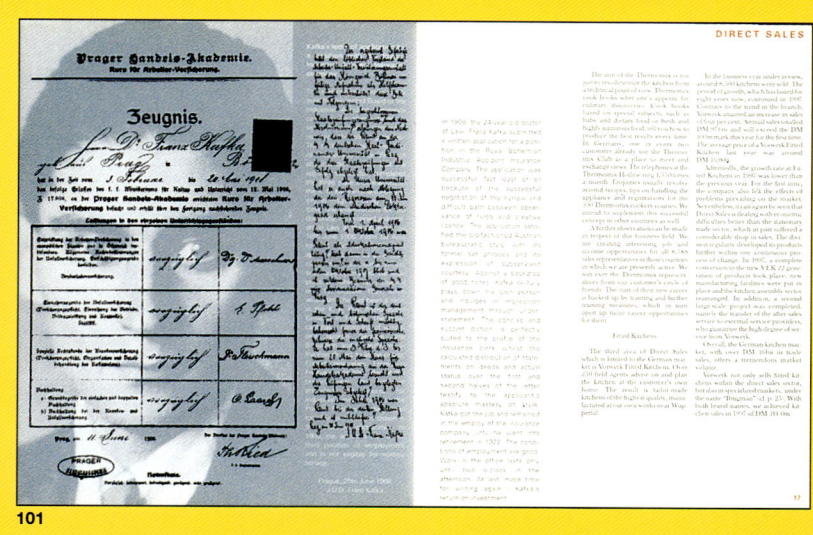

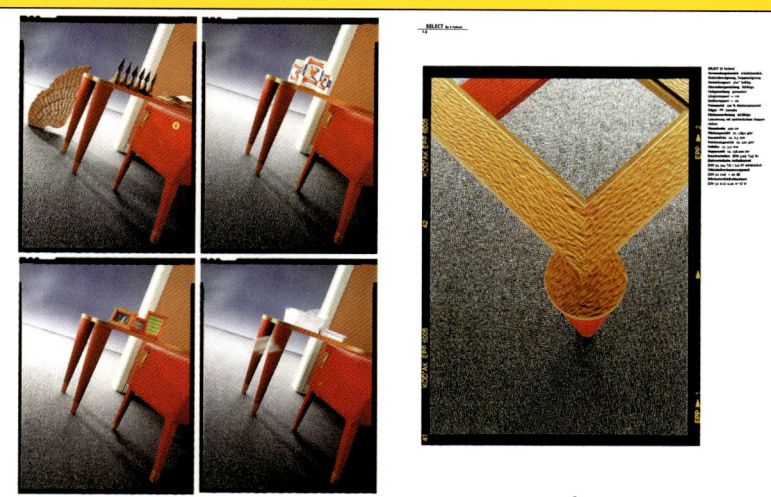

Germany 47

Hungary Gazetteer

Restaurants & bars

Fészek
VII, Kertész u. 36 (corner of Dob u.)
Budapest
T +36 1 322 6043
Hidden inside the 100 year old Fészek Artists' Club in downtown Pest is this large neoclassical dining room. An extensive menu offers Hungarian classics (the venison stew with tarragon is outstanding). In summer dine outdoors in a Venetian-style courtyard.

Náncsi Néni ("Aunt Nancy's")
II, Ördögárok út 80
Budapest
T +36 1 397 2742
The dining room is incredibly cosy and feels like a country kitchen with garlands of paprika and garlic dangling from the ceiling. The shelves are crammed with jars of home-pickled vegetables. Generous Hungarian menu.

New York Café
VII, Erzsébet körút 9-11
Budapest
A Budapest institution since 1895 with its fin-de-siècle décor. Open from noon until midnight.

Coquan's Kavé
V, Nádor utca 5 and IX Ráday utca 15
Budapest
Come here for the best coffee in town.

Places of Interest

Thermal baths in Budapest
This is a major spa town with numerous thermal baths to choose from. Try the Gellért Baths (off XI, Kelehegyi út) which maintain a constant temperature of 40°C or the Rudas Baths (I, Döbrentei tér 9), built by the Turks in 1566 and still retaining a strong Turkish ambience.

Jánoshegy (János Hill)
Take the chairlift to the summit and the highest point in Budapest. Climb the lookout tower for the best view of the city.

Museums & Galleries

Néprajzi Múzeum (Museum of Ethnography)
V, Kossuth Lajos tér 12
Budapest
T +36 1 332 6340
Elegant both inside and out, this museum has impressive and exhaustive exhibits of folk costumes and traditions. These are the authentic pieces you can't find in the tourist shops.

Mücsarnok (Palace of Exhibitions)
XIV, Dózsa György út 37
Budapest
Striking structure built in 1895 holding exhibitions of contemporary Hungarian and international art and a rich series of films, plays and concerts.

Kovács Margit Múzeum
Vastag György u.1
Szentendre
The lively artist's colony was first settled in the 14th century and the narrow cobbled streets are lined with painted houses, many now art galleries. Visit the Museum devoted to Margit Kovács a ceramic artist whose pottery blended the vernacular with motifs from modern art, now housed in an 18th-century merchant's house.

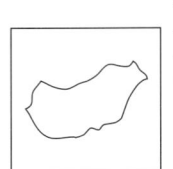

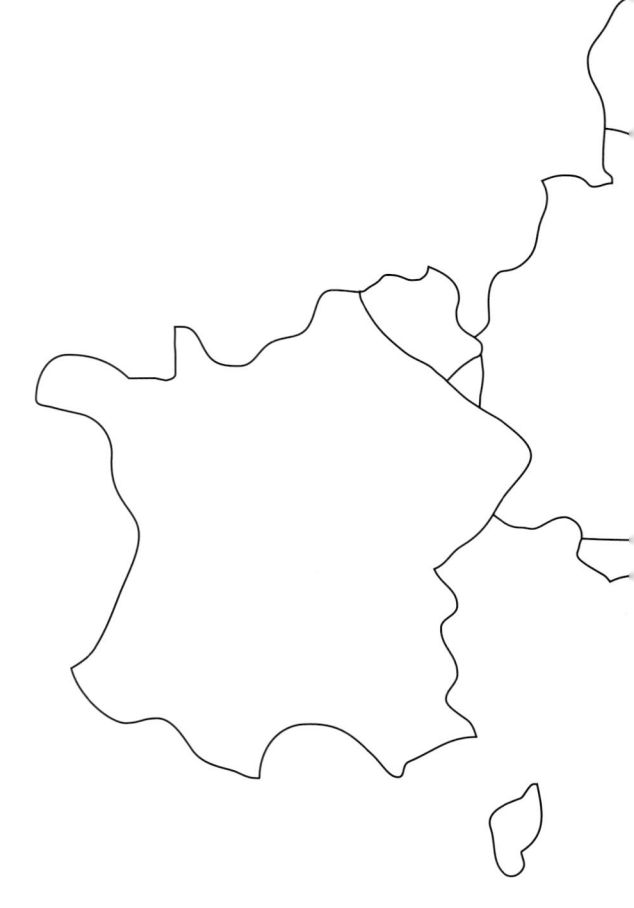

Hunguary

Local name	**Magyarorszag**
Coordinates	**47 00 N, 20 00 E**
Population |1000	**10,208**
Design Population |1000	**000**.7
Languages	**Hungarian, Other**
Capital	**Budapest**
Monetary unit	**Forint (Ft)**

Area 1000 km | 2

Austria	**083**.9	Germany	**357**.0	Russia	Belarus	**17,075**.0	**207**.6
Belgium	**030**.5	Ireland	**070**.3	Slovenia	**020**.3
Croatia	**056**.5	Italy	**301**.0	Spain	**505**.0
Denmark	**043**.1	Lithuania	**065**.2	Sweden	**450**.0
Finland	**338**.0	The Netherlands	**041**.5	Switzerland	**041**.3
France	**552**.0	Norway	**324**.0	Turkey	**779**.2
		Poland	**313**.0	United Kingdom	**243**.3
		Portugal	**092**.4	Yugoslavia	**103**.2
		Hungary	**093**.0		

1 Promotional brochure for Fortuna, an ad agency owned by Hungary's largest gaming company
Design firm Sárkány Graphics Design, Budapest
Designer/illustrator/photographer Roland Sárkány

2-5 Pages from calendar for Malev Hungarian Airlines
Designer Mátyás Kóbor, Székesfehérvár

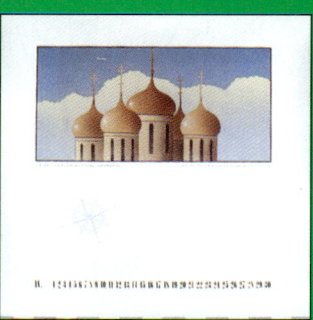

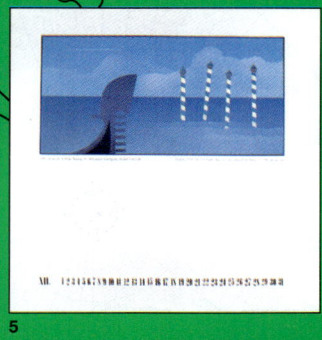

6 Exhibition poster
Design firm Art-Core, Budapest
Designer Krisztina Zékány

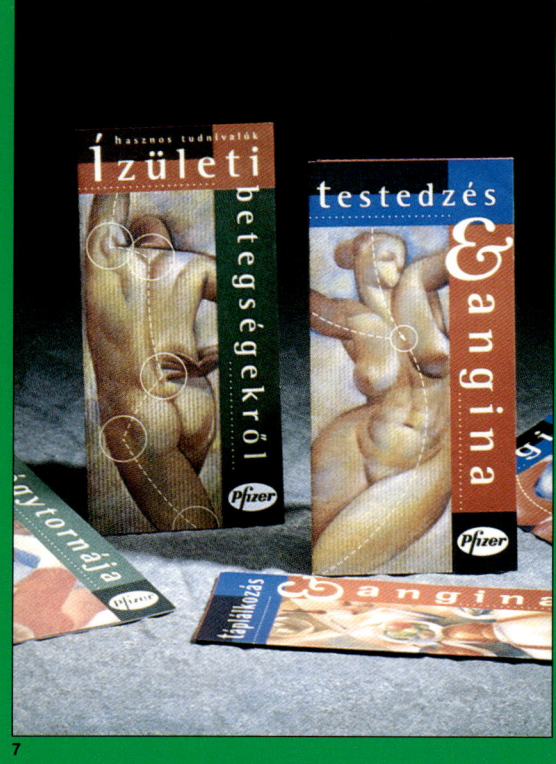

7 Patients' information sheet for Pfizer
Design firm Art Force Studio, Budapest
Designer Veress Tamás
Client The Rowland Company

Hungary 49

Ireland Gazetteer

Hotels

Marlfield House
Gorey, Co. Wexford
This is a country house hotel of great charm, comfort and modest cost.

Restaurants & Bars

Moran's Oyster Cottage
The Weir
Kilcolgan
Co. Galway
T +353 91 96113 / 91 96083
Overlooking a river and a small quay Moran's has been converted into an oyster bar and small restaurant, specialising in seafood of all descriptions.

Bewley's Coffee House
12 Westmoreland Street
Dublin
A Dublin institution that has been supplying Dubliners with coffee and buns since 1842. Not far from Trinity College where Ireland's greatest treasure, the Book of Kells, is on view.

John M. Keating
14 Mary Street / 23 Jervis Street
Dublin
T +353 1 873 1567
For a real Irish pub lunch, sit at a low table upstairs and warm up with a bowl of soup and a sandwich.

Mrs McDonagh's
Quay Street
Co. Galway
No fish'n chips here—but wonderful freshly caught and cooked fish which still tastes of the sea.

Places of interest

Marsh's Library
St. Patrick's Close
Dublin
Reached through a tiny and charming cottage garden is Ireland's first public library, opened in 1701. Its interior is virtually unchanged and still contains the "cages" used by perusers of the rarest books in the collection.

Old Jameson Distillery
Bow Street
Dublin
T +353 1 872 5566
The birthplace of one of Ireland's most celebrated whiskeys offers a fascinating insight into the making of "uisce batha" (or "holy water").

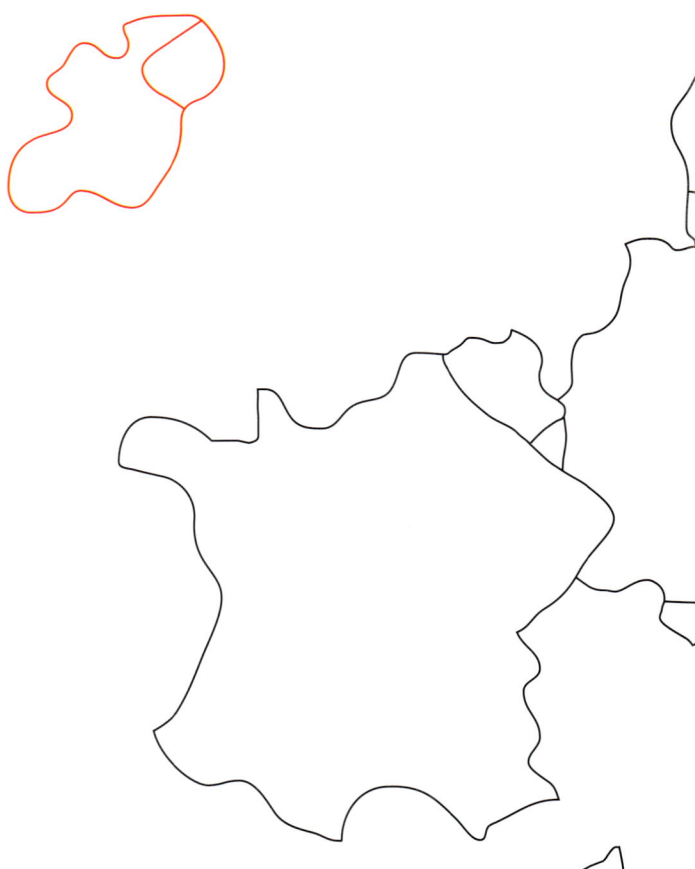

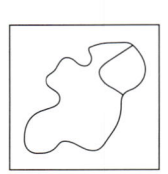

Ireland

Local name	Ireland
Coordinates	53 00 N, 8 00 E
Population ∣ 1000	3,619
Design Population ∣ 1000	000.5
Languages	English, Irish (Gaelic)
Capital	Dublin
Monetary unit	Irish pound (£Ir)

Area 1000 km ∣ 2

Austria	083.9	Germany	357.0	Russia ∣ Belarus	17,075.0 ∣ 207.6
Belgium	030.5	Hungary	093.0	Slovenia	020.3
Croatia	056.5	Italy	301.0	Spain	505.0
Denmark	043.1	Lithuania	065.2	Sweden	450.0
Finland	338.0	The Netherlands	041.5	Switzerland	041.3
France	552.0	Norway	324.0	Turkey	779.2
Ireland	070.3	Poland	313.0	United Kingdom	243.3
		Portugal	092.4	Yugoslavia	103.2

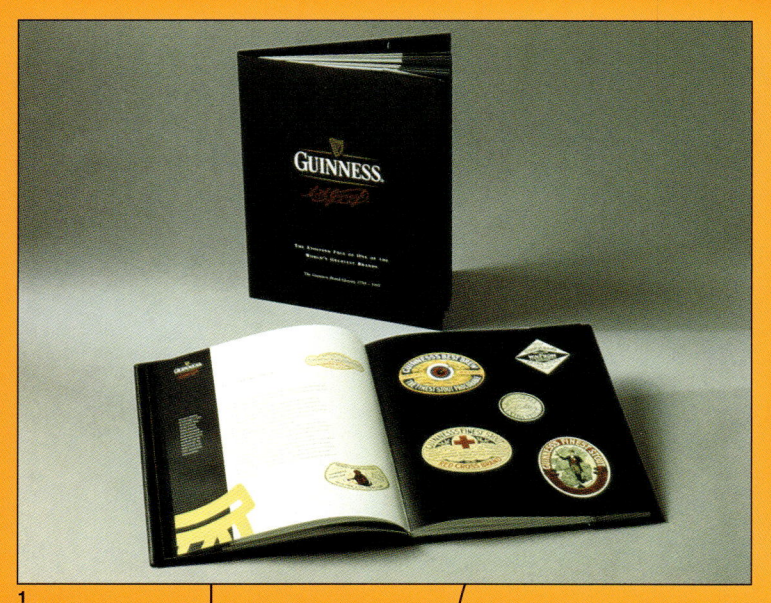

1 A book on the history of Guinness
Design firm Index Creative Communications, Dublin
Art directors Vince Murphy, Geoff Kirk
Designer Kevin Boyle
Photographer Gordon Ireland
Client Guinness

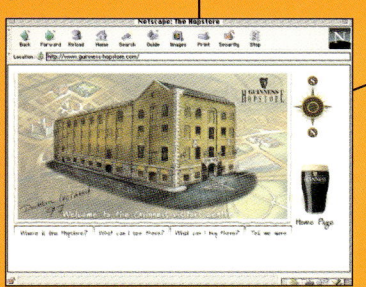

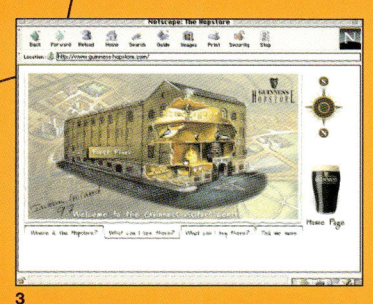

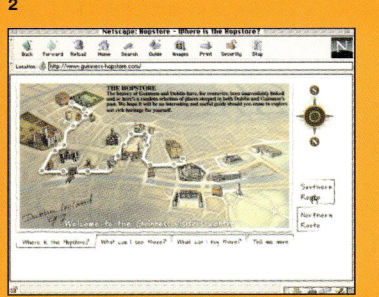

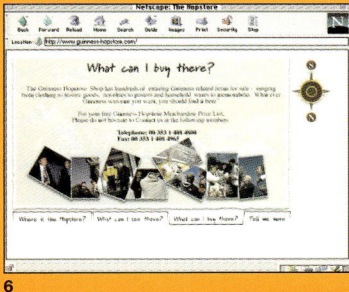

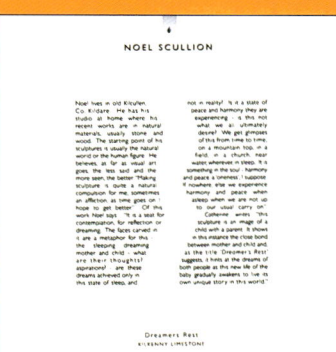

2–6 Guinness Hopstore Web site (www.guinness-hopstore.com)
Design firm Webfactory, Dublin
Art director Marcus Lynam
Designers Marcus Lynam, Ken O'Brien
Copywriter Richard Callanan
Illustrator Olivia Golden
Photographers Ken O'Brien, Bobby Nevill
Client Guinness

7 U2 tour programme
Design firm Averill Brophy Associates, Dublin
Art director Steve Averill
Designer Shaughn McGrath
Photographers Anton Corbijn, Rankin, et al
Client U2

8 Wedding invitation
Designer/illustrator Carla Daly, Dublin
Clients Barbara Cruise, Clive O'Sullivan

9 Guidebook to Shekina Sculpture Garden, in Glenmalure, County Wicklow
Design firm Creative Inputs, Dublin
Designer Peter Monaghan
Photographer Con Brogan
Client Dúchas The Heritage Service

Ireland 51

Gazetteer

Hotels

Hotel J & J
via di Mezzo
Florence
T +39 055 240 951
Hotel converted from a 16th-century monastery is a gem and you may get a room with a frescoed ceiling or with its own courtyard.

Restaurants & Bars

Castello di Gargonza
52048 Monte San Savino,
Arezzo
T +39 0575 847021/2

L'Albereta
via V. Emanuele
Erbusco
T +39 030 776 05 50
69 km from Milano, between Brescia and Bergamo an inn/restaurant opened by Gualtiero Marchesi in 1994.

Il Paradiso
Carrara
Toscana
After visiting the spectacular marble quarries, wash the dust away with the local Grappa at Il Paradiso (above the village of Querceta and near the Henraux quarries). They serve fresh trout from a mountain lake, where you can also swim on a warm afternoon.

Ristorante Rigolo
via Solferino 11
Milan
T +39 02 805 9768
A neighbourhood trattoria favoured by artists and writers where the food is often superb and always reasonably priced. Make sure you make a reservation first.

Places of interest

Il Bisonte Print Workshop
via San Nicolo 24
Florence
T +39 055 234 425 85
The leading Fine Arts print workshop and school in Italy since the 1950s, Il Bisonte attracts major present-day artists and offers short courses in print techniques, taught by the best practitioners. Located in the elegantly restored stables of the Palazzo Demidoff across the river from the Uffizi.

Bookshops & Shopping

L'Archivolto
via Marsala 2
Milan
T +39 02 659 2734
One of the best bookstores in town for architecture, graphics and design and rare books. Good coffee shops in the vicinity and an excellent restaurant, La Bricola, across the street.

Cesare Crespi
28A via Brera
Milan
T +39 02 86 28 93
Near the Scala Theatre, this old-fashioned art supplies store, established in 1840, stocks the largest range of hand-made, rare, western and oriental papers and cards.

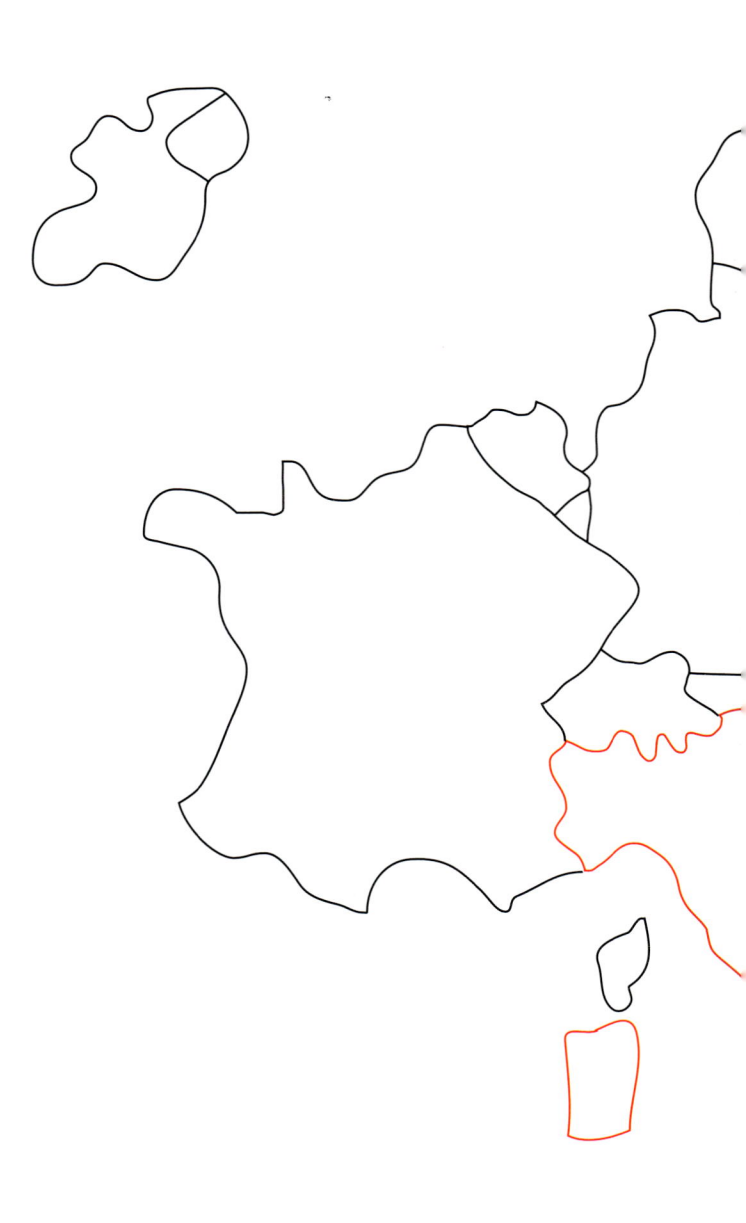

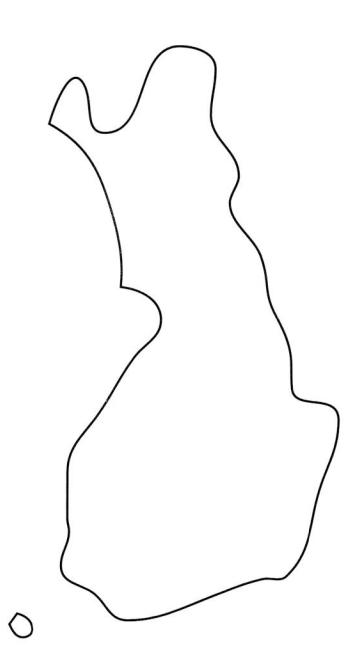

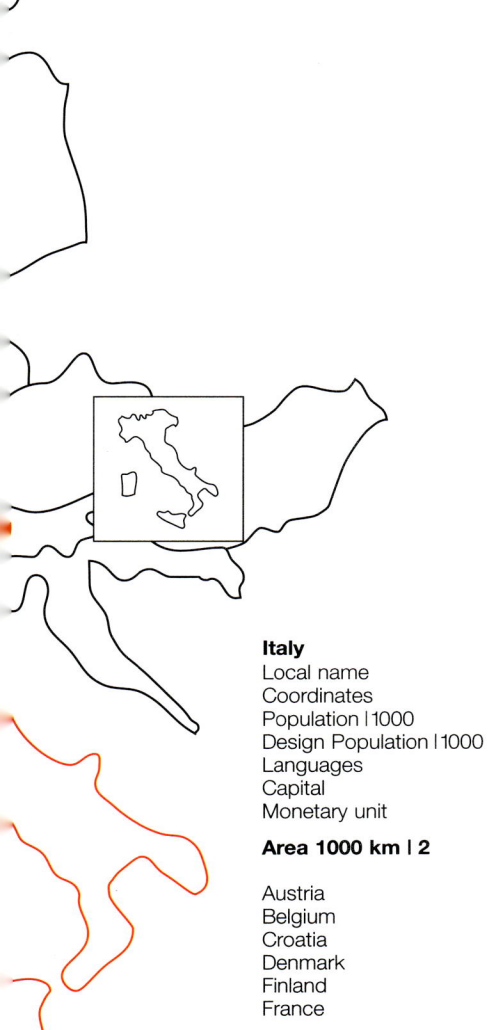

Italy

Italy
Local name　　　　　　　Italia
Coordinates　　　　　　　42 50 N, 12 50 E
Population | 1000　　　　56,782
Design Population | 1000　005.0
Languages　　　　　　　Italian, German, French, Slovene
Capital　　　　　　　　　Rome
Monetary unit　　　　　　Italian lira (Lit)

Area 1000 km | 2					
		Germany	357.0	Russia | Belarus	17,075.0 | 207.6
		Hungary	093.0	Slovenia	020.3
Austria	083.9	Ireland	070.3	Spain	505.0
Belgium	030.5	Lithuania	065.2	Sweden	450.0
Croatia	056.5	The Netherlands	041.5	Switzerland	041.3
Denmark	043.1	Norway	324.0	Turkey	779.2
Finland	338.0	Poland	313.0	United Kingdom	243.3
France	552.0	Portugal	092.4	Yugoslavia	103.2
		Italy	**301**.0		

1, 2 Posters promoting a theatre festival for Italian State Theatre Corp.
Design firm Fausta Orecchio Design, Rome
Art director Fausta Orecchio
Designer Silvana Amato
Illustrator Fabian Negrin

3, 4 Covers of Etinforma, a monthly magazine on the performing arts
Design firm Fausta Orecchio Design, Rome
Art director Fausta Orecchio
Designers Silvana Amato (Figs.3, 4), Sara Verdone (Fig.4)
Illustrators Lorenzo Mattotti (Fig.3), Stefano Ricci (Fig.4)
Client Italian State Theatre Corp.

5-7 Calendar for Vespa
Design firm AreA Strategic Design, Rome
Art director Antonio Romano
Designer Stefano Aureli
Illustrator Francesca Montosi
Photographer Giuseppe Fadda

8, 9 Covers of Nessuno Tocchi Caino (Hands off Cain), a bimonthly magazine on literature, politics, and art
Design firm Fausta Orecchio Design, Rome
Art directors Fausta Orecchio, Rosa Schiavello
Designers Fausta Orecchio (Figs.8, 9), Theo Nelki (Fig.8), Silvana Amato (Fig.9), Sara Verdone (Fig.9), Simone Tonucci (Fig.9)
Illustrators Brad Holland (Fig. 8), Lorenzo Mattotti (Fig.9)

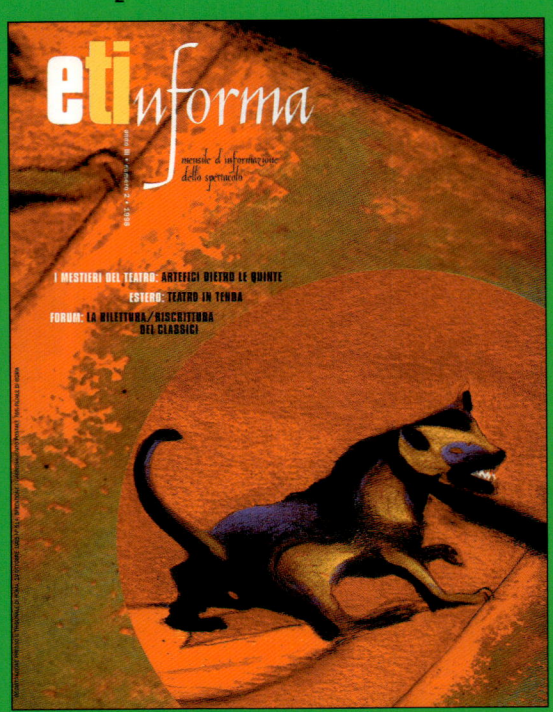

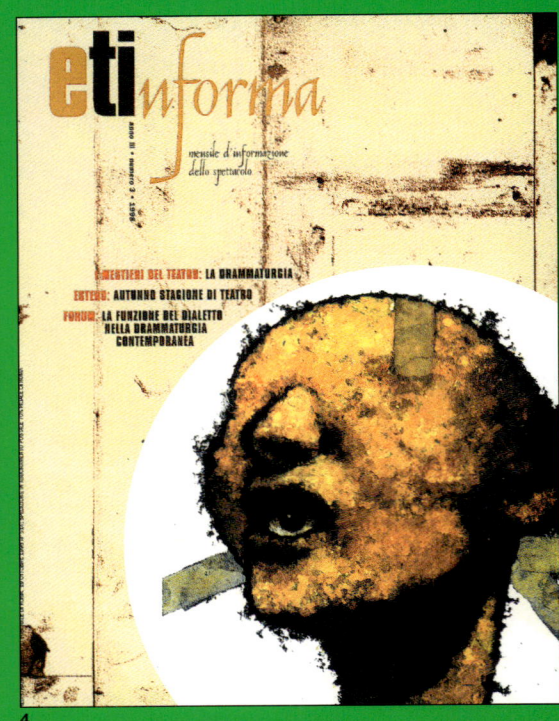

10 Self-promotional logo
Design firm Cap Design, Potenza
Designer/illustrator Carlo Alberto Perretti

11 Logo for Saralva,
a hosiery manufacturer
Design firm Studio Gianni Bortolotti, Bologna
Designer Gianni Bortolotti

12 Catalogue for Bacirubati,
a manufacturer of lingerie
Design firm Maiarelli+Rathkopf, Bologna
Art director Giona Maiarelli
Designers Giona Maiarelli, Sonia Tinelli
Photographer Serge Leblon

13 Spread from a book catalogue
for Arte
Design firm CDM Associati, Udine
Art directors Giovanna Durì, Laura Morandini
Designers Marina Biasutti, Susi Grion

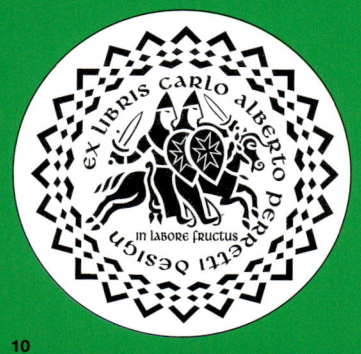

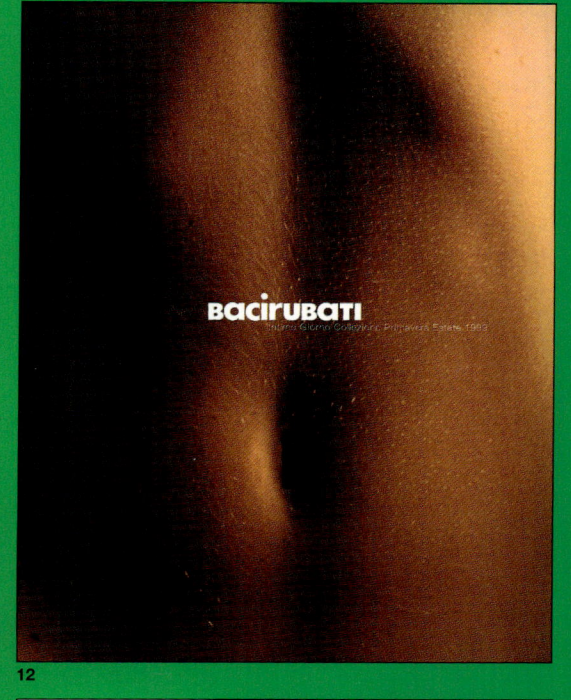

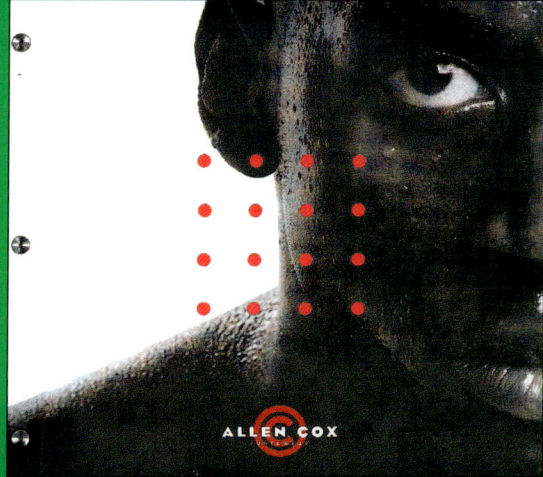

14 Catalogue for Allen Cox,
an underwear manufacturer
Design firm Maiarelli+Rathkopf, Bologna
Art directors Giona Maiarelli, Tiziano Campolmi
Designers Giona Maiarelli, Davide Premuni
Photographer Luca Castelli

15 Yearly planner for Tipolito Maggioni
Design firm Tipolito Maggioni, Milan
Art director/illustrator Guido Pigni

16 Calendar for Hand Made Group,
an ad agency
Design firm Maiarelli+Rathkopf, Bologna
Art director Giona Maiarelli
Designers Giona Maiarelli, Davide Premuni
Photographer Alessandro Esteri

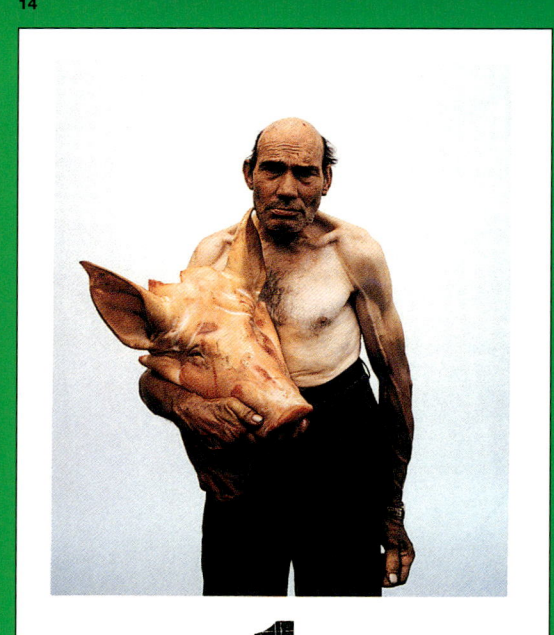

Italy 55

17 Newsletter celebrating 150th anniversary of Lanificio del Casentino
Design firm Maiarelli+Rathkopf, Bologna
Art director Giona Maiarelli
Designers Giona Maiarelli, Davide Premuni

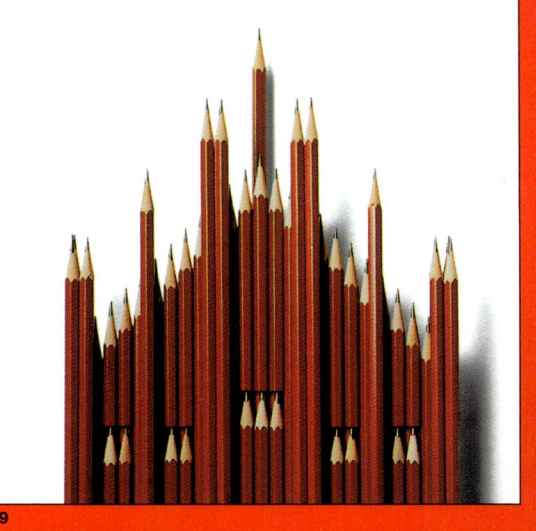

18 Self-promotional material
Design firm no.parking, Vicenza
Art directors Caterina Romio, Sabine Lercher

19 Poster for Comune di Milano
Design firm AreA Strategic Design, Rome
Art director Antonio Romano
Designer Stefano Aureli
Illustrator Francesca Montosi
Photographer Giuseppe Fadda

20 Exhibition catalogue
Design firm Fausta Orecchio Design, Rome
Designer Fausta Orecchio
Illustrator Roberto Innocenti

21 Wine labels for Azienda Vitivinicola Marianna, a wine seller
Agency McCann-Erickson Italiana s.p.a., Rome
Creative directors Paola Manfroni, Claudia Chianese
Photographer Marco Biondi

22 Spread from self-promotional book for photographer Pino Usicco
Design firm IMDCR, Vicenza
Art director/photographer Pino Usicco
Designers Paolo Renier, Alberto Michieli
Publisher Reggiarni Editore

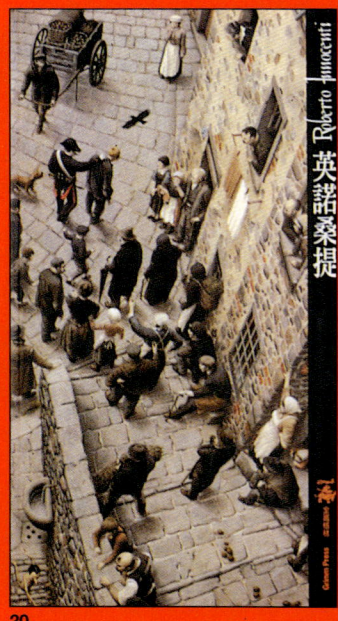

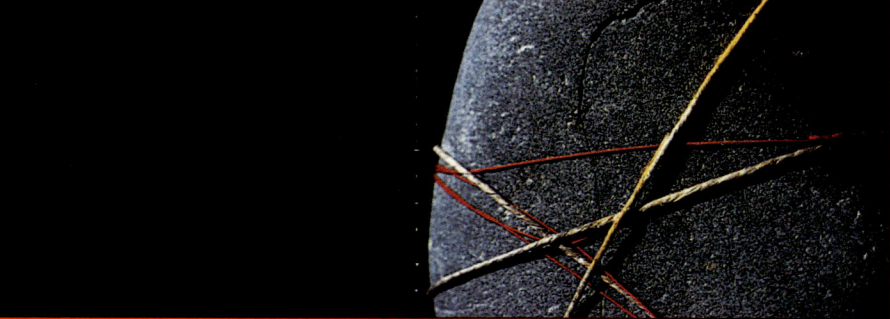

23 Catalogue for Bianchi menswear
Design firm Maiarelli+Rathkopf, Bologna
Art director Giona Maiarelli
Designers Giona Maiarelli, Davide Premuni
Photographer Alessandro Esteri

24 Catalogue cover for Alparda, an office furniture manufacturer
Design firm Studio Karavil, Milan
Art director Defne Koz
Designer Bessi Karavil
Photographer Erdal Baydas

25 Self-promotional calendar for Alberto Ruggieri
Illustrator Alberto Ruggieri, Rome
Art director Roberto Menelao
Designer Interno Otto

26-28 Book covers from a literature series for Editori Laterza
Design firm Fausta Orecchio Design, Rome
Designer Fausta Orecchio

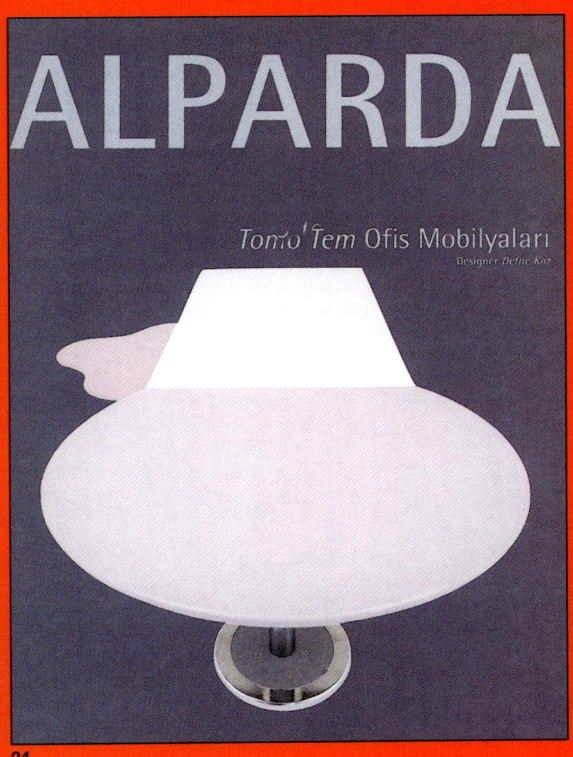

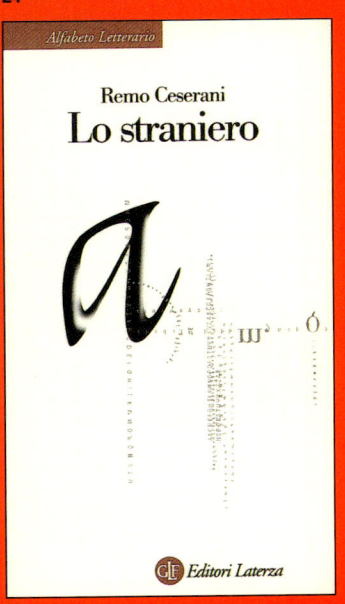

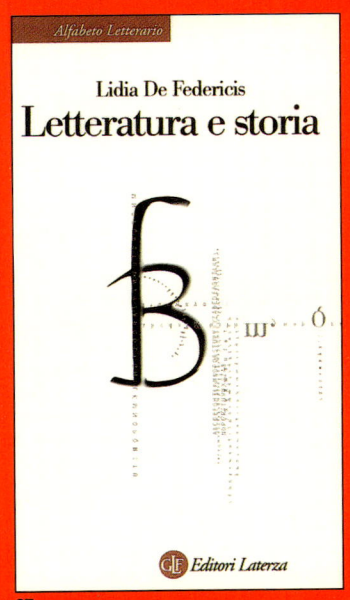

29 Promotional material for ENEC
Design firm Pavese Toscano Studio, Rome
Designers Francesca Pavese, Maria Grazia Toscano

30 Self-promotional booklet for Dudka Sala Design Strategy, Milan
Designers Artur Dudka, Paolo Sala

31 Booklet containing statistics on Rome's population for Comune di Roma
Design firm Fausta Orecchio Design, Rome
Designer Fausta Orecchio

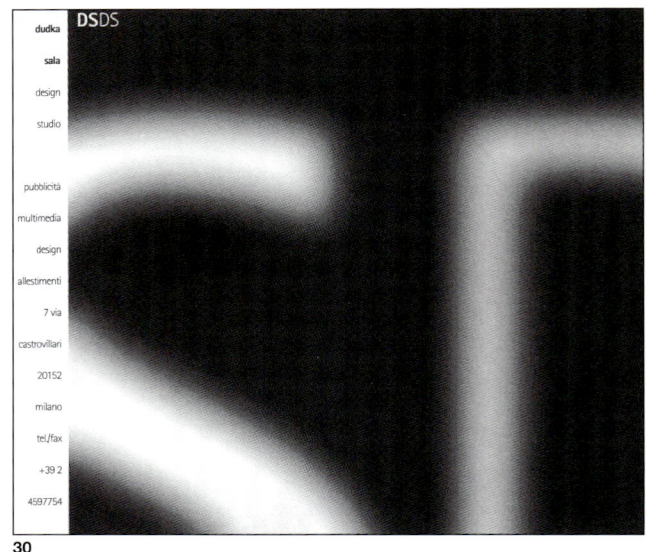

32 Brochure and bookmarks for Central Institute for the Union Catalogue of Italian Libraries
Design firm Fausta Orecchio Design, Rome
Art director Fausta Orecchio
Designers Fausta Orecchio, Simone Tonucci
Illustrator Sabrina Marconi, Blue Omelette

33 Promotional materials for Area Qualita, an environmental protection programme
Design firm Carmi e Ubertis Associates, Casale
Art directors Elio Carmi, Andreina Angelino
Illustrator Andreina Angelino

34 Calendar for Azienda Vitivinicola Marianna, a wine seller
Agency McCann-Erickson Italiana s.p.a., Rome
Art director Claudia Chianese
Photographer Marco Biondi

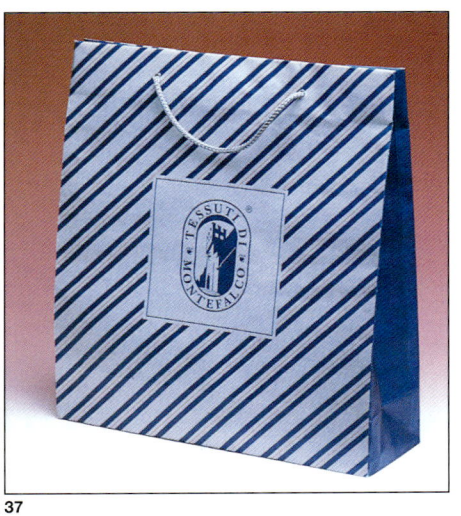

35 Promotional illustrations for Le Monde
Design firm CDM Associati, Udine
Illustrator Lorenzo Mattotti
Client Nuages, publishers

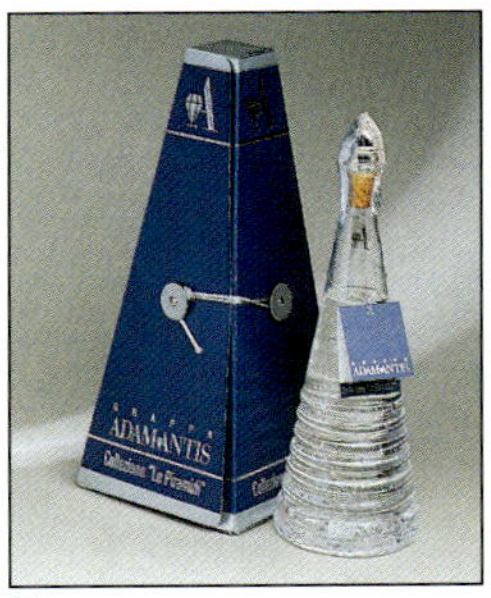

36 Self-promotional calendar for Fausta Orecchio
design firm Fausta Orecchio Design, Rome
Designer Fausta Orecchio
Illustrator Fabian Negrin

37 Shopping bag for Artigianato Umbro, a fabric store
Design firm Studio GT&P, Foligno (PG)
Designer Gianluigi Tobanelli

38 Packaging for Penta Star, a manufacturer of spirits
Design firm Studio GT&P, Foligno (PG)
Designer Gianluigi Tobanelli

39 Promotional poster for Crest Theatre
Designer/illustrator Chiara Caproni, Rome

40 Poster for Pallastrada '98, an athletic event
Design firm Studio Emo Risaliti, Agliana (PT)
Designer/illustrator Emo Risaliti
Client Polisportiva Aurora

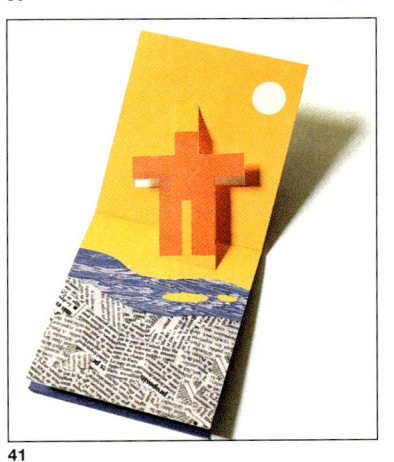

41 CD package for Night & Day Recording
Design firm Studio Tam, Venice
Designer Raul Pantaleo

42, 43 Booklet covers from a series on child rearing
Art director Chiara Caproni, Rome
Illustrators Chiara Caproni, N. Costa

Italy 59

Lithuania Gazetteer

Restaurants & bars

Indigo
Traku 3/2
Vilnius
The newest club in town with all the makings of a groovy club. Retro canteen, dancefloor, cocktail bar on the three floors and chessboard painted tables outside in the courtyard.

Bookshops

Humanitas
Donelaicio 52
Kaunas
T +370 7 229 555
For graphic design books.

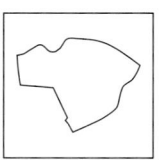

Lithuania

Local name	**Lietuva**
Coordinates	**56 00 N, 24 00 E**
Population | 1000	**3,600**
Design Population | 1000	**000**.2
Languages	**Lithuanian, Polish, Russian**
Capital	**Vilnius**
Monetary unit	**Lithuanian lita**

Area 1000 km | 2

		Germany	**357**.0	Russia | Belarus	**17,075**.0 | **207**.6
		Hungary	**093**.0	Slovenia	**020**.3
Austria	**083**.9	Ireland	**070**.3	Spain	**505**.0
Belgium	**030**.5	Italy	**301**.0	Sweden	**450**.0
Croatia	**056**.5	The Netherlands	**041**.5	Switzerland	**041**.3
Denmark	**043**.1	Norway	**324**.0	Turkey	**779**.2
Finland	**338**.0	Poland	**313**.0	United Kingdom	**243**.3
France	**552**.0	Portugal	**092**.4	Yugoslavia	**103**.2
		Lithuania	**065**.2		

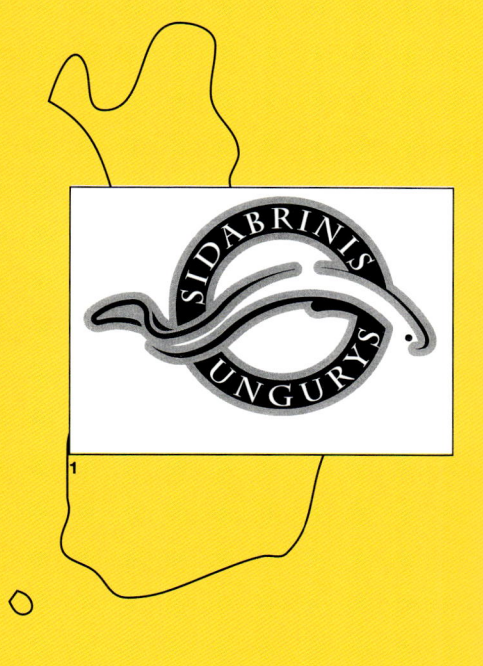

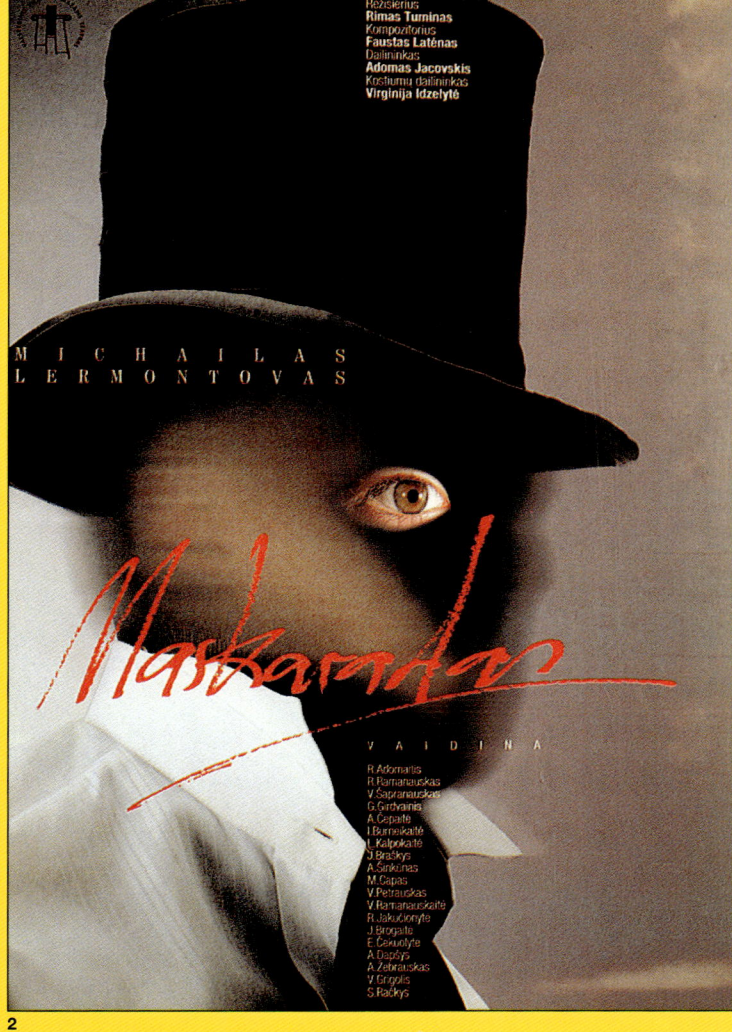

**1 Logo for Sidabrinis
Ungurys, an eel farm**
Design firm RIC Ltd., Vilnius
Art director Giedrius Laurušas
Designer Vilmas Narečionis

**2 Poster for Masquerade by Small
Theatre of Vilnius**
Design firm RIC Ltd, Vilnius
Designer/illustrator Giedrius Laurušas

Gazetteer

Hotels

Hotel 'New York'
Koninginnehoofd
Rotterdam
T +31 10 439 0500
A new hotel and restaurant housed in an historic Art Nouveau building where each bedroom is different and there's a splendid view over the harbour. The restaurant is excellent.

Restaurants & Bars

Seafood Restaurant Lucius
Spuistraat 247
Amsterdam
T +31 20 624 1831
A small and popular restaurant serving delicious seafood. Reservation recommended.

Pancake Bakery
Prinsengracht 191
Amsterdam
T +31 20 625 1333
Pancakes laden with sweet and savoury fillings. Not far from the Anne Frankhuis.

De Pijp
90 Gaffel Street
Rotterdam
T +31 10 436 68 96
A wonderful restaurant, supposedly used as head-quarters for the Dutch resistance during World War II. The walls are hung with ties from different regiments around the world. Moules et frittes are an absolute must here.

L'Orage
Oude Delft 111b
Delft
T +31 15 212 3629
A fresh and classically-designed restaurant serves delicious fish dishes on the canalside by award-winning chef.

Museums & Galleries

New Metropolis
(Science & Technology Museum)
Oosterdok 2
Prins Hendrikkade
Amsterdam
T +31 20 531 3233
A stunning and very modern science and technology centre designed by Renzo Piano, architect of the Pompidou Centre in Paris. Get a fantastic view of the city from the rooftop terrace.

Kröller-Müller Museum
National Park De Hoge Veluwe
Apeldoorn
T +31 318 591 241
In the middle of the woods of the Hoge Veluwe Park is one of the world's best collections of modern art, housing nearly 300 works by Vincent Van Gogh, as well as paintings, drawings and sculpture from masters like Seurat, Redon, Braque, Picasso and Mondriaan.

Rijksmuseum van Speelklok tot Pierement
(National Museum of Mechanical Musical Instruments)
Buurkerkhof 10
Utrecht
T +31 30 231 2789
Devoted solely to music machines—from music boxes to street organs and musical chairs to a self-playing Steinway grand piano—this museum is located in a medieval church house in the centre of town.

Places of interest

De Waag (The Weighhouse)
Nieuwmarkt
Amsterdam
T +31 20 557 9844
Dating from 1488 this turreted, red brick building looks out over the Nieumarkt (New Market) in the oldest part of Amsterdam and was once the head-quarters for the ancient professional guilds of the city. Now home to the Society of Old and New Media, it puts on occasional exhibitions

IMAX Rotterdam
Leuvehaven 77
Rotterdam
T +31 10 40 48844
Enormous movie theatre projecting films on to a six-storey screen.

Bookshops

Bruil & Van de Staaij
Zuidelinde 64
Meppel
T +31 522 261 303
For graphic design books.

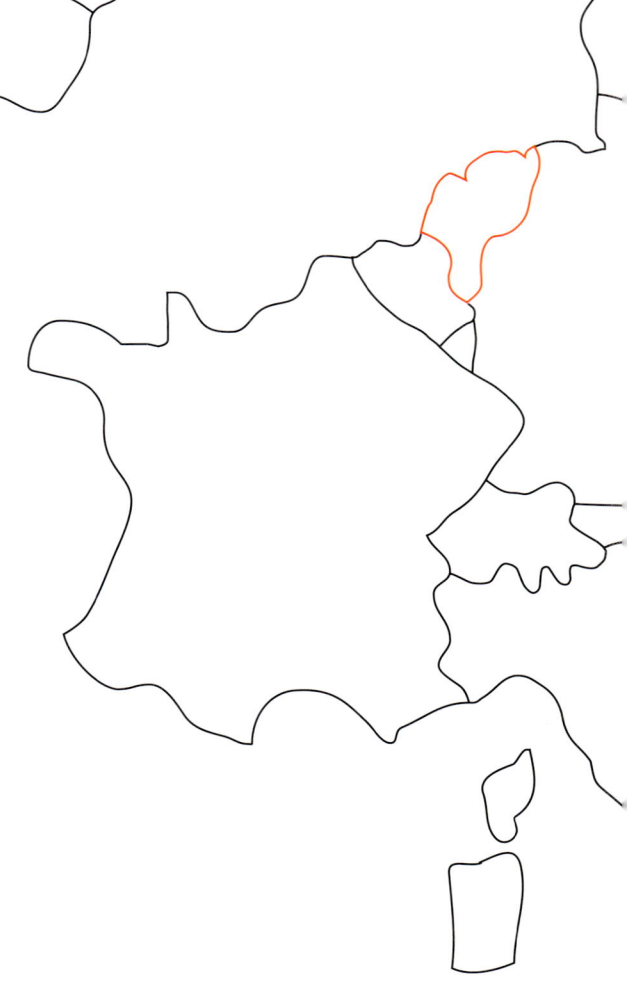

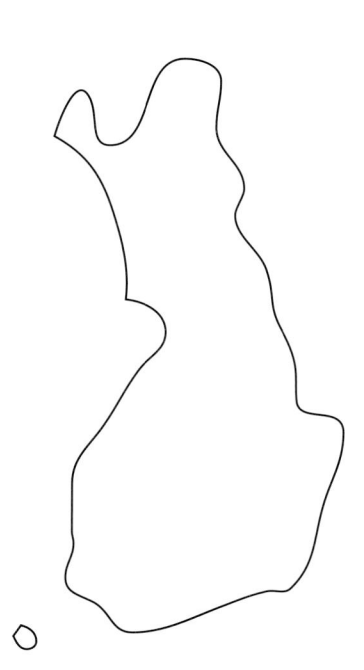

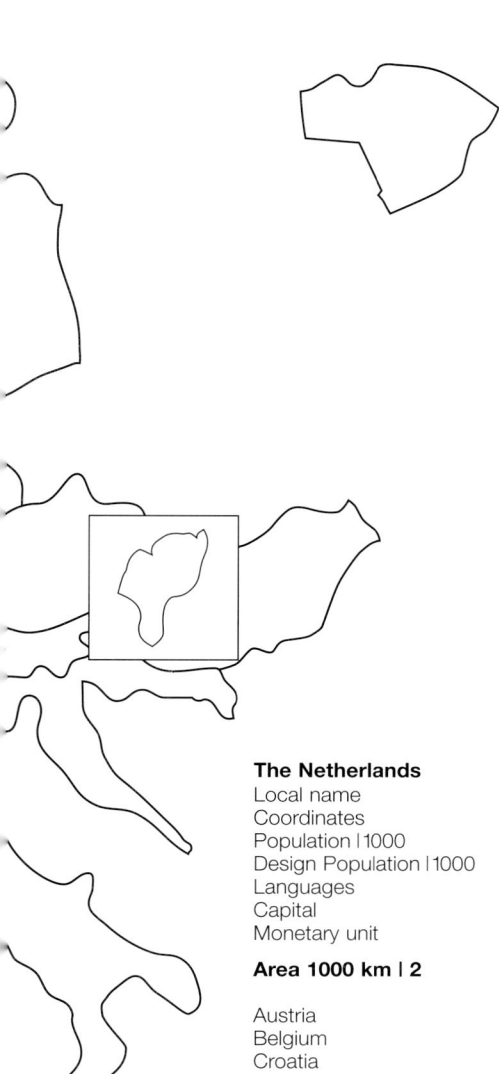

The Netherlands

The Netherlands
Local name | **Nederland**
Coordinates | **52 30 N, 5 45 E**
Population | 1000 | **15,731**
Design Population | 1000 | **003**.0
Languages | **Dutch**
Capital | **Amsterdam (The Hague is the seat of government)**
Monetary unit | **Netherlands guilder, gulden (Nlg) or florin (f.)**

Area 1000 km | 2

		Germany	**357**.0	Russia	Belarus	**17,075**.0	**207**.6
		Hungary	**093**.0	Slovenia	**020**.3
Austria	**083**.9	Ireland	**070**.3	Spain	**505**.0
Belgium	**030**.5	Italy	**301**.0	Sweden	**450**.0
Croatia	**056**.5	Lithuania	**065**.2	Switzerland	**041**.3
Denmark	**043**.1	Norway	**324**.0	Turkey	**779**.2
Finland	**338**.0	Poland	**313**.0	United Kingdom	**243**.3
France	**552**.0	Portugal	**092**.4	Yugoslavia	**103**.2
		The Netherlands	**041**.5		

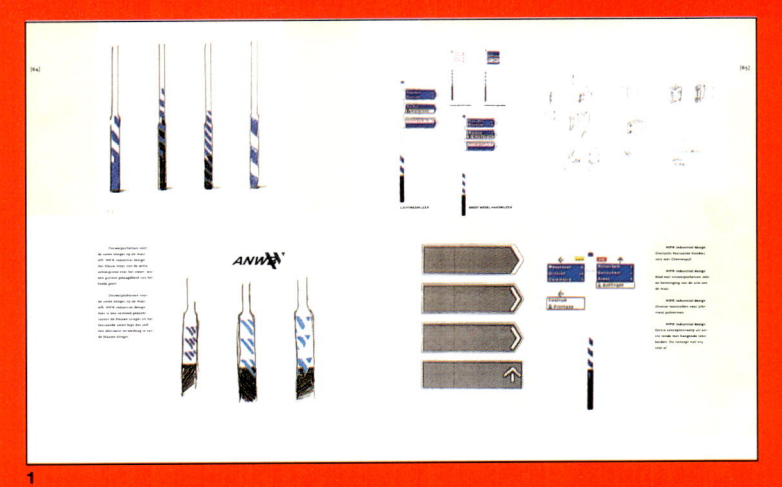

1 Street signage and graphics for ANWB, an independent highway organization that is creating new road signage for the whole of the Netherlands
Design firms n/p/k industrial design, Leiden and Gerard Unger Design, Bussum
Project leaders Peter Krouwel, Gerard Unger
Typography Gerard Unger

2 Identity and 1997 annual report for the Open Universiteit Nederland
Design firm BRS Premsela Vonk/DC3 interaction, Amsterdam
Art director René van Raalte
Designers Selmar de Jager, Erwin Slaats, Philippe Wegner

3 Promotional booklet showcasing the work of artist Dorine de Vos
Design firm Proforma Grafisch Ontwerp & Advies, Rotterdam
Art director Marisa Klaster
Designer Joost van Daalen
Illustrator Dorine de Vos

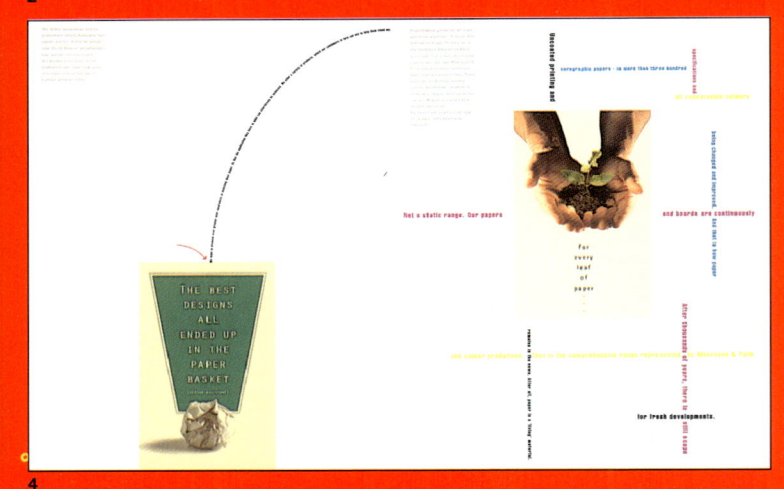

4 Corporate brochure for Meersson & Palm Papierfabrieken
Design firm Addition Advertising, Hilversum
Art director Peter Frühman
Photographer Frank van Biemen

5 Exhibition catalogue for Holland Papier Biënnale
Design firm Kader, The Hague
Designer Loes Schepens

6 Promotional brochure showcasing 12 projects by landscape architects Buro Kromwijk, Maastricht
Design firm Ontwerpbureau FAH BV, Nuth
Designer Fabrice Hermans

7 Graphics detailing neighbours' behaviour developed for SVW (Stichting Verenigde Woningcorporaties), a rental company
Design firm Openbaar Gevoel, Amsterdam
Designer Robert Vulkers

8 Poster for a production of Medea by the Aluin theatre troupe
Design firm Anker x Strybos, Utrecht
Art directors Hans Strybos, Menno Anker
Designer Hans Strybos
Photographer Willem Odendaal

9 Web site for NS, Dutch Railways (www.ns.nl)
Design firms BRS Premsela Vonk and DC3 interaction, Amsterdam
Art director Rik Koster
Designers Elma Wolschrijn, Joost Holthuis, Ralf Mitsch, Ellen van de Sande

10 Promotional brochure for design firm Kesselskramer, Amsterdam, featuring portraits of uniform launderers employed by the Dutch Football League
Art directors Erik Kessels, Johan Kramer
Designer Erik Kessels
Photographer Hans van der Meer

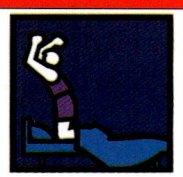

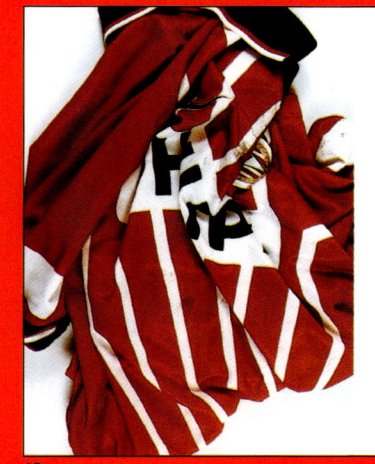

11, 12 Stationery and course binder for the Shell Learning Center
Design firm Tel Design, The Hague
Designer D. Hermelink (Fig. 12)

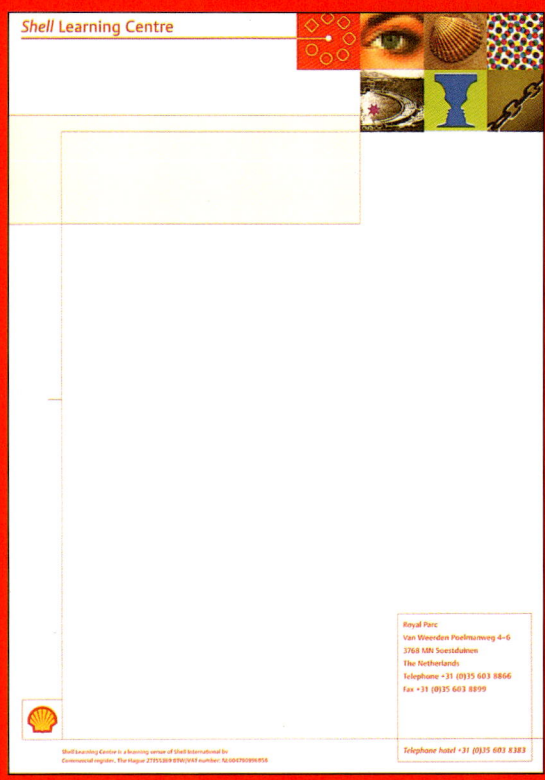

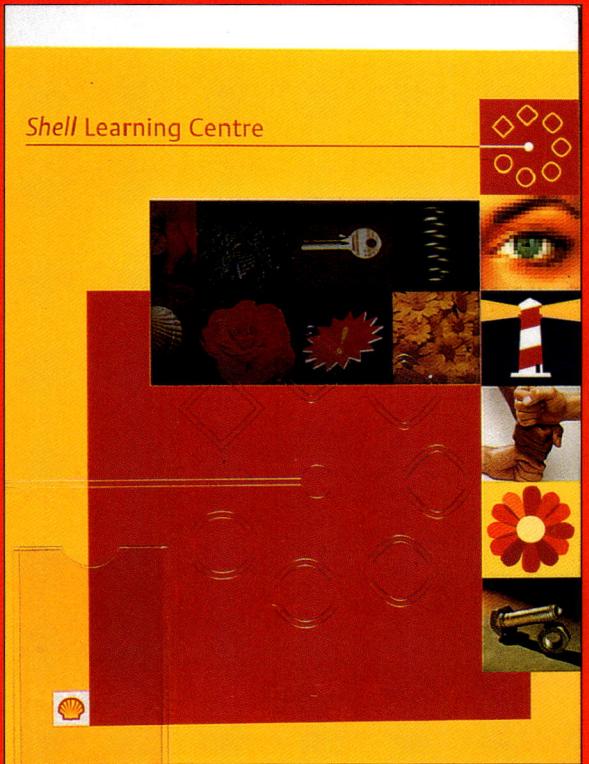

The Netherlands 65

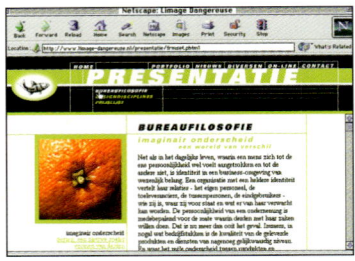

13 Copyright manual published
by Stichting Beeldrecht
Design firm Studio Knegtmans, Amsterdam
Designer Marise Knegtmans
Photographer Reinier Gerritsen

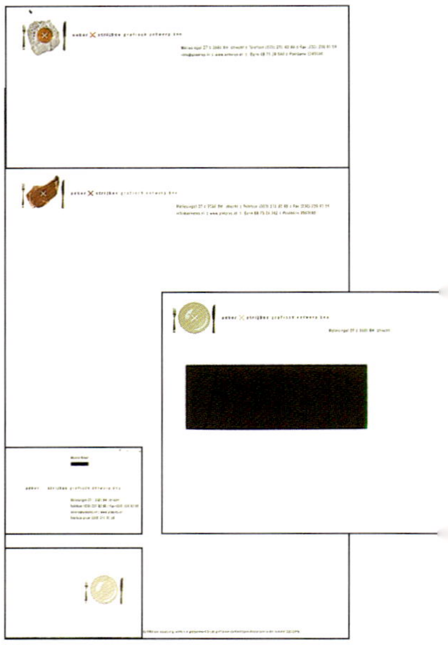

14 Fifty-year jubilee book
published by Eefdese Tehuizen
Design firm M+M Grafisch Ontwerpers, Arnhem
Designers Michelle Clay, Marsel Stoopen

15 Self-promotional Web site
(www.limage-dangereuse.nl)
Design firm Limage Dangereuse, Rotterdam

16 Promotional booklet for Nike Europe
featuring Heinrich Blümchen, the oldest
runner in the Berlin Marathon
Design firm Kesselskramer, Amsterdam
Designer Karen Heuter
Photographer Frans Jansen

17 Dance club flyers for Factor-Y
Designer Jan Heijnen, The Hague
Client 't Paard

18 Stationery for design firm
Anker x Strybos, Utrecht
Art directors Hans Strybos, Menno Anker
Designer Hans Strybos

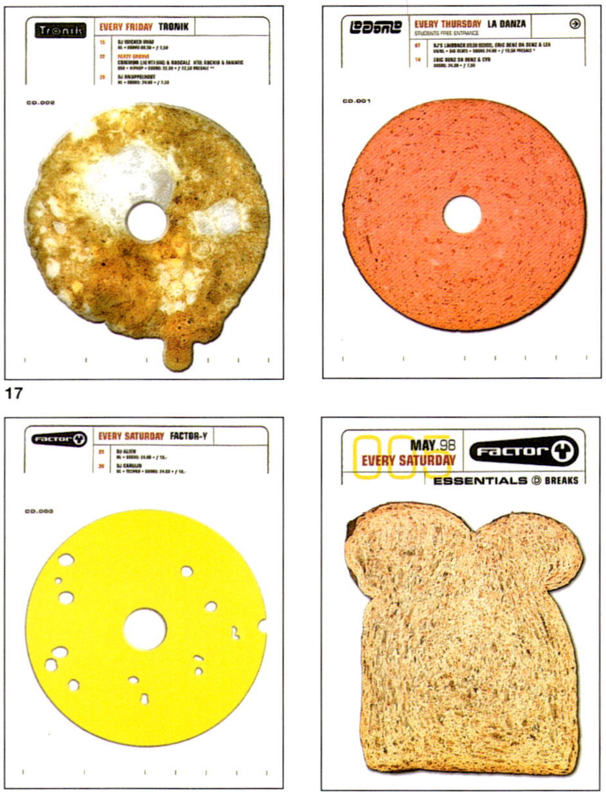

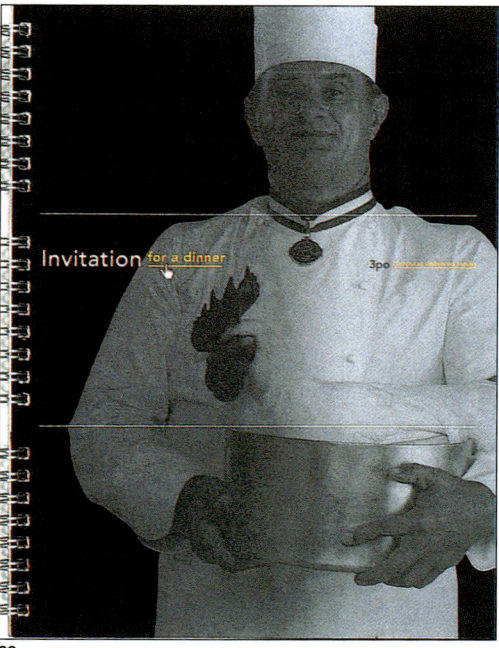

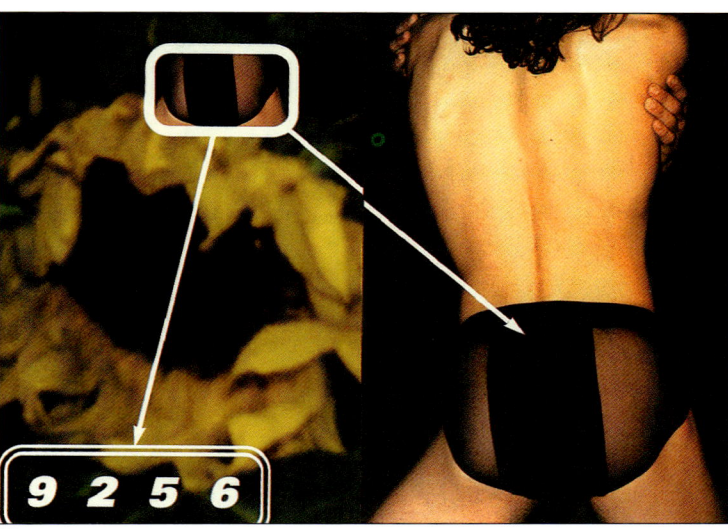

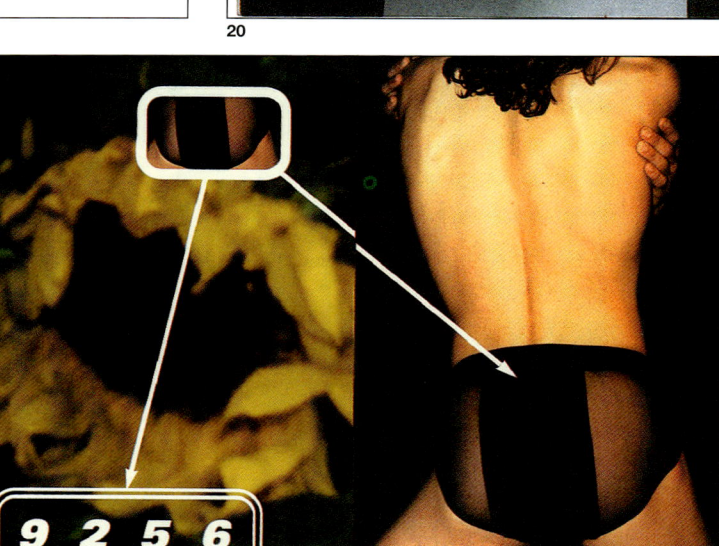

19 Biology textbook
Design firm Malmberg, Den Bosch
Art director Elsbeth Volker

20 Promotional brochure and invitation to a dinner given by 3po Computer Delivered Media
Design firm Proforma Grafisch Ontwerp & Advies, Rotterdam
Art director Marisa Klaster
Designer Joost van Daalen
Photography Jaap van der Beuke

21 Lingerie catalogue for Undressed by Marlies Dekkers
Design firm Limage Dangereuse, Rotterdam

22 1997 annual report for Westland Utrecht Hypotheekbank
Design firm Total Design Amsterdam BV
Designer Bas Masbeck
Photographer Reinier Gerritsen

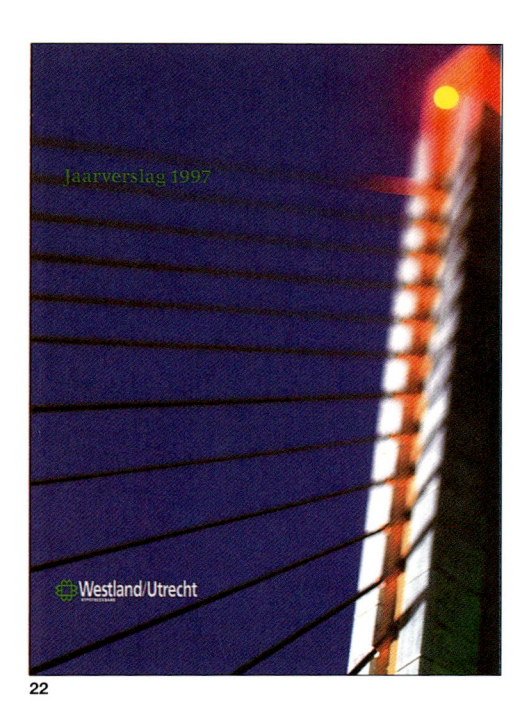

23 Promotional calendar for GITP Human Resource Management
Design firm Ad Broeders Graphic Design BV, Middelbeers
Designer Ad Broeders
Photographer Bart Versteeg

24 Stationery for Beeldrijk, an offline editing house for film and audiovisual programs
Design firm Langtry Associates, Hilversum
Art director Emilia Langtry

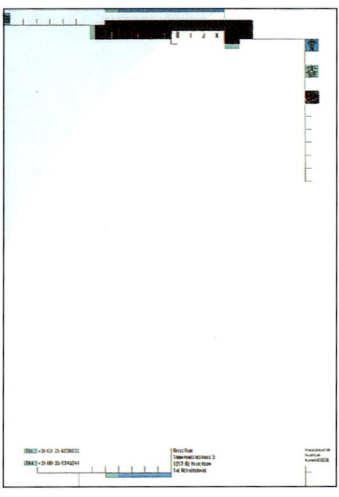

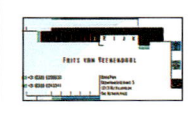

The Netherlands 67

25 1997 annual report for the RAI Group, an organizer of trade fairs, exhibitions, and conferences
Design firm Shape BV, Amsterdam
Designer Hans Versteeg
Photographers Taco Anema, C. Barton van Flymen

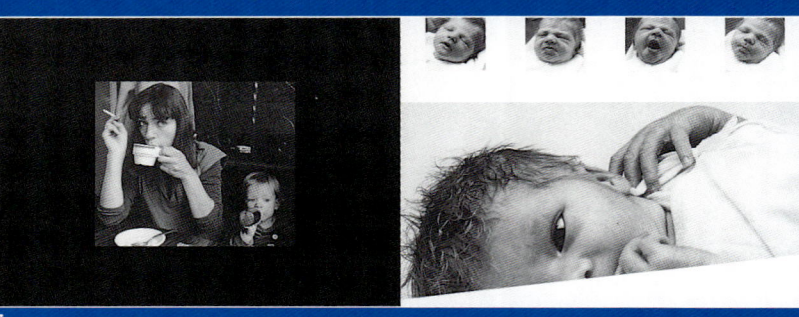

26 Typometer and measuring set for desktop publishing
Design firm Polka Design, Roermond
Designer/illustrator Joep Pohlen
Client Verlag Fontana

27 New Year's gift book for the customers of Polka Design, Roermond, and Valkenburg Printers
Art director Joep Pohlen
Designers Joep Pohlen, Tedje Pohlen
Photographers Joep Pohlen, Tedje Pohlen, Paul Maessen

28 Book showcasing Leiden as the 1997 city of culture
Design firm Kader, The Hague
Designer Vivienne van Leeuwen
Photographer Taco van der Eb
Client Kunstgebouw

29 Artist book titled Amorphophallus
Design firm Ontwerpbureau 3005, The Hague
Designer/photographer Marc Vleugels
Illustrators Karin Peulen, Marc Vleugels

30 Stage cards for the Tour de France
Design firm Kesselskramer, Amsterdam
Art directors Erik Kessels, Tyler Whisnand
Designer Erik Kessels
Illustrator Leendert Masseling
Client Nike Europe

31 Promotional brochure for Hans Brinker Budget Hotel
Design firm Kesselskramer, Amsterdam
Art director Erik Kessels
Designer/illustrator Bless the Artist

32 Catalogue for a show of the work of artist Wim T. Schippers at the Centraal Museum
Design firm Studio Gonnissen en Widdershoven, Amsterdam

33 Book titled Eternally Yours, published by 010 publishers, Rotterdam, offering design guidelines for creating lasting products that reduce waste
Design firm Studio Gonnissen en Widdershoven, Amsterdam

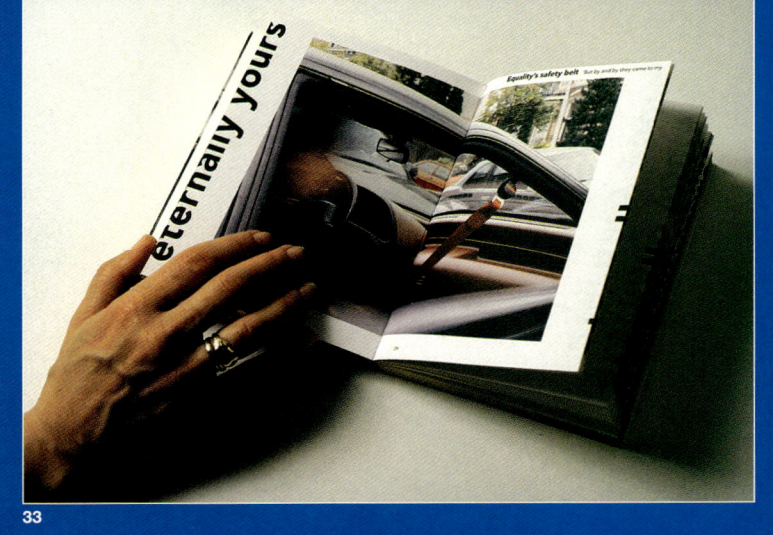

34 Promotional book for the city and port of Rotterdam
Design firm Proforma Grafisch Ontwerp & Advies, Rotterdam
Art director Marisa Klaster
Designers Jeroen Berg, Marisa Klaster
Photography Aeroview, Freek van Arkel, dS+V, Ben Wind, Marco de Nood, Peter van Rhoon, Huib Rutten, Rotterdams Dagblad, Dejong & van Es

Norway Gazetteer

Hotels

Holmenkollen Park Rica
Kongevn. 26
Oslo
T +47 229 22000
An imposing hotel near one of the world's highest ski jumps in Holmenkollen. Romantic, folkloric rooms, many with balconies and excellent views of the city and the fjord.

Walaker Hotel & Galleri
Solvorn
Sognefjord
T +47 5 68 42 07
For sheer natural beauty and a small, quaint fjord-side hotel with home cooking in the heart of the country try this one sitting in its garden of fruit trees. Wonderful walks abound and the ferry will take you across the fjord to one of Norway's best stave churches.

Restaurants & Bars

Theatercafeen
Stortingsgt 24-26
Oslo
T +47 233 3200
A fun café with music (like you may have found in Paris in the 1930s). Very simple, very noisy, always packed, and one of the last Viennese-style cafés in northern Europe. The pastry chef here makes desserts for Norway's royal family.

Finnegaardstue
Rosenkrantzgt. 6
Bergen
T +47 55550300
This is a classic Norwegian restaurant with four snug rooms and an emphasis on seafood. However the venison and reindeer are outstanding and the traditional Norwegian desserts, like cloudberries and cream, are to die for.

Museums & Galleries

Kon-Tiki Muséet
Bygdøynesvn. 36
Oslo
T +47 224 38050
Take a ferry from Rådhusbryggen (City Hall Wharf) to this museum where Thor Heyerdahl's Kon-Tiki raft and his reed boat RA II are on view. He crossed the Pacific on the raft and the Atlantic in the boat.

**Norsk Folkemuseum
(Norwegian Folk Museum)**
Museumsvn. 10
Oslo
T +47 221 23700
Again, the ferry from Rådhusbryggen will take you over to this park where historic farmhouses have been collected and reassembled from all over the country. A section of 19th-century Oslo and a 12th-century wooden stave church have been moved here.

Bookshops

Luth
Ostre Aker vei 213
Oslo
T +47 22 25 48 20
For graphic design books.

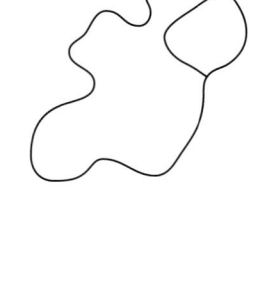

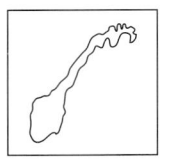

Norway

Local name	Norge
Coordinates	62 00 N, 10 00 E
Population	1000	4,420
Design Population	1000	000.6
Languages	Norwegian (small Lapp and Finnish-speaking minority)
Capital	Oslo
Monetary unit	Norwegian krone (NKr)

Area 1000 km | 2

Country	Area	Country	Area	Country	Area
Austria	083.9	Germany	357.0	Russia	Belarus	17,075.0	207.6
Belgium	030.5	Hungary	093.0	Slovenia	020.3
Croatia	056.5	Ireland	070.3	Spain	505.0
Denmark	043.1	Italy	301.0	Sweden	450.0
Finland	338.0	Lithuania	065.2	Switzerland	041.3
France	552.0	The Netherlands	041.5	Turkey	779.2
		Poland	313.0	United Kingdom	243.3
		Portugal	092.4	Yugoslavia	103.2
		Norway	324.0		

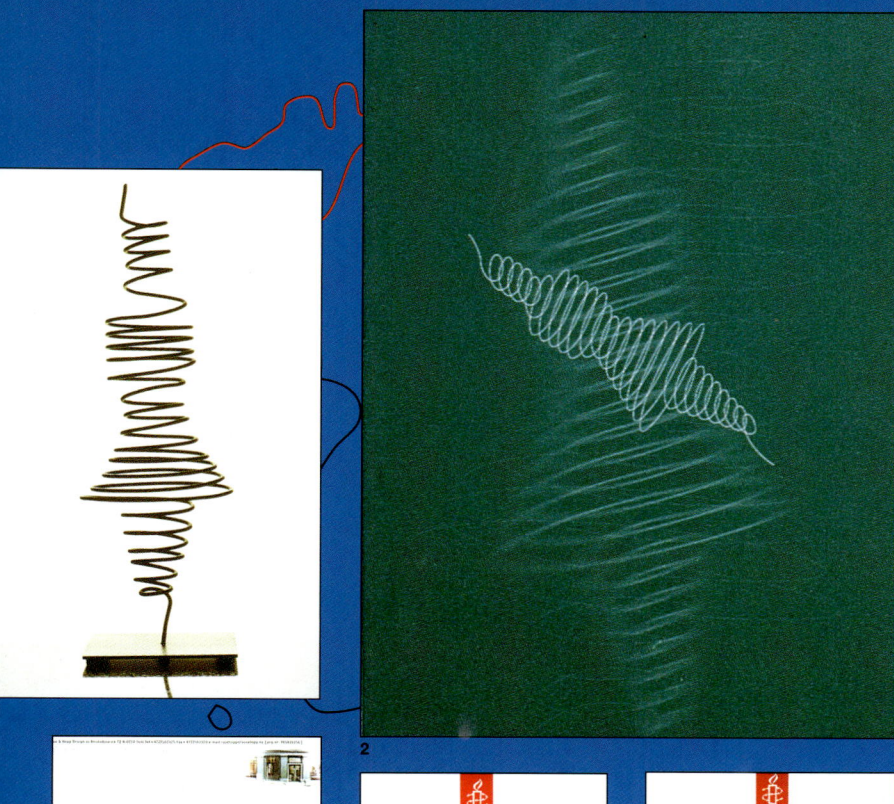

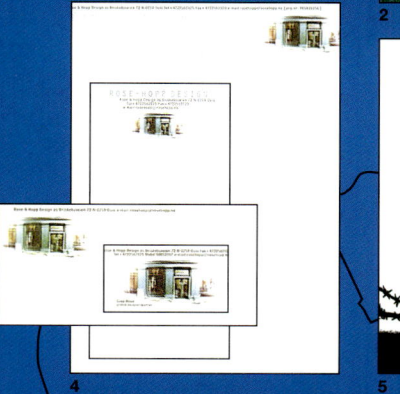

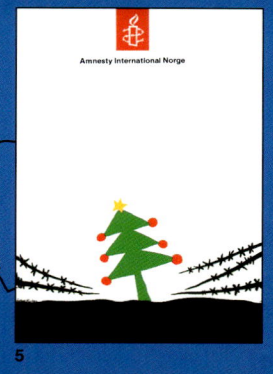

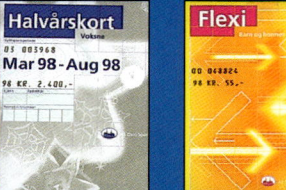

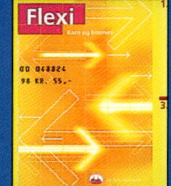

1, 2 Brochure cover (Fig.2) employing a spiral motif adapted from a sculpture (Fig.1) for NTKD, a textile design company
Design firm Ashley Booth Design AS, Oslo
Designer Ashley Booth

3 Self-promotional brochure for a web design and information company
Design firm Gazette AS, Oslo
Art directors Irène Sæthre, Heidi Bakken
Designer Erik Sand
Photographer Morton Krogvold

4 Stationery for Rose+Hopp Design
Design firm Rose+Hopp Design, Oslo
Art director Gina Rose
Designers Gina Rose, Magne Hopp

5, 6 Christmas cards for Amnesty International
Design firm Kutal Graphic Design AS, Oslo
Designer Firuz Kutal

7 Poster for the Quart Music Festival. (After losing its place to a new ID last year, the mackerel was brought back by popular demand as the symbol for this rock festival)
Design firm Trigger Design, Kristiansand
Art directors Bjørn Hoydal, Johan Olsen
Designer Bjørn Hoydal
Photographer Michael M. Krohn

8 Passes for Norwegian Public Transportation
Design firm Ashley Booth Design AS, Oslo
Designer Ashley Booth

9 Stationery for TTS, a theatre and stage management company
Design firm Rose+Hopp Design, Oslo
Art director Gina Rose
Designers Gina Rose, Magne Hopp

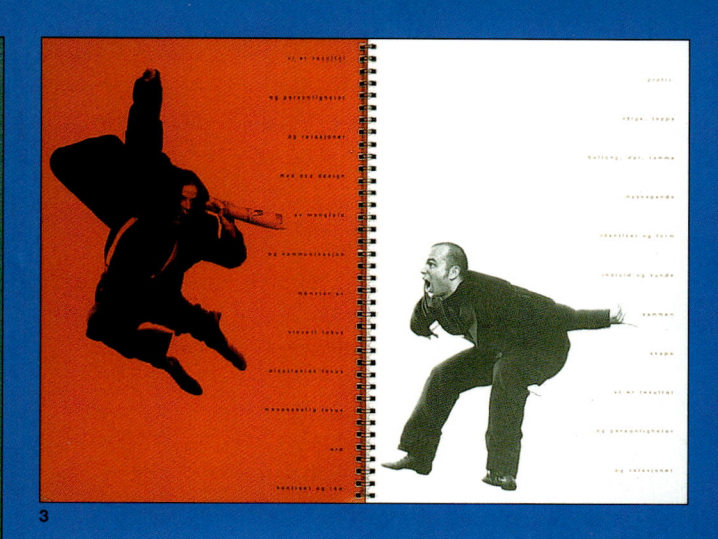

Norway 71

Gazetteer

Restaurants & Bars

Chimera
Sw. Anny 3
Krakow
T +48 12 23 21 78
A fancy restaurant at street level and a salad bar in the cavernous cellar (in the summer you can eat in the ancient courtyard). Traditional Polish dishes with a good choice of warm and cold soups and great desserts.
Ask for pasha.

Pod Lososiem
Ul. Szeroka 54
Gdansk
T +48 58 301 76 52
The restaurant's name refers to salmon (which is highly recommended if it's available when you visit). Other fish and wild fowl dishes are good choices. "Goldwasser", the famous Gdansk liqueur, used to be made in the basement.

Floranska
Cafe Cabaret
The Green Balloon
Krakow
A beautifully preserved fin-de-siecle café chantant with Art Nouveau fittings and furniture. Murals were drawn by Polish artists of the day and there are examples of the marionettes which were used in the performances.

Museums & Galleries

Galeria Foksal
Foksal 1/14
Warsaw
T +48 22 27 62 43
A small space in a 17th-century Palace not far from the University. Good Polish and avant-garde art is on show, and there's a pleasant café.

**Muzeum Plakatu
(Poster Museum)**
Wilanów Palace
Warsaw
T +48 22 42 07 95
Housed in the former Royal stables beside the palace the Poster Museum mounts changing exhibitions of Polish posters and is well worth a visit. Closed Mondays. There's also a gallery of contemporary art in the grounds.

Bookshops

Artes
Ul. Mazowiecka11a
Warsaw
T +48 22 282 64758 ext. 112
For graphic design books.

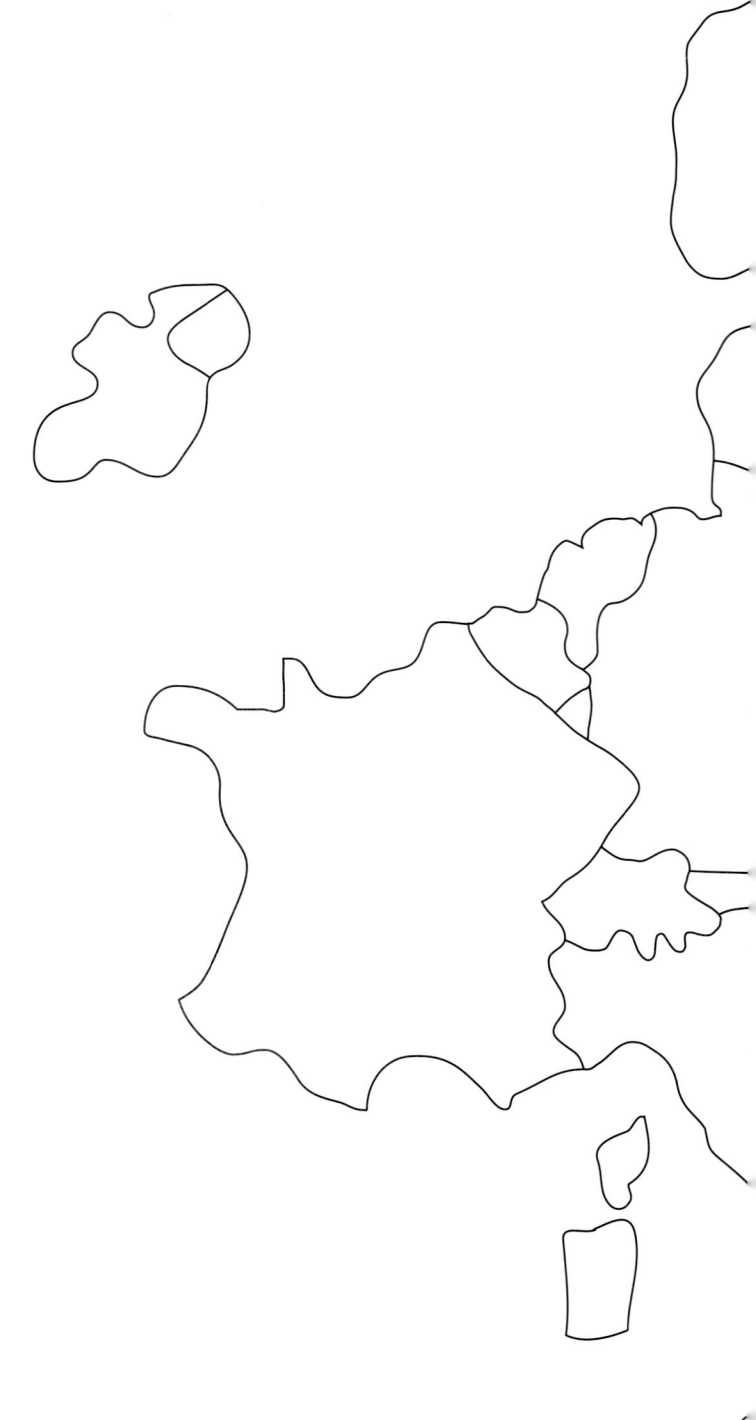

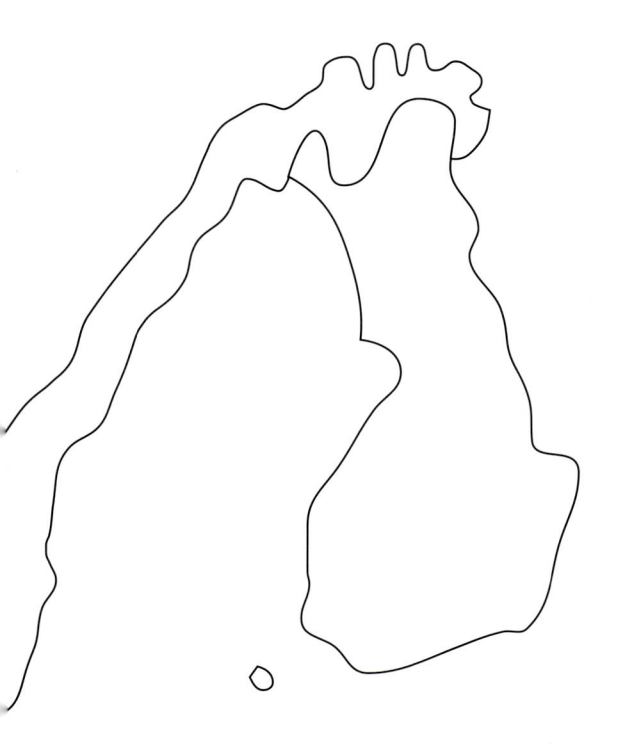

Poland

Poland
Local name — Polska
Coordinates — 52 00 N, 20 00 E
Population |1000 — 38,607
Design Population |1000 — 000.8
Languages — Polish
Capital — Warsaw
Monetary unit — Zloty (Zl)

Area 1000 km | 2

		Germany	357.0	Russia I Belarus	17,075.0 I 207.6
		Hungary	093.0	Slovenia	020.3
Austria	083.9	Ireland	070.3	Spain	505.0
Belgium	030.5	Italy	301.0	Sweden	450.0
Croatia	056.5	Lithuania	065.2	Switzerland	041.3
Denmark	043.1	The Netherlands	041.5	Turkey	779.2
Finland	338.0	Norway	324.0	United Kingdom	243.3
France	552.0	Portugal	092.4	Yugoslavia	103.2
		Poland			313.0

1
1 Self-promotional booklet
Design firm Studio Pro, Toruń
Art director Edward Malinowski
Designer/illustrator Krzysztof Bialowicz
Photography Studio Pro, Jacek Szczure

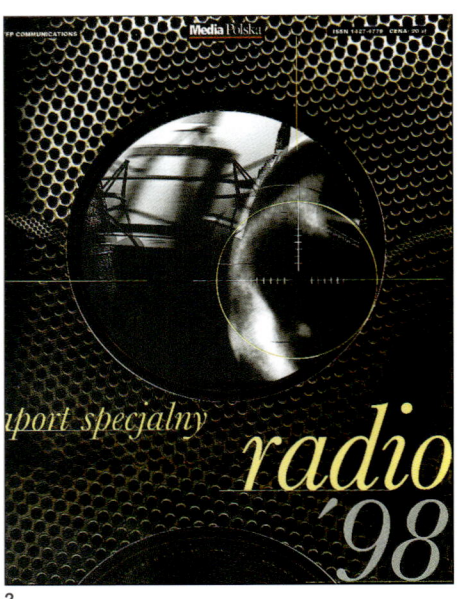

2
2, 6 Covers of supplements for Media Polska magazine, on the TV and radio industries
Art director Mark Rozycki, Warsaw
Illustrators Mark Rozycki (Figs. 2, 6), Andrzej Saganowski (Fig. 2)
Client VFP Communication Sp.zo.o.

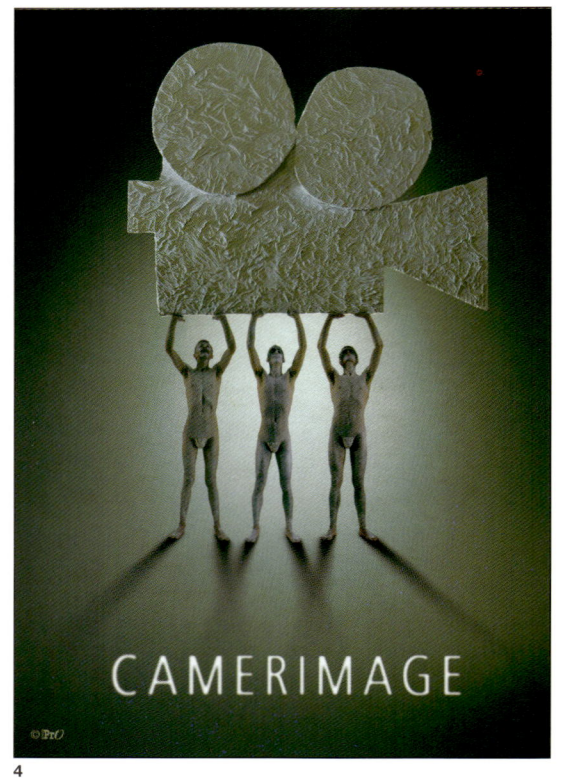

4

3
3 Calendar promoting the city of Toruń
Design firm Studio Pro, Toruń
Art director Edward Malinowski
Designer/illustrator Maciej Bochuzyński

4 Poster for International Film Festival of the Art of Cinematography
Design firm Studio Pro, Toruń
Art director Edward Malinowski
Designer/illustrator Krzysztof Bialowicz
Photography Studio Pro
Client Tumult

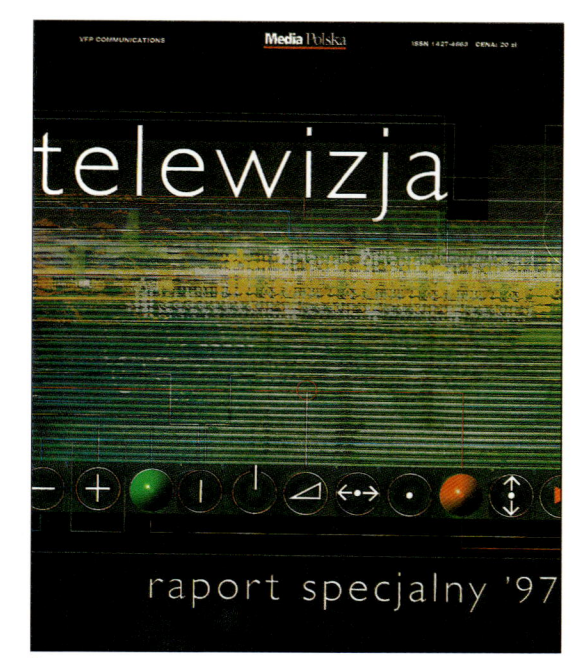

5 Symbol promoting anti-fascism
Design firm Moby Dick Group, Szczecin
Art director/designer/illustrator
Wojciech Mierowski

7 Poster for a conference
by Ośrodek Kultury Ochota
Design firm Korek Studio, Warsaw
Designer/illustrator
Wojciech "Korek" Korkuć

8 Poster for a theatre performance
Design firm Korek Studio, Warsaw
Art director Wojciech "Korek" Korkuć
Client Teatr Powszechny, Łódź

9 Calendar for Polar appliances
Agency Agencja Reklamowa Fart, Wroclaw
Creative director Wieslaw Jurewicz
Designer Julita Gielzak
Photographers Tomasz Zieliński,
Piotr Gielec, Lukasz Kajchert,
Wieslaw Jurewicz

Poland 75

10 Poster for "Stypendysci"
exhibition at Galeria Internetowa, Łódź
Design firm Atelier Tadeusz Piechura, Łódź
Designer Tadeusz Piechura

11 Corporate ID design
for airline Eurolot
Design firm Definition Design, Warsaw
Designer Tomasz Lachowski

12, 13 Egri wine packaging
Design firm Studio DN Design Group, Warsaw
Art director Andrzej Roszkowski (Fig. 12)
Designer Joanna Roszkowska

14 Poster promoting recycling
Design firm Studio Pro, Toruń
Art director Edward Malinowski
Designer/illustrator Krzysztof Bialowicz
Photographer Jacek Szczurek

15 Page from promotional calendar
for PTK Centertel
Design firm Korek Studio, Warsaw
Designer/illustrator
Wojciech "Korek" Korkuć

16 Spread from Media Polska magazine
Design firm Korek Studio, Warsaw
Art director/illustrator
Wojciech "Korek" Korkuć
Client VFP Communication Sp.zo.o.

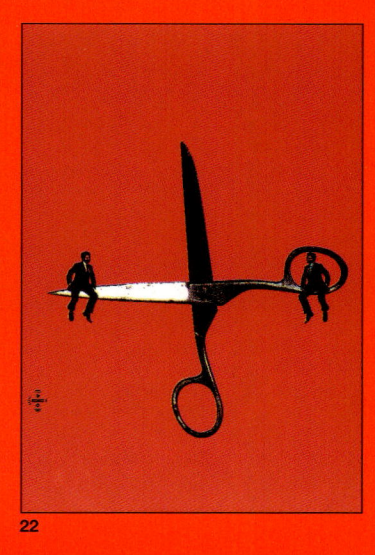

17-19 Spreads from
Media Polska magazine
Art director Mark Rozycki, Warsaw
Illustrator Andrzej Saganowski (Fig. 17, 18),
Mark Rozycki (Fig. 19)
Client VFP Communication Sp.zo.o.

20 Calendar promoting
a wire and rope factory
Design firm Agencja-Vi, Toruń
Art director Tomasz Sobecki
Designer Malgorzata Sobecka,
Tomasz Sobecki
Photographer Grzegorz Przyborek
Client Drumet SA

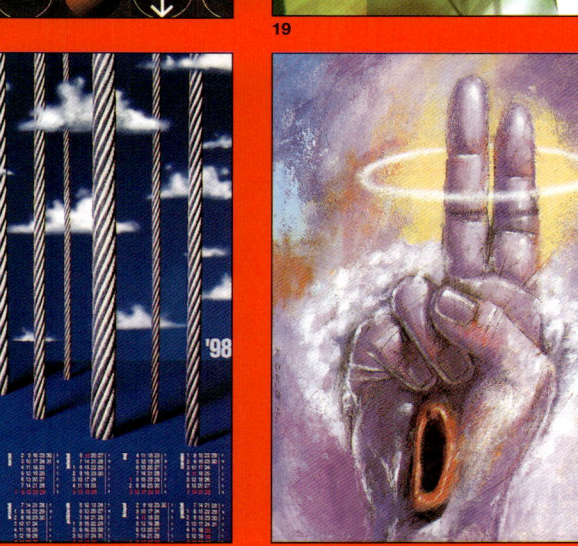

21, 22 Illustrations from
Media Polska magazine
Design firm Korek Studio, Warsaw
Art director/illustrator
Wojciech "Korek" Korkuć
Client VFP Communication Sp.zo.o.

Poland 77

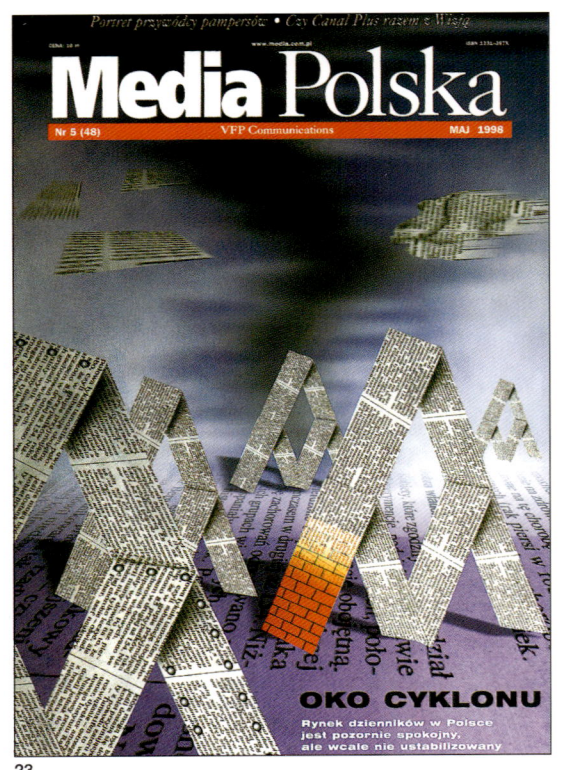

23, 24 Covers of Media Polska magazine
Art director Mark Rozycki, Warsaw
Illustrators Andrzej Saganowski (Fig.23), Piotr Leśniak (Fig. 24)
Client VFP Communication Sp.zo.o.

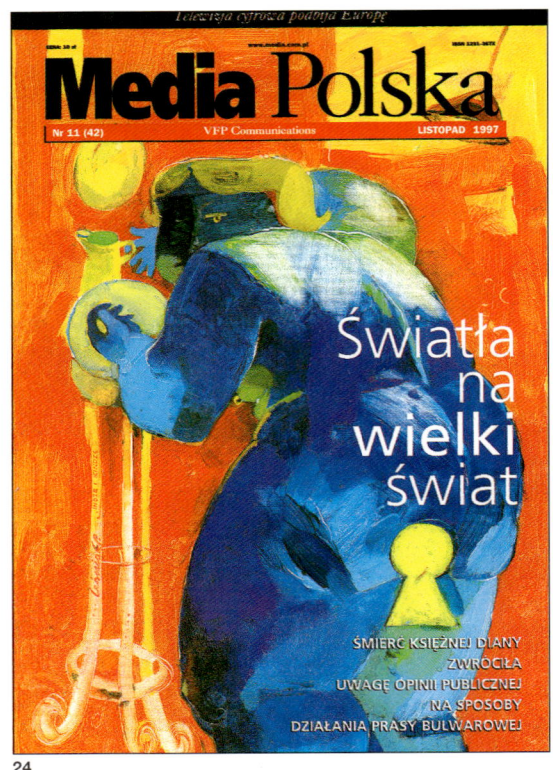

25, 26 Logo and packaging for Metsa Tissue's Prymus toilet paper brand
Design firm Definition Design, Warsaw
Art director Tomasz Lachowski
Designer/illustrator Sebastian Szumigaj

27 Cover of Media Polska magazine
Design firm Korek Studio, Warsaw
Art director/illustrator Wojciech "Korek" Korkuć
Client VFP Communication Sp.zo.o.

28 Page from Media Polska magazine
Design firm Korek Studio, Warsaw
Designer/illustrator Wojciech "Korek" Korkuć
Client VFP Communication Sp.zo.o.

29 Promotional booklet for Cipher, a clothing company
Design firm Studio PK, Łódź
Designer Piotr Karczewski
Photographers Piotr Karczewski, Robert Laska

30 Annual report for Hestia Insurance
Agency Hestia Art, Sopot
Art director Wojciech Fulek
Designer/illustrator Wieslaw Grubba
Photographers M. Karewicz, K. Ladebski, Wieslaw Grubba

31 Self-promotional ad
Design firm Korek Studio, Warsaw
Art director/illustrator Wojciech "Korek" Korkuć
Photography Focus Studio

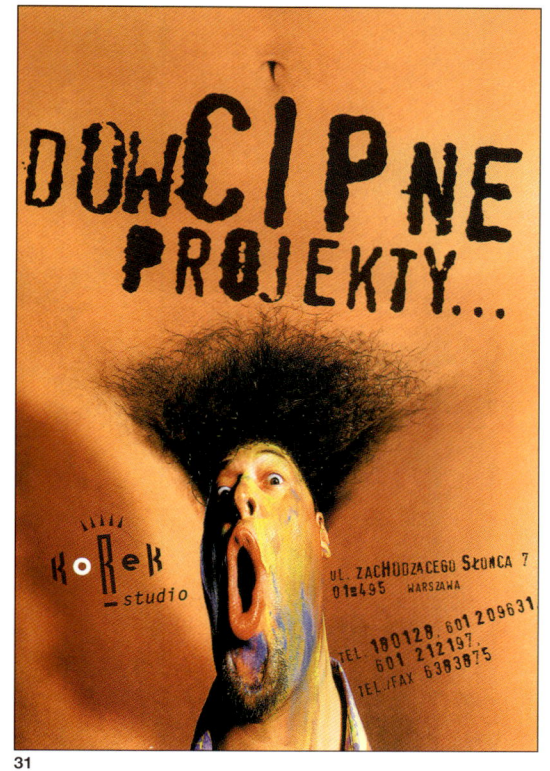

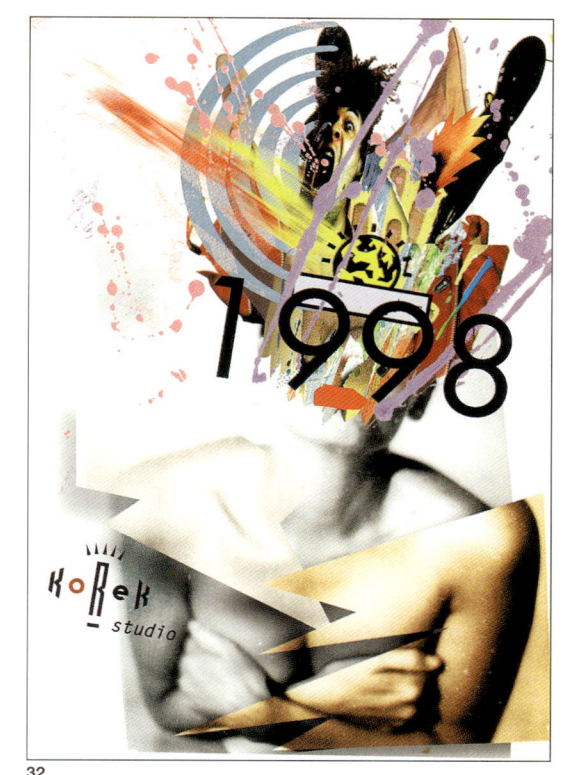

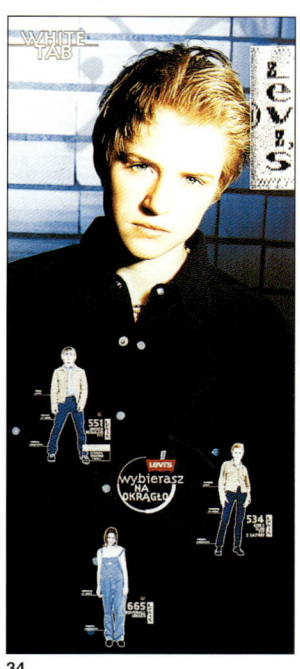

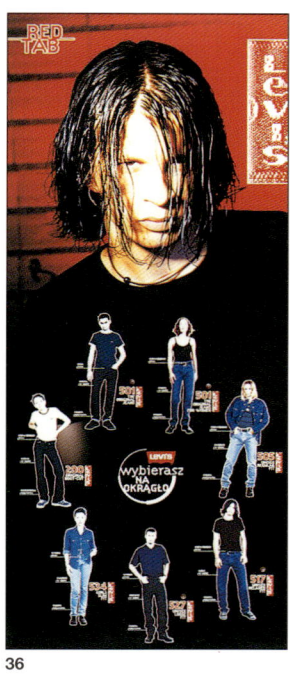

32 Cover of self-promotional calendar
Design firm Korek Studio, Warsaw
Art director/illustrator Wojciech "Korek" Korkuć

33–36, 38 Promotional brochure (Fig. 33) and posters (Figs. 34-36, 38) for Levi Strauss's Red Tab jeans brand
Agency Corporate Profiles DDB, Warsaw
Art directors Jacek Dyga, Filip Gebski
Photographers Jacek Poremba (Figs. 34-36), Christian Coigny (Fig. 38)

37 Poster image for No More Jeanswear
Design firm Moby Dick Group, Szczecin
Designer/illustrator Wojciech Mierowski
Photographer Beata Wielgosz

Poland 79

Gazetteer

Hotels

Residencia York House
Rua das Janelas Verdes 32
Lisbon
T +351 1 60 66 36
Small hotel in a 16th-century convent above the River Tagus. Beautiful courtyard. Clean simple rooms (no luxuries, but sublime peace). Get one of Lisbon's wonderful trams and eat in the city centre 5 minutes away.

Estalagem Santa Catarina
Rua Santa Catarina 1347
Oporto
Wonderful hotel tucked away around a lovely inner garden with tropical plants and fountains. Bedrooms are sumptuous and full of antiques.

Restaurants & Bars

Solmar Restaurant
Rua das Portas de Santo Antão
Nos. 106A-108
Lisbon
T +351 1 342 3371
Solmar belongs to another era and this has a magnificent 1950s interior complete with lots of curves and great murals. The food is pretty good too, all fish, fresh from the Atlantic.

CAM (Centro d'arte Moderna)
Fundaçao Gulbenkian
Lisbon
T +351 1 795 0236
A modern museum of modern art with perhaps the best café of its kind in Lisbon.

Museu Nacional do Azulejo
Rua Madre de Deus 4
Lisbon
T +351 1 814 7747
Housed in a former monastery founded in 1509 is a collection of tiles from the 15th century to the present. The tiles are mainly from Portugal, but there are additional examples from Antwerp, the Netherlands and Spain.

Portugal

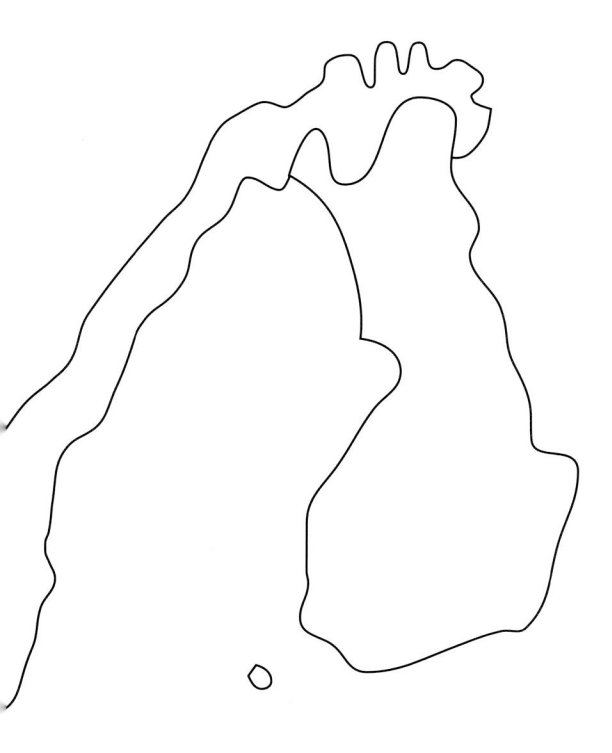

Portugal
Local name — **Portugal**
Coordinates — **39 30 N, 8 00 E**
Population | 1000 — **9,928**
Design Population | 1000 — **002**.0
Languages — **Portuguese**
Capital — **Lisbon**
Monetary unit — **Portuguese escudo (Esc)**

**Area 1000 km	2**					
		Germany	**357**.0	Russia	Belarus	**17,075**.0	**207**.6
		Hungary	**093**.0	Slovenia	**020**.3
Austria	**083**.9	Ireland	**070**.3	Spain	**505**.0
Belgium	**030**.5	Italy	**301**.0	Sweden	**450**.0
Croatia	**056**.5	Lithuania	**065**.2	Switzerland	**041**.3
Denmark	**043**.1	The Netherlands	**041**.5	Turkey	**779**.2
Finland	**338**.0	Norway	**324**.0	United Kingdom	**243**.3
France	**552**.0	Poland	**313**.0	Yugoslavia	**103**.2
				Portugal	**092**.4

1 Package of cultural guidebooks for CulturPorto/Rivoli
Design firm PĀ Design, Porto
Designers Ana Menezes, Né Santelmo, Miguel Freitas

2, 4 Promotional posters for DDD gallery in Osaka, Japan
Design firm João Machado Design LDA, Porto
Designer/illustrator João Machado

3 Promotional booklet for Marca-Artes Gráficas, a printer
Design firm PĀ Design, Porto
Designers Ana Menezes, Né Santelmo
Copywriter Miucha Carvalhal
Photographer Óscar Almeida

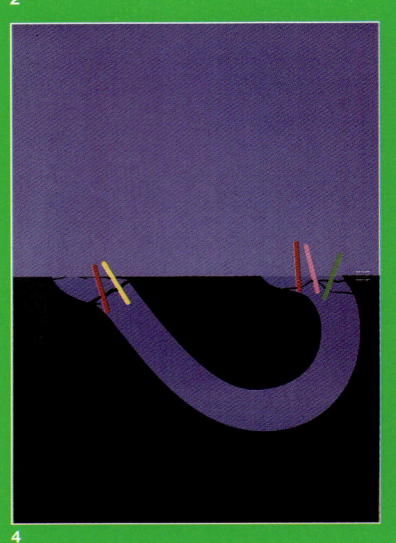

5, 6 Book covers for Pergaminho Publishing
Designer Carlos Reis, Lisbon
Art (Fig.6): Hieronymus Bosch
Illustrator (Fig.5): Bruno Carriço

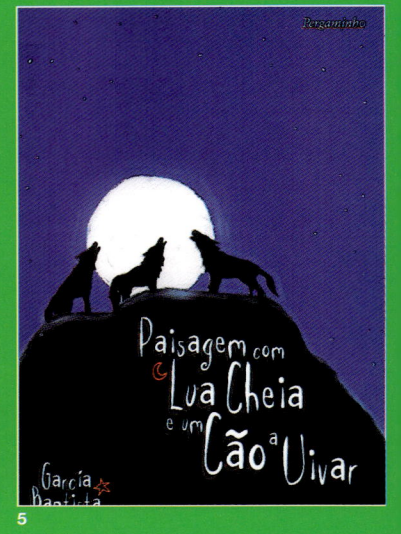

7 Book cover for "Dive into the Future," an event at Expo '98
Design firm Ricardo Mealha–Atelier, Lisbon
Art director Ricardo Mealha
Designer/illustrator Carlos Reis

8 Self-promotional T-shirt
Design firm Planet Design, Carnaxide
Art director Maria do Céu Vasconcelos
Designer Nuno Luz
Photographer Nuno Constantinto

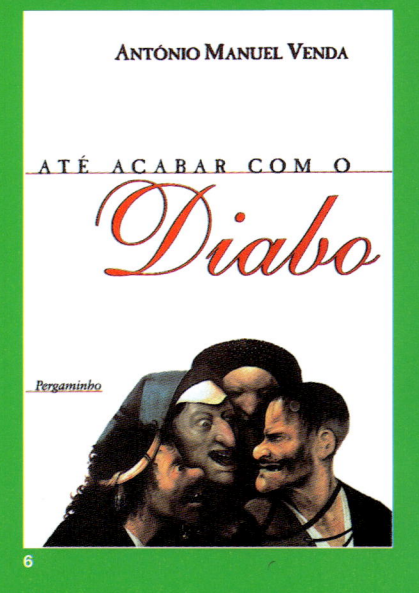

9 Catalogue cover for a Christmas exhibition about children
Design firm Ricardo Mealha–Atelier, Lisbon
Designer Ricardo Mealha

10 Covers of cultural guidebooks for CulturPorto/Rivoli
Design firm PÁ Design, Porto
Designers Ana Menezes, Né Santelmo

11–14 Promotional posters representing the seasons for Carreira Paper
Design firm João Machado Design LDA, Porto
Designer/illustrator João Machado

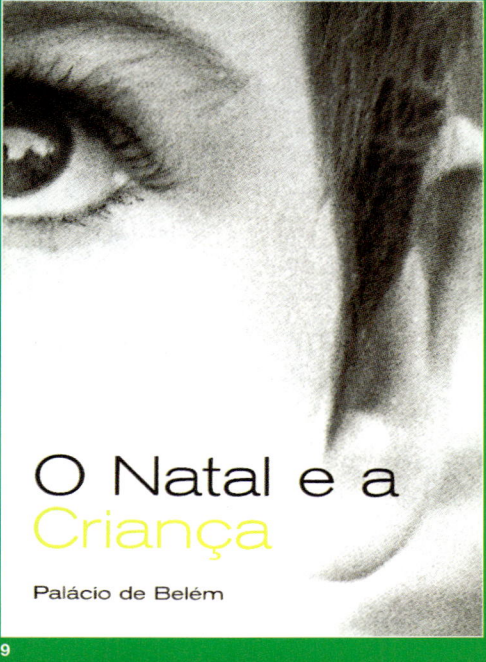

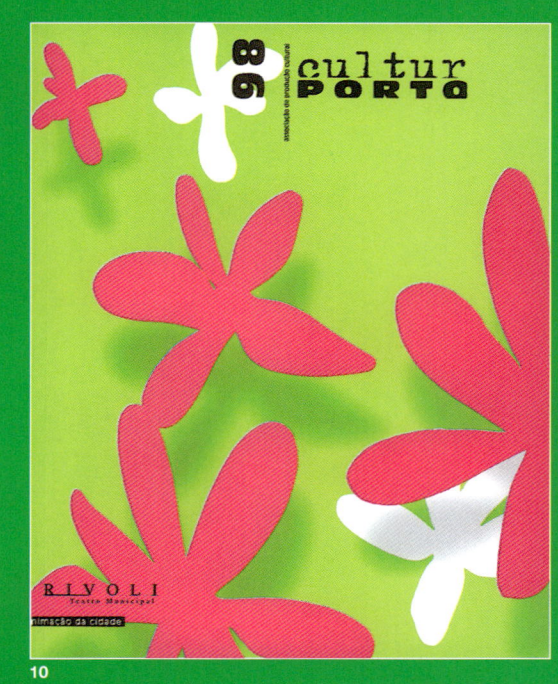

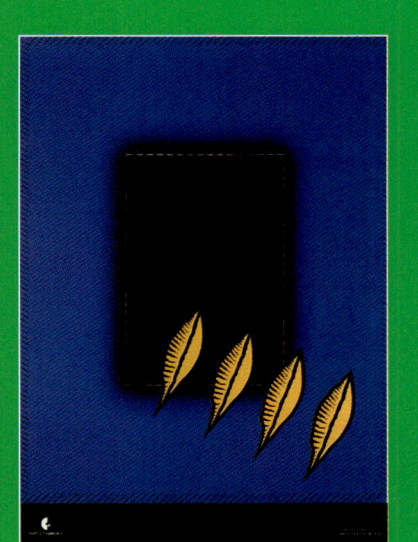

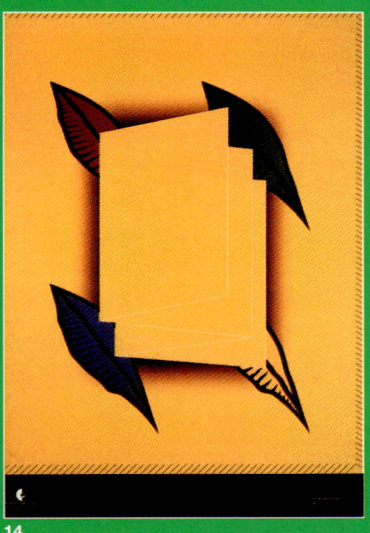

15 Booklet for Unicer, a Portuguese beverage company at Expo '98
Design firm Publicis Design, Lisbon
Art director José Dionísio
Designer Miguel Diniz
Photographer João Pádua

16 Promotional flyers for a nightclub
Design firm Ricardo Mealha–Atelier, Lisbon
Designer/illustrator Ricardo Mealha

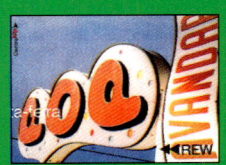

portugal 83

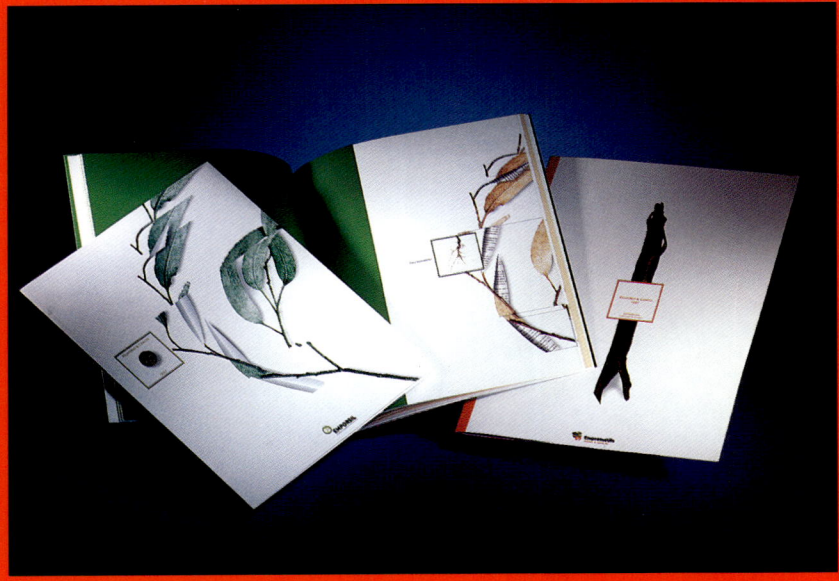

17 1997 annual report for Soporcel
Design firm Novodesign, Lisbon
Art director Luis Alvoeiro
Designer/illustrator Maria João Lima

18 Poster promoting
National Water Day, 1997
Design firm
João Machado Design LDA, Porto
Client SMAS
Designer/illustrator João Machado

19 Logo for Mayer & Fish,
a company specializing in fish food
Design firm R2 Design, Matosinhos
Designers Lizá Defossez Ramalho,
Artur Rebelo

20 Cover of cultural guidebook
for CulturPorto/Rivoli
Design firm PÃ Design, Porto
Designers Ana Menezes, Né Santelmo

21, 26 Book covers
for Pergaminho Publishing
Designer Carlos Reis, Lisbon

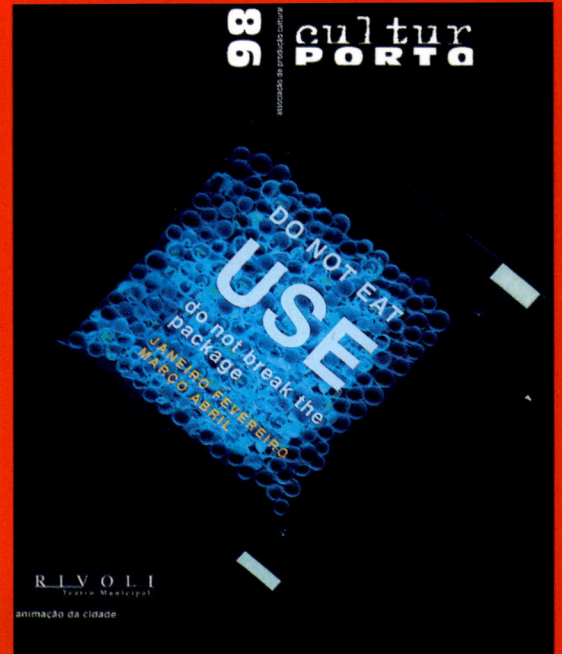

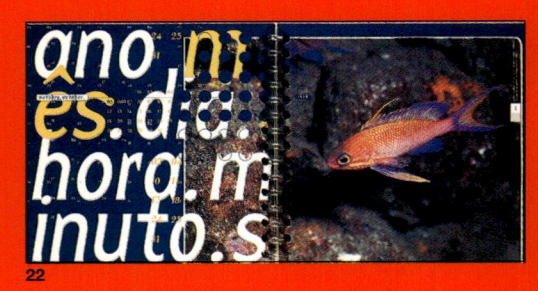

22 Yearly planner for
Raiz Quadrada for Expo '98
Design firm Publicis Design, Lisbon
Art director José Dionísio
Designer João Paulo Pádua
Illustrators Les Gallagher, João Barreiros

23 Brochure and stationery for a shoe manufacturer
Design firm Ricardo Mealha–Atelier, Lisbon
Art director Ricardo Mealha
Designer Ana Margarida Cunha
Client Uns & Outros

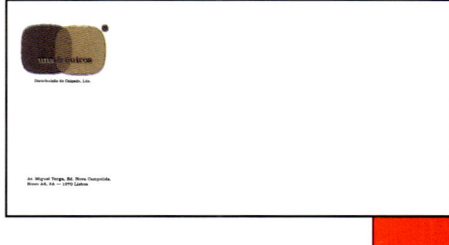

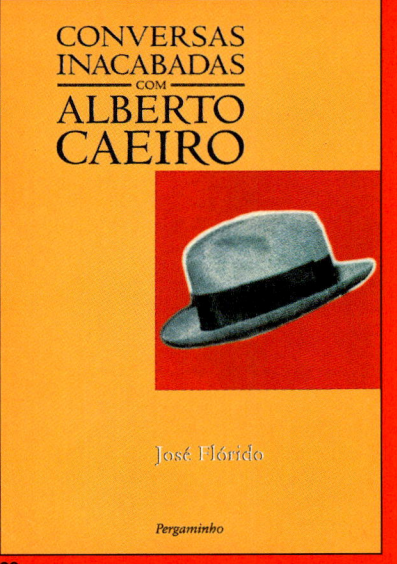

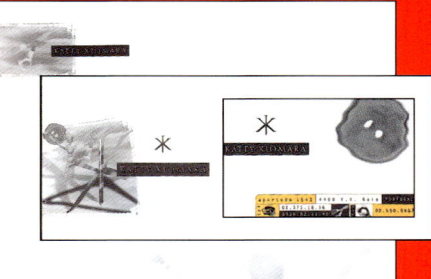

24 Promotional booklet for Pregaia
Design firm PA Design, Porto
Designers Ana Menezes, Né Santelmo
Illustrator Né Santelmo
Photographers Alexander Koch, António Pinto

25 Signage for a soup stand
Agency Euro RSCG, Oeiras
Art director Eugénio Chorão
Designer Luisa Toffolo

27 Stationery for Katty Xiomara, a fashion designer
Design firm Setezeroum, Vila Nova de Gaia
Designer José Manuel Da Silva

28 Logo for Digidoc Information Technologies
Design firm Atelier de Design e Comunicação, Lisbon
Art director Nuno Frazão
Designer Nuno Alves

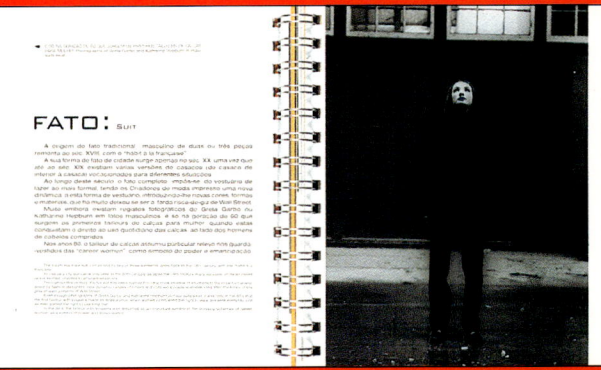

29 Logo for Made in Hell Productions, producers of raves and alternative events
Design firm Atelier de Design e Comunicação, Lisbon
Designer Nuno Alves

30 Invitation to 10th annual fashion show, ModaLisboa
Design firm Ricardo Mealha–Atelier, Lisbon
Designer Ricardo Mealha

31 Catalogue and yearly planner for 10th annual fashion show, ModaLisboa
Design firm Ricardo Mealha–Atelier, Lisbon
Art director Ricardo Mealha
Designer Ana Margarida Cunha
Photographers Inês Gonçalves, Pedro Claudio

Portugal 85

Russia & Belarus Gazetteer

Hotels

Hotel Metropol
1 Prospekt Marxa
Moscow
T +95 927 6100
This hotel by the oldest part of the Kremlin Wall was Stalin's first Moscow headquarters before he moved into the Kremlin. Dining rooms in the classic Empire style and the Breakfast Room has a fountain in gold. A haven.

Museums & Galleries

Tolstoy House Museum
21 Lev Tolstoy Street
(Ulitsa L'va Tolstovo 21)
Moscow
After the Tolstoy Museum. take a taxi to the writer's house, a beautiful wooden building in a run-down part of Moscow.

The Tile Museum at The Novo-Devichi Convent
Moscow
Down a little path in the convent grounds, this little museum displays in chronological order a fascinating collection of wonderful tiles, dating from the 16th to the 19th Centuries.

Russia
Local name	Rossiya
Geographic coordinates	60 00 N, 100 00 E
Population l1000	146,861
Design population l1000	000.5
Languages	Russian, other
Capital	Moscow
Monetary unit	Ruble (R)

Belarus
Local name	Byelarus
Geographic coordinates	53 00 N, 28 00 E
Population l1000	10,409
Design population l1000	000.1
Languages	Byelorusssian, Russian, other
Capital	Minsk
Monetary unit	Belarusian rubel (BR)

Area 1000 km l 2

Austria	083.9	Germany	357.0	Portugal	092.4
Belgium	030.5	Hungary	093.0	Slovenia	020.3
Croatia	056.5	Ireland	070.3	Spain	505.0
Denmark	043.1	Italy	301.0	Sweden	450.0
Finland	338.0	Lithuania	065.2	Switzerland	041.3
France	552.0	The Netherlands	041.5	Turkey	779.2
		Norway	324.0	United Kingdom	243.3
		Poland	313.0	Yugoslavia	103.2

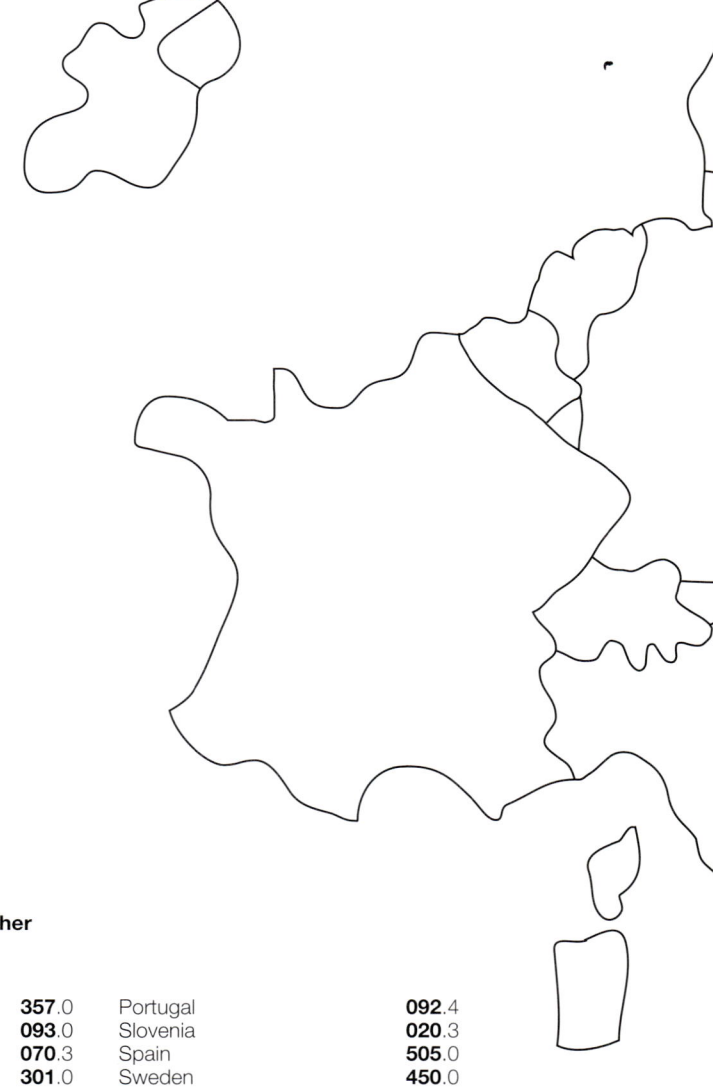

Russia | Belarus   17,075.0 | 207.6

1 Logo for Razgulyai,
a military supply chain
Art directors/designers/illustrators
Gelena Melnikova, Denis Kusnetzov, Moscow

2 Logo for Kino-Art Project,
a cinema culture project
Art directors/designers Gelena Melnikova,
Denis Kusnetzov, Moscow

3 Corporate ID for Garmoniya,
a stationery company
Art directors/designers Gelena Melnikova,
Denis Kusnetzov, Moscow

4 Logo for Videoryad, a TV company
Art directors/designers Gelena Melnikova,
Denis Kusnetzov, Moscow

5 Promotional poster
for AIDS prevention
Design firm Belaya Karona (The White Crown), Minsk
Art director Oleg Usstinovich
Designer Shamil Hayrulin
Photographer Andrej Gerassimchuk

Russia & Belarus 87

Gazetteer

Restaurants & Bars

Vinoteka
Dunajska 18
Ljubljana
T +386 61 131 5015
Offering the best in national dishes including seafood and vegetarian food, it also serves an excellent selection of Slovenian wines.

Terasa Neboticnik
Corner of Slovenska cesta and Stefanova ulica. A café with a view atop an Art Deco skyscraper.

Spajza
Gornji trg 28
Ljubljana
T +386 61 125 3094
This restaurant is tucked into a rose-coloured building and has the best décor in the city with its meandering rooms full of colour. Excellent food.

Museums & Galleries

Moderna Galerija
(Museum of Modern Art)
Cankarjeva ulica 15
Ljubljana
T +386 61 214 106
Strikingly modern gallery displaying paintings, sculpture and prints by 20th-century Slovenian artists. The International Biennial of Graphic Arts is held here every other summer in odd-numbered years. Free entry on Sundays.

Places of Interest

Centromerkur
Trubaljeva 1
Ljubljana
T +386 61 126 3170
One of the most glorious of all the Vienna Secessionist-style buildings. Inside this department store you'll find an extraordinary curved wrought-iron staircase leading to the upper floors. Built 1903.

Piran
A medieval walled city perched on a peninsula in the Adriatic Sea, its narrow walkways, charming harbour and grand plaza are overlooked by a Romanesque church.

Bookshops

Mladinska Kniga
Slovenska 29
Ljubljana
T +386 61 159 7527
For graphic design books.

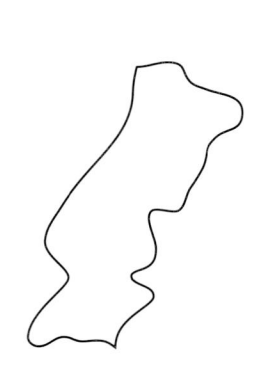

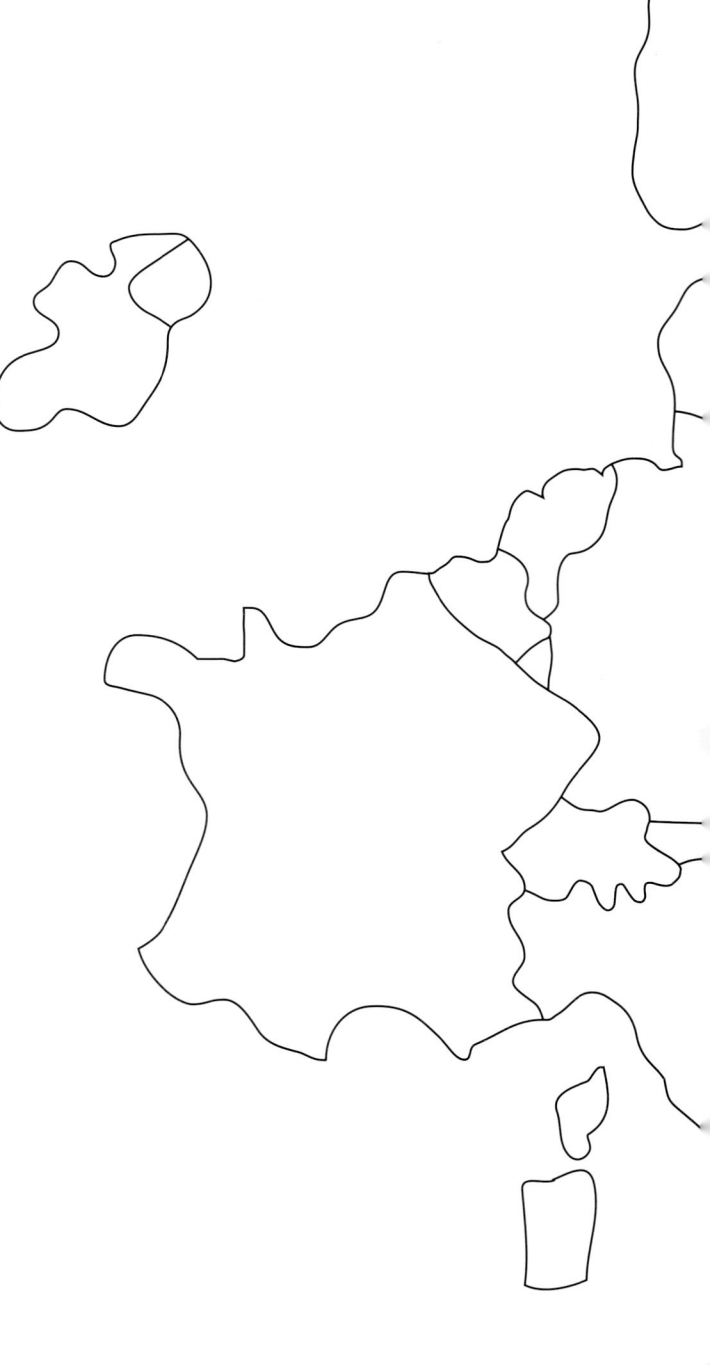

Slovenia

Slovenia
Local name — **Slovenija**
Geographic coordinates — **46 00 N, 15 00 E**
Population | 1000 — **1,972**
Design population | 1000 — **000**.1
Languages — **Slovenian, Serbo-Croatian**
Capital — **Ljubljana**
Monetary unit — **Tolar (SIT)**

Area 1000 km | 2

Austria	**083**.9	Germany	**357**.0
Belgium	**030**.5	Hungary	**093**.0
Croatia	**056**.5	Ireland	**070**.3
Denmark	**043**.1	Italy	**301**.0
Finland	**338**.0	Lithuania	**065**.2
France	**552**.0	The Netherlands	**041**.5
		Norway	**324**.0
		Poland	**313**.0
Portugal	**092**.4		
Russia	Belarus	**17,075**.0	**207**.6
Spain	**505**.0		
Sweden	**450**.0		
Switzerland	**041**.3		
Turkey	**779**.2		
United Kingdom	**243**.3		
Yugoslavia	**103**.2		
Slovenia	**020**.3		

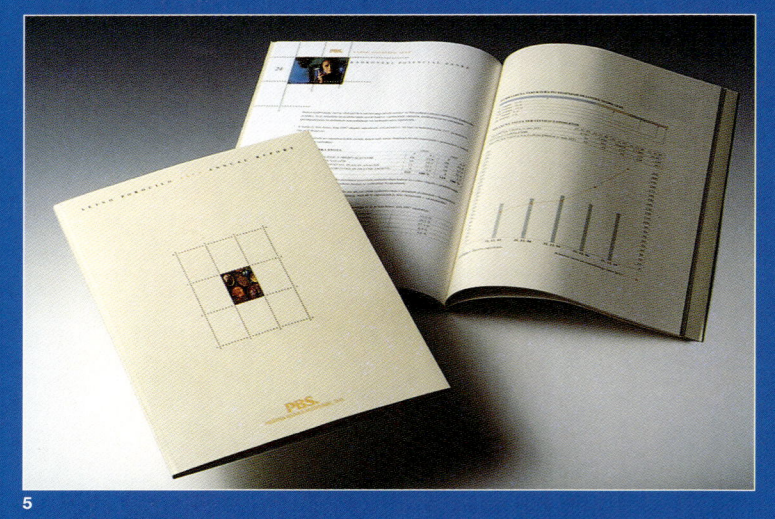

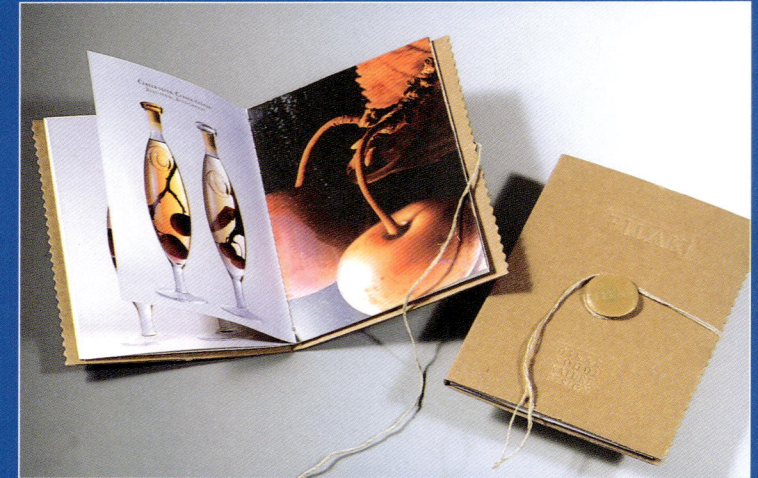

1 Annual report for Dolenjska Banka, a regional bank
Design firm Kompas Design, Ljubljana
Designer Žare Kerin
Photographer Janez Pukšič

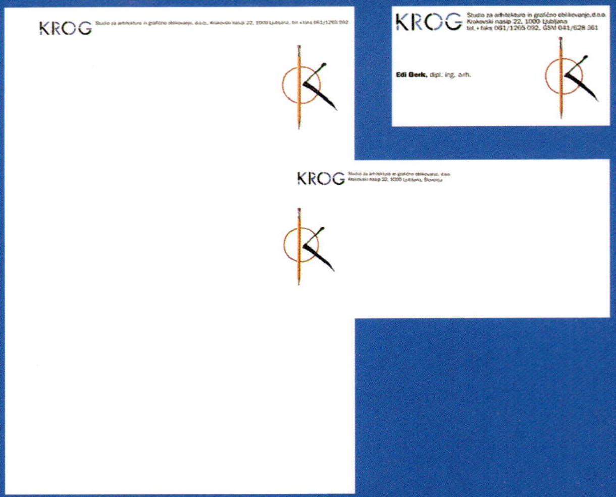

2 Stationery for KROG, a Ljubljana design firm
Designer Edi Berk
Photographer Janez Pukšič

3 Promotional publication for Janez Pukšič, a photographer
Design firm Kompas Design, Ljubljana
Designer Žare Kerin
Photographer Janez Pukšič

4 Spread from Gaudeamus Igitur, a book about the traditions at schools in Slovenia
Design firm KROG, Ljubljana
Designer Edi Berk
Copywriter Janez Bogataj
Photographer Janez Pukšič and others
Client Državni Izpitni Center

5 Annual report for Poštna Banka SLO, a Slovenian post bank
Design firm Kompas Design, Ljubljana
Designer Žare Kerin

6 Promotional publication for business gifts
Design firm Kompas Design, Ljubljana
Designer Žare Kerin
Photographer Janez Pukšič.
Client Janez Filak

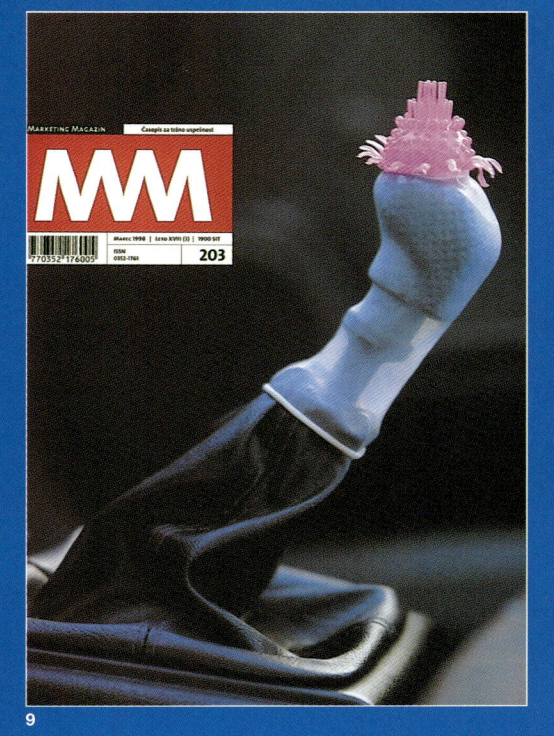

7 Logo for a birthday celebration
for Anno Aetatis, an attorney
Design firm KROG, Ljubljana
Designer Edi Berk
Client Miro Senica

8 Logo for the book club of
publisher Slovenska Knjiga
Design firm KROG, Ljubljana
Designer Edi Berk

9–12 Covers of MM,
a marketing magazine
Design firm Medja & Karlson, Ljubljana
Designer Matevz Medja
Photographer Dragan Arrigler

13 1998 calendar issued by
Kmečki glas, a publisher, using
the theme of traditional Slovenian
materials and crafts
Design firm KROG, Ljubljana
Designer Edi Berk
Copywriter Janez Bogataj
Photographer Janez Pukšič

14 "The Light Out of Darkness,"
an exhibition catalogue of paintings
by the artist Tisnikar, sponsored by
KRKA, a pharmaceutical company
Design firm Movera, Ljubljana
Designer Bojan Straže
Photographer Antonio Živkovič

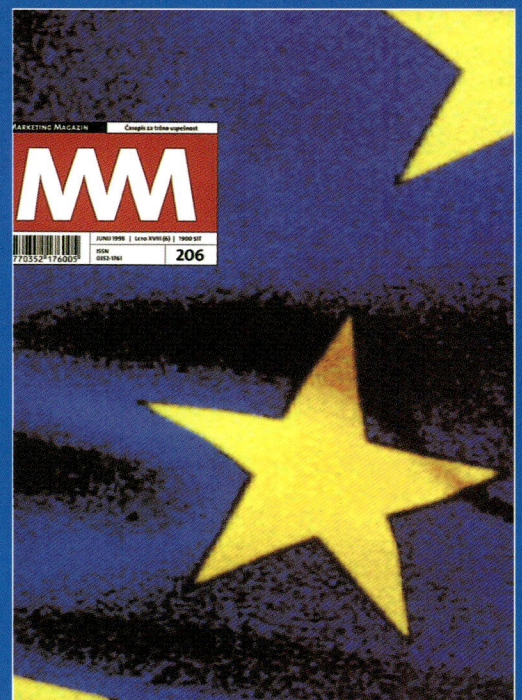

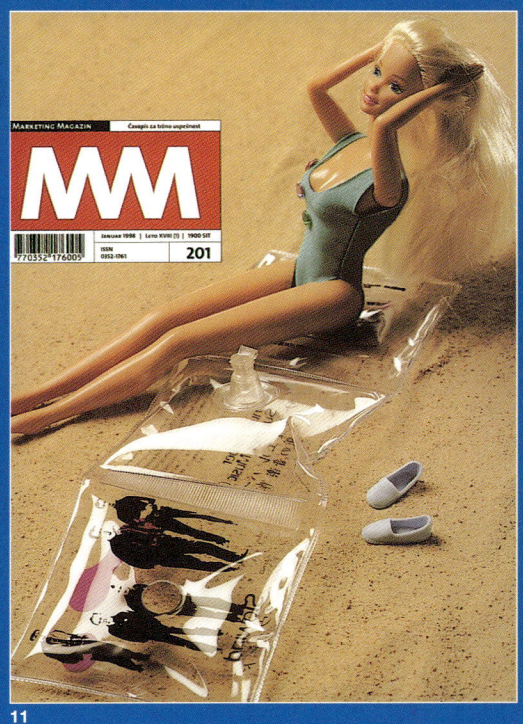

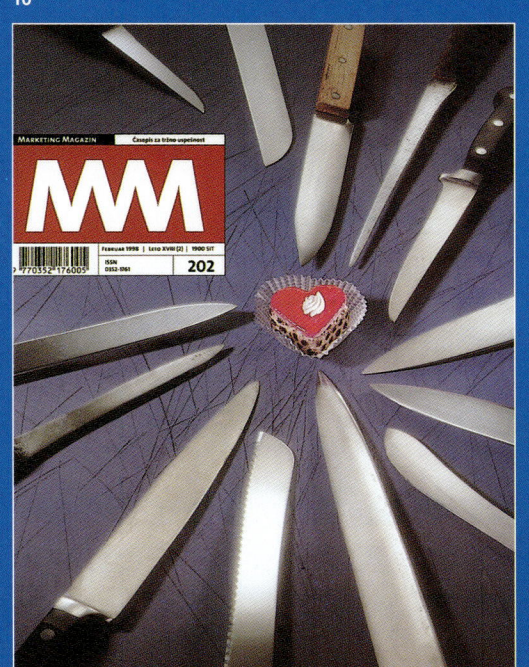

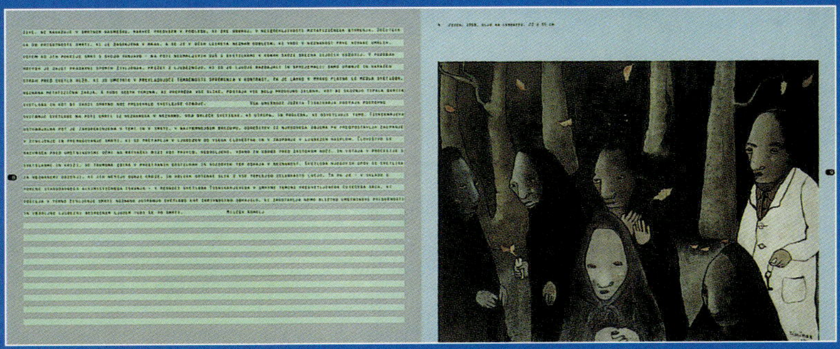

Slovenia 91

Gazetteer

Hotels

Hotel Suecia
Marqués de Casa Riera 4
Madrid
T +34 91 231 6900
Wonderfully crisp, bright and clean, well-run hotel with a great location half-way between the Prado and the Plaza Mayor.

Pintor El Greco
Alamillos del Tránsito 13
Toledo
Next door to the painter's house and museum this is a friendly hotel that was once a 17th-century bakery. Inside it is warm and modern with brick vaulting and terracotta tile floors.

Restaurants & Bars

Beltxenea
Calle Mallorca 275
Barcelona
Quiet and very private restaurant in a traditional house with courtyard garden. Fantastic food of all types and sublime desserts–try the wild strawberries with vanilla custard and pepper in season.

Casa Cuelleretes
Quinta 5
Barcelona
T +34 93 317 3020
This is the oldest restaurant in Barcelona and it doesn't seem to have changed much since 1786 with its wrought-iron chandeliers, hand-painted wall tiles and cavernous fireplace. Food, too, is delicious and moderately priced.

La Biotika
Amor de Dios 3
Madrid
T +34 91 429 0780
A vegetarian's heaven, this small and cosy restaurant servies macrobiotic cuisine with enormous salads, great soups and creative tofu.

La Trucha
Plaza de Santa Ana
Madrid
Small and popular fish restaurant. Very Spanish with a great atmosphere. Delicious and cheap.

Places of Interest

Convento de las Descalzas Reales
(Convent of the Royal Barefoot Nuns)
Plaza de las Descalzas
Madrid
T +34 91 559 7404
A little off the beaten track, but one of Madrid's best kept secrets, this convent is still in use and has been endowed with a wealth of jewels, ornaments, wonderful Flemish tapestries and Old Master paintings.

Art Popular
2 BIS
Barcelona (Barrio Gótico)
T +34 93 315 0954
In an alleyway at the back of the Cathedral is this beautiful shop full of designer's stuff and an amazingly diverse and unique collection of papier maché.

Santa Maria del Mar
(St. Mary of the Sea)
Plaça Santa Maria
Barcelona
Perhaps the best example of Mediterranean Gothic architecture and one of Barcelona's loveliest churches, built between 1329 and 1383. Stunning rose window.

Bookshops

Index Books
Consejo de Ciento 160
Barcelona
T +34 93 454 5547
For graphic design books.

Spain

Spain
Local name   **España**
Geographic coordinates   **40 00 N, 4 00 E**
Population | 1000   **39,134**
Design Population | 1000   **000**.3
Languages   **Castilian Spanish, Catalan, Galician, Basque**
Capital   **Madrid**
Monetary unit   **Peseta (Pta)**

Area 1000 km | 2

		Germany	**357**.0	Portugal	**092**.4
		Hungary	**093**.0	Russia	Belarus	**17,075**.0	**207**.6
Austria	**083**.9	Ireland	**070**.3	Slovenia	**020**.3
Belgium	**030**.5	Italy	**301**.0	Sweden	**450**.0
Croatia	**056**.5	Lithuania	**065**.2	Switzerland	**041**.3
Denmark	**043**.1	The Netherlands	**041**.5	Turkey	**779**.2
Finland	**338**.0	Norway	**324**.0	United Kingdom	**243**.3
France	**552**.0	Poland	**313**.0	Yugoslavia	**103**.2
				Spain	**505**.0

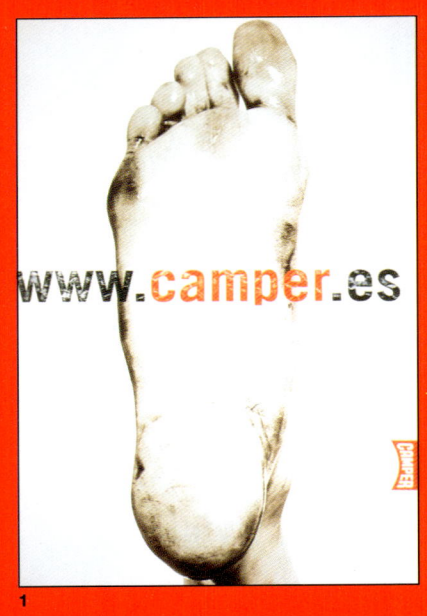

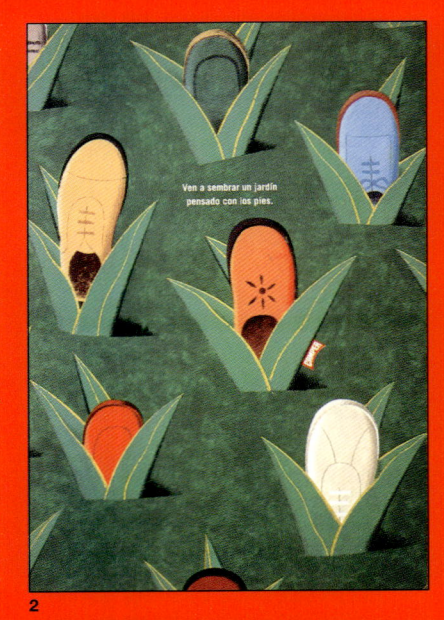

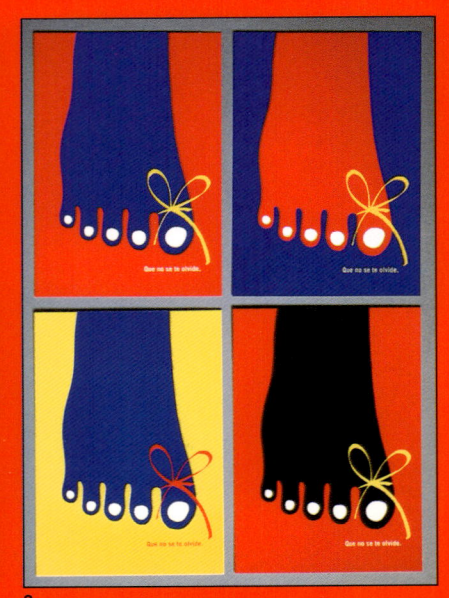

1, 2 Self-promotional poster for Web site (Fig. 1) and invitation to a fundraiser (Fig. 2) for Camper, a shoe manufacturer
Design firm Camper Communication Service, Madrid
Art directors Pep Carrió, Sonia Sánchez, Ipsum Planet
Photographer Miguel Oriola (Fig. 1)
Illustrator Angel de Pedro (Fig. 2)
Creative director Quico Vidal

3, 4 Self-promotional postcards announcing a new store for Camper
Design firm Camper Communication Service, Madrid
Art directors Pep Carrió, Sonia Sánchez
Illustrators Angel de Pedro (Fig. 3), Pep Carrió (Fig. 4)
Creative director Quico Vidal

5 Shopping bags for Camper.
Design firm Camper Communication Service, Madrid
Art directors Pep Carrió, Sonia Sánchez
Photographer Álvaro Villarrubia
Creative director Quico Vidal

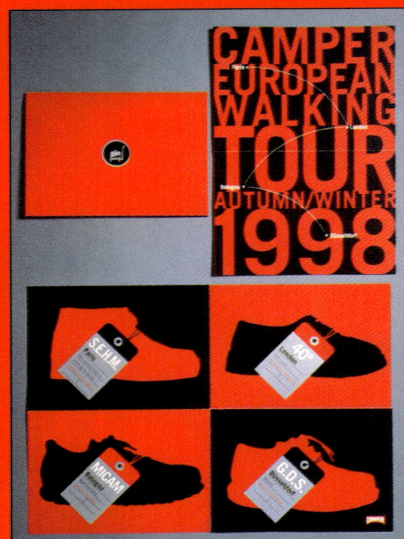

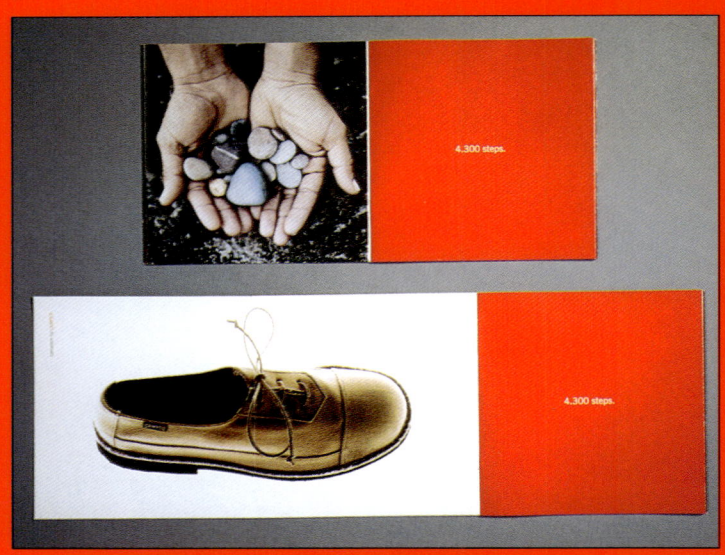

6, 7 Self-promotional mailer (Fig. 6) and booklet (Fig. 7) for Camper
Design firm Camper Communication Service, Madrid
Art directors Pep Carrió, Sonia Sánchez
Illustrator Pep Carrió (Fig. 6)
Photographers Salvador Fresneda, Bela Adler (Fig. 7)
Creative director Quico Vidal

8 Promotional booklet for Roig Rob', a restaurant
Design firm Sonsoles Llorens Studio, Barcelona
Art director/designer Sonsoles Llorens
Photographer Rafael Vargas

9 Promotional clay figurine for Joan Miró Foundation
Design firm Osoxile S.L., Barcelona
Designer Carmelo Hernando

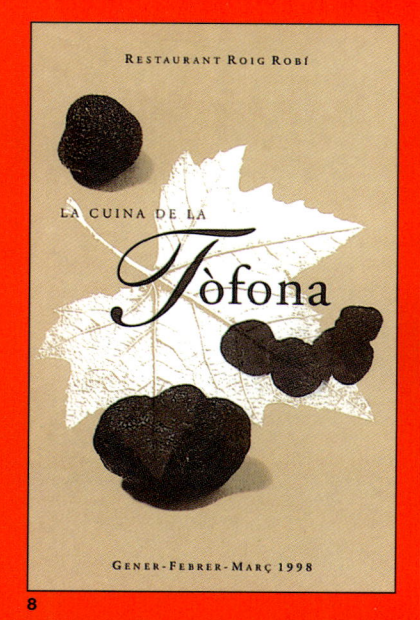

10 1997 annual report for Indra,
a telecommunications company
Design firm Tau Diseño, Madrid
Art director Emilio Gil
Designers Emilio Gil, Harriet Miller
Photographer Paco Ortigosa

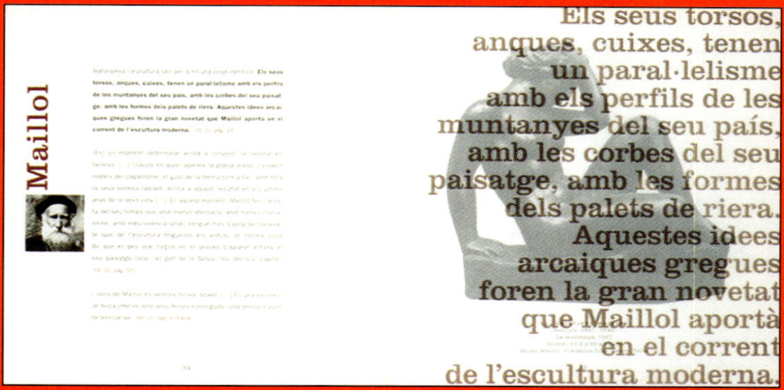

11 Cover and pages from Own News-
The Magazine, a promotional magazine
for fashion designer Frederic Homs
Design firm Pep Valls, Studio, Igualada
Art director/designer Pep Valls
Photographer Daniel Riera
Production Cristina Pons

12 Pages from a cookbook published
by El Pa's
Design firm Tau Diseño, Madrid
Designer Emilio Gil
Illustrator Jorge Garcia
Photographer Paco Ortigosa

13 Book cover for Tribuna
Ciudadana Publishing
Design firm Impreso Estudio, Oviedo
Designers Victoria Ocio, Helios Pandiella

14 Promotional booklet for an exhibition of
art by Josep Pla
Design firm Sonsoles Llorens Studio, Barcelona
Designer Sonsoles Llorens
Client Fundació la Caixa

15 Catalogue for Rocersa Cerámica
Design firm ABM Serveis de Comunicació,
Barcelona
Art director Jaume Anglada
Designer Maurici Palouzié
Illustrator Rolando del Porto
Photographer Jaume Diana-Globus

Spain 95

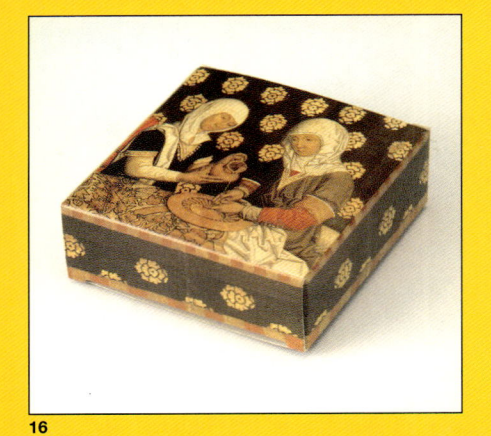

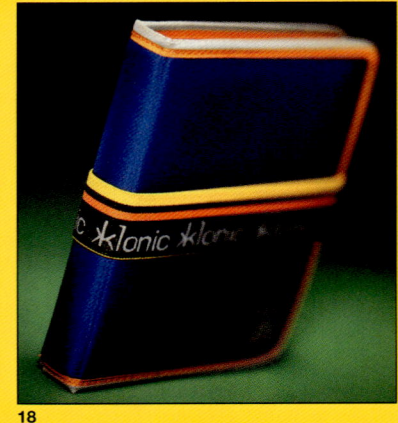

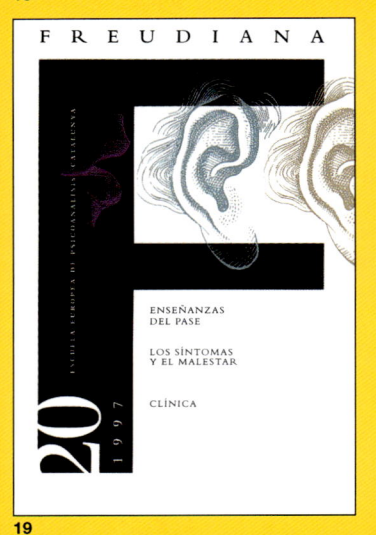

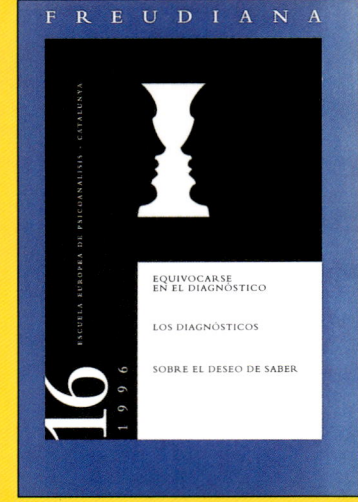

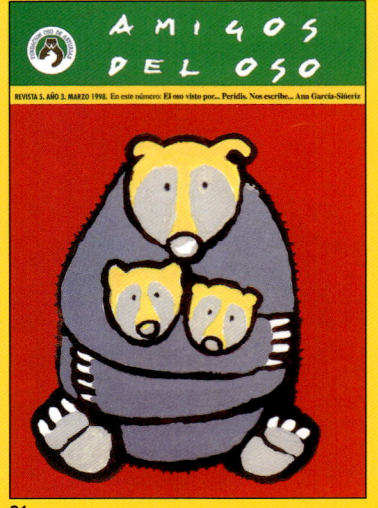

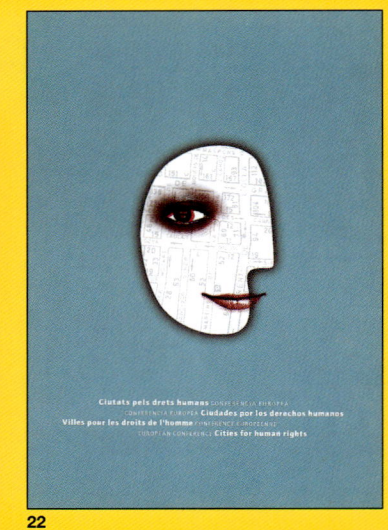

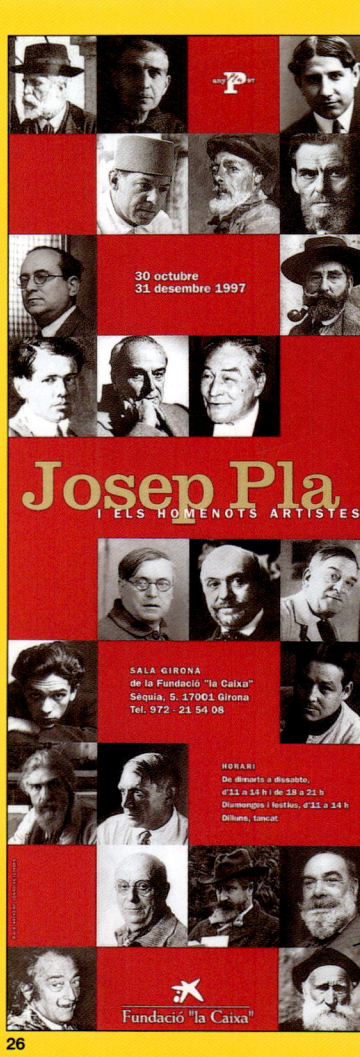

16, 17 Packaging and soap for National Museum of Art of Cataluña
Design firm Osoxile S.L., Barcelona
Designer Carmelo Hernando

18 Organizer for Manuel Cabero S.A.
Design firm Artimaña, Disseny I Comunicació, Barcelona

19, 20 Covers of Freudiana, a publication featuring essays on psychoanalysis
Design firm The Design Workshop, Barcelona
Designer/illustrator Carlos Rolando
Client European School of Psychoanalysis, Catalonia

21, 27 Illustration (Fig. 21) and cover (Fig. 27) from Amigos del Oso, a children's magazine about the preservation of bears
Design firm Estudio Forma, Oviedo

22 Promotional material for a conference on human rights
Design firm Sonsoles Llorens Studio, Barcelona
Designer Sonsoles Llorens

23, 24 Covers of the publication Cuadernos de Psicoanálisis
Design firm The Design Workshop, Barcelona
Designer Carlos Rolando
Client Spanish Freudian Institute

25 Menu for Inmortales, an Italian restaurant
Design firm The Design Workshop, Barcelona
Designer/illustrator Carlos Rolando

26 Poster for an exhibition of art by Josep Pla
Design firm Sonsoles Llorens Studio, Barcelona
Designer Sonsoles Llorens
Client Fundació la Caixa

28, 29 Promotional Christmas
gift for Paradis Restaurants
Design firm Ososxile S.L., Barcelona
Designer Carmelo Hernando

30, 31 Promotional posters
for 1h Clean, a laundromat
Design firm Puig Falco Associates,
Barcelona
Art director Sergi Puig
Designer Katja Nüschen

32 Brochure for IDEP School of Design
Design firm Hetcett, Barcelona
Art director Jesús del Hoyo Arjona

33 Promotional poster for 16th
International Furniture Design
Competition
Design firm Pepe Gimeno, S.L.,
Godella, Valencia
Designer Pepe Gimeno
Client Feria Internacional del Mueble
en Valencia

34 Ad for Dry Martini, a martini bar
Design firm The Design Workshop,
Barcelona
Art director Carlos Rolando

35 Birth announcement for a grandson
Design firm The Design Workshop,
Barcelona
Designer/illustrator Carlos Rolando

36 Yearly planners for Manuel Cabeno, S.A.
Design firm Artimaña, Disseny I
Comunicació, S.L., Barcelona

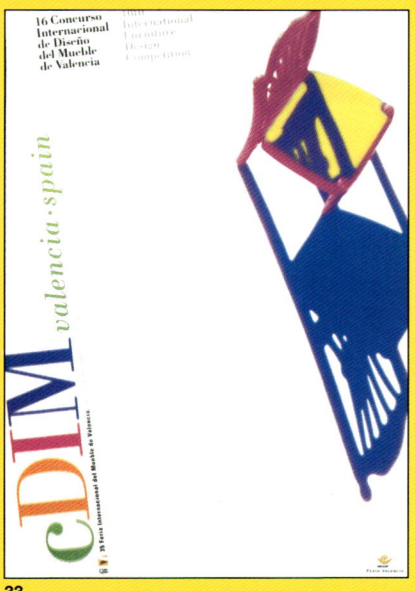

Gazetteer

Hotels

Berns Hotel
Näckströmsg. 8
Stockholm
T +46 8 614 0700
Cosy but very modern hotel in a 19th-century building recently converted. Art Deco and Italian-inspired in design with gorgeous wooden floors.

John Bauer Hotel
Södra Strandg. 15
Jönköping
T + 46 36 349 000
Modern hotel named after a local artist whose speciality was fairytale depictions of trolls and mystical landscapes. Close to the centre of town, overlooking Munksjön Lake.

Restaurants & Bars

Wedholms Fisk
(Wedholm's Fish Restaurant)
Nybrokajen 17
Stockholm
T +46 8 10 48 74
A fabulous fish restaurant, and probably the best in Scandinavia where the fish is extremely fresh and impeccably presented. The Scandinavian artwork on display is part of the owner's personal collection.

Café Opera and Opera Bar
Stockholm
T +46 8 11 00 26
Housed in the old Opera House Grill with mirrored walls, old stucco ceilings it's one of Europe's largest and most beautiful watering holes. The bar offers a genuine Art Nouveau shelter for the arts and letters people.

Räkan
Lorensbergsg. 16
Gothenburg
T +46 31 169 839
Tables are arranged around a long tank. Order shrimp, a speciality here, and watch them arrive at your table in radio-controlled boats you navigate yourself.

Museums & Galleries

Carl Larsson Gården
Carl Larssonsv. 12
Sundborn
T + 46 23 60053
In a lovely lakeside setting, the former home of the celebrated Swedish artist where you can see a selection of his paintings.

Tändsticksmuseet
(The Match Museum)
Tändsticksgr. 7
Jönköping
T +46 36 105 543
Jönköping was the birthplace of the match, and this museum, built on the site of the first factory, contains exhibits on the history and manufacture of matches.

Places of Interest

Loppmarknaden
Skärholmen shopping centre
Stockholm
One of the largest flea markets in Northern Europe open every day and a 20 minute subway ride from the city centre.

Grythyttan
Grtythyttan
T +46 591 147 00
To see Sweden's forests and rivers try this exclusive country inn. A 3-hour car ride from Stockholm.

Bergianska Botaniska Trädgården
(Bergianska Botanical Garden)
Frescati
T +46 8 162 853
North of Stockholm, see the world's largest display of water lilies.

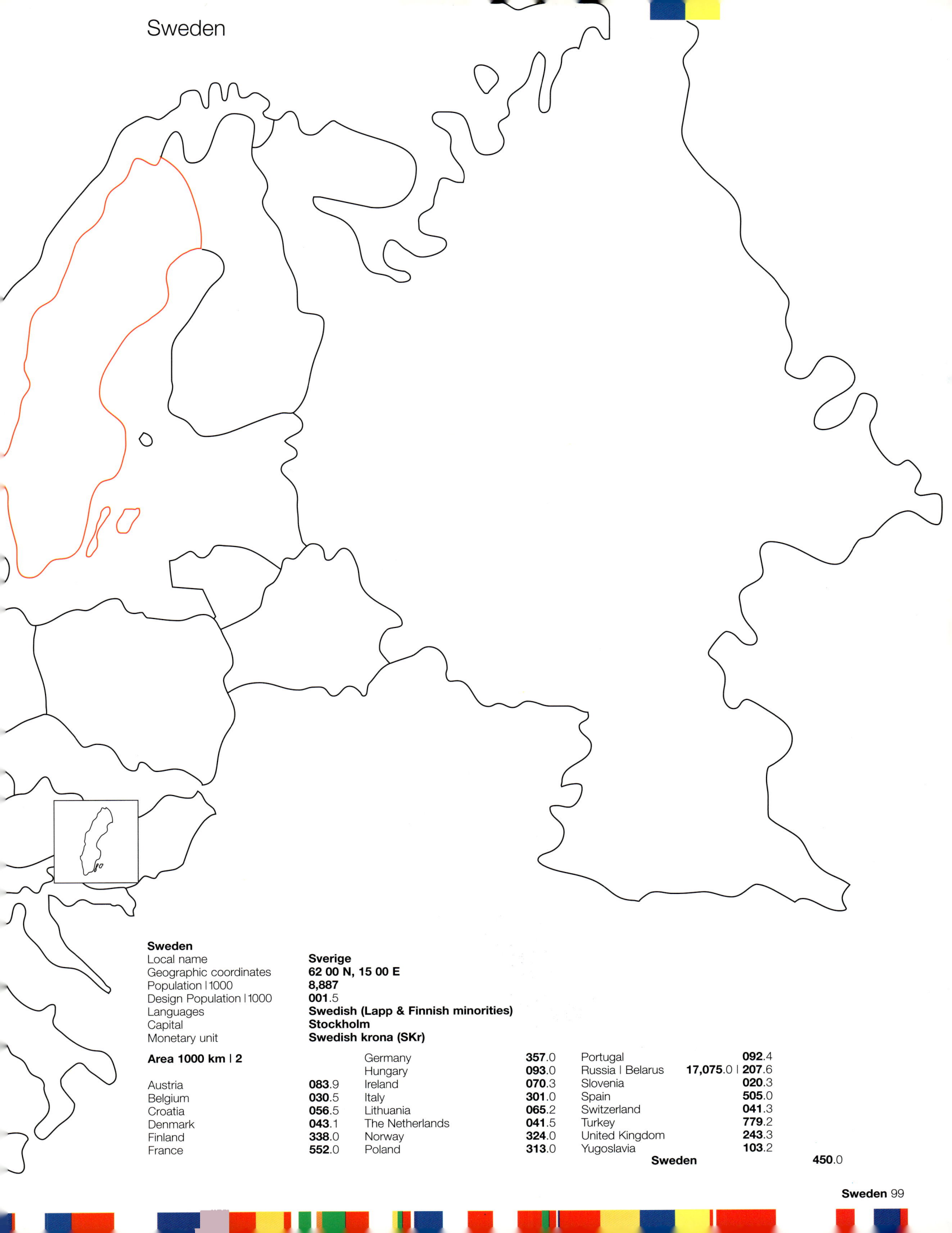

Sweden

Sweden
Local name — Sverige
Geographic coordinates — 62 00 N, 15 00 E
Population | 1000 — 8,887
Design Population | 1000 — 001.5
Languages — Swedish (Lapp & Finnish minorities)
Capital — Stockholm
Monetary unit — Swedish krona (SKr)

Area 1000 km | 2

		Germany	357.0	Portugal	092.4
		Hungary	093.0	Russia	Belarus	17,075.0	207.6
Austria	083.9	Ireland	070.3	Slovenia	020.3
Belgium	030.5	Italy	301.0	Spain	505.0
Croatia	056.5	Lithuania	065.2	Switzerland	041.3
Denmark	043.1	The Netherlands	041.5	Turkey	779.2
Finland	338.0	Norway	324.0	United Kingdom	243.3
France	552.0	Poland	313.0	Yugoslavia	103.2
				Sweden	450.0

1 1997 annual report for HSB, owners of apartment houses
Illustrator/designer Lasse Skarbovik, Stockholm
Design firm Svea Reklambyrå

2 1998 annual report cover for the Norwegian Department of Oil and Energy
Illustrator Lasse Skarbovik, Stockholm
Design firm Melvar & Lien
Designer Ivar Oftedahl

3 Scotch whiskey packaging
Design firm Fältman & Malmén AB, Stockholm
Designer Anders Eliasson
Desktop Jonas Cleaström
Client Vin & Sprit

4 Illustration for a product brochure promoting a portable chair ("The Walking Chair")
Illustrator Lasse Skarbovik, Stockholm
Agency Brunkell & Strömberg
Art director Christer Mortensen

5 Cover illustration of the Y2K problem for Fastighetstidningen, a magazine about housing
Illustrator Lasse Skarbovik, Stockholm
Art director Cia Killander

6 Postcard announcing a new telephone number for Appelberg Store Danmark, a store and magazine publisher
Illustrator Lasse Skarbovik, Stockholm
Design firm Magazine AB
Designer Lotta Vareman

7 Annual report cover for Monark, a bicycle and games company
Illustrator Lasse Skarbovik, Stockholm
Design firm Sandberg & Co.
Art director Per Ohlsson

8 Packaging for "The Hot Spot," a line of salsas, sauces, and pastes.
Design firm Tennis, anyone?, Gothenburg
Designer/illustrator Fredrik Ganslandt
Client Ridderheims Delikatesser

9 Three Dostoevsky novels published by Wahlström & Widstrand.
Design firm Nina Ulmaja Grafisk Form, Stockholm
Art director Nina Ulmaja

10 Logo for a brand of BIOS AB flyfishing products
Agency CEMK AB (Centrum för Målinriktad Kommunikation), Gothenburg
Art director Ola Inser

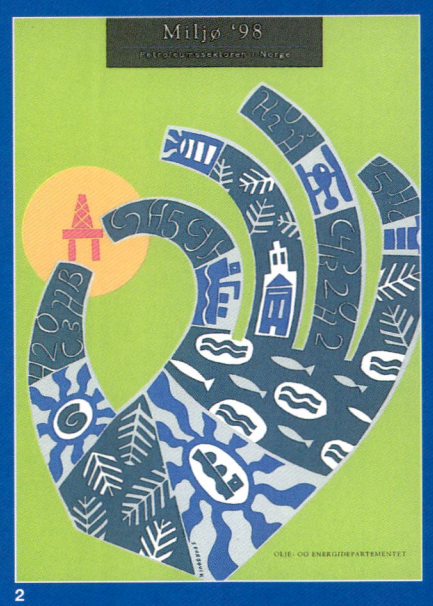

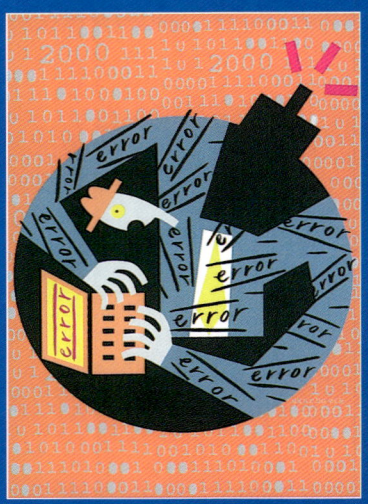

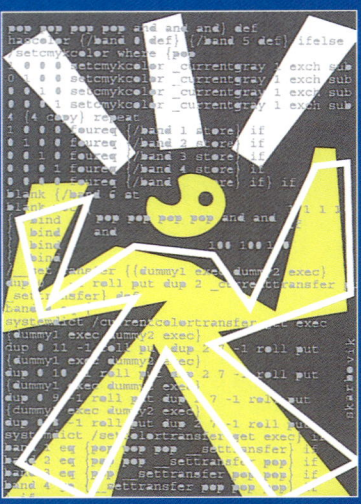

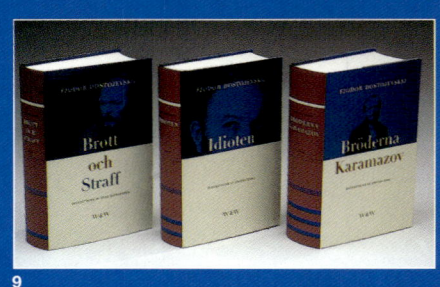

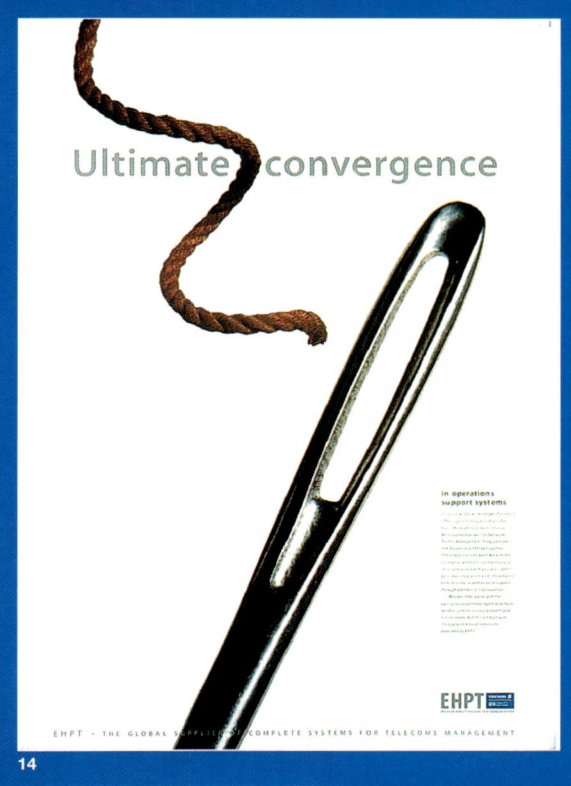

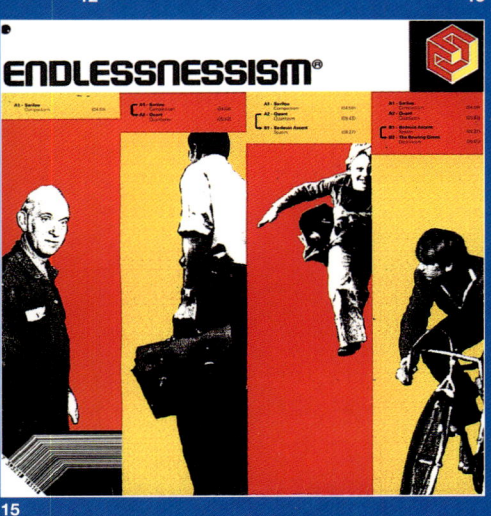

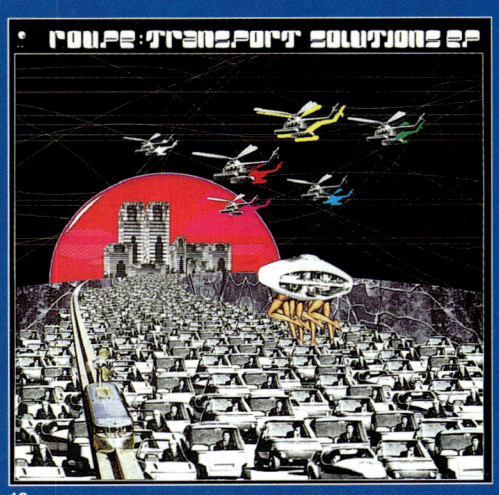

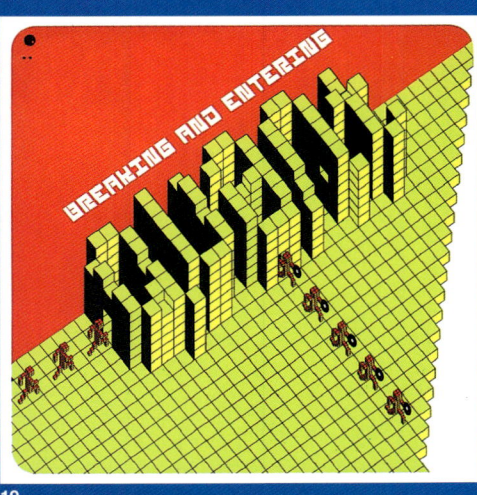

11 Logo for a magazine published by Finansförbundet, the banking and finance workers union
Design Firm Neo Media AB, Stockholm
Art director Magdalena Taubert

12, 17 Packaging and beer glass for Tomtefar, a Christmas ale produced by Kungsholmens Kvarters-Bryggeri
Design firm OCH-Herrmann, Liljendahl & Co. AB, Stockholm
Designer Lars Liljendahl
Illustrator Håkan Lundgren

13, 14 Ads for EHPT Ericsson Hewlett-Packard Telecommunications AB
Design firm GRITS, Stockholm
Art director Bo Sundin
Designer Johan Skogh
Photographer Christian Pohl

15, 16, 18, 19 Record covers for Dot Records
Design firm SWEDEN, Stockholm

Sweden 101

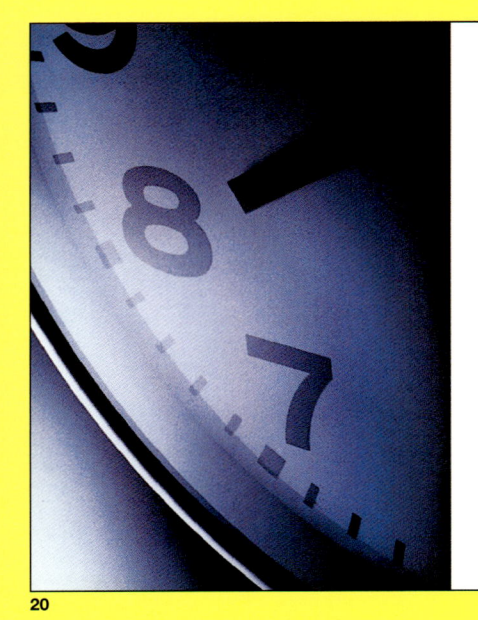

20

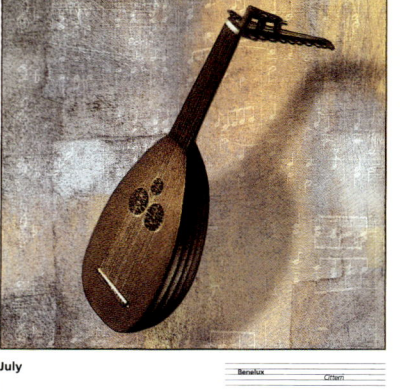

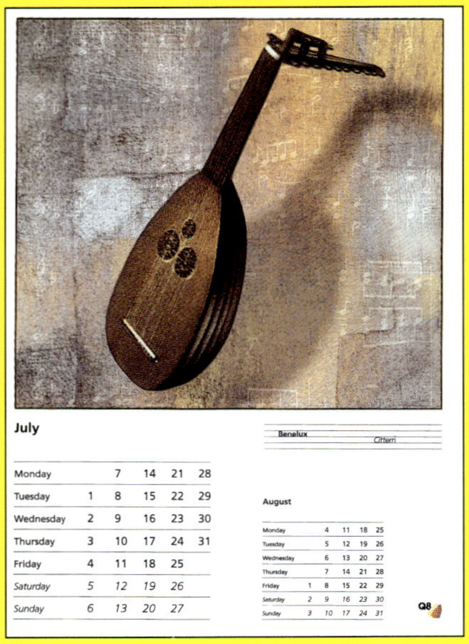

20 Self-promotional brochure for Glitter & Company, Stockholm, a new ad agency
Art director Carl Carlsson
Photographer Anders Hansen

21 Promotional calendar for Q8
Design firm Anders Lindholm Prod AB, Stockholm
Designer Malcolm Farrar
Illustrator Anders Lindholm

22 Logo from a menu for Hamburger Börs
Design firm Design X Stockholm
Designer Monica Eskedahl
Illustrator Marie Sandin

23 Beer packaging
Agency CEMK AB, Gothenburg.
Art director Ola Inser

21

22

23

24

25

26

24 Spread from Form, a Swedish design magazine
Illustrator Lasse Skarbovik, Stockholm
Designer Jacob Nordström

25, 26 Ads for Laura Ashley, Inc.
Agency Jerlov & Co., Gothenburg
Art director Maria Midby
Photographer Mats Bengtsson

27 Spread from Smart ID no. 4
Illustrator Annika Skiöld-Lindau
Design firm Publicis Welinder, Stockholm
Art director Per Börjesson
Photographer Björn Tesc.

28, 29 Covers of Fotografi magazine
Design firm Neo Media AB, Stockholm
Art director Magdalena Taubert
Photographers Jan Saudek (Fig. 28), Andreas Lind (Fig. 29)

30 Illustration for a Nordic Mail brochure
Illustrator Lasse Skarbovik, Stockholm
Design firm Manne & Co.
Art director Petra Handin

31 Brochure for Trygghetsstiftelsen, a governmental job security agency, offering advice to job seekers and employers
Illustrator Bo Lundberg
Design firm Log Kommunikation, Stockholm
Art director Chatarina Nyman

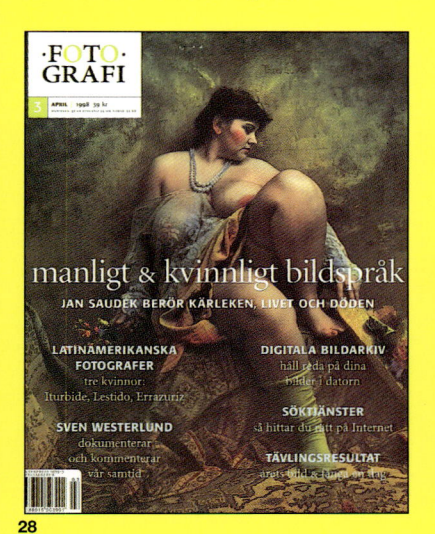

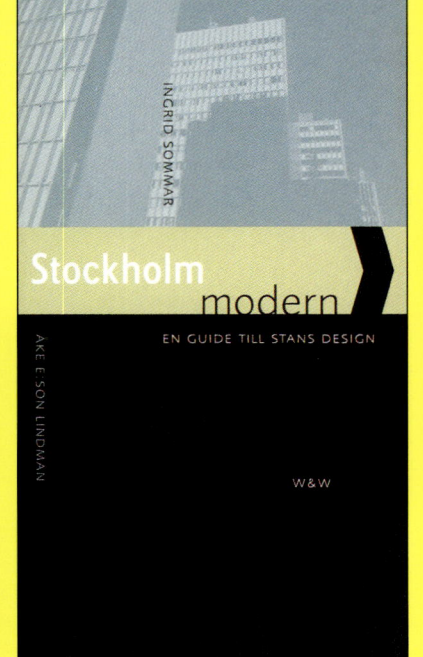

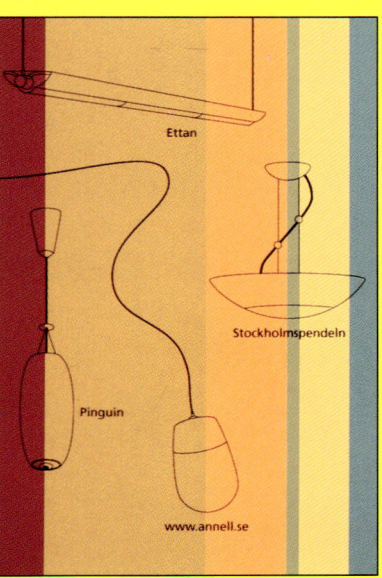

32 Design guide to Stockholm
Design firm Nina Ulmaja Grafisk Form, Stockholm
Designer Nina Ulmaja
Photographer Åke E:son Lindman

33 Print ad promoting the Web site of Annell Ljus+form
Design firm Brand Internet, Stockholm
Art director Fredrik Lewande

34 1997 annual report for AMF Insurance
Design firm Log Kommunikation, Stockholm
Art director Maria Gaenger
Photographer Pål Allan

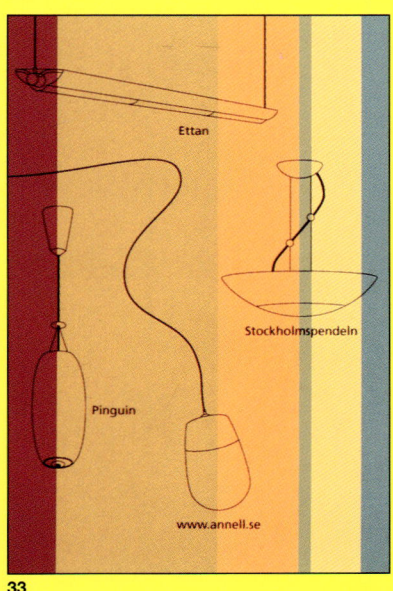

Sweden 103

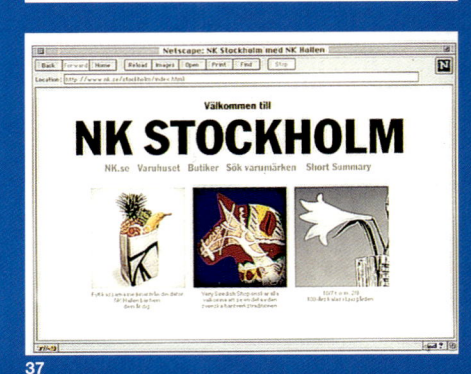

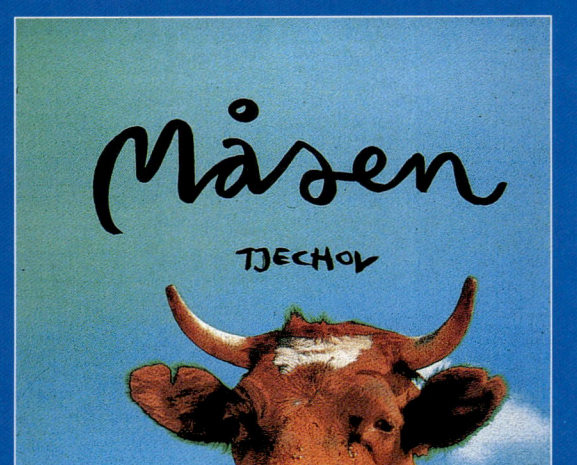

35 Poster for a permanent exhibition on the human body and health
Photographer Ivar Sviestins, Stockholm
Designer Joakim Söderquist
Client Tom Tits Experiment, Science Center

36 Promotional poster for Language Land
Agency Glitter & Company, Stockholm
Art director/illustrator Carl Carlsson

37 Web site for Nordiska Kompaniet, a department store (www.nk.se)
Design firm Brand Internet, Stockholm
Designer Fredrik Lewander
Programmer Johan Eklund
Creative director Ajje Ljungberg

38 Theatre poster for The Seagull by Anton Chekhov
Design firm Nina Ulmaja Grafisk Form, Stockholm
Designer Nina Ulmaja
Client Unga Klara/Stockholm City Theatre

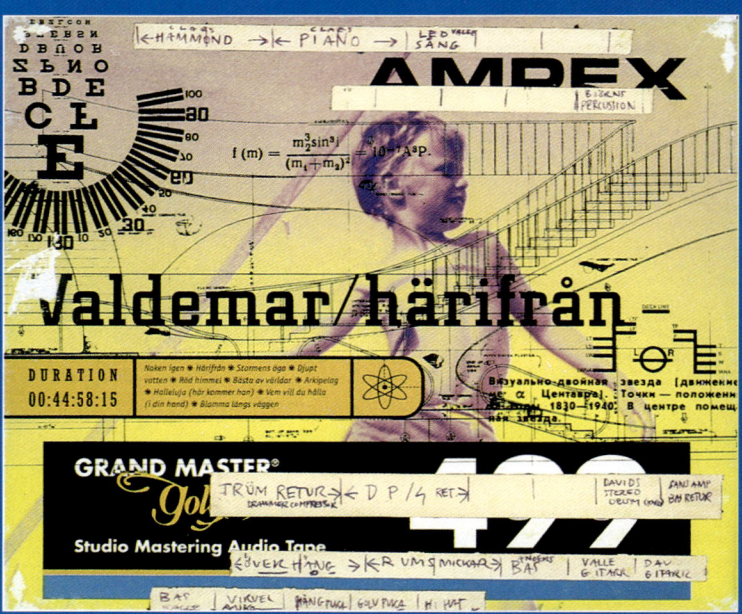

39 Spread from a CD package titled "Living in Sweden" promoting Swedish design in Milan
Design firm Design X Stockholm
Designer Monica Eskedahl
Illustrator Gabriella Agnér
Photographer Denise Grünstein

40 CD packaging for Zebra Art Records
Design firm Dagnå Grafisk Design, Stockholm
Designer Gunnar Dagnå
Concept Valle Erling

41 Theatre poster for play about a "fairly confused lady who has killed her husband"
Design firm Typisk Form designbyrå, Stockholm
Art director Pelle Björkman
Photographer Martin Skoog
Client Riksteatern

42 Logo for Fässbergsgymnasiet, a grammar school
Design firm Bodebeck Grafisk Form AB, Gothenburg
Illustrator Anders Bodebeck

43 Spread from Little People, a book of photographs of children by Micke Berg
Design firm Neo Media AB, Stockholm
Art director Stefan Lundström

44 Spread from a cookbook published by Albert Bonniers Förlag/Sturehof
Design firm Design X Stockholm
Designers Monica Eskedahl, Karl-Magnus Olsson
Illustrator Jonas Bohlin

45 Web site for Annell Ljus+form, a lighting company (www.annell.se)
Design firm Brand Internet, Stockholm
Designer Fredrik Lewander
Programmer Johan Eklund

46 Corporate identity for Apoteket AB, the Swedish pharmaceutical company
Design firm Göthberg & Co. Design, Gothenburg
Designer Bengt Göthberg

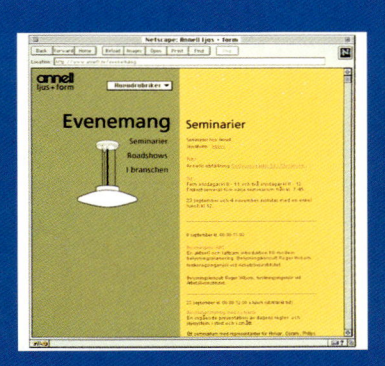

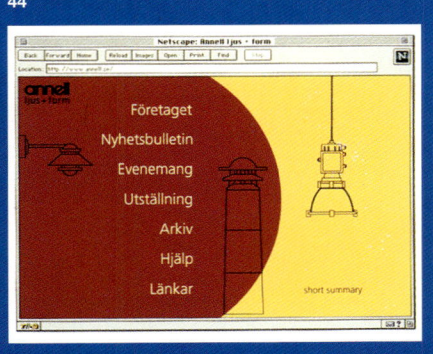

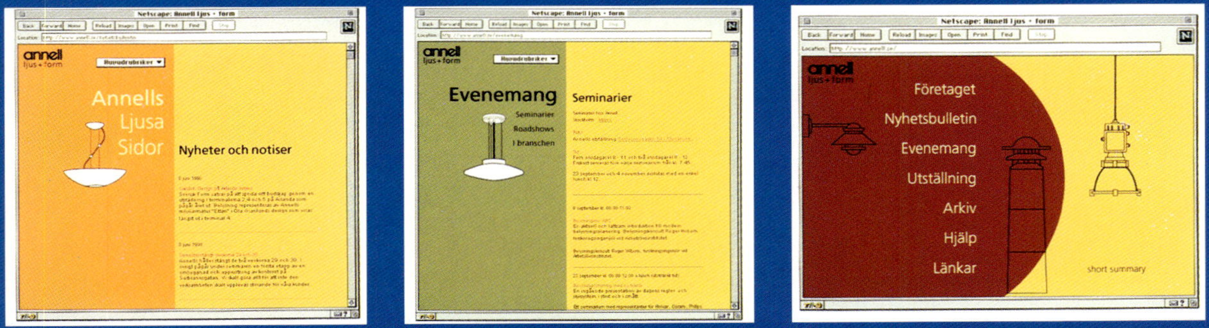

47 Promotional materials and mailers for Electrolux Laundry Systems
Design firm Agitator i Helsingborg AB, Helsingborg
Designer/illustrator Jesper Gustafson
Designer Martin Holm
Photographers Jesper Gustafson, IKANO Studios, Bogren & Co.

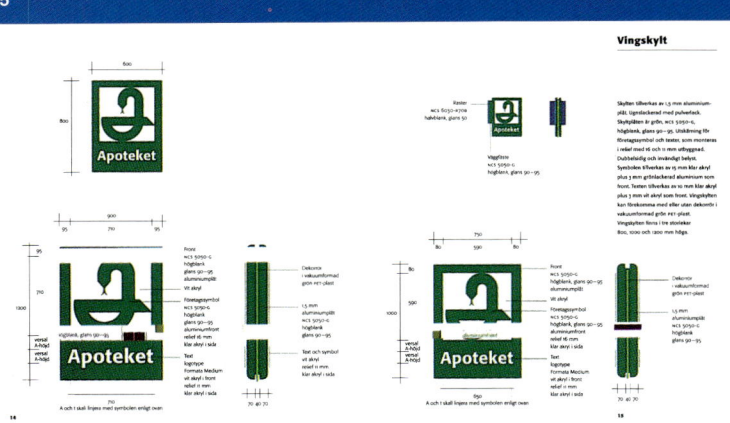

Sweden 105

Switzerland Gazetteer

Hotels

Der Teufelhof Basel
Das Kultur-und Gasthaus
Leonhardsgraben 47
Basel
T +41 61 25 10 10
Hotel/restaurant converted from a middle class family house with eight rooms, each individually designed by a different artist and re-done every two years. The award-winning restaurant has a daily-changing menu and offers a choice of over 450 wines.

Hotel Richemont
Restaurant 'Zur Bäckerstube'
Rigistrasse 28
Luzern
T +41 41 51 22 15
Small and cosy hotel up on the hill overlooking Lake Luzern and surrounding mountains. The breakfast buffet is particularly delicious (your table is covered with every kind of fresh bread imaginable. There is a bakery school below which is probably the source).

Restaurants & Bars

Restaurant & Bar Kronenhalle
Ramistrasse 4
Zürich
T +41 1 251 02 56
Superb food, good wine and friendly service, the walls are adorned with fine art. Look out for the bizarre lamps designed by Giacometti, and in the corridor between the bar and the restaurant pause to wash your hands in Switzerland's most beautiful washbasin.

Restaurant Blaue Ente
Seefeldstrasse 223
Zürich
T +41 1 422 77 06
Restaurant located in a converted flower mill which has become a centre for art and design. The charming interior is a mixture of remains of the industrial era and high tech. A meeting place for the beautiful people and the avant garde, the food is creative and interesting.

Würstli Bar
Bellevueplatz
Zürich
Stop at this small bar for the best Würstli sausage in Zürich. Short on comfort, but long on ambience.

Boeuf Rouge
17 rue Alfred-Vincent
Geneva
T +41 22 732 7537
Try hand-stuffed pistachio sausage and authentic tarte tartin in this kitsch-packed fin-de-siècle setting. Closed weekends.

La Favola
15 rue Jean Calvin
Geneva
T +41 22 311 7437
A quirky little restaurant and one of the most picturesque in town at the top of a dizzying spiral staircase. The food combines country simplicity with city chic.

Museums & Galleries

Sammlung Karikaturen & Cartoons
(Caricature & Cartoon Collection)
St. Alban-Vorstadt 9
Basel
T +41 61 22 13 36
In the centre of Basel a unique museum with a rare collection of international caricatures and cartoons. Open Wednesdays and Saturdays.

Collection de l'Art Brut
('Art Brut' Collection)
Musée du Château de Beaulieu
11-13 Avenue des Bergières
Lausanne
T +41 21 37 54 35
An extensive and disturbing collection of art by recluses, eccentrics and lunatics well worth the brisk walk from the town centre. Closed Mondays.

Haus für Konstruktive und Konkrete Kunst
(Foundation for Constructivist Art)
Seefeldstrasse 317
Zürich
T +41 1 381 3808
Changing presentations, workshops and exhibitions by Swiss and international artists of the constructivist movement.

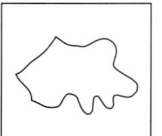

Switzerland

Local name	Schweiz/Suisse/Svizzera
Geographic coordinates	47 00 N, 8 00 E
Population | 1000	7,260
Design Population | 1000	001.5
Languages	German, French, Italian, Romansch, other
Capital	Bern
Monetary unit	Swiss franken/franc/franco (SFR)

Area 1000 km | 2

		Germany	357.0	Portugal	092.4
		Hungary	093.0	Russia | Belarus	17,075.0 | 207.6
Austria	083.9	Ireland	070.3	Slovenia	020.3
Belgium	030.5	Italy	301.0	Spain	505.0
Croatia	056.5	Lithuania	065.2	Sweden	450.0
Denmark	043.1	The Netherlands	041.5	Turkey	779.2
Finland	338.0	Norway	324.0	United Kingdom	243.3
France	552.0	Poland	313.0	Yugoslavia	103.2

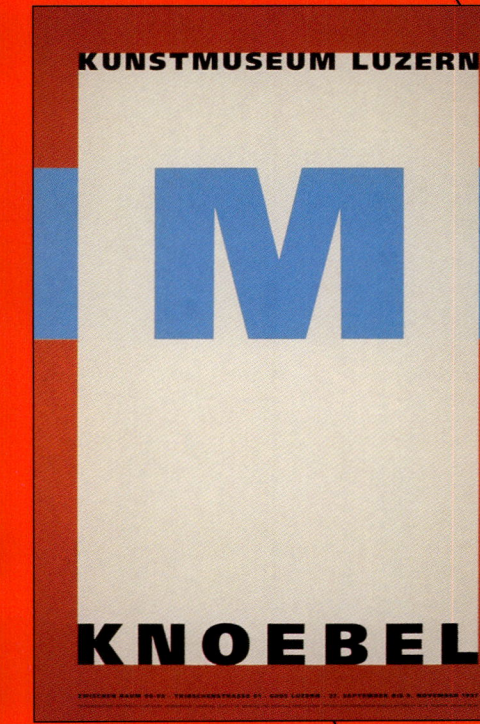

1 Poster for Kyoto
Committee for the Environment
Design firm Odermatt & Tissi, Zürich
Designer Rosmarie Tissi

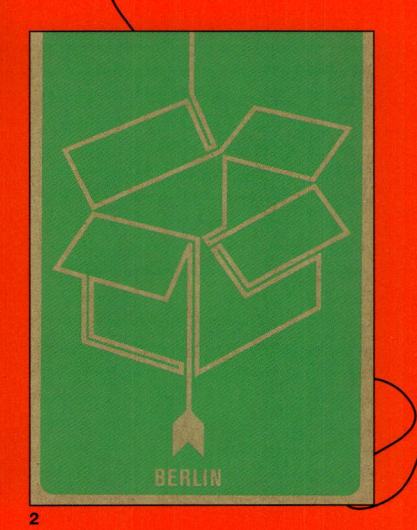

2 Moving announcement
Design firm Neeser & Müller, Basel
Designers Thomas Neeser, Thomas Müller
Client Marlis Kaulich

3 Poster promoting a
Swiss poster exhibition
Design firm Odermatt & Tissi, Zürich
Designer Rosmarie Tissi

4 Poster for Associazione Piazza Blues
Design firm G/D/S Agenzia
Publicitaria, Lugano
Designer Mirko Nesurini

5 Poster for an exhibition of
IMI Knoebel
Designer Melchior Imboden, Buochs
Client Lucerne Art Museum

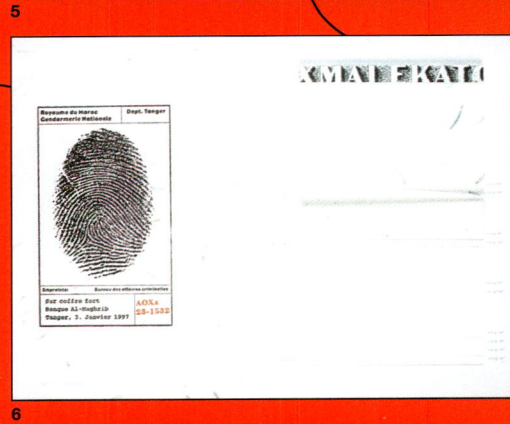

6 Spread from "Money,"
a paper promotion
Design firm Wild & Frey, Zürich
Designers Lucia Frey, Heinz Wild
Client Büttenpapierfabrik Gmund

Switzerland 107

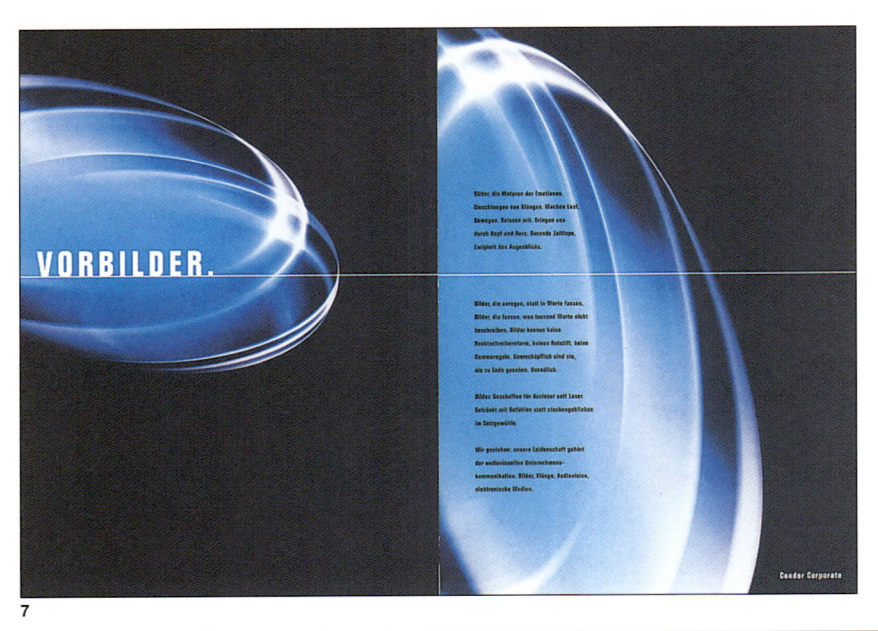

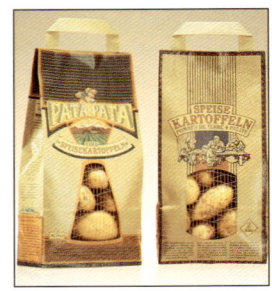

7 Brochure promoting corporate movies
Design firm Eclat AG, Erlenbach
Art director Robert Krügel-Durband
Designer Bastien Aubry
Client Condor Films

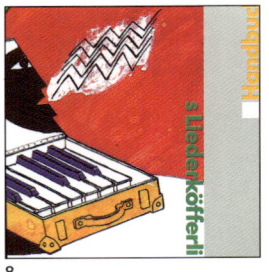

8 Book jacket for Lehrmittel Publishing
Design firm Albert Gomm Design Factory, Basel
Designer Albert Gomm
Illustrator Juerg Tramer

9 Packaging for a supermarket
Design firm Bolt, Koch & Ko, Zürich
Designer/illustrator Corinta Cito
Client Volg Konsumwaren AG

10 Poster for a children's village
Design firm Odermatt & Tissi, Zürich
Designer Rosmarie Tissi
Client SOS Kinderdorf

11 Packaging for a supermarket
Design firm Bolt, Koch & Ko, Zürich
Designer/illustrator Halo Moro
Client Volg Konsumwaren AG

12 Packaging for a supermarket
Design firm Bolt, Koch & Ko, Zürich
Art director/illustrator Heike Grein
Client Volg Konsumwaren AG

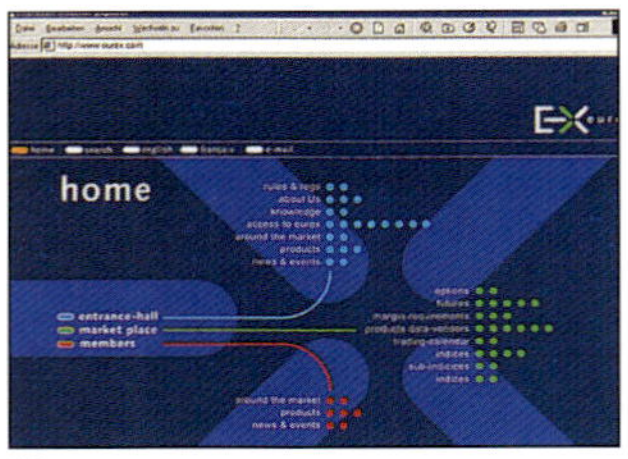

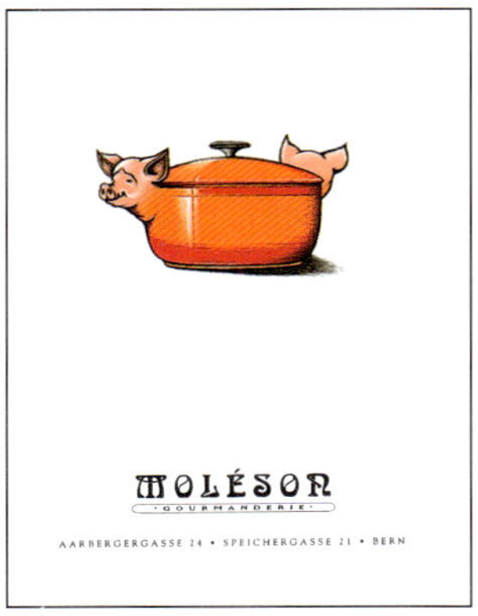

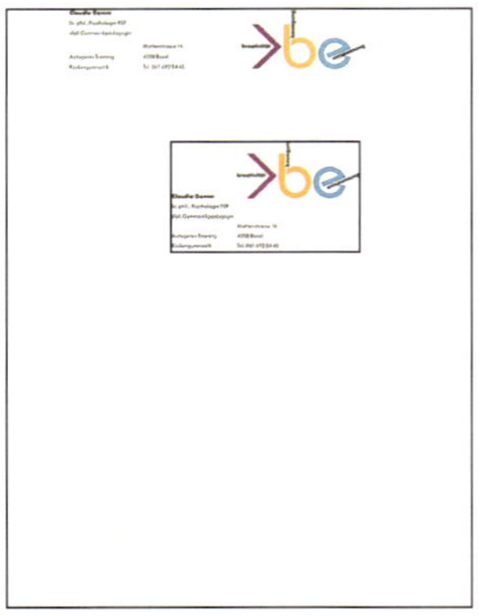

13–15 Web site for Eurex, a finance company (www.eurex.com)
Design firm Eclat AG, Erlenbach
Art director Robert Krügel-Durband
Designers Elke Schultz, Romano Bassi, Katarina Lang

16 Postcard promoting the relaunch of Restaurant Moléson
Design firm LineUp, Bern
Art director Robert Riesen
Designer/illustrator Boris Pilleri

17 Letterhead and business card for a psychologist
Design firm Albert Gomm Design Factory, Basel
Designer Albert Gomm

18 Poster for a children's village
Design firm Niklaus Troxler Design, Willisau
Designer Niklaus Troxler
Client SOS Kinderdorf

19 Poster for jazz concert featuring Steve Coleman & Five Elements
Design firm Niklaus Troxler Design, Willisau
Designer Niklaus Troxler
Client Jazz in Willisau

20 Poster for a jazz concert featuring Fred Frith and Tense Serenity
Design firm Niklaus Troxler Design, Willisau
Designer Niklaus Troxler
Client Jazz in Willisau

21 Poster for a jazz concert featuring Marc Ribot
Design firm Niklaus Troxler Design, Willisau
Designer Niklaus Troxler
Client Jazz in Willisau

22 Annual report for Expo.01
Design firm Sandra Kunz Visuelle Gestaltung, Basel
Designer Sandra Kunz
Photographers Roland Kniel, Sandra Kunz
Copywriters Barbara Groher, Christian Rintelen

23 Poster for an exhibition of work by design firm Odermatt & Tissi at the Ginza Graphic Gallery, Tokyo
Design firm Odermatt & Tissi, Zürich
Designer Rosmarie Tissi

24, 25 Cover and page from Smart Mart, a book of short stories and cocktail recipes
Design Firm IDEART, Lucerne
Designer/illustrator/photographer Ludek Martschini
Copywriters Alex Breuer, Dany Bucher
Client Buchecker AG Glas

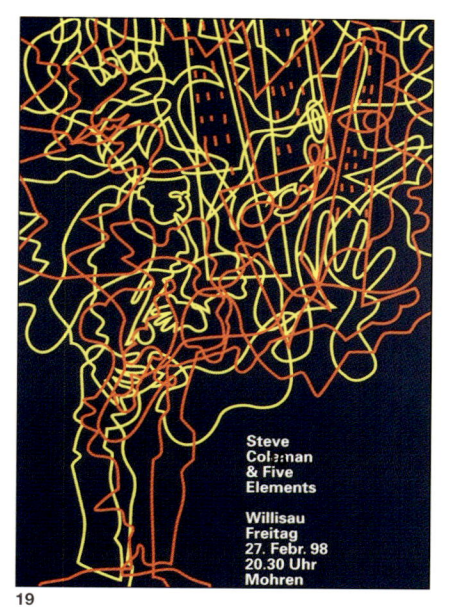

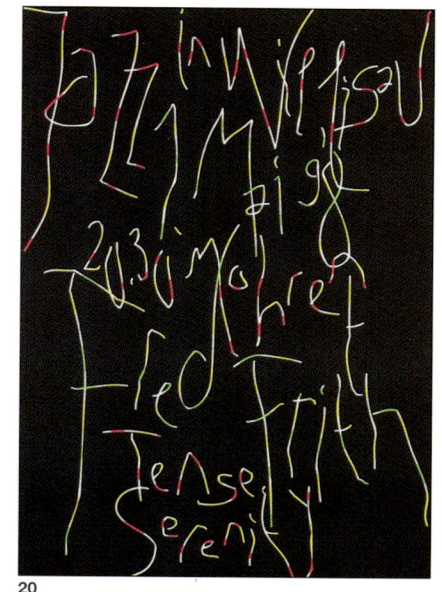

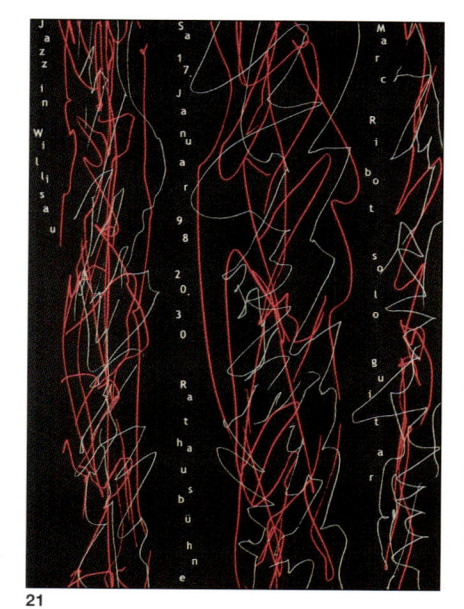

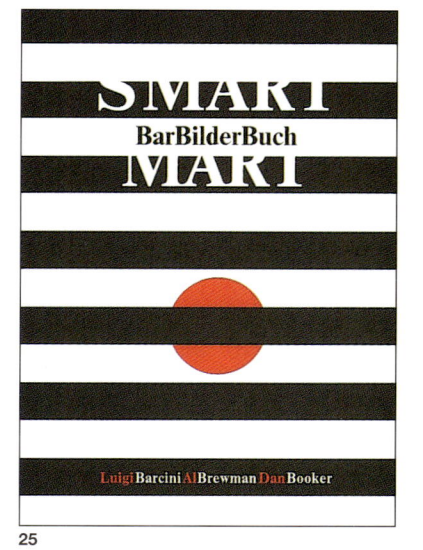

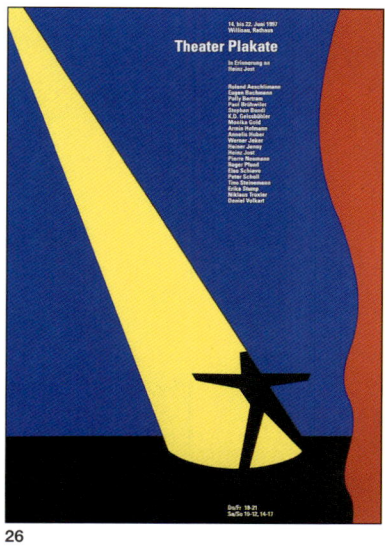

26 Poster for exhibition of theatre posters
Design firm Niklaus Troxler Design, Willisau
Designer Niklaus Troxler
Client Rathaus Willisau

27 Corporate identity programme for BIC (Business Information Technology & Consulting)
Design firm Communication Graphic Design, St. Gallen
Designer/illustrator Mario Romano

Switzerland 109

Turkey Gazetteer

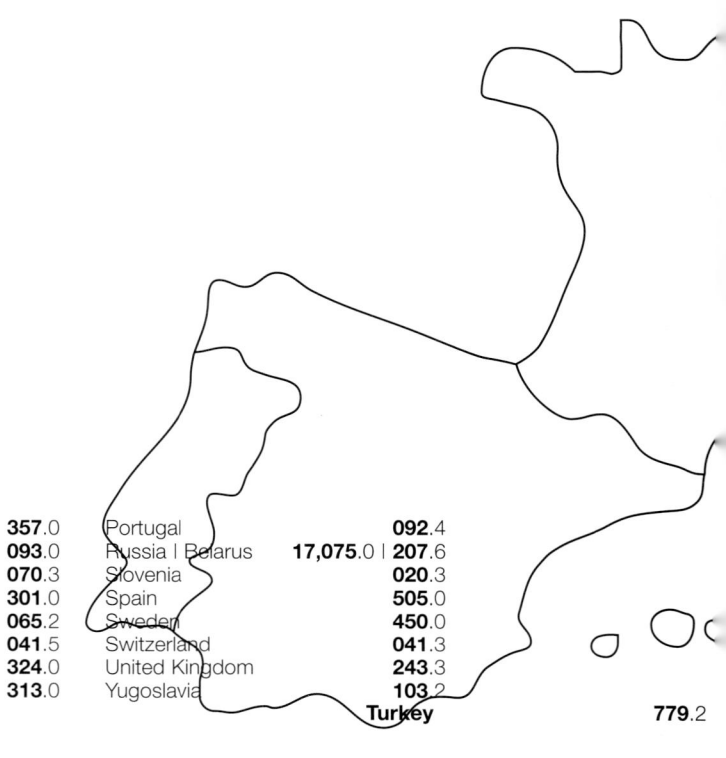

Restaurants & Bars

Pandeli's Restaurant
Misir Carsist - the Spice Bazaar
Hamidiye Caddesi
Istanbul
An excellent restaurant in domed rooms above the entrance to the Spice Bazaar with views over the Golden Horn, and an exotic approach.

Place of Interest

Sultan Ahmet Cami
(Blue Mosque)
Sultanahmet Meyd.
Istanbul
With its shimmering blue tiles, 260 stained-glass windows and six minarets, this mosque is a beautiful monument to Islam. Built in the early 17th century. There is a carpet and kilim museum in the cellars
T +90 212 518 1330

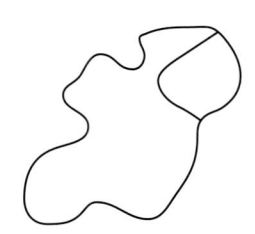

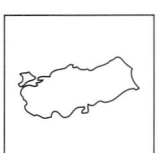

Turkey
Local name	Turkey
Coordinates	39 00 N, 35 00 E
Population |1000	64,567
Design population |1000	000.5
Languages	**Turkish, Kurdish, Arabic**
Capital	Ankara
Monetary unit	Turkish lira (TL)

Area 1000 km | 2

		Germany	357.0	Portugal	092.4
		Hungary	093.0	Russia | Belarus	17,075.0 | 207.6
Austria	083.9	Ireland	070.3	Slovenia	020.3
Belgium	030.5	Italy	301.0	Spain	505.0
Croatia	056.5	Lithuania	065.2	Sweden	450.0
Denmark	043.1	The Netherlands	041.5	Switzerland	041.3
Finland	338.0	Norway	324.0	United Kingdom	243.3
France	552.0	Poland	313.0	Yugoslavia	103.2
				Turkey	779.2

**1 Stationery for
Istanbul Surgery Hospital
Design firm** G.C. Graphic Design, Istanbul
Designer/illustrator Gulizar Cepoglu

Gazetteer

Restaurants & Bars

The Willow Tea Room
217 Sauchiehall Street
Glasgow
T +44 141 332 1521
Sample a delightful traditional tea in this pioneering example of interior design by Charles Rennie Mackintosh.

Rules
35 Maiden Lane
London
T +44 171 836 5314
London's oldest restaurant, the oak walls are packed with theatrical and literary memorabilia, playbills, paintings and prints. Charles Dickens was a regular here. The food is a feast for the eyes as well as the palate. Near Covent Garden.

Museums & Galleries

The Burrell Collection
Pollock Country Park
Glasgow
T +44 141 649 7151
Housed in an extraordinary building, the collection is that of Burrell, a sea captain whose compulsive acquisitiveness has left a hugely varied showcase of art and antiquities from monastery doors to Chinese ceramics.

The Courtauld Gallery
Somerset House
Strand
London
T +44 171 873 2526
Internet http://www.kcl.ac.uk/inst/courtauld/int.htm
A fine collection of Impressionist and Post-Impressionist paintings as well as Old Masters, housed in one of the most beautiful 18th-century buildings in London.

The Design Museum
Butler's Wharf
Shad Thames
London
T +44 171 407 6261
The first museum dedicated to product design, its floors contain a graphics gallery, films, video and library as well as a riverside café/bar.

Sir John Soane's Museum
13 Lincoln's Inn Fields
London
T +44 171 405 2107
A real museum, little known or visited housing a superb collection of Hogarths in a dusty, crowded setting.

Museum of the Moving Image
South Bank Arts Centre
London
T +44 171 928 3535
Part of the British Film Institute this is the most comprehensive museum of cinema (and television) history, from silent movies to the latest special effects.

Places of Interest

The Glasgow School of Art
167 Renfrew Street
Glasgow
T +44 141 332 9797
Functional and lovely rectangular form of the Vienna Secessionist movement, and the building is still used as an art school. Book yourself onto a guided tour.

Atlantis European Ltd
146 Brick Lane
London
T +44 171 377 8855
Cathedral-like space selling paints, brushes, paper and every tool an artist could wish for. More artists live in close proximity to London's East End than any other place in the world.

Cecil Court
London
A one-block mews filled with a fantastic array of curiosity shops: old print dealers, theatre memorabilia, cigarette card shops (a must for graphic designers) and a fine book store devoted to design (Ann Creed Books).

The Print Room
37 Museum Street
London
T +44 171 430 0159
Close to the British Museum this little shop carries a wonderful selection of antique prints, maps and books as well as political cartoons, military, botanical and architectural prints. Ideal for passing away a rainy afternoon.

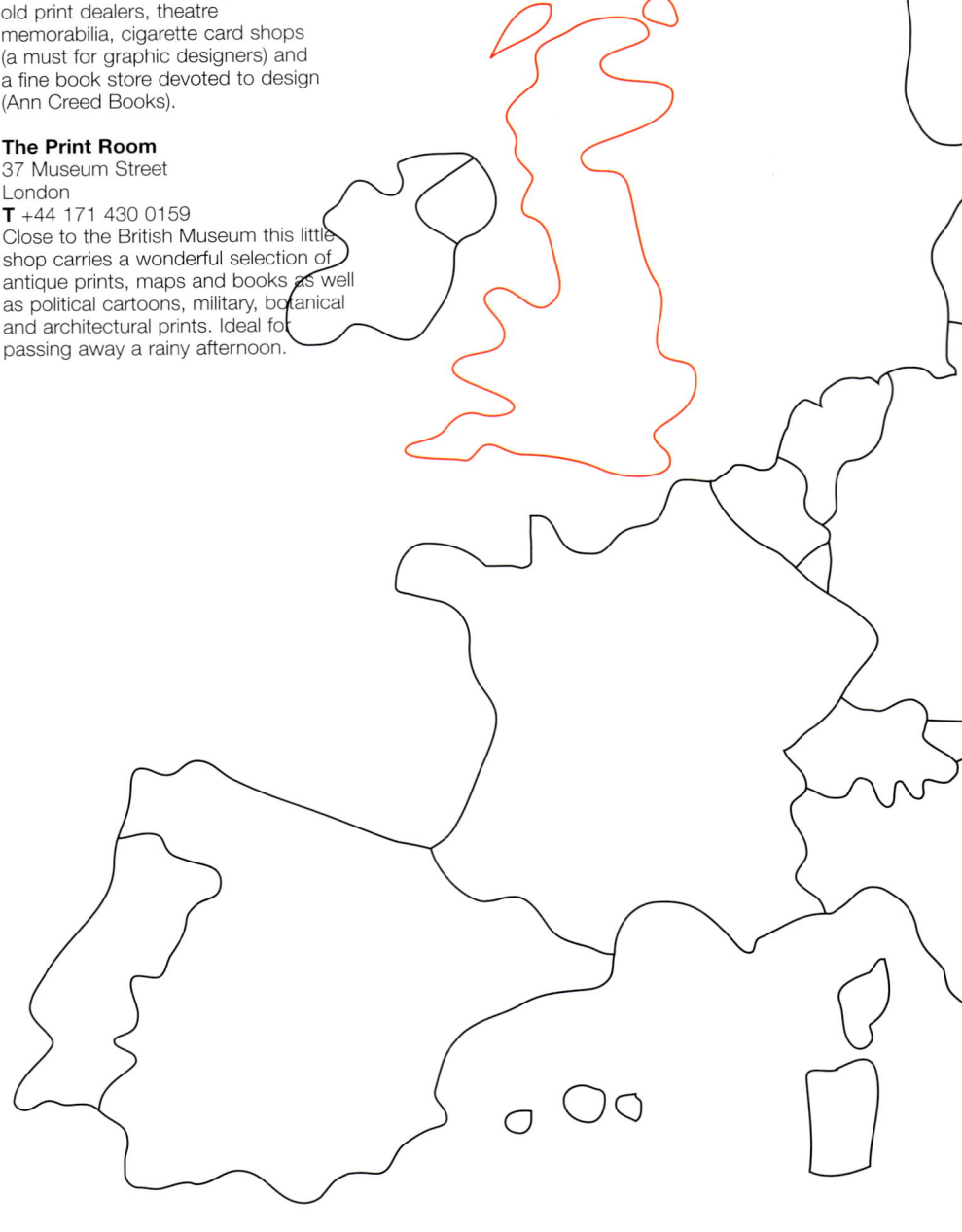

United Kingdom

United Kingdom
Local name   **United Kingdom**
Coordinates   **54 00 N, 2 00 E**
Population |1000   **58,970**
Design Population |1000   **006**.0
Languages   **English, Welsh, Scottish Gaelic**
Capital   **London**
Monetary unit   **GBP Sterling (£)**

Area 1000 k/m2

		Germany	**357**.0	Portugal	**092**.4
		Hungary	**093**.0	Russia	Belarus **17,075**.0	**207**.6
Austria	**083**.9	Ireland	**070**.3	Slovenia	**020**.3
Belgium	**030**.5	Italy	**301**.0	Spain	**505**.0
Croatia	**056**.5	Lithuania	**065**.2	Sweden	**450**.0
Denmark	**043**.1	The Netherlands	**041**.5	Switzerland	**041**.3
Finland	**338**.0	Norway	**324**.0	Turkey	**779**.2
France	**552**.0	Poland	**313**.0	Yugoslavia	**103**.2

United Kingdom

United Kingdom 113

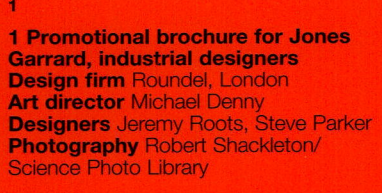

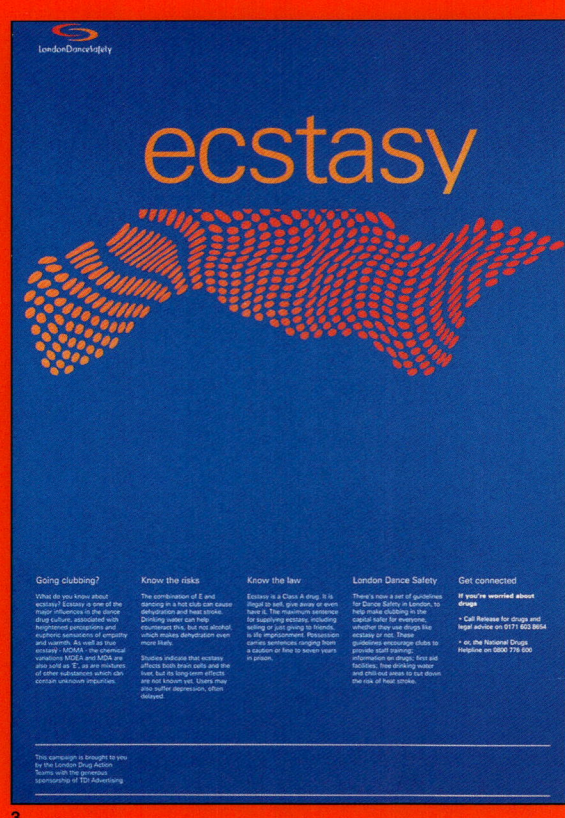

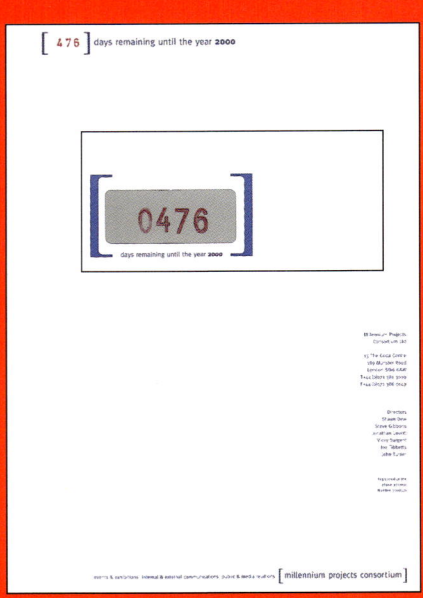

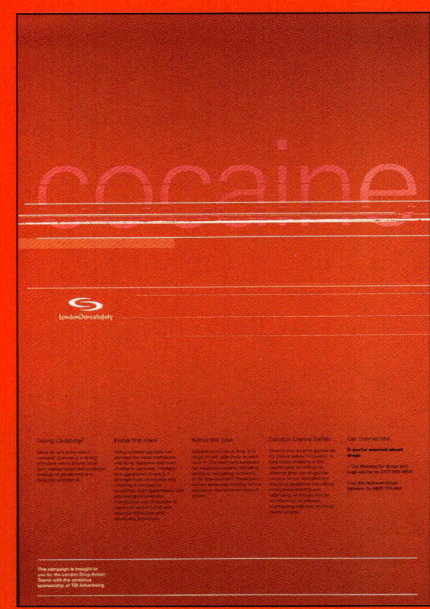

1 Promotional brochure for Jones Garrard, industrial designers
Design firm Roundel, London
Art director Michael Denny
Designers Jeremy Roots, Steve Parker
Photography Robert Shackleton/ Science Photo Library

2 Stationery for Millennium Projects Consortium, highlighting the countdown of days to the year 2000
Design firm Dew Gibbons, London
Art directors Shaun Dew, Steve Gibbons
Designers Joanne Fairey, Lee Wilson

3, 4 Drug awareness posters aimed at London dance clubbers
Design firm Ideology, London
Art director Michael Lindley
Designers Michael Lindley, Paul Gallagher
Client 26 London Drug Action Teams

5 1997 annual report for Severn Trent Water PLC, a utility services company
Design firm Addison, London
Designer Nick Jones
Photographer Robin Broadbent

6 Self-promotional Christmas poster
Design firm Minale Tattersfield+Partners, Richmond
Photographer Nigel Stead

7 1997 annual report for Severn Trent Water PLC
Design firm Addison, London
Art director Nick Jones
Designers Nick Jones, Sinclair Ashman
Photographer Robin Broadbent

8 Brochure promoting Ikono paper
Design firm Roundel, London
Art director John Bateson
Designers Alec Law, Mark McConnachie, Paul Ingle
Photographers Neil Bailey, Tim Flak (cover)
Client Zanders Finepapers

United Kingdom 115

**9 Packaging for Howling
Monkey Black and Tan Beer
Design firm** Turner Duckworth, London
Art directors Bruce Duckworth,
David Turner
Designer David Turner
Illustrator Thomas Hennessy
Client McKenzie River Corp

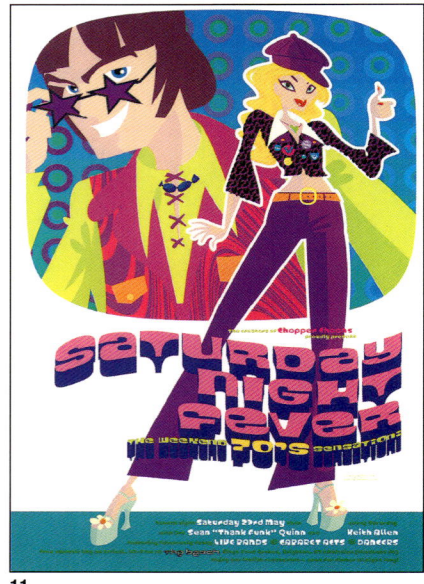

**10 Packaging for Vinopolis house wines
Design firm** Lewis Moberly, London
Designer Mary Lewis
Client Wineworld PLC

**11 Poster for '70s disco event
Design firm** Device, London
Designer/illustrator Rian Hughes
Client The Beach

**12 Directional poster
for Space Restaurants
Design firm** The Chase Creative
Consultants, Manchester
Art director Ben Casey
Designers Damian Nowell, Stephen Royle,
Tom O'Shaughnessy

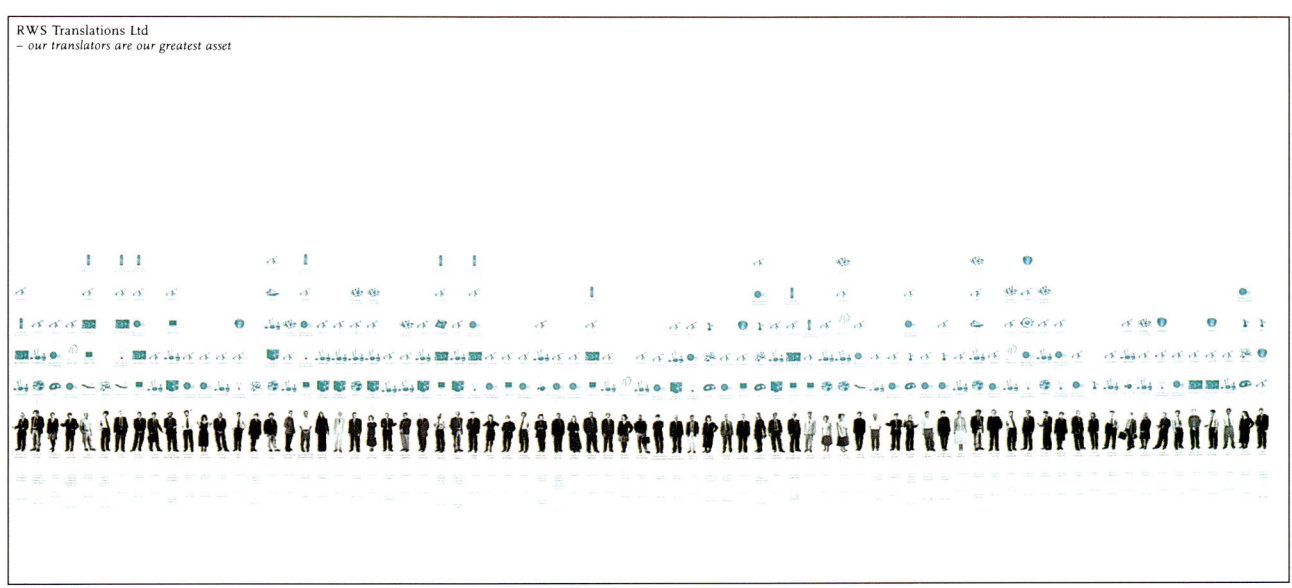

13 Christmas card in the form of a booklet whose subject is "witness."
Design firm Lippa Pearce Design, Twickenham
Designer Harry Pearce
Photographers Richard Foster, Harry Pearce.

14 Folder for RWS Translations, diagramming the expertise of its staff of translators
Design firm Jannuzzi Smith, London
Art directors Richard Smith, Michele Jannuzzi
Designers Alexia Cox, Michele Jannuzzi, Richard Smith

15 Page from portfolio of photographer Christopher Griffith, originally published in German Elle
Design firm D.design, London
Designer Derek Samuel
Client Christopher Griffith

16 Brochure for Paragraphics
Design firm Struktur Design, London
Designer Roger Fawcett-Tang

United Kingdom 117

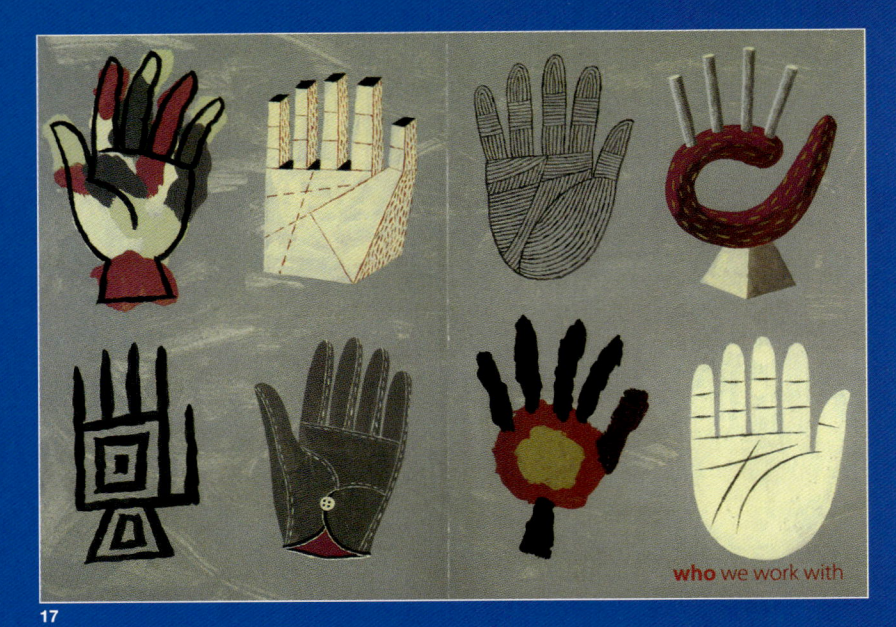

17

18

19 20

17 "Handbook" a promotional booklet for Touchstone Exhibitions & Conferences
Design firm Trickett & Webb, London
Designers Lynn Trickett, Brian Webb, Katja Thielen
Illustrator Jeffrey Fisher

18 Logo for Clare Simmons Associates, a conference and event production company
Design firm Imagine, Manchester
Designer David Caunce

19 CD cover for "Flaming Pie"
Design firm The Team, London
Designer Richard Ward
Photographer Linda McCartney
Client Paul McCartney

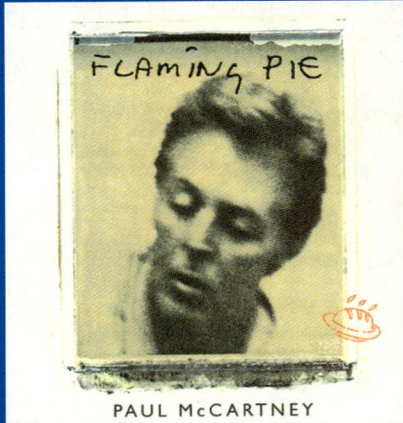

21

20 Self-promotional book called "(noise)3"
Design firm The Attik, Huddersfield

21 Brochure promoting Phillipe Starck–designed furniture produced by Cassina
Design firm Michael Nash Associates, London
Art directors/designers Stephanie Nash, Anthony Michael
Photographer Matthew Donaldson

22 Cover of self-promotional magazine for design firm Baber Smith, London
Art director Simon Smith
Designer Hayden Berman
Photographer Kulbir Alandi

23 1997 annual report for The London Institute, a group of five London art colleges
Design firm Trickett & Webb, London
Designers Lynn Trickett, Brian Webb, Heidi Lightfoot

24 1997 annual report for London Business School
Design firm Addison, London
Art director David Freeman
Designer Sinclair Ashman
Photographers Davy Jones, John Ross

25 Cover of Handlines, a book promoting the cause of banning landmines by showing the hands of 45 people who rely on them to make their living (artists, musicians, surgeons, etc.)
Design firm Omnific Studios, London
Art director Derek Birdsall
Designers Derek Birdsall, John Morgan
Photographer Ken Griffiths
Client Rebekah Gilbertson

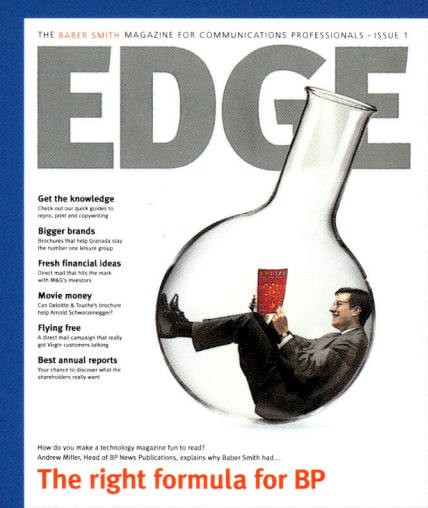

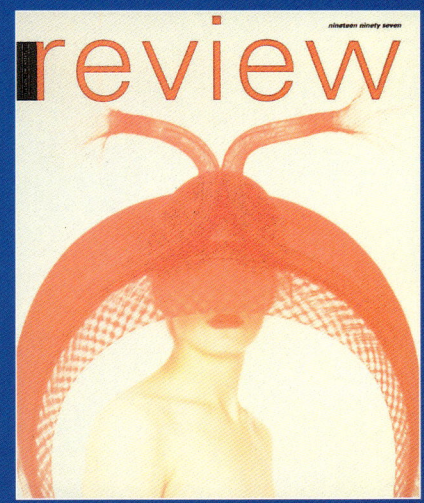

26 Packaging for Sundsvall Vodka, a premium vodka for the U.S. market
Design firm Pearlfisher, London
Art director Jonathan Ford
Designers Kate Barsby, Jonathan Ford

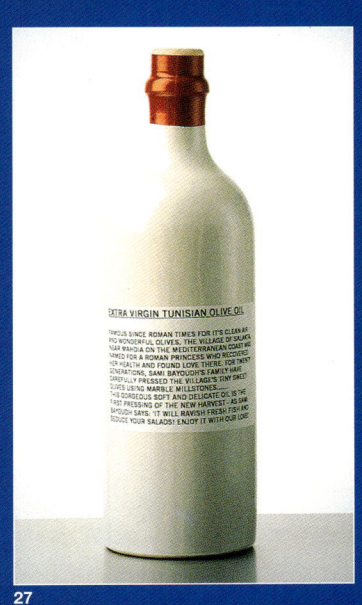

27 Packaging for Extra Virgin Tunisian Olive Oil
Design firm Michael Nash Associates, London
Art directors Stephanie Nash, Anthony Michael, David Hitner
Designers Kevin Gould, David Hitner
Client Joy of Real Food

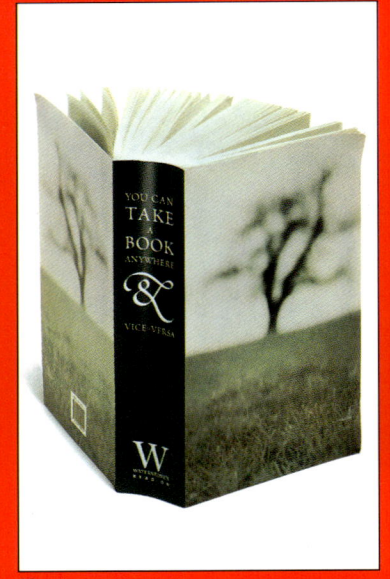

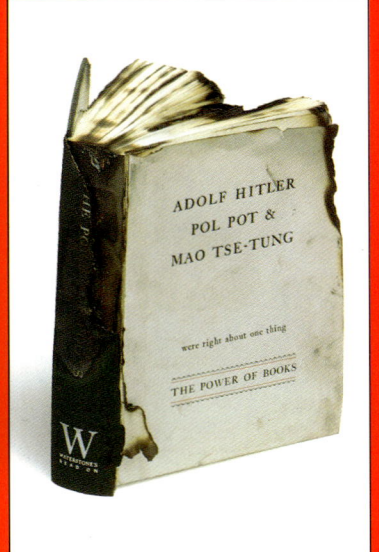

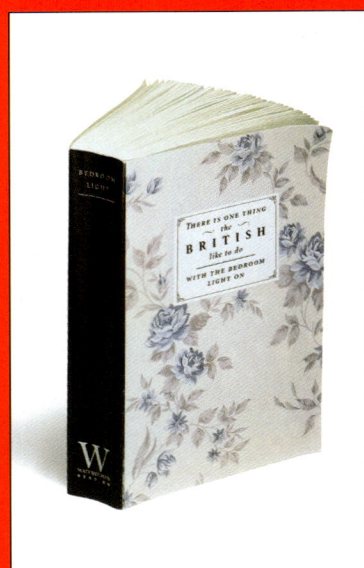

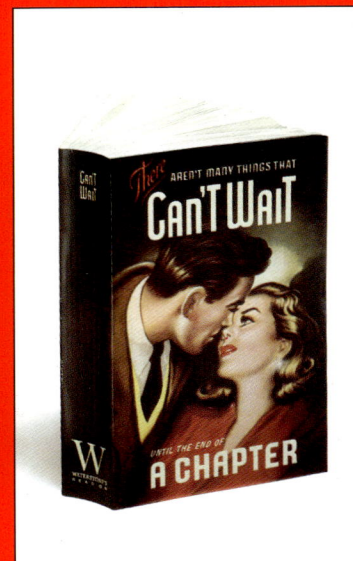

28–31 Ad campaign for Waterstone's Booksellers
Agency TBWA GGT Simons Palmer, London
Art director Paul Belford
Copywriter Nigel Roberts
Typographers Paul Belford, Nigel Ward (Figs. 28, 30), Alison Wills (Fig. 29), Alan Dempsey (Fig. 31)
Photographers Laurie Haskell, Glen Erler (Fig. 28)

32 Cover of catalogue for Fourth Estate, book publishers
Design firm Frost Design, London
Art director Vince Frost
Designers Vince Frost, Andrew Collier
Photographer James Cant

33 Promotional brochure for the design firm Stocks Austin Sice, London
Art director David Stocks
Designers David Stocks, Kin Ip Yu
Photographer Colin Grey

34 Spread from book Angels from the Vatican, published by Art Services International
Design firm Omnific Studios, London.
Designer Derek Birdsall

35 Logo for Vinopolis, a wine emporium
Design firm Lewis Moberly, London
Art director Mary Lewis
Designer Nin Glaister
Client Wineworld PLC

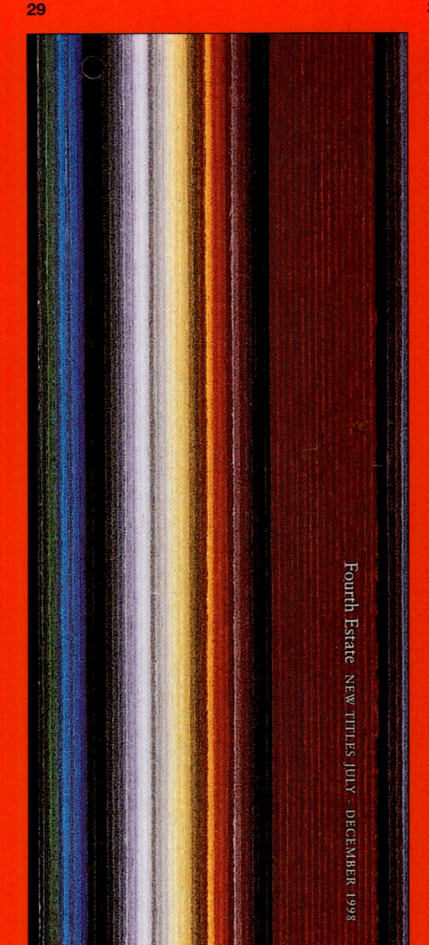

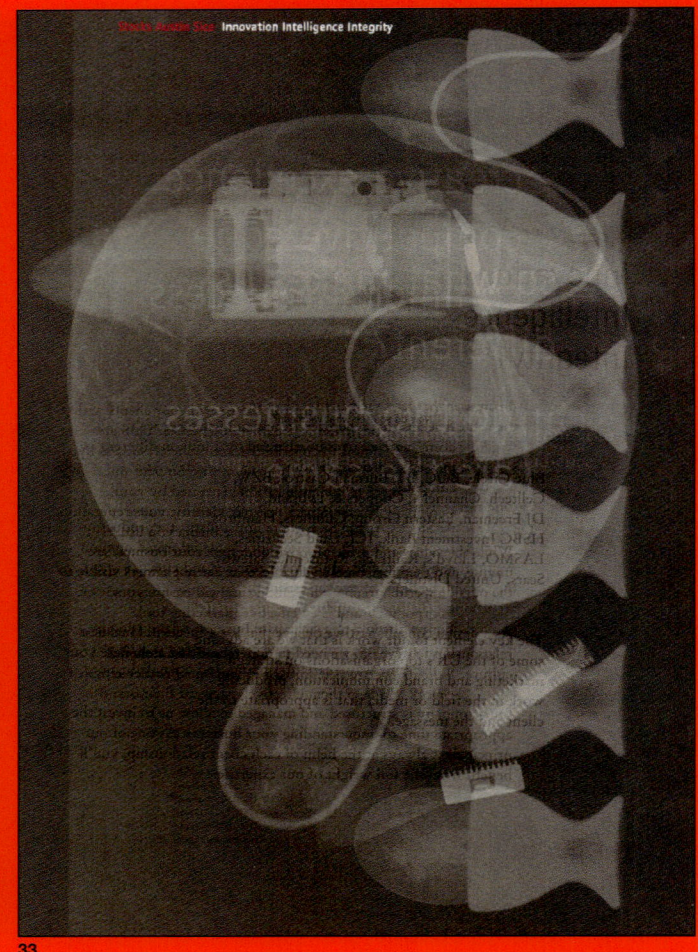

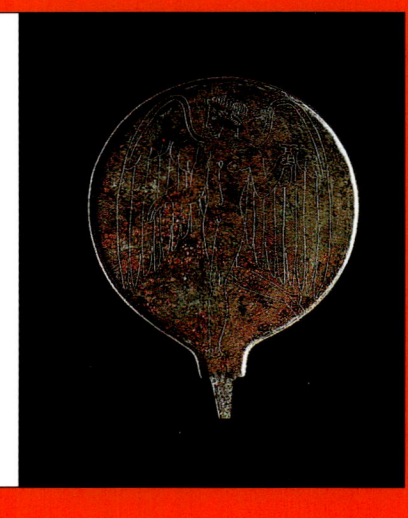

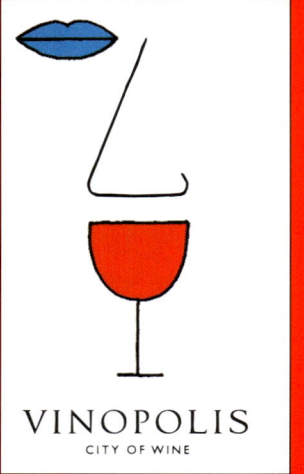

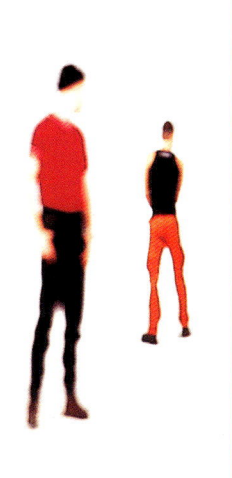

36-39 AIDS awareness posters
Photographer Peter Dazeley, London
Design firm Spencer Landor
Art directors Juliet Barclay,
Shaun Whelan
Designer John Spencer
Client The Terrence Higgins Trust

40 Spread from Into the Red, a book about 21 classic racing cars
Design firm The Team, London
Art director Julian Grice
Designer Adrian Mewitt
Photographers Mike Johnson,
Simon Childs
Client Nick Mason

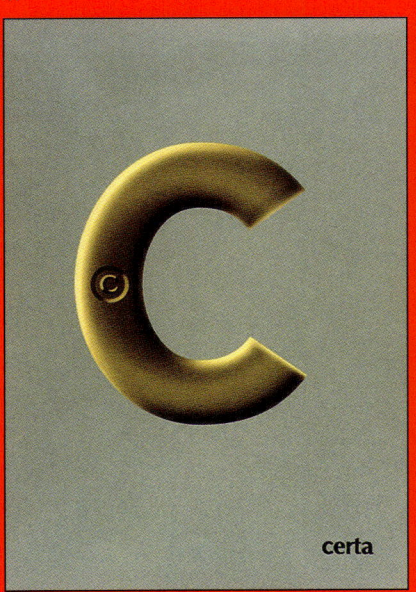

41 Cover of book catalogue for Fourth Estate
Design firm Frost Design, London
Designer/typographer Vince Frost

42 Spread from The Swanstock Collection of fine art photography
Client The Image Bank, London
Design firm Mervyn Kurlansky Design
Art director Mervyn Kurlansky
Designers Mervyn Kurlansky,
Simon Engelbrecht
Photographer (spread shown) Kirk Anderson

43 Identity brochure for Certa (Contamination Assessment and Land Certification)
Design firm Lippa Pearce Design, Twickenham
Art director Domenic Lippa
Designer Rachael Dinnis
Photographer Tim Flak

United Kingdom 121

44 Underwear packaging for Exté
Design firm Minale Tattersfield+Partners, Richmond

45 Brochure for CWB, information technology specialists
Design firm HGV, London
Art directors Pierre Vermeir, Jim Sutherland
Designer Stuart Radford

46 Symbol for National Botanic Garden of Wales
Design firm Lippa Pearce Design, Twickenham
Designer Domenic Lippa
Illustrator Geoffrey Appleton

47 Booklet for research department of The Design Council
Design firm HGV, London
Art directors/designers Pierre Vermeir, Jim Sutherland

48 ikono attributes brochure
Design firm Roundel, London
Art director John Bateson
Designers Alec Law, Mark McConnachie, Paul Ingle
Client Zanders Finepapers

49 "Matthew's Way," a booklet commemorating the life of an infant who died before his first birthday with a short tour of the locale in which he lived
Design firm The Graphics Team, Aylesbury
Art director M. Goodwin
Designer Linda Jones
Illustrators Linda Jones and schoolchildren

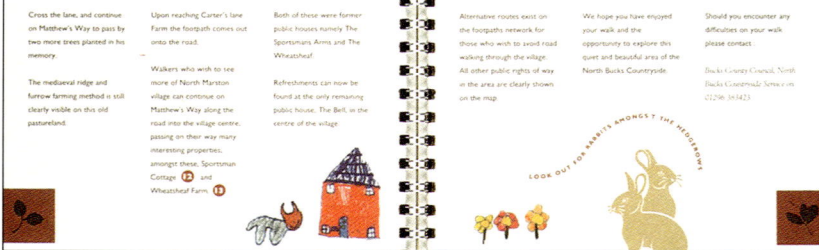

50 Logo for Big Bang,
an event decoration company
Design firm HGV, London
Art director Pierre Vermeir
Designer Stuart Radford

51 National Portrait
Gallery retail identity
Design firm FOUR IV, London
Art director Andy Bone
Designer Kim Hartley

52 Boots camera packaging
Design firm Lewis Moberly, London
Art director Mary Lewis
Designers Stewart Devlin, Mary Lewis, Ann Marshall
Client The Boots Company PLC

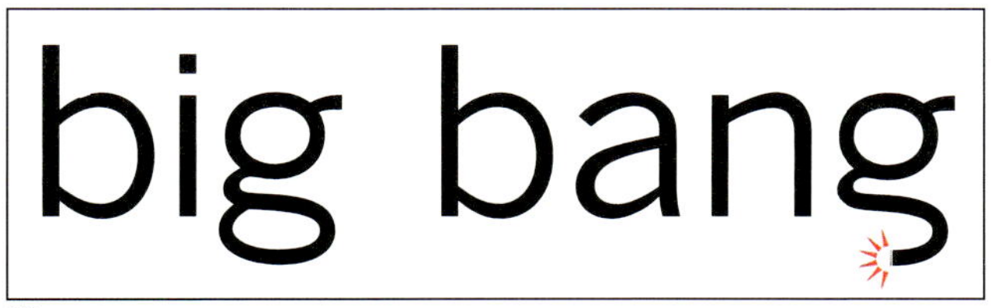

53 Nikon compact camera packaging
Design firm Brewer Riddiford
Art director John Brewer
Designer Richard Haywood
Client Nikon (UK)

54 CD-ROM for Virtual Showroom, a major source of British contemporary furniture
Design firm Paper White, London
Art director Jonathan Howkins
Designer Paul Fennell

55 Poster for Sun Devil Alcoholic Lemon Drink
Design firm Turner Duckworth, London
Art directors Bruce Duckworth, David Turner
Designers David Turner, Allen Raulet
Client McKenzie River Corp

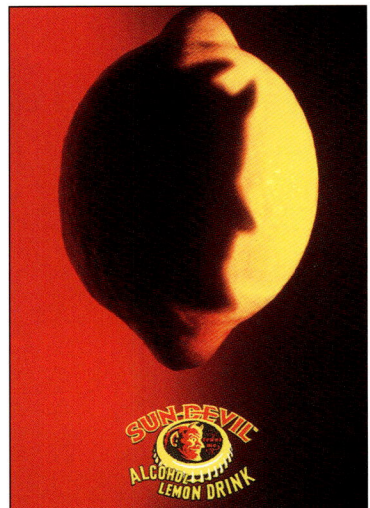

56 "A New Perspective" booklet for Marlin construction management
Design firm HGV, London
Art directors Pierre Vermeir, Jim Sutherland
Designer Stuart Radford
Photographer Duncan Smith

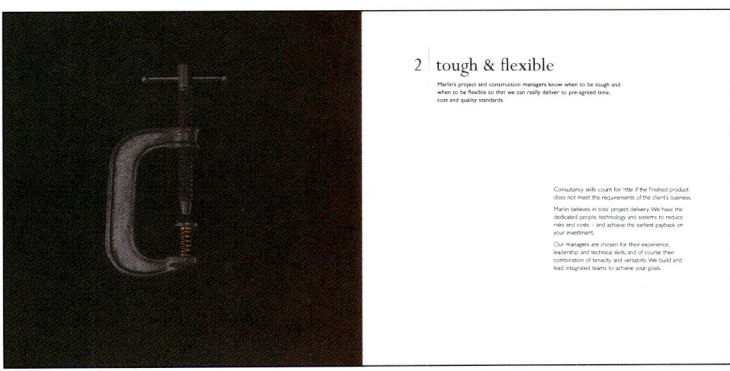

United Kingdom

57 Packaging for Neals Yard Remedies
Design firm Turner Duckworth, London
Art directors Bruce Duckworth, David Turner
Designers Bob Celiz, Bruce Duckworth
Illustrator Mike Pratley

58 Recipe booklets for a bakery
Design firm Fitch, London
Art director Carol Dean
Designers Carol Dean, Matt Merrett
Client Pieter Totte

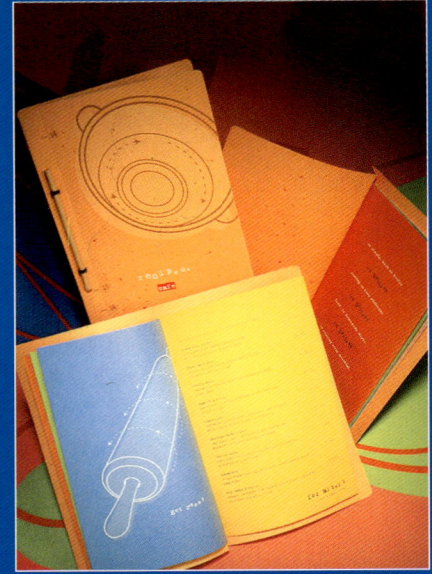

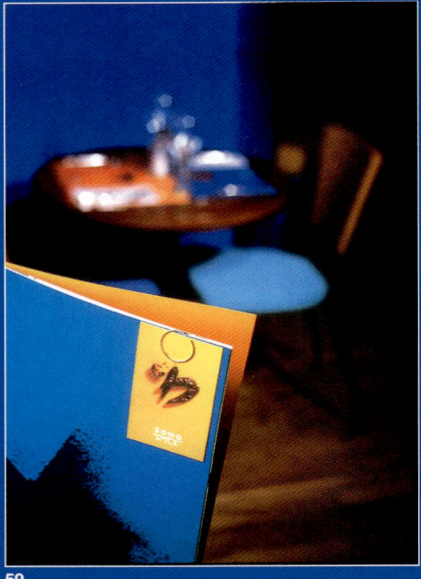

59 Soho Spice restaurant menu cover
Design firm Fitch, London
Art director Giles Marking
Designer Nick Richards
Photographer Chris Gascoigne
Client Amin Ali

60 Packaging for Boots specialist vitamins
Design firm Roundel, London
Art director John Bateson
Designers Paul Ingle, John Bateson
Illustrator Paul Ingle

61 Food packaging for Massarella Catering Group.
Design firm WPA Pinfold, Leeds
Art director Richard Hurst
Designer/illustrator Hayley Wall

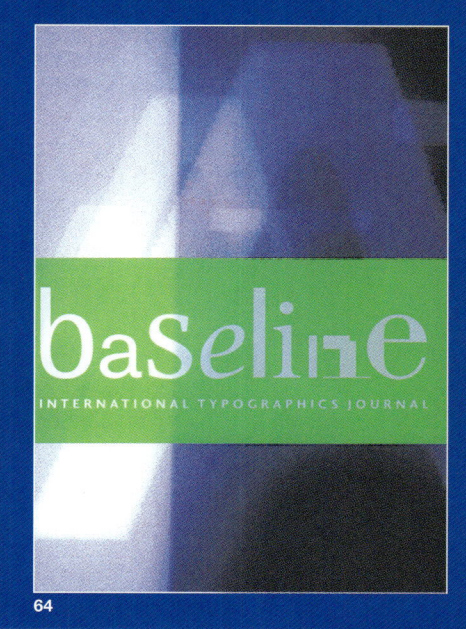

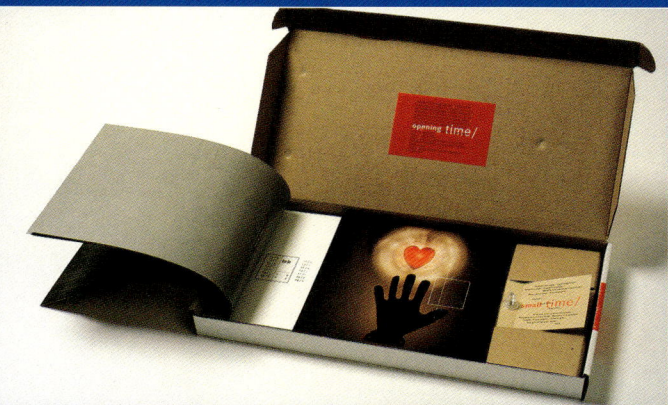

62–64 Covers of Baseline journal
Publisher Bradbourne Publishing Ltd., East Malling
Design firm HDR Design
Art director Hans Dieter Reichert
Designers Hans Dieter Reichert, Peter Black, Debi Ani, Dean Pavit

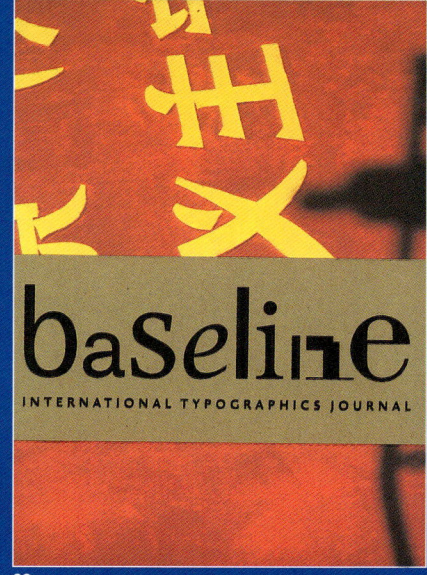

65 "Just in Time" calendar, joint promotion of design firm Pure Design, Edinburgh, and Nimmos Colour Printers
Designer Mick Dean
Photographers Colin Gray, Reuben Paris, Iain Stewart, Chris Hall, Neil Leslie, Warren Sanders, Laurence Winram, Mick Dean

66 Flos Lighting brochure
Design firm Michael Nash Associates, London
Art directors Anthony Michael, Stephanie Nash, David Hitner
Designer David Hitner
Photographers Fasanotto Piacentini (product shots), Ramak Fazel (lifestyle shots), Nick Veasey (cover and dividers)

67 Bookplates, sent as gifts to the design firm's clients and friends
Design firm Lippa Pearce Design, Twickenham
Designer Rachael Dinnis
Photographer Paul Reeves

68 A(S)P Handbook, showcasing the work of members of the Association of Scottish Photographers
Design firm Pure Design, Edinburgh
Designer Mick Dean photographer (spread shown) David Boni

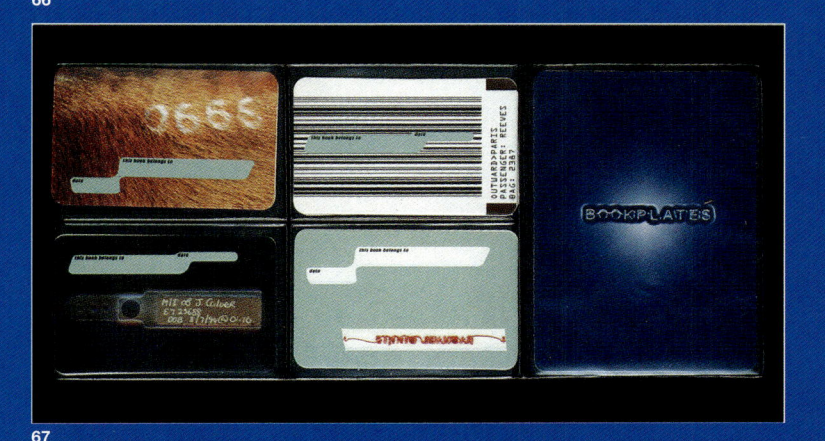

United Kingdom 125

69

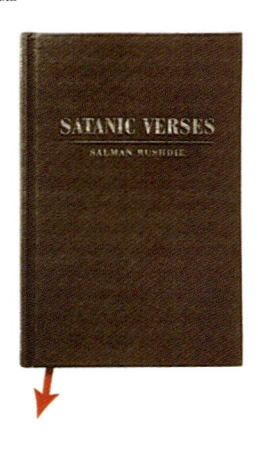

70

69 News at Ten, a promotional book commemorating HGV's 10th anniversary by satirizing news events of the last decade
Design firm HGV, London
Art directors Pierre Vermeir, Jim Sutherland
Designers Stuart Radford, Dominic Edmunds, Jamie Roberts

70 Tupperware-style packaging for Exedo shoes
Design firm Minale Tattersfield+Partners, Richmond
Client Bally

71 Brand identity for Soup Opera, a soup retailer
Design firm Lippa Pearce Design Ltd., Twickenham
Designer Rachael Dinnis

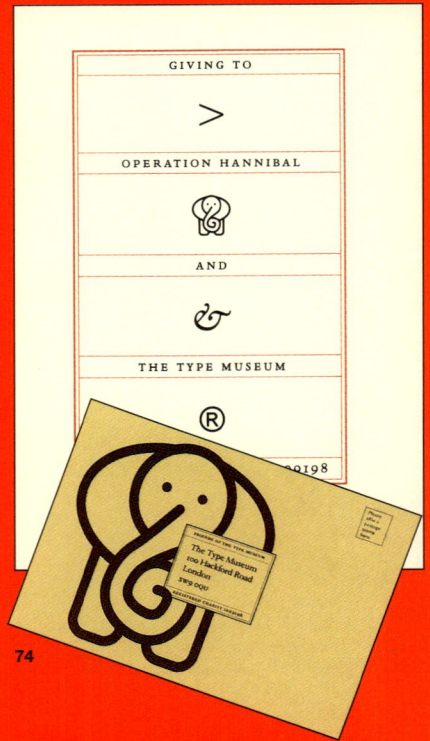

71

72

73

74

72 Booklet promoting customized ATMs (automated teller machines)
Design firm Graphic Partners, Edinburgh
Designer Jack Rodgers
Illustrators David Sim, Diane Lumley
Photographer Ian Atkinson
Client NCR

73 Self-promotional calendar for design firm WPA Pinfold, Leeds
Art directors Andy Probert, Richard Hurst
Designers Andy Probert, Phil Morrison
Illustrators Andrew Robinson, Simon Henshaw, Nigel Burton, Peter Beard
Photographer Michael Jones

74 Booklet and return envelope for "Operation Hannibal," a fundraising effort for The Type Museum
Design firm Cleaver et al, London
Art director Phil Cleaver
Designers Phil Cleaver, Eiichi Kono, Susan Shaw, Aurobind Patel

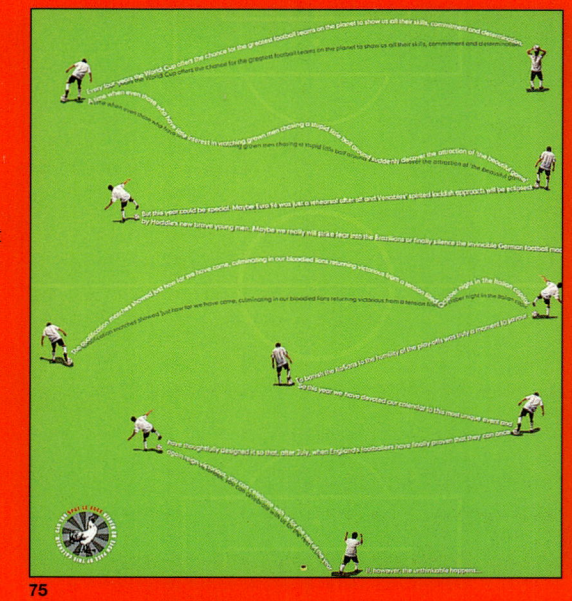

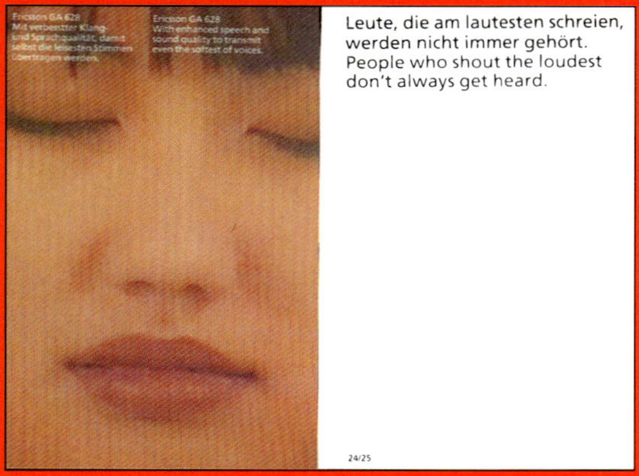

75 Page from World Cup Football Calendar 1998
Design firm Stocks Austin Sice, London
Art director Nick Austin
Designer Ben Tomlinson

76 Packaging for St. Edmund beer
Design firm Brewer Riddiford, Bury St. Edmunds
Art director Steve Booth
Designer Mike Harris
Illustrator Peter Garland
Client Greene King PLC

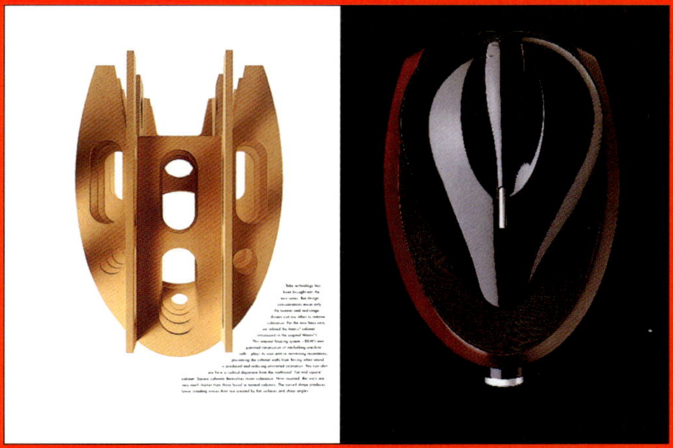

77 Litigation brochure for law firm Linklaters & Paines
Design firm Saatchi & Saatchi Design, London
Designer Nicola Penny
Illustrator M.H. Jeeves

78 "Voice," product catalogue for Ericsson Mobile Communications AB
Design firm Imagination, London
Art director Stuart Jane
Designer Melissa Price
Photographer Mark Livemore
Illustrator Martin Brown

79 Wine packaging for Gatão Vinho Verde, a Portuguese brand
Design firm Blackburn's, London
Art director Belinda Duggan
Designers Belinda Duggan, Roberta Oates
Illustrator James Marsh
Client Sociedade Dos Vinhos Borges

80 Promotional booklet "The Minale Tattersfield Book of Colour"
Design firm Minale Tattersfield+Partners, Richmond

81 Brochure announcing launch of top range of B&W loudspeakers
Design firm Thomas Manss & Co., London
Art director Thomas Manss
Designer David Lovelock
Copywriter Richard Butterworth
Photographers Steve Rees, Andreas Schmidt, Ken Kirkwood

United Kingdom 127

82

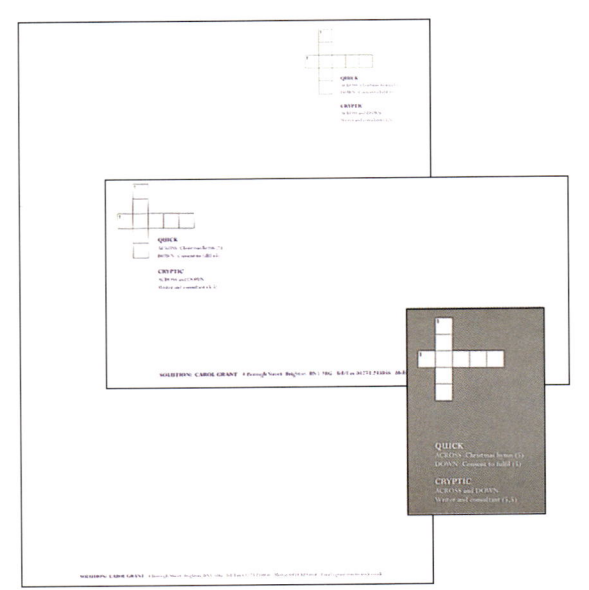

83

82 Virtual receptionist—a stand-in signaling to visitors to design firm Dew Gibbons, London, that the firm's reception area is unstaffed
Art directors Shaun Dew, Steve Gibbons
Designer Peter Hale

83 Stationery for copywriter Carol Grant, using a cryptic clue to portray her work
Design firm The Team, London
Art director Matt Frost
Designer Jon-Paul Winter

84 Board game direct-mail piece sent to potential clients from NE6 Design Consultants, Newcastle
Art directors Alan Whitfield, David Coates
Designers Alan Whitfield, Tom Grathes
Illustrator Anthony Sidwell

85 Retail packaging for SPACE, NK, Apothecary
Design firm Michael Nash Associates, London
Art directors Anthony Michael, Stephanie Nash, David Hitner
Designers David Hitner, Stephanie Nash

86 Carton for Courvoisier V.S. Cognac
Design firm Blackburn's, London
Art director John Blackburn
Designers Matt Thompson, Sarah Roberts
Client Allied Domecq Spirits & Wine

87 Stationery for Kate Besley Garden Design
Design firm Jones & Co. Design, Farnham
Designer/illustrator Jack Jones

84

85

86

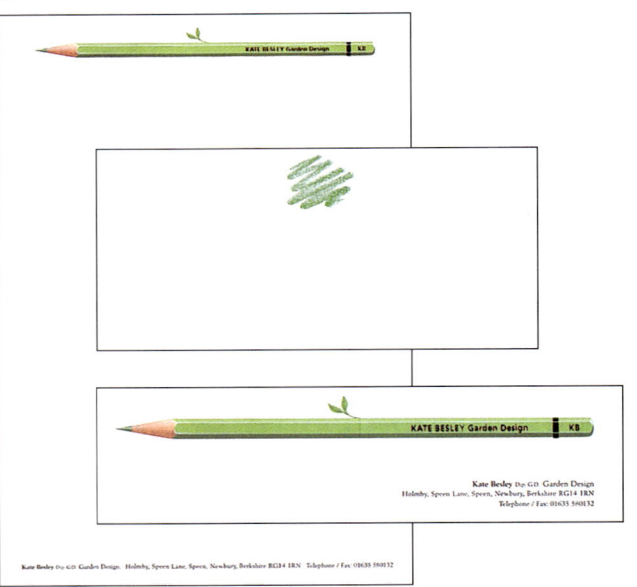

87

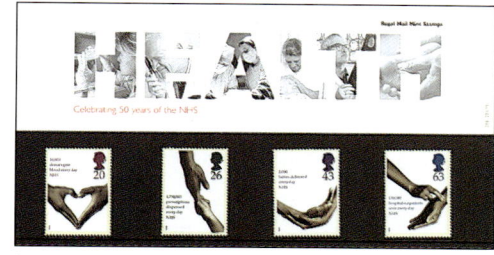

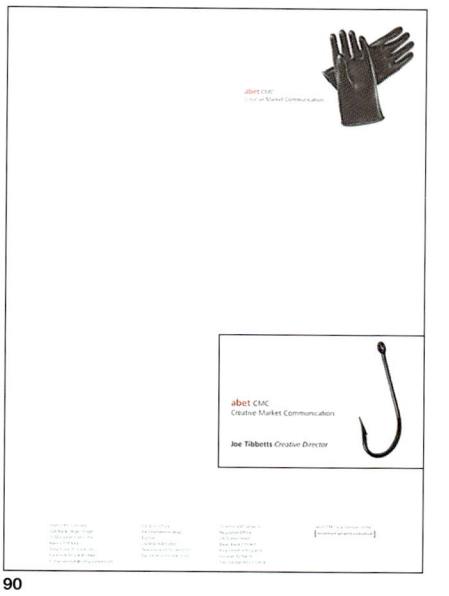

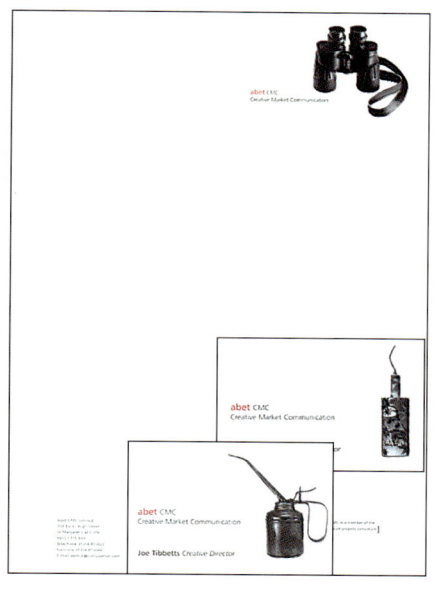

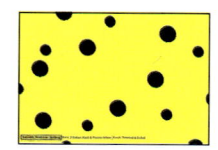

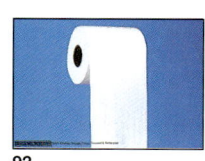

88 Stamp issue commemorating the 50th anniversary of the National Health Service
Design firm Frost Design, London
Designer Vince Frost
Photographer Albert Watson
Client Royal Mail

89 Page from "The Definitive Portrait," first in a series of prestige stamp books for Royal Mail
Design firm Dew Gibbons, London
Art directors Shaun Dew, Steve Gibbons
Designers Peter Hale, Sine Sørensen
Copywriter Jim Davies

90 Stationery for Abet CMC, a marketing consultancy specializing in communications solutions
Design firm Dew Gibbons, London
Art directors Shaun Dew, Steve Gibbons
Designer Lee Wilson
Photographer John Edwards

91 Wedding invitation
Design firm The Chase Creative Consultants, Manchester
Designer Stephen Conchie
Clients Stephen and Erica

92 Four in a series of postcards promoting the services of Highlight, a printer
Design firm The Chase Creative Consultants, Manchester
Art director Richard Scholey
Designers Richard Scholey, Janet Neil, Billy Markcom, Craig Webster, Grant Mitchell

93 Brochure for Fusion Glass Designs
Design firm Frost Design, London
Designer Vince Frost

94 Booklet announcing the launch of a fast U.K. parcel service by train
Design firm HGV, London
Art directors/designers Pierre Vermeir, Jim Sutherland
Client Esprit Europe

95, 96 Identity for an in-flight meal service
Design firm Luxon Carrà, London
Art director Peter Smith
Designer Robert Cachia
Client Britannia Airlines

United Kingdom 129

Yugoslavia Gazetteer

Hotels

Hotel Beograd
Nemanjina 6
Belgrade
T + 381 11 645 199

Restaurants & Bars

The Znak Pitanje (Question Mark)
Kralja Pitanje 6
Belgrade
An old Balkan inn with an excellent range of traditional meat dishes and salads washed down with an intriguing flat beer.

Museums & Galleries

Palace of Princess Ljubice
Belgrade
Sited on the corner of Svetozara Markovica and Kralija Petra, this Balkan-style palace is well worth a visit with its period furnishings.

Places of Interest

National Theatre
Trg Republike
Belgrade
Built in 1869 this elegant building is the home for opera during the winter months. Dress code – unpretentious (jeans acceptable)

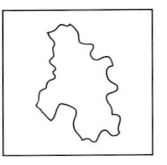

Yugoslavia

Local name	Srbija-Crna Gora
Geographic coordinates	44 00 N, 21 00 E
Population ǀ1000	11,206
Design Population ǀ1000	000.3
Languages	Serbo-Croatian, Albanian
Capital	Belgrade
Monetary unit	Yugoslav Novi Dinar (DIN)

Area 1000 k/m2

Austria	083.9	Germany	357.0	Portugal	092.4
Belgium	030.5	Hungary	093.0	Russia I Belarus 17,075.0	207.6
Croatia	056.5	Ireland	070.3	Slovenia	020.3
Denmark	043.1	Italy	301.0	Spain	505.0
Finland	338.0	Lithuania	065.2	Sweden	450.0
France	552.0	The Netherlands	041.5	Switzerland	041.3
		Norway	324.0	Turkey	779.2
		Poland	313.0	United Kingdom	243.3

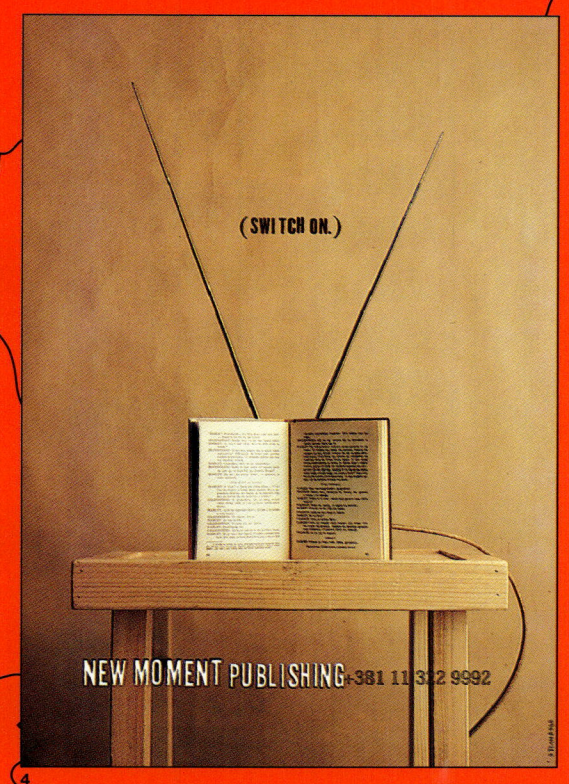

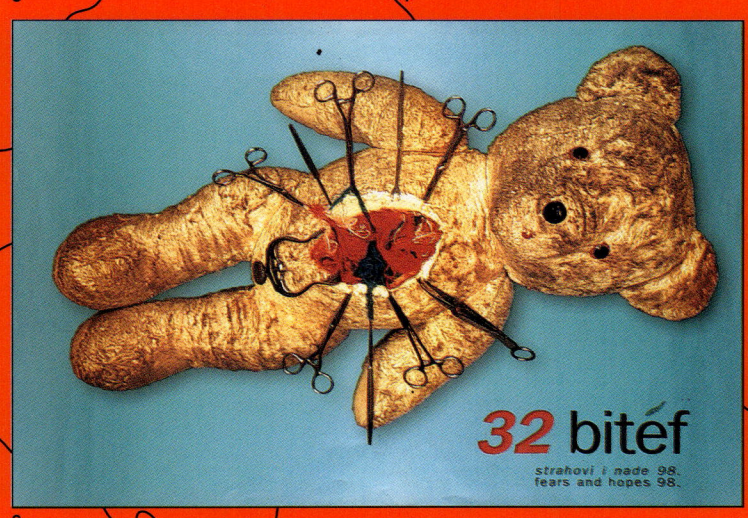

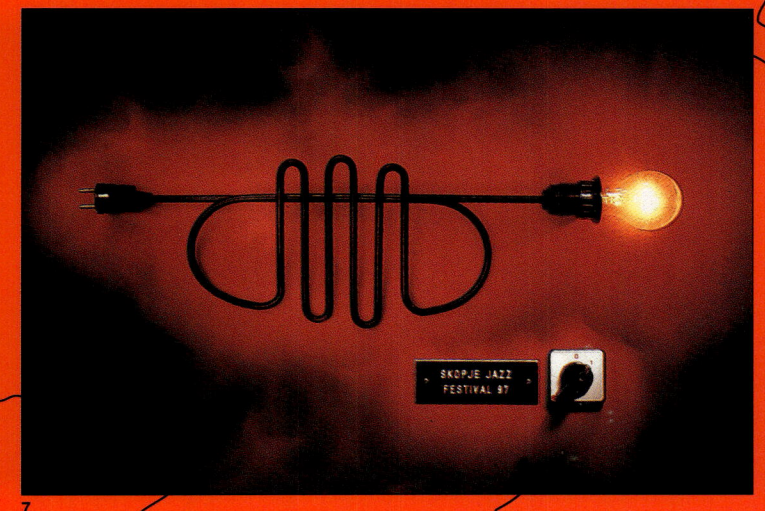

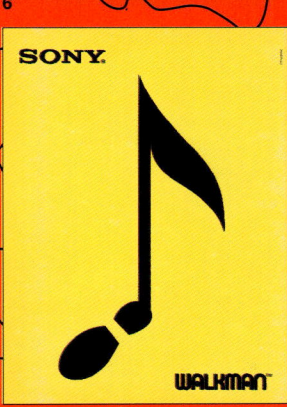

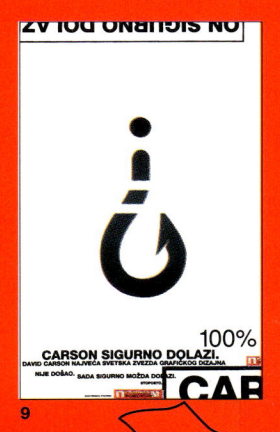

1 Symbol for Cinema Café, a café in the lobby of a Belgrade movie theatre
Agency S Team Saatchi & Saatchi, Belgrade
Art director Slavimir Stojanović

2 Logo for Vincent Production, a music production house owned by rock band Van Gogh
Agency S Team Saatchi & Saatchi, Belgrade
Art director Slavimir Stojanović

3 Logo for Informa, a magazine about the applied arts
Agency S Team Saatchi & Saatchi, Belgrade
Art director Slavimir Stojanović

4 Newspaper ad for New Moment Publishing.
Agency S Team Saatchi & Saatchi, Belgrade
Art director Slavimir Stojanović
Photographer Aleksandar Kujučev

5 Outdoor ad for the Belgrade International Theatre Festival
Agency S Team Saatchi & Saatchi, Belgrade
Art directors Slavimir Stojanović, Miloš Ilić
Photographer Aleksandar Kujučev

6 Poster for the Belgrade International Theatre Festival's 32nd Annual International Festival of Avant-Garde Theatre
Agency I&F McCann-Erickson, Belgrade
Art director Sanja Rudić
Photographer Vladimir Perić

7 Poster for Skopje Jazz Festival 97
Agency S Team Saatchi & Saatchi, Belgrade
Art director Slavimir Stojanović
Photographer Aleksandar Kujučev
Client Oliver Belopeta

8 Outdoor ad for Sony Walkman
Agency S Team Saatchi & Saatchi, Belgrade
Art director/illustrator Slavimir Stojanović

9 Poster for a lecture by David Carson, sponsored by Publikum, a print shop
Agency S Team Saatchi & Saatchi, Belgrade
Art director Slavimir Stojanović

Yugoslavia 131

Concept and Design
1-571 European Design Annual 5 | 2000.

Design firm Navy Blue Design Consultants
Art director Geoff Nicol
Designer Clare Lundy
Client RotoVision SA

Navy Blue Communications Group
Navy Blue Design Consultants | London | **T** +44 171 253 03 16
Navy Blue Design Consultants | Edinburgh | **T** +44 131 553 50 50
Navy Blue Interiors & Exhibitions | **T** +44 131 553 09 90
navyblue.com | Edinburgh | London | **T** +44 131 553 50 50
www.navyblue.co.uk

Design Exports Register
For consultancies to register the products and projects they are designing for non-UK clients to enable them to be included in BDI export promotion activities.

Design News Service
For journalists, editors and researchers seeking the latest press material from British consultancies. For consultancies seeking international media exposure.

Design Directory
For design buyers seeking to obtain details of and view the work of Britain's leading design consultancies. For consultancies seeking to promote internationally.

Design Awards Planner
For consultancies seeking to obtain details of all the international, commercial design awards they can enter.

Design Advisory Service
For design buyers who require more in-depth knowledge of design consultancies' skills, processes and fee structures – and how to appoint them.

Design Export Events
For organisations who wish to participate in, or appoint BDI to organise, design led events in Britain or overseas.

Design Export News
A quarterly publication promot British design successes. Obta editorial schedule and submit your details to qualify for a fre subscription.

Design Export Register | Design News Service | Design Directory | Design Awards Planner | Design Advisory Service | Design Export Events | Design Export News

The British Design Initiative
2-4 Peterborough Mews
Parsons Green
London SW6 3BL

Telephone
+44 (0)171 384 3435
Facsimile
+44 (0)171 371 5343

E-mail
initiative@britishdesign.co.uk

Internet
http://www.britishdesign.co.

If there's one thing guaranteed to make an industry feel as though its cutting edge has been blunted, it's praise from politicians. Britain's New Labour government has been attempting to prove its funky young credentials by targetting the creative industries. Measures such as the Creative Industries Task Force (a committee to promote these areas) are all very laudable, but the overall effect of hearing Labour politicians profess their love for design is like listening to vicars talk about rock and roll.

These thoughts occurred while at a Downing Street reception, watching Chancellor Gordon Brown work a room of creative notables. Among the great and good gathered there was Pentagram partner John Rushworth. Pressed for his predictions as to what the next big graphic trend may be, Rushworth replied simply: "Big type".

Yes, it seems that large, clear, simple typography is to make a comeback. Designers beloved of setting pages of text in 7 pt beware: legibility is back. Distressed, distorted, Carson-esque grunge has had its day: expect to see Swiss Modernism re-evaluated and reinterpreted.

Perhaps a new design hero will emerge to lead this old/new wave. As past stars such as tomato and Designers Republic have matured, the field is open for the next new graphic guru. It is quite likely that such a hero will emerge not from print but from new media.

Young designers can expect to earn around 30 per cent more if they have multimedia skills and colleges have not been slow in responding to the demand such opportunities create. New media courses are springing up all over the country (and will need monitoring to ensure that they are turning out graduates with good skills and not just taking advantage of a new market with an underdeveloped quality control procedure).

With the chance to earn good money plus the attraction of being part of a pioneering industry on a mission to change the world, it is not surprising that a great deal of design talent is heading toward a digital future. Some more traditional areas are suffering: good young packaging designers in particular are increasingly thin on the ground. Each year Creative Review runs a scheme to highlight the talent of tomorrow called Creative Futures. Last year we were told by just about every packaging creative director in London that there was a dire shortage of talent in their field. Not one could name a potential star.

Despite such gloom, the overall standard of work coming out of Britain remains encouragingly high. If the future of design is to be digital, it is exciting to see that the UK has already set itself up as a centre of multimedia creativity to rival anything San Francisco has to offer. And in the meantime, the end of print is still a long way off.

Creative Futures, Patrick Burgoyne, Editor, Creative Review magazine

the almighty euro

By Todd Pruzan On the first day of 2002, eleven European countries will share one official currency. Designers are divided on the look of the new money.

The inhabitants of the continental landmass known as Europe know a thing or two about division. European unity is an oxymoron with several thousand years of strife and bickering to back it up, resulting in a fascinating patchwork of languages, cultures, heroes, villains, and wars and treaties and music and architecture and soccer teams.

But commonality is encroaching, following the 1992 establishment of the European Union, with membership extended to the continent's most powerful nations. And from the morning of New Year's Day 2002, the citizens of 11 European countries, from Portugal to Austria, will begin exchanging their own national currencies for new euro notes and coins.

A new monetary lingua franca won't erase national borders, of course; many Europeans are predictably unhappy about having to rally around an untested financial standard uniting their strong national economies with their neighbours' weaker ones. But the issues are hardly limited to economics. A nation's currency—embodied by the design of the notes and coins everyone carries around in pockets and purses—is possibly the most immediate, tangible expression of its culture, history, and identity. So the passing of the franc, lira, peseta, mark, and other currencies may provoke mourning as the 12 billion new euro notes and 80 billion euro coins—most of them lacking any imagery to stir national pride—replace them. To make matters more confusing, there's a new typographic symbol for the euro that ultimately will need to be on nearly every computer keyboard in the world.

The European Monetary Institute, precursor of the new European Central Bank, established the money's design with a contest won, for the notes, by Robert Kalina of Austria's Österrichische Nationalbank, and for the faces of the coins, by Luc Luycx of Belgium's mint, Monnaie Royale de Belgique. (Each member nation will supply its own design for the reverse.) Criticism has been extensive of both the currency designs and of Belgian designer Alain Billiet's new euro typographical symbol—essentially an uppercase C with two horizontal bars running through it, evoking the Greek epsilon.

Among those most dissatisfied with the results are European and European-born graphic designers. "It's a great opportunity gone down the drain, as usual," fumes Massimo Vignelli of Vignelli Associates in New York. "People without knowledge of design, and having done no homework, were in charge of doing a job they're no good at," he says of the Monetary Institute's procedure for selecting a design. "The right way to do it would be to examine all the good currency in Europe, go to one designer, and ask that person to do it," Vignelli says. "Some great designers have done great money in Europe—number one, R.D.E. Oxenaar in the Netherlands, and Jorg Zintzmeyer, who designed beautiful money for Switzerland rather recently. But this is more a political design than anything, to please everybody—it's very undefined, very blurred. It's just plain corny."

Not surprisingly, some designers in the Netherlands—whose currency has been heralded as innovative and attractive since Oxenaar's designs were introduced—agree with that assessment. (For the record, Oxenaar, himself an entrant in the euro design competition, dismissed Kalina's euro design as "really miserable" last year in The New York Times.)

Bruno Ninaber van Eyben's existing Dutch coin design, featuring Queen Beatrix, will be revised for the reverse of the Dutch euro, largely unchanged but for a ring of stars, the symbol of the EU, surrounding it. "I'm

1 The euro typographical symbol, created by Belgian typographer Alain Billiet and selected by the European Commission. The EC originally declared that the euro symbol would appear identically, with these proportions and dimensions, in every typeface; it has since backed down from its stance.
2-8 The front sides of seven denominations of euro coins, designed by Luc Luycx of Belgium and distinguished by color, weight, and, in the case of the 20 euro cent coin (Fig. 5), shape. The coins' front sides will appear uniformly among the nations using the euro.
9-12 Various denominations of Dutch paper currency, designed by R.D.E. Oxenaar and cited by some

not wholly satisfied with the existing coins," he says. "A coin should express a trust in the future, and this coin expresses the border of Europe with nothing inside. What are we uniting? Are we building a fence around Europe? It's really a lost opportunity. I'm disappointed about it."

While some designers can't get into the spirit of unification as a theme, others tried a nationalistic approach with a satirical edge. Lo Breier, a designer at Hamburg's Büro X Kommunikation, proposed a design for Germany's version of the two-euro coin bearing the BMW and Mercedes-Benz logos. Another Breier approach uses a pair of holes—designed, apparently, so the euro coins can be made into buttons. (His proposals weren't selected.)

The European Commission says the face of its new coin was intended to be simple and attractive, with identification possible not only on the basis of prominent numeric denominations but also by size, shape, and colour. The 2-euro coin has a diameter of 2.58 cm, with a white ring around a yellow circle; the slightly smaller one-euro coin has a yellow ring around a white circle. And the yellow 20-euro cent coin isn't even exactly round: the EC identifies its shape as "Spanish flower."

The notes are identified by a spectrum of colours as well as varying sizes; the largest, the 500-euro note, is a whopping 16 cm x 8.2 cm. (U.S. bills are 15.5 cm. x 6.5 cm.) Each of the notes' seven denominations, identified by a predominant colour scheme and numbers expressed in sans-serif type, depicts one historic European architectural style—classical, Romanesque, Gothic, Renaissance, Baroque and Rococo, the Age of Iron and Glass, and 20th-century—emphasizing windows, gateways, and bridges, intended to symbolize cooperation and communication.

But anyone travelling Europe in search of these "landmarks" will be crushed to discover that the EMI approved illustrations of hybrid structures rather than real ones.

That, too, has proved a controversial decision. "I think it's a travesty," says Kenneth R. Windsor, executive VP/creative director at corporate identity agency Siegel & Gale's London office. Vignelli backs him up: "It's terrible, what they've done with the bridges and buildings that don't belong to any country."

Marc Gobé, the New York–based founder of corporate identity specialist Desgrippes Gobé, disagrees; he feels the design is successful. "You can't be partisan in designing something like this," he says. "I think anyone can identify any of the structures depicted, because the history of architecture in Europe is very common. I can look at a Roman bridge and identify something very similar in France, as would a German, an Italian, and a Spanish person, because we were all at some point occupied by the Romans."

Gobé also appreciates the notes' many cues indicating their value. Windsor does not. "From a design principle, how many variables do you use to create elements of distinction within a system? Do you use size, colour, and a graphic element of layout? Or can you keep just one?"

Perhaps the strangest manifestation of this confusion is the repetition of the word "euro" on the note, in Latin and Greek alphabets—despite the fact that only countries using Latin alphabets have signed on to adopt the currency standard. (Russia, with its chaotic economy, and Cyrillic alphabet is not currently under consideration to become a Member State of the EC; Greece may yet drop its drachma.)

Windsor is unsurprised by howls from some parts of the continent: "I can understand the Dutch being a little more critical, because their note design is more forward-looking than the rest of Europe." Still, the problem may demand a larger perspective. "People fear they'll be losing their identity. But what they don't realize is that in ten years we're going to be cashless," he says, predicting an economy running solely on electronic and other cash-free transactions. "Coins and currency will be potentially a moot point."

The currency itself aims to be an enduring institution, even if the cash becomes obselete—but the design of the euro typographic symbol has encountered some opposition of its own. Many typographers weighed in on the matter on a Web site run by a Montreal typographer, Neil Kandalgaonkar, who says, "Most people really didn't care who'd done it, but they were annoyed by the fact that it was produced by fiat—produced by a company that apparently didn't know much about typography."

Kandalgaonkar's site documented a host of complaints in early 1998. The symbol, designers said, was hard to draw by hand, requiring three strokes instead of two (e.g., $ and £); it was ugly, particularly with regard to the stems of the horizontal bars protruding beyond the back of the curving C; and, perhaps worst of all, it functioned more as a logo than a new character, unaccommodating to the constraints of varying typefaces. (The EC originally mandated that the symbol's exact dimensions were always to be reproduced identically, regardless of the font it lives in, but quietly backed down from this suggestion in March 1998.)

Typographers were miffed at the EC's lack of understanding on how to integrate a new character into the vernacular of typography, a problem necessitating revisions to existing and forthcoming computer

designers as a superior design to the paper euro notes that will replace its use in the Netherlands. Oxenaar's 10-guilder note (front, Fig. 9; reverse, Fig. 10) first circulated in 1971; his 50-guilder note (front, Fig. 11; reverse, Fig. 12) in 1982; and his 1000-guilder note in 1973.

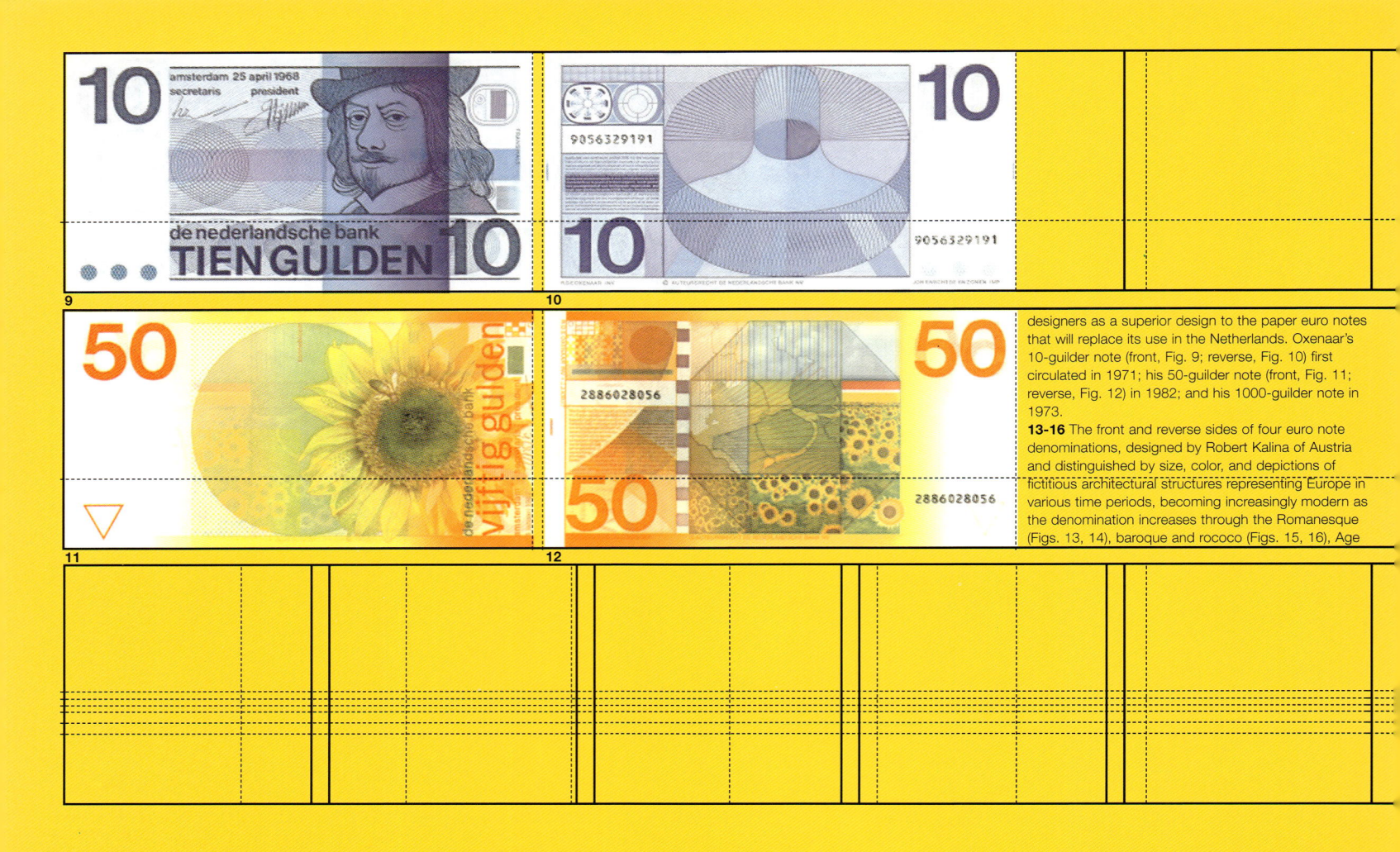

13-16 The front and reverse sides of four euro note denominations, designed by Robert Kalina of Austria and distinguished by size, color, and depictions of fictitious architectural structures representing Europe in various time periods, becoming increasingly modern as the denomination increases through the Romanesque (Figs. 13, 14), baroque and rococo (Figs. 15, 16), Age

hardware and software as well as fonts. "You can't force anyone to just use one symbol," notes Petr van Blokland, founder of an eponymous design studio in Delft, Netherlands. "If they had made any inquiries about how this kind of thing works in a typographic sense, they would have known."

Still, he may be grateful for the extra work resulting from this special headache. His studio, Buro Petr van Bloklund, has been busy formulating euro symbol designs for its original fonts, including those commissioned by Dutch corporate giants IGBank and Nationale Nederlands insurance. Production costs for the new symbol amount to roughly 90 percent of creating a new font from scratch, he says. (Some hand-drawn fonts' hinting codes, which improve onscreen and laser-printed images of the fonts, will be lost when the font is opened with a commercial font application; a manually drawn hinted character is vastly more expensive and time-consuming to create but is more accurate and precise.) Consequently, most of his clients have opted for the full monty.

The problem is slightly stickier on a larger scale, says Simon Daniels, a typographic engineer at Microsoft in Redmond, WA. His department is concerned with establishing the design of the euro symbol in each Microsoft font. (Another department handles the task of making the symbols printable.) "This is the first time we've altered the code pages, which from the old days have basically contained 255 characters," he says. Whereas Microsoft merely added the new symbol to its code pages, archrival Apple had no room to do so and instead resorted to replacing the obscure international currency symbol, a circle studded with points at regular intervals.

Another engineer, John Gray in Redhill, Surrey, England, has created extensive notes on how to produce the euro symbol for Microsoft Office software; his paper includes many examples of "euro-enabled" Hewlett-Packard FontSmart fonts. In several cases, the euro is based heavily on the uppercase C—including serifs—a character that, like the standard accepted design of the symbol, has been criticized as too wide to function properly in tables of narrower numeral characters.

Of course, the symbol's designer, Alain Billiet, had a formidable task. "The target was to obtain a symbol with non-aggressive lines expressing a large content and an open door to the future," he explains. "I had to consider the fact that it had to be applied to different typefaces"—despite the EC's original intentions to the contrary. "And it has to look coherent to other countries too," he says. "There can't be a double interpretation in India or Japan."

Despite criticism that the euro lacks real meaning, Billiet says his typographic symbol is loaded with significance. "A round symbol gives the idea of an expectation, and the ideal form is open, not a closed sphere. It gives expectations of what the euro has to be in the future—it's unlimited, a circle without limits."

Today, the currency symbol seems to have emerged from the firing line more unscathed than the cash it represents. (Even Kandalgoankar has softened his stance: "I think the graphic language of typography can accommodate that symbol, the more I've looked at it with some changes.") That's a promising sign. On January 1, the euro became a legal national currency in Austria, Belgium, Finland, France, Germany, Ireland, Italy, Luxembourg, the Netherlands, Portugal, and Spain. By July 1, 2002, national currencies will be good only for exchange at banks. And, ready or not, 370 million Europeans, who have rarely agreed on anything, will be trying to get used to sharing their money.

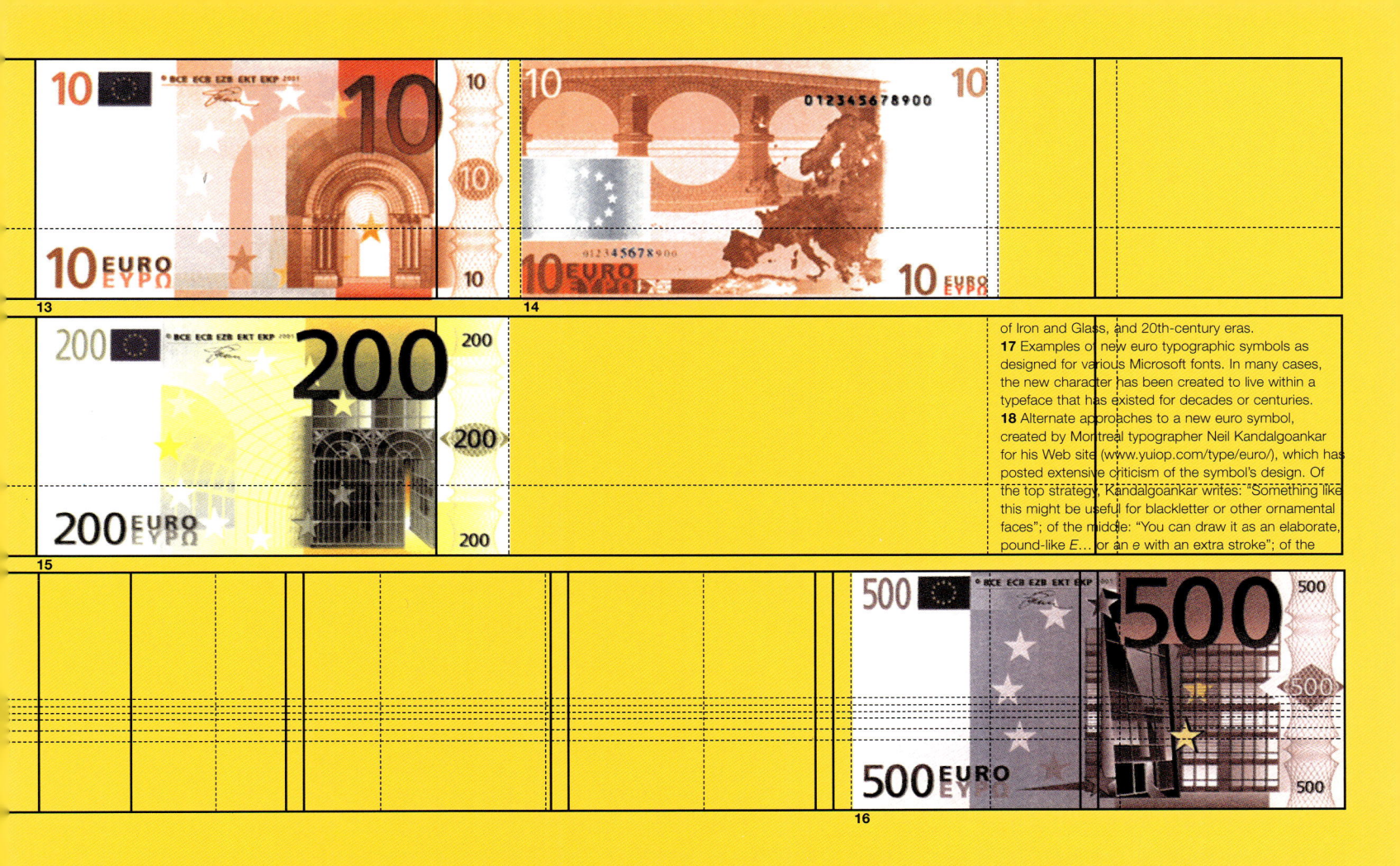

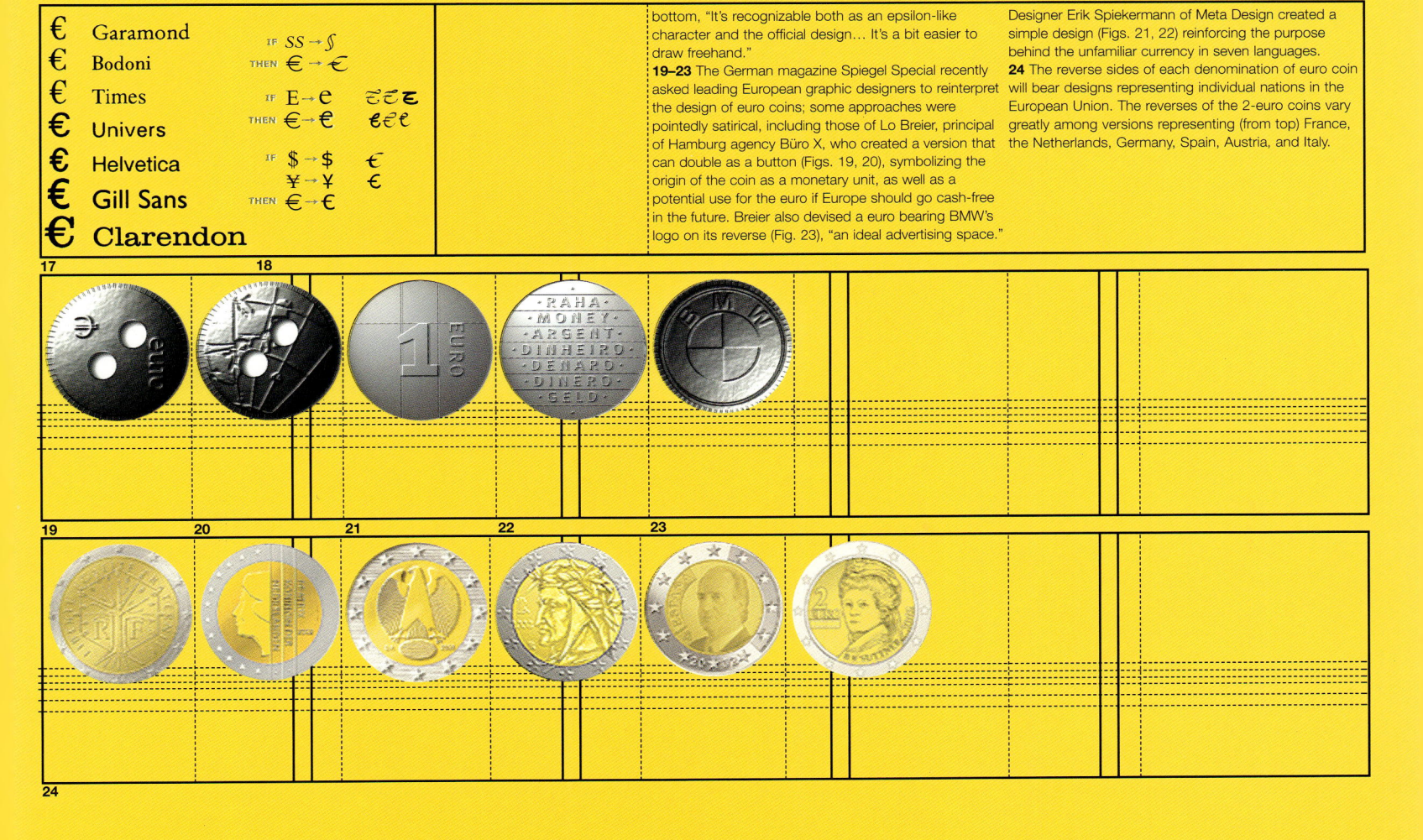

of Iron and Glass, and 20th-century eras.
17 Examples of new euro typographic symbols as designed for various Microsoft fonts. In many cases, the new character has been created to live within a typeface that has existed for decades or centuries.
18 Alternate approaches to a new euro symbol, created by Montreal typographer Neil Kandalgoankar for his Web site (www.yuiop.com/type/euro/), which has posted extensive criticism of the symbol's design. Of the top strategy, Kandalgoankar writes: "Something like this might be useful for blackletter or other ornamental faces"; of the middle: "You can draw it as an elaborate, pound-like *E*… or an *e* with an extra stroke"; of the bottom, "It's recognizable both as an epsilon-like character and the official design… It's a bit easier to draw freehand."
19–23 The German magazine Spiegel Special recently asked leading European graphic designers to reinterpret the design of euro coins; some approaches were pointedly satirical, including those of Lo Breier, principal of Hamburg agency Büro X, who created a version that can double as a button (Figs. 19, 20), symbolizing the origin of the coin as a monetary unit, as well as a potential use for the euro if Europe should go cash-free in the future. Breier also devised a euro bearing BMW's logo on its reverse (Fig. 23), "an ideal advertising space."
Designer Erik Spiekermann of Meta Design created a simple design (Figs. 21, 22) reinforcing the purpose behind the unfamiliar currency in seven languages.
24 The reverse sides of each denomination of euro coin will bear designs representing individual nations in the European Union. The reverses of the 2-euro coins vary greatly among versions representing (from top) France, the Netherlands, Germany, Spain, Austria, and Italy.

Distant Relations

By Clare Dowdy

If design firms in London want to expand into the U.S., they usually plump for New York City. U.K. identity stalwart Wolff Olins is the latest such group to choose that option, establishing an East Coast office around Thanksgiving 1997, and multi-award-winning advertising agency Bartle Bogle Hegarty ventured to the city two months earlier.

London firms who have set up in San Francisco, on the other hand, tend to treat that city as their second U.S. port of call. Pentagram did not open there until 1986, eight years after it planted itself in New York. The Attik set up in New York at the beginning of 1997 before adding an office in San Francisco later in the year to target the film industry.

For British consultancies, the advantages of a New York base are self-evident. A number of big European client companies operate there, and it is home to many major U.S. clients—Wolff Olins works for Mobil and General Motors, for example. And the time difference and distance from London is manageable. But what does San Francisco have to offer?

London-based brand-packaging specialist Turner Duckworth certainly broke with convention when it leapfrogged New York and set up a second studio in San Francisco six years ago. The company could offer a string of strategic reasons for its actions, but such rationale is in marked contrast to the romantic reality behind the situation. "I was chasing a girl," admits U.K.-born David Turner, who runs the San Francisco office, explaining that the fact that he ended up in San Francisco is accidental. (Had he been chasing, let's say, a Polish girl, it could have been Warsaw.)

Given the haphazard nature of its beginnings, the arrangement has proved highly productive. Both offices are littered with design awards and citations, and the firm has built a reputation as small and professional but innovative.

The partnership was formed when Turner skipped the country, on the understanding that if things didn't work out he would return to the London office. Six years on—Turner caught the girl—Turner Duckworth is thriving. The West London office is housed in the Chiswick area—rather than design consultancy-drenched Soho—in an old printer's building named after turn-of-the-century British architect

Rather than providing obstacles, the 5300 miles separating Turner Duckworth's design offices in London and San Francisco have been a boon.

1 San Francisco staff (from left): David Turner, Allen Raulet, Anthony Biles, Jonathan Warner, Joanne Chan, Elise Thompson, John Givens, Jeanette Hodge.
2 London staff (back row, from left): Jon Sleeman, Cath Lloyd, Sarah Moffat, Justine Penruddocke, Mark Waters; (front row): Jules Crosthwaite, Janice Davison, Bob Celiz, Bruce Duckworth.

Charles Voysey. The San Francisco office, twice the size, has the more glamorous location of South Beach, a scenic drive from Turner's home in Marin County and over the Golden Gate Bridge. Known also as Multimedia Gulch, South Beach has attracted a plethora of new-media and design groups.

Turner and London-based partner Bruce Duckworth have honed an unusual creative method. Rather than being allowed to hinder the design process, the long-distance arrangement is treated as the company's USP. Exploited to its full advantage, the setup allows the two teams (nine in London, eight in San Francisco) to operate as one studio.

While 5300 miles and an eight-hour time difference create practical problems, the partners try to minimize the inconvenience with daily phone conversations and copious use of ISDN and fax machines. "We have very understanding wives," concedes Duckworth, who frequently finds himself on the phone to Turner at 11 P.M. Greenwich Mean Time.

However, the success of the partnership cannot be explained away by time-management skills and tolerant families. A stable business strategy, a respect for cultural differences, a mutual passion for design, and similar life stages are key factors, too. Turner attributes much of the firm's success to the latter: Both partners, now in their mid-30s, married at about the same time, with first children appearing within a couple months of each other and second children imminent.

"Inadvertently, we have mirror lives," says Turner, demonstrating his mastery of West Coast vernacular. "We go through the same things and feel the same pressures. It would be much more difficult if Bruce was single, but we have the same life forces, so it's easier to make decisions."

This contributes to their shared approach to running the business. "Each of us is responsible for his office as a profit-making centre, and we are equal partners," says Duckworth. Turner elaborates: "We felt strongly that it had to be split down the middle to keep both partners involved in each other's business."

While there is no lead arm, the design process is generally managed by the office that picks up the pitch or project, with the other in a collaborating role. A brief is faxed to the distant office, which will work up perhaps one design, with the local group creating two or three concepts. "We believe a good design is going to work from a scribble," says Turner. These initial ideas will all be sent back and forth for comment or input. It is at this point that the time difference helps, allowing in effect a 24-hour studio operation.

Both partners believe this process of long-distance

assessment pushes up the quality of their work. "For most designers, the time they hold their breath and hope is when they show work to the client. For me, it's showing it to Bruce," says Turner. "It's good to have someone detached from the little problems to have an influence."

And offer encouragement, which "fills you with confidence," says Duckworth. It was Turner's egging on that pushed the London team to be more daring than it might have been with tights packaging for U.K. retailer Superdrug. The private-label Dare range, which went on-shelf last fall, features a grid image to give a voyeuristic feel to the packaging.

The partners stress that their long-distance relationship has to be worked at. As well as speaking every day, they meet up as often as possible. For client Nike they met halfway, in New York, last year. (They were both "knackered," jokes Turner.)

However, they understand that while they know each other very well, their respective staffs do not. "We are trying to make staff in each office recognize each other better," to improve collaboration, says Duckworth. There was a month-long design director exchange two years ago, but the cost of a two-office meeting would be high. Video conferencing is being explored as an alternative.

The advantage of the long-distance relationship is that phone conversations are mostly focused on design rather than on the humdrum day-to-day business and petty grievances that owner-managers can sometimes be caught up in. And in some respects the distance aids Turner Duckworth's understanding of cultural issues. Duckworth feels he is pretty much in tune with the U.S. market, and the consultancy expects to benefit as Turner's vantage point becomes ever more detached from the U.K. "The two points of view are what give us a leading edge," Turner explains. But they are wary of kowtowing to cultural stereotypes. "The stereotypes are pretty much all wrong," says Turner, with Duckworth adding that the U.S. is not just a "bigger and brasher" Britain.

Duckworth warns of "the added danger of falling into the cliché of being derogatory about each other's culture." And while there is a huge Middle American market, the niche markets can be as big as a single European territory. Duckworth cites the company's work for Levi's Re-threads—a niche U.S. brand of jeans made of recycled material.

The exploitation of this multicultural understanding can be seen in projects such as the packaging for Howling Monkey beer, which appeared last fall. Designed for U.S. client Steel Brewing Company, it is steeped in references to English Victoriana. And when Coca-Cola Schweppes Beverages decided to launch Oasis as an adult soft drink in the U.K., the London team could draw on Turner's knowledge of U.S. brands Fruitopia and Snapple. "We knew what the market looked like and how it behaved," says Duckworth.

Conversely, the London office had seen the U.K.'s "alcopop" sector take off and mature rapidly. The sweet, alcoholic fizzy drink pioneer brands were Two Dogs and Hooper's Hooch in 1995, followed by a raft of similar brands. Alcopops makers were accused of targeting underage drinkers, and a code of practice for brand naming and packaging design was drawn up. Duckworth and his team were able to provide useful knowledge on the pitfalls of branding this controversial sector for San Francisco's Sun Devil product for McKenzie River Brewing.

Despite the cultural differences, clients are not dissimilar. "The big corporation is an international animal now," explains Turner. "The forces that influence the commissioning of design are pretty much the same wherever you are—budgets, timing, and bosses to please."

However, Duckworth has noticed a more go-for-it attitude in California's vibrant business climate. Turner agrees: "It has a reputation for being a hotbed of innovation."

Like any small company anywhere, as the business grows, the founders have to reassess the management structure. And as creative directors, they would both rather be designing than managing. "We would never lose creative control," says Duckworth. "No, because every piece of work literally has our names on it," Turner adds.

As we bring a conference call between the West Coast and West London to an end, the partners can't resist talking business and start discussing concepts for a current job. Turner hangs up to take his very pregnant wife for her last hospital checkup.

The next day, Duckworth calls me with the news that Turner's wife has had a baby girl. Another creative solution to a demanding brief—and delivered well before the deadline.

Distant

3 Packaging for Superdrug Vitamins
Art directors David Turner, Bruce Duckworth
Designer Bruce Duckworth
Illustrator Justin Davison.

4 Packaging for Oasis energy drinks.
Art directors David Turner, Bruce Duckworth
Designer Bruce Duckworth
Illustrator Anton Morris
Client Schweppes UK.

5 Howling Monkey Black and Tan Beer packaging.
Art directors David Turner, Bruce Duckworth
Designer David Turner
Illustrator Thomas Hennessy
Client Steel Brewing Co.

6 Steel Reserve lager packaging.
Art directors David Turner, Bruce Duckworth
Designer David Turner
Client Steel Brewing Co.

7, 12, 13 Steel Reserve Web site.
Art directors David Turner, Bruce Duckworth
Designer Corwin Stone
Site execution Thunk Design, San Francisco
Photographer Michael Lamotte
Illustration (Fig. 16) Thomas Hennessy
Client Steel Brewing Co.

8 Levi's Re-threads labels.
Art directors David Turner, Bruce Duckworth
Designers David Turner, Bruce Duckworth, Janice Davison
Photographer Lloyd Hryciw
Client Levi-Strauss.

9–11 Dare tights packaging.
Art directors David Turner, Bruce Duckworth
Designer Bruce Duckworth
Photographer Tim Platt
Client Superdrug.

Relations

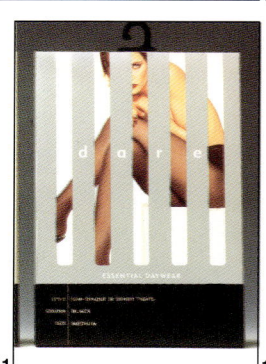

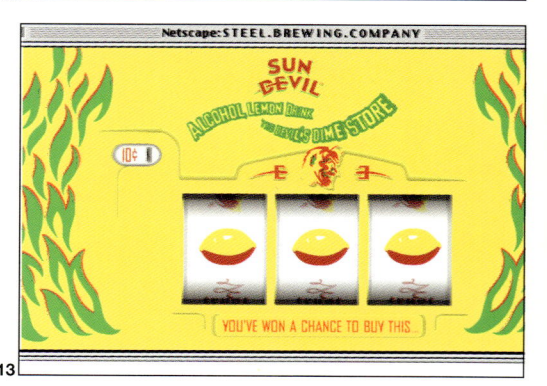

Clare Dowdy is news editor of the London-based publication Design Week.

NEW EUROPE - NEW CREATIVITY

New Moment Magazine For Art & Advertising East & Central Europe

New Moment - magazine for new advertising man - philosophy, art, advertising, culture, society, life,...
New Moment Nº 9/10 - PEEP SHOW - 200 color pages
Founder & Publisher Dragan Sakan New Moment
sakan@EUnet.yu   http://www.sd-newmoment.si
Sponsored by SAATCHI & SAATCHI
Subscription for New Moment › Bezigrad 10, 61000 Ljubljana, Slovenia tel. +386611336126 fax. +386611336002
New Moment Nº 9/10 PEEP SHOW..................16U$D

Type design in Russia is a precarious business. Commercial graphic design has proliferated since the end of the Soviet era, with designers creating new typefaces for every purpose, overwhelming the pages of slick new magazines with a wealth of Cyrillic letterforms. But within this creative anarchy there is virtually no copyright law, no protection against piracy—and therefore no market for selling commercial fonts.

Moscow graphic designer Yuri Gordon has made a dramatic splash in this chaotic field over the last few years, creating typefaces and designs that wed the cutting edge of Western typography with the power and energy of Russian graphics. Far from being a Young Turk, however, Gordon recently turned 40 and collaborates with his own son, Illarion, on designing type at his foundry, Letterhead. Both produce work that is fresh, works well in both Cyrillic and Latin alphabets, and shows a well-honed Russian sense of irony, sarcasm, and oblique reference.

Two of Yuri Gordon's typefaces, Dve Kruglyh Cyrillic and FaRer Cyrillic, won awards last year from the Type Directors Club in New York, in its first type-design competition, TDC². And in Moscow in September, the alternative-design festival Grafit gave awards to Gordon's Letterhead colleague Valery Golyzhenkov for his typography and to Gordon for his typeface Respublicana, which he conceived as a "reply" to the Emigre face Democratica.

"Before this year, not only did we not sell our fonts, we didn't even think of doing so," says Gordon. "We used to prepare typefaces for ourselves and for some of our friends. Several almost simultaneous events made us change our intentions. First, some of our typefaces, mine and my son Illarion's, were licensed by ParaGraph, the only genuine professional type manufacturer in Russia. Second, the results of the TDC typeface competition made us take a second hard look at our work as something that may be of interest to society. And besides, my Letterhead colleague Valery Golyzhenkov came up with an extremely provocative conceptual project, an enterprise to generate graphical trash [the Garbage Type Foundry].

"As a result, we now have around 40 fonts. We came up with the typeface library as a major theme of our display at the Dizayn i Reklama [Design and Advertising] exhibition in Moscow. That allowed us to finally assert ourselves in the Moscow design community as manufacturers of nonstandard designs."

Gordon's background is in book publishing, as both an illustrator and a book designer. In 1990, he and his wife, Olga Vasilkova, won an award at the National Book Design Competition for their collaboration on a textbook, The Secrets of Orthography. In more recent years, with the advent of true commercial activity, Gordon has done a lot of trademarks and logos, and he won another prize in the burgeoning field of business-card design, at the recent exhibition "Best Business Cards of Russia." He has been working in magazine design since 1992, and currently art-directs the Russian editions of the magazines Sesame Street and Sesame Street Parents.

The vogue in Moscow today is for English words, names, and phrases to pop up everywhere. (Even the name of the primary Russian digital type foundry, ParaType, is a non-Russian, English-based word.) For that reason, as well as for the needs of an increasingly global type business, most Russian type designers create both Latin and Cyrillic character sets in the same font. This practice makes the fonts saleable to Western

russian eclectic

PROBBARIUS REGULAR

ABCDEFGHIJKLMNOPQRSTUVWXYZ
abcdefghijklmnopqrstuvwxyz
1234567890

PROBBARIUS

АБВГДЕЁЖЗИЙКЛМНОПРСТУФХЦЧ
ШЩЪЫЬЭЮЯ
абвгдеёжзийклмнопрстуфхцчш
щъыьэюя

graphic designers who want Latin letters, and it makes it easy to mix languages for pragmatic or stylistic reasons.

The mixing of languages and writing systems grows out of a general sense of the jumble of influences, images, styles, and conflicting messages that make up the cultural surroundings of urban Russians in the 1990s. Gordon and his colleagues have applied this eclecticism to the design of individual fonts. His first complete typeface, FaRer, designed in 1993–94, started life as a logo for the "official" advertising agency Soyuzreklama. "FaRer is dedicated to Vladimir Favorsky and Ivan Rerberg—the two most prominent Russian typeface designers," says Gordon. "Since FaRer was in part a commission, and the client, Soyuzreklama, looked to me like a most obvious representative of Soviet officialdom, some traits of Soviet eclecticism started creeping into the type's esthetics. I consider the style of the Moscow Metro the most typical example of that style, which incorporates everything from Constructivism to Stalinist Baroque to the most modern post-Brezhnev esthetics of the restrooms. Thus, a second dedication was born: to the Moscow Metro."

Typography and printing under the Soviet regime were closely regulated, and an enforced standard of mediocrity gave Russian printed matter the tatty gray quality that now seems quaintly appealing to some Westerners. Very few typefaces were available, in very few sizes, and access to printing facilities was closed. With the post-Soviet freedom came a revived interest in all the styles of typography that do not speak of life in the Soviet Union: hip Western postmodern type, pre-Revolutionary Art Nouveau, the rationalist revision of the alphabet under Peter the Great in the 17th century, even the deep roots of Cyrillic orthography in medieval scripts and the earliest printing, which have been preserved largely in ecclesiastical documents.

Maxim Zhukov, typographic adviser to the United Nations and a friend of Gordon's, laments that despite the creativity in display type in his native Russia today, "the typographic underpinnings simply aren't there." The basics of setting text in a readable fashion are barely taught, and even fewer book publishers in Russia than in the U.S. pay attention to how well the type is set in the books they publish. For advertising and job work, however, the choices are tremendous.

A large number of typefaces are being adapted from the Latin alphabet into the Cyrillic, for use in Russian and the other languages that use Cyrillic letters. ParaType, for instance, has a standing arrangement with International Typeface Corp. to extend some of ITC's typefaces into Cyrillic versions. ParaType began as part of ParaGraph, the Russian software company that also developed the handwriting-recognition software for the Apple Newton. But when Silicon Graphics bought ParaGraph in 1997, the orphaned type-design group formed its own company, ParaType, to carry on its unique role in the business of Russian typographic design. Other type companies have come and gone, but ParaType seems to remain the standard by which all other Russian typographic businesses measure themselves. And ParaType is the source for buying the Letterhead typefaces (www.paratype.com).

Gordon's own first attempt at creating a Cyrillic version of a Western type was illegal, an unlicensed version of Copperplate Gothic. "I have only one excuse," he says. "I did the

FARER NORMAL

ABCDEFGHIJKLMNOPQRSTUVWXYZ
abcdefghijklmnopqrstuvwxyz
1234567890

DVE KRUGLYH (LATIN)

ABCDEFGHIJKLMNOPQRSTUVWXYZ
abcdefghijklmnopqrstuvwxyz
1234567890

DVE KRUGLYH (CYRILLIC)

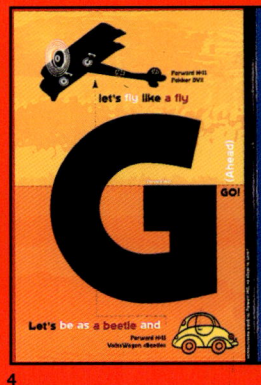

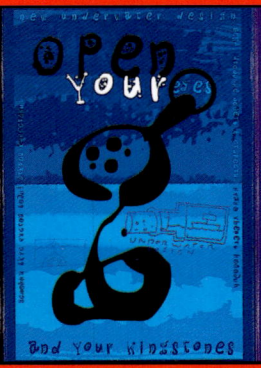

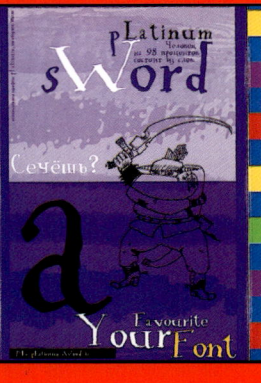

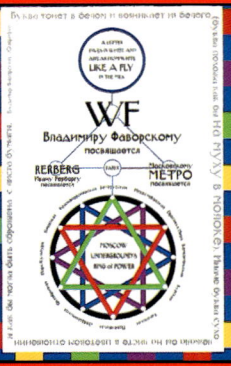

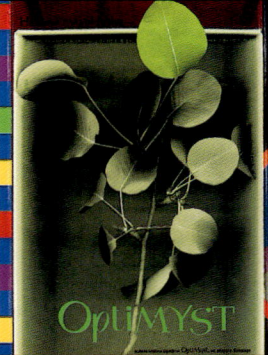

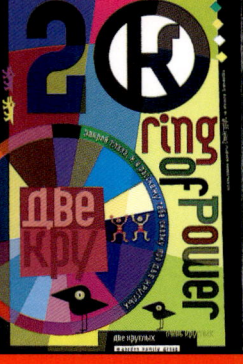

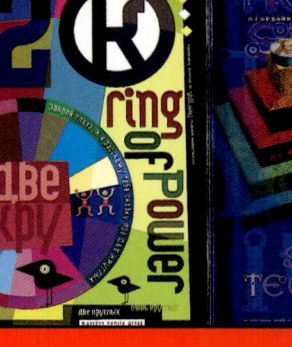

АБВГДЕЁЖЗИЙКЛМНОПРСТУ ФХЦЧШЩЪЫЬЭЮЯ

translation exclusively for non-commercial use. Interesting that I did my layout of the special composition, called Damascus Steel, well before seeing Matthew Carter's typeface Sophia, or similar typefaces by Emigre."

Gordon's more recent type designs would look right at home in the catalogues of Emigre or FontShop International. Dve Kruglyh was given the name of a typographic measurement in hot-metal composition ("Two Em"). "I chose the name for its political resonance, not for the direct meaning," he says. "It started as an experiment in the shapes of glyphs, and later I liked it for its awkwardness and arrhythmia, which is most pronounced in Russian texts. Dve Kruglyh reminds me of the abstract sculpture made by pieces of plumbing."

Bistro and Hot Sauce both show a painterly freedom that is highly readable but barely looks like type. Some of Letterhead's "garbage" fonts are inspired by the typefaces of Neville Brody and other Western designers. And Gordon's OptiMYST, which shares some traits with FaRer, is described by Gordon as a jazz composition. "Its subject is the Roaring '50s. There is no definite baseline to this: All the glyphs are different sizes, all the stroke weights are different, and the typeface's esthetics address those heady times before the sexual and student revolutions, before the hippies and the Beatles. Its second subject is a parody of Optima, to which in my youth I had quite an attachment, like a passion for the boss's secretary."

Vladimir Yefimov a principal at ParaType, says of Gordon's type designs, "Yuri Gordon's fonts are so funny. They are light, they are flying and smiling. That's why they are so popular now among our modern graphic designers and other young people. They may be the fonts of our next generation, the generation that does not feel the ideological suppression of Soviet times, that senses the

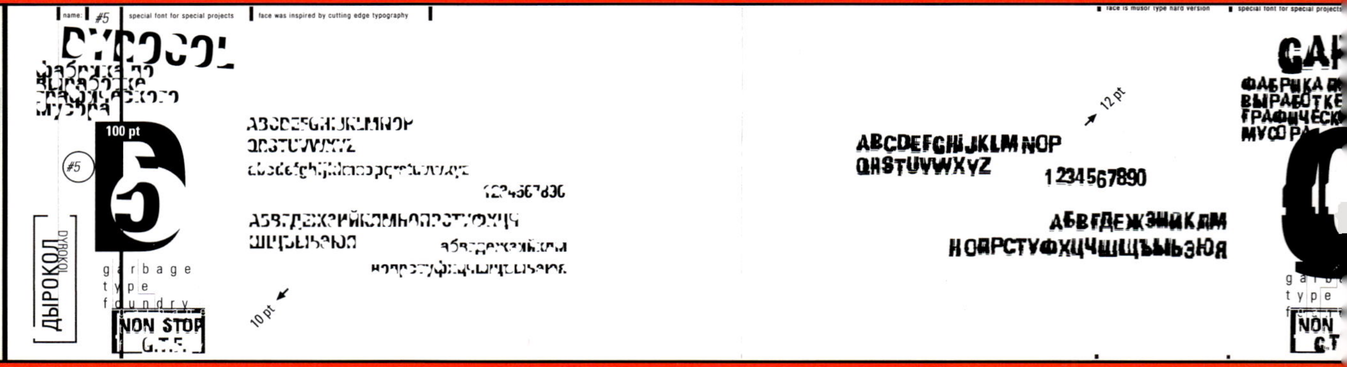

DVE KRUGLYH (CYRILLIC)

абвгдеёжзийклмнопрстуфхц
чшщъыьэюя

freedom to know the whole world, without the Iron Curtain and other barriers. Yuri Gordon's fonts express that feeling of the freedom to play with varied letterforms. Thus they are very original.

"Nevertheless, the fonts are not lightweight," Yefimov continues. "I can't judge how Western people perceive such typeface games, but to me, Yuri Gordon's fonts are full of type associations and connotations, based on a good knowledge of art and of the history of type design. The connotations may be very humorous or quite ironic, but they're by no means dull. Maybe his fonts will partially destroy the impression that Russians are always gloomy and never smile."

The Russian economic crisis of last summer threw the type business, like every other aspect of commerce in Russia, into uncertainty and turmoil. "Everything that could break, broke," says Gordon, "starting with the ruble and ending with the presidential republic." Despite this chaos and its attendant worries, design work continues to be commissioned, he says. Letterhead created more than 10 new fonts last spring and summer, and interest in type design is rising. And Gordon sees some hope in the overall situation because "the newspapers are boring again"—a sure sign of stabilization, in Russian terms.

Looking ahead, Gordon sees Russian type designers becoming "designers for designers," who will do two very different sorts of work: "seasonal typefaces," display faces intended for a season or a moment, and typefaces that "don't address fashion," pure experiments. "Unfortunately," he adds, "in Moscow I know no one who would design a new original text typeface, one that is not an extension of a Western design. You probably shouldn't expect to see a new Carter emerging from Russia—but a new Carson is very likely."

John D. Berry is a typographer, book designer, and editor and publisher of U&lc and U&lc Online.

1, 2 Promotional cards for Letterhead fonts: FaRer (Fig. 2) and Arrow Header (Fig. 1).

3, 4 Accordion-fold brochure for Letterhead fonts (Fig. 4, front; Fig. 3, back).

5 Page from a limited-edition chapbook, in portfolio style, of a Russian translation of Blaise Cendrar's Prose du Transibérien et de le Petite Jeanne de France, published by Leonid Tishkov/Dablus and printed at the Moscow-American Silk Screen Print House, 1994.

6, 7 Spreads from a promotional booklet for "Garbage" fonts: Dyrokol and Garbage (Fig. 5), and Pseudotype and Grammatika (Fig. 6). Designer: Valery Golyzhenkov.

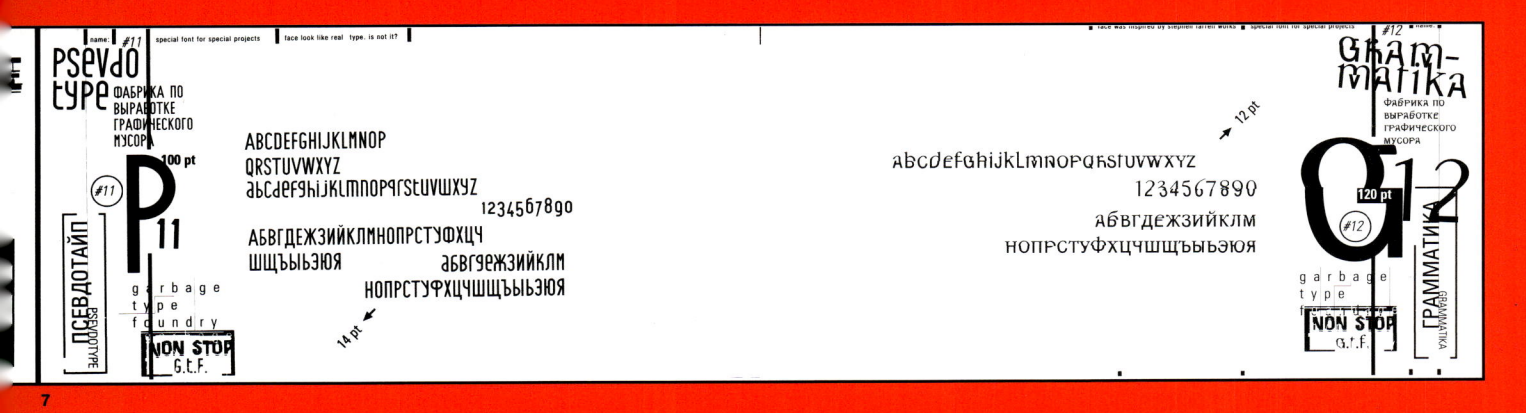

"No great man lives in vain," wrote the 19th-century steel manufacturer and philanthropist Andrew Carnegie. "The history of the world is but the biography of great men." This view of history, of a narrative peopled by kings and queens, wars and treaties, dates and events, informed the teaching and general understanding of that subject until comparatively recently. The proletariat was lumpen, the huddled only recognized in their masses. Historical source material was to be found at battlegrounds, in Papal proclamations, in temples and palaces, and in the doings and sayings of those great men. The backdrop to this rattling read was the rest of the world, which only figured in history when it had organized into a movement or fallen prey in great numbers to war, sickness, or religious dissent.

More recently, however, a new breed of historian has begun to construct a new history, a more personal history that goes beyond the "drums and trumpets" to look into the daily lives of the not so great—those who just got on with their business, producing and consuming in their inconsequential way. And the historians have had to come out of the libraries, out of the government records, and out of ivory towers to find information on these lives. This new history is to be found in what the endeavours of ordinary people left behind: not in parliaments, or in cathedrals, but in nondocumentary forms of evidence—stamps, coins, bills, advertising, packaging, comics, cigarette cards—virtually anything that illustrated the life and mores of a section of society.

Historians' interest in the "ordinary," which has been growing since World War II, is not entirely new. A tension between what might be called the "aristocratic" and the "democratic" approach to history exists in the writings of the two earliest historians in the 5th century b.c. Thucydides is all about great men and battles and politics, while Herodotus is far more interested in the customs, social habits, and religious beliefs of the Greeks and their neighbours.

Since that time, however, it has predominantly been the "aristocratic" version of events that has held sway. But it was the social and political changes of the 1960s, and the heavy impression they made on academia, that gave currency to what English historian G.M. Trevelyan said "might be negatively defined as history with the politics left out." A generation of historians was given the freedom and academic legitimacy to explore a new past through the social and cultural changes that swept the world in the postwar years. Growing interest in the U.S. about the history of Africa and Asia, of slaves, women, homosexuals, the "poor"—marginal groups "hidden from history"—was complemented on the other side of the Atlantic by the expansion of the university system in Europe, the rise of the New Left in the 1960s, the interest by historians in disciplines like sociology and anthropology, and the collation of archives by trade unions, craft associations, workingmen's clubs, and the like. Many scholars who did pursue the new history have risen to become the preeminent historians of today, including E.P. Thompson, Eric Hobsbawn, and Asa Briggs, former provost of Worcester College, Oxford.

It was Lord Briggs's interest in social history that led the Centre for Ephemera Studies to invite him to be its patron. The Centre is, in a sense, the physical manifestation of the Foundation for Ephemera Studies, a body set up by photographer/graphic designer/author Maurice Rickards. Ephemera, as defined by Rickards, who died last year, are "the minor transient documents of everyday life." Rickards did not collect for profit; in fact, he was annoyed to discover that some elements of his

far from ephemeral

By Chris Foges

collection were valuable. But beyond collecting for fun, he had a serious purpose: to raise the study and presentation of handwritten and printed graphic ephemera to the level of an academic discipline.

Rickards was a committed pacifist, so many of his political beliefs chimed with those on the left who were seeking a new perspective on history. But Rickards's initial interest in graphic design was essentially professional rather than intellectual. His design career began when he was still at school, where he produced a poster for a local grocer, and he went on to create items for organizations such as Christian Aid, The Missionary Society, the YMCA, and the Save the Children Fund.

Simultaneously, he was collecting and archiving examples of printed ephemera, a practice he put on a semiformal footing in 1975 by founding, with other enthusiasts, the Ephemera Society. Its first president was poet laureate John Betjeman. The Society was devoted to the conservation, study, and presentation of handwritten ephemera. "We aim to bring the subject above the level of trivia," said Rickards. "The collecting of ephemera is the use of apparent garbage to be educational. It is the other side of history from what sits on the library shelves." To that end, the Society publishes a journal, The Ephemerist, and Rickards himself wrote several books, notably Banned Posters, The Public Notice: An Illustrated History, and Collecting Printed Ephemera. It was with the establishment in 1993 of the Centre for Ephemera Studies, part of the Department of Typography & Graphic Communication at the University of Reading, however, that Rickards made his most significant contribution to the elevation of ephemera to the status of a subject suitable for academic study.

The University, situated just outside London, is one of the few places in England where students can focus on the study of typography in all its aspects: practice, theory, and history. The course leader, until his retirement last summer, was Michael Twyman, himself a distinguished typographer, historian, and now custodian of the Rickards collection. The collection is housed in a single-story prefabricated building, where the clanking and whirring of old and new printing machinery and the smell of ink fills the air. Like Rickards, Twyman's interest in the robust qualities of vernacular design led him to discover the value of ephemera as a historical resource. "I realized that printing told one an enormous amount about societies of the past," Twyman says. "The ordinary things that people throw away told you about things that you wouldn't find in libraries—that you wouldn't find in books."

Twyman's association with Rickards began in the early 1970s, but it was not until the Centre for Ephemera Studies was formed in 1993, and Rickards's collection was moved to the Centre on semipermanent loan, that the pair began to collaborate on what might be described as a vision for the study of ephemera. The cataloging of Rickards's collection, which contains over 20,000 items, was the immediate task of the new Centre. It was from this that its role as a resource for the historical study of what is now called graphic design began to take shape. "The first thing to do was devise a way of cataloging ephemera, something that there is no standard for doing," says Twyman. "We did spend quite a lot of time working it out and agreed that there were two different approaches. First of all, by the subject that the item of ephemera in some way represented—for example, railways, or dancing. And then there was another route, by artifactual description—whether it was a ticket, or a poster, or a menu, or a programme. We felt it was important to document both of those strands. So a dance programme would be

A centre for the study of graphic ephemera is moving the research of everyday printed artifacts toward academic respectability.

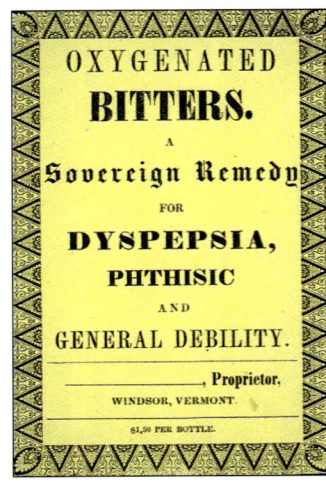

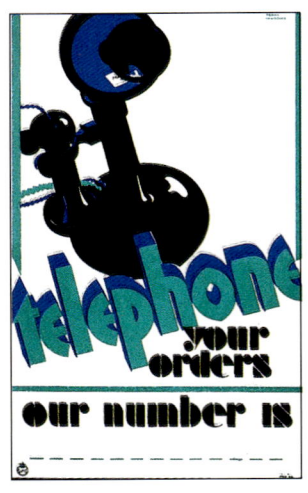

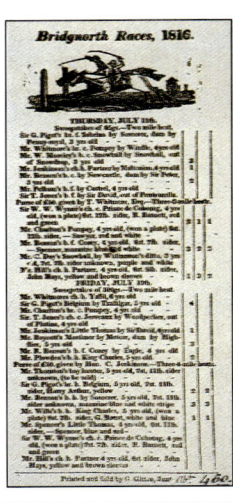

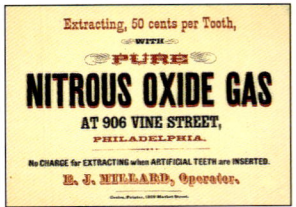

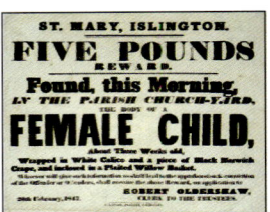

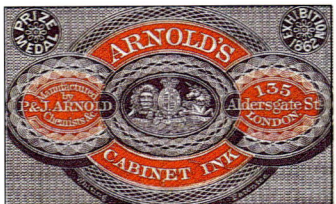

On this spread: selected items from the Rickards Collection, archived and maintained by the Centre for Ephemera Studies, University of Reading, England. Most of the items in the collection were produced by "jobbing printers" or anonymous designers, and Maurice Rickards made no distinction between items produced by designers and those that were not.

Chris Foges is a London-based journalist and the author of two books, on letterhead design and magazine design, published by RotoVision.

catalogued in terms of when the dance was, where it was, what sort of dance it was, and also that the programme was four-page, single-fold, with a pencil and tassel attached."

The Rickards collection is significant in that it is what Twyman refers to as an "exemplary" collection, i.e., it does not contain every theatre programme or wine label ever produced, but rather contains carefully selected items to exemplify types of ephemera. "Maurice Rickards, in building up his collection, had an intellectual framework to it that collections built according to what you are given don't have," explains Twyman. "There's no single approach to collecting, displaying, and recording." Rickards's collection is unique in that it is about the range and breadth of printed material in general, rather than a particular subject matter or period. "He was quite remarkably self-disciplined," observes Twyman. "If someone offered him 5000 orange labels, he might have said, 'Thank you very much, I'll have three.'" Rickards wanted to keep the collection manageable and make it almost a teaching tool. If someone is passionate about orange labels, he might find in the Centre's register of ephemera collections a listing for a collection of 500,000 orange labels. But if he wants to see what type of information is generally recorded by orange labels, he can do that from this collection.

It is as an "index" of ephemera that the Rickards collection and the Centre for Ephemera Studies are most important. The professed intention of the Centre is to act as a nucleus or hub, a global starting point for historical research into ephemera. "We have a grant from a foundation—The Pilgrim Trust—to begin to compile a register of ephemera collections in Great Britain," explains Twyman. "This project has been going on for two years, and we've sent a questionnaire around to about 1000 museums and institutions. We've had about 500 replies, and are well on the way to compiling a register which will be published electronically and on paper." From there, the hope is to create a global register, so that whether the interest is in 18th-century German almanacs or 1950s American baseball cards, the Centre will have a listing for an archive containing them.

"The aim of the Centre is to look outwards to Great Britain and indeed the world," says Twyman. "We have good connections with the American Ephemera Society and similar societies in other countries. But broadly speaking, such societies consist of dealers and collectors who tend to be single-minded. There are people who collect only beer labels, say, and aren't interested in anything else. So you can see why the Centre has a real role: It can demonstrate how those specialties—and there are thousands of them—can make sense in a social context."

Although connected to a university, the Centre relies on grants and private donations to continue its work, and is staffed by volunteers. As Twyman observes, it stands in danger of becoming a victim of its own success, as the more it is seen as a resource, the more people will use it, "and everyone thinks information should be free these days."

Funding notwithstanding, the Centre has several projects currently under way that promote the collection and study of printed materials. An Encyclopedia of Ephemera, which Rickards was writing before his death, is being completed and prepared for publication. Further contacts are being made and strengthened with societies and institutions around the world. Seminars and exhibitions are being organized. While the Rickards collection continues to grow and major gaps in it are filled, Twyman also hopes that the Centre will eventually provide supervision for students wishing to undertake research into aspects of ephemera and the history of graphic design or printed communication, as well as become a resource for other historians.

Collectors and enthusiasts have wallowed since time immemorial in the deep sense of nostalgia that antiquities can evoke, and figures such as Benetton advertising supremo Oliviero Toscani have spoken of the responsibility of today's image-makers in recording our times for the people of tomorrow. But this new initiative, which for the first time sets out to make the history of graphic communication of wider interest and significance than to historians of the subject itself, gives the study of information encoded in the graphic communications of an era not only increased academic legitimacy but also a focus and a standard.

Lineagrafica is a historical Italian graphic design magazine. Since fifty years the periodical has observed, with a critical eye, the development of the sector of graphic design. In recent years Lineagrafica has followed the digital revolution: an international observation of the new instruments of planning and design of new supports and new media, of the debate on the profession and its new languages.

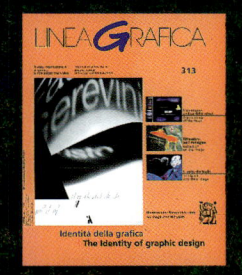

Lineagrafica
towards new graphic design

subscription application

Please send me a year's subscription (6 issues) to LINEA**G**RAFICA at the price of $135, starting with issue .... for foreign countries.

Name and Surname .... Address ....

Town .... Postcode .... Country ....

Profession .... Telephone ....

☐ Cheque to Progetto Editrice Srl - corso Garibaldi, 64 - 20121 Milano - Italy

☐ Mastercard ☐ Eurocard ☐ American Express ☐ Visa

n° |_|_|_|_|_|_|_|_|_|_|_|_|_|_|_|_| Expiry date |_|_|_|_|_|

Credit card holder ....

Date .... Signature ....

klein aber fein

By Christian Küsters

Despite its glowing reputation for impeccable design, Germany's Baumann & Baumann has been criticized for its ideological rigidity.

The Baumann & Baumann Büro für Gestaltung is a pillar of the German design establishment. An impressive client list, a prestigious reputation among its peers, and many awards—both national and international—have given the name Baumann & Baumann weight in those circles that value creative excellence.

But the company and its founders, the husband-and-wife team of Gerd and Barbara Baumann, have not enjoyed an entirely blissful time in the limelight. Their signature use of the Rotis typeface has stirred intense debate in a German design industry pulled between the dual impulses of creative expression and ordered clarity. For some critics and designers, the studio's commitment to Rotis smacks of anachronistic rigidity. The typeface controversy has also led some observers to go further and question whether the Baumanns' unmistakable visual style is too much about them as designers and not enough about the demands of the client and the project.

When I meet the designers in a hotel in Mayfair, London, they're easy to spot, standing in the lobby among business people with suitcases and a group of Scotsmen in kilts. Gerd looks like a distinguished elder statesman of German design. Barbara is dressed elegantly, in black leather trousers and a simple black jumper. Both are in their late 40s.

The Baumanns are on a trip to discuss an architectural project with Norman Foster's firm (the discussion subsequently turns into their first large-scale design project in the U.K.). In conversation, they complement each other extremely well. Their opinions hardly differ, and a sentence started by one is often concluded by the other. It's like talking with a single person.

Gerd and Barbara belong to the generation that shaped the identity of German design. They met during their studies at the Fachhochschule für Gestaltung (School for Design) in Schwäbisch Gmünd, a college staffed by professors from the bastion of archmodernist thinking, Ulm, and with a strong modernist tradition of its own. After graduation, they married and moved to Berlin, but they didn't feel comfortable there and swapped metropolitan for provincial life by moving back to Schwäbisch Gmünd. According to Gerd, Baumann & Baumann was the first design practice in town, and the Baumanns were the first married couple to set one up. They must have been excellent role models: Schwäbisch Gmünd has a population of only 60,000, but it now boasts the highest concentration of design studios in Europe. This is partly due to the design school, but mostly to the quality of life in this prosperous section of southern Germany.

An old soap factory converted by a former Bauhaus architecture student provides the spacious environment the Baumanns need for their complex projects. It is a large, square building covered by a flat pyramid roof; its two high-ceilinged floors house as many as 10 designers and interns. The steady influx of designers and high turnover of interns are regarded by the duo as positive factors in the studio's work that influence their design process. Gerd explains that "the diversity of attitudes in our studio forces Barbara and me to question our relationship to design and to our projects." The result, he says, is a conscious engagement with issues beyond design and a constant assessment of attitudes.

The firm's clients are predominantly large industrial companies (most notably DaimlerChrysler AG), augmented by German cultural institutions and a host of small clients. According to Gerd, his friend Otl Aicher, the late, legendary German designer, once said, "There aren't any big or small cakes, only good ones." The Baumanns are extremely particular in their choice of cakes: They once resisted an offer from Mitsubishi but agreed to work for DaimlerChrysler. "We are klein aber fein"—small but sophisticated, Gerd says, laughing.

Clients like DaimlerChrysler have built a platform for the company to forge a strong reputation—strong enough to withstand criticism, though the Rotis debate clearly roiled the German design scene. Created by Aicher, Rotis was first introduced to a mass audience when the Baumanns began using it. Criticism of its use focuses on the ideological nature of the font—or perhaps more accurately, on the controversial nature of Aicher himself. Once head of the Visual Communications Department at Ulm, he was renowned for highly systematized work for Lufthansa and the 1972 Olympic Games in Münich. Aicher believed that all individual elements in a work of design should be subservient to the overall corporate message, and his outspoken declarations along these strict lines were (and continue to be) seen by many as overly constraining and orthodox. Like Paul Renner's Futura, Rotis is a typeface whose design objective—clarity of message—constructively informs the shape of each individual letterform. Some observers argue that by using this particular font, designers knowingly or unknowingly associate themselves with Aicher's tenets. "Dogmatic" seems to be the key term here.

Gerd regards the Rotis criticisms as an affront to thinking designers. He disagrees with the criticisms but seems reluctant to engage in debate, insisting that the work—Aicher's and Baumann & Baumann's—speaks for itself. "For me, Rotis is the font of the '90s and the next millennium," he says.

It is surely misguided to dismiss the Baumanns' work due to its association with this font. Close inspection reveals great sensitivity to the German and European context in which the work is produced. No European country has been through more dramatic changes in this century than Germany, both esthetically (from Jugendstil to Postmodernism) and politically (from the Weimar Republic through two World Wars, the Cold War, and reunification). The Baumann approach is one articulation of this history. At its best it represents a conscious act of balance. Whether that balance forms an effective means of communication in today's world, however, is open to argument.

Before the Baumanns discuss their work in detail, our conversation gets snagged on terminology. Both of them react strongly to the English terms used in discussing design. They are opposed to the word designer, preferring Gestalter (literally, form-giver, but also implying a high degree of self-consciousness in designing). Asked to explain their design philosophy, they say they prefer "purpose" to "philosophy," as the former term is more suggestive of the designer's role in society. They define themselves as craftsmen rather than artists and condemn quick solutions, which they regard as superficial and without social responsibility. They see themselves in a broad cultural context as communicators, and believe their communication has a political component. Gestaltung (form-giving) gains an importance in society that design simply cannot achieve, Gerd contends: "Gestaltung begins with the actual contents."

Does the Baumanns' work succeed in ensuring and enhancing the effective communication of such "contents"?

The answer changes by example, and by discipline. Last year's most important project, and one of the best

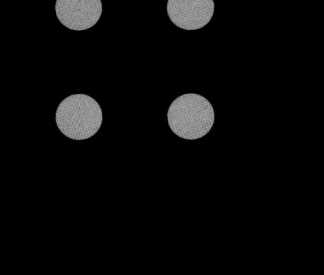

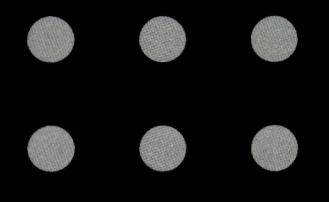

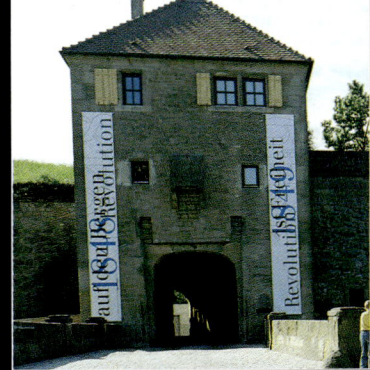

All work shown is credited to Baumann & Baumann Büro für Gestaltung.
1, 2 Gerd and Barbara Baumann, founders of Baumann & Baumann Büro für Gestaltung.
3-4 House of History, Stuttgart. Exhibition in the castle Hohenasperg commemorating the 150th anniversary of the Revolution of 1848–49.

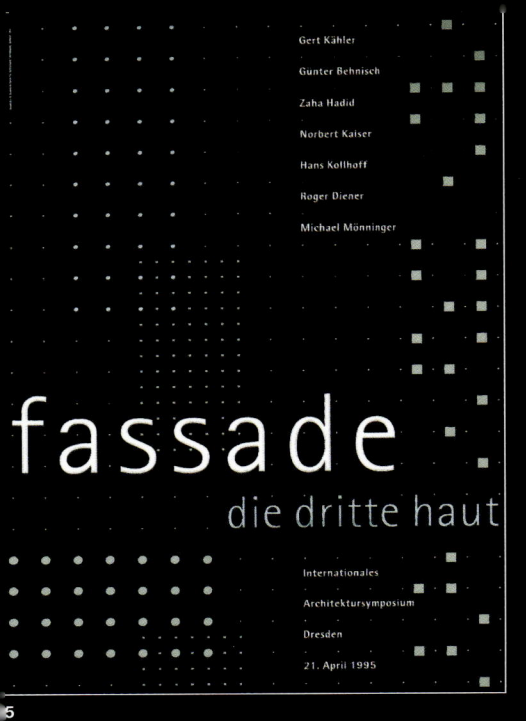

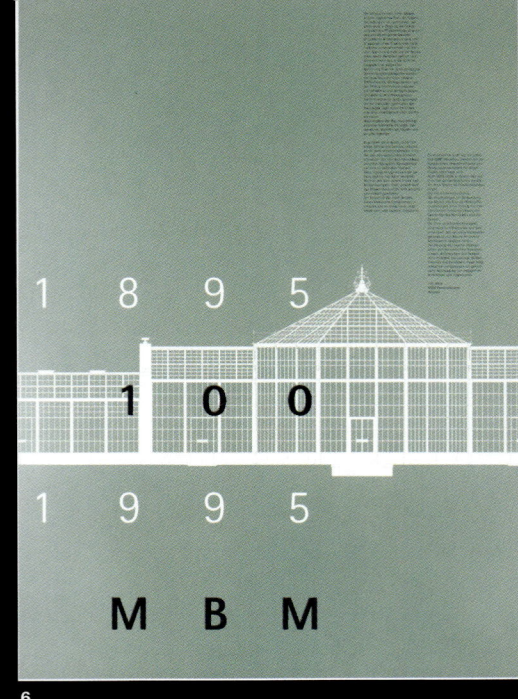

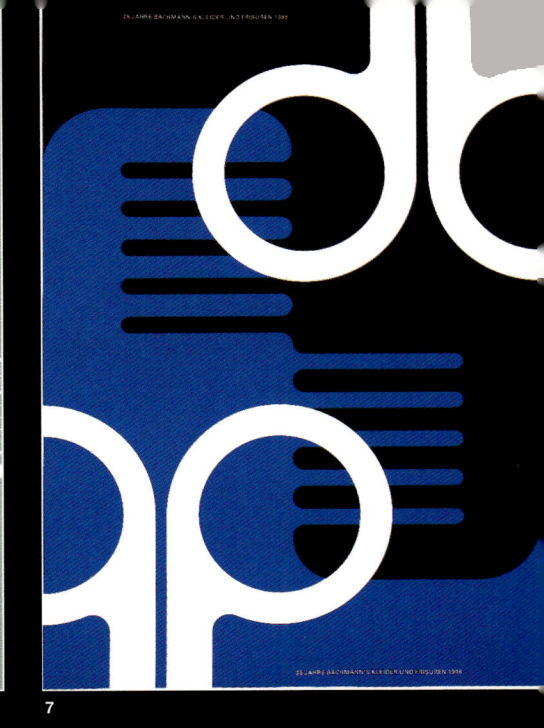

examples of the Baumanns' capabilities, was the design of an exhibition commemorating the 150th anniversary of the Revolution of 1848–49. In collaboration with an historian, they developed the concept for the entire project. "It was important for the overall design of this exhibition not to teach but rather to inform on many different levels, without becoming too overbearing," Barbara says.

Entering the exhibition, visitors found themselves on the site of a prison of the period. They were led along a path with a wall displaying general historical information on the right side and seven rooms on the left, each with personal items pertaining to everyday life in the prison. Visitors were left to explore and find out as much as they wished by entering one or more of the rooms. The exhibition was complex but accessible, its design enhancing the historical experience for audiences as diverse as schoolchildren and pensioners.

On another front, the Baumanns also organize architectural conferences. The first, Façades, was held in Dresden in 1995. They invited some of the profession's most prominent names to lecture, including Iranian architect Zaha Hadid. The daylong event was attended by 1200 architects from all over the world. The poster for the event, Fassade (façades), is an exceptionally well-produced piece whose vibrant yet subtle surface results from a creative use of a transparent gloss ink. By reducing the meaning of the word façades to a simple visual metaphor—a composition of various grid systems—the poster attempts to function as an invitation to the viewer to fill in the space furnished with individual interpretations or imagery. The objective is to provide a neutral framework that will allow the viewer to form his or her own opinion. But does it work? Visually translating façades into a set of grid systems reduces the complexity of the word and concept to a single expression. While his approach is intended to reflect a symposium of a wide variety of speakers addressing one topic, it also reflects the designers' narrow visual translation, which, because of its bare minimalism, fails to engage the viewer fully with the idea of façades.

Baumann & Baumann has also been involved in packaging, like that for a new range of Ritterwerks Ritter cutting machinery. The packaging displays abstract line drawings as opposed to a conventional colour representation of the products. The formal simplicity of these premium items finds an equivalent in the simple but highly effective two-colour scheme of the packaging. "In the context of the supermarket, these products/packs gain a higher value than all the colourful packaging that surrounds them," Gerd maintains. "The increasing pace of society often leads to visual pollution," he says. "Most products disappear from the market as quickly as they are introduced. We are more interested in creating products that last several years."

The Ritter packaging does stand out on the shelf. It is commercially effective. But the Baumanns' solution might be less a conscious decision on their part than a successful matching of their standard visual approach to this particular "quality" brief. In other words, the design solution was not chosen for a contextual reason, but rather conformed to their established design principles.

And then there are the posters. Some have gained almost iconic status and have been displayed in exhibitions all over the world. The Baumanns' formal language is illustrated in Bachmann's Kleider und Frisuren 1996 (Bachmann's Fashion and Hairstyles 1996). The poster creates a simple abstract composition, combining several Superzeichen (larger-than-life pictograms): two scissors and two combs. The type is set in uppercase and acts as a subtle name tag to contextualize the work. Again, the viewer is invited to create his or her own associations on the simple platform provided. The poster is aimed at every age group. Yet once again, despite the open character of the Baumanns' design, the predominance of their principles seems to hamper clear communication. They encourage their audience to interact with the work but appear to avoid any specific message that might relate to a place or time. The design is more about their abstract ideas than about the here and now of the product and its very specific conditions.

Even those with a high regard for the Baumanns' work must admit that their passion for functionalism has resulted in one particular way of approaching any subject. But in a world of increasing visual awareness, it becomes ever more challenging to transmit messages to their intended audiences. The formal language of modernism—of ordered systems and reduction to essentials—falls short if it cannot capture and engage the viewer. Surely, design escapes its responsibility when no one responds to it.

In his Bauhaus manifesto of 1923, Walter Gropius stated that "the objective of all creative effort in the visual arts is to give form to space." Consequently, the interaction between form and audience defines the success and failure of communication. While the Baumanns surprise us with their incredible love of detail and impress us with their impeccable technique, their work may not be flexible enough to grab today's diverse audiences. Over the years they have developed a template that they apply to a variety of projects—with distinctive results—but it has seemed gradually less engaging.

With notable exceptions, such as the 1848–49 Revolution exhibition, Baumann & Baumann's work is developing into a series of static statements rather than being a critical engagement with society. The result is exclusive rather than inclusive design. In fact, their work might even face the danger of becoming—God and Aicher forbid—superficial.

5 Promotional poster for Fassade: Die Dritte Haut (Façades: The Third Skin), a 1995 international architecture conference commemorating the 100th anniversary of MBM Constructions, Dresden. The poster is part of a larger identity effort, from letterhead to banners.
6 Poster commemorating MBM's 100th anniversary, depicting a palmhouse built in 1858 that MBM was commissioned in 1995 to restore and reconstruct.
7 Poster commemorating 25th anniversary of Bachmann's, a hairstylist and boutique.
8, 9 Promotional posters introducing a corporate identity for Ritterwerk's Ritter knives and personal household products.
10-12 Posters commemorating Siemens's 150th anniversary. palmhouse built in 1858 that MBM was commissioned in 1995 to restore and reconstruct.
13-15 Exhibition of Daimler Chrysler AG utility vehicles at the 68th International Automobile Fair, Geneva, 1998.

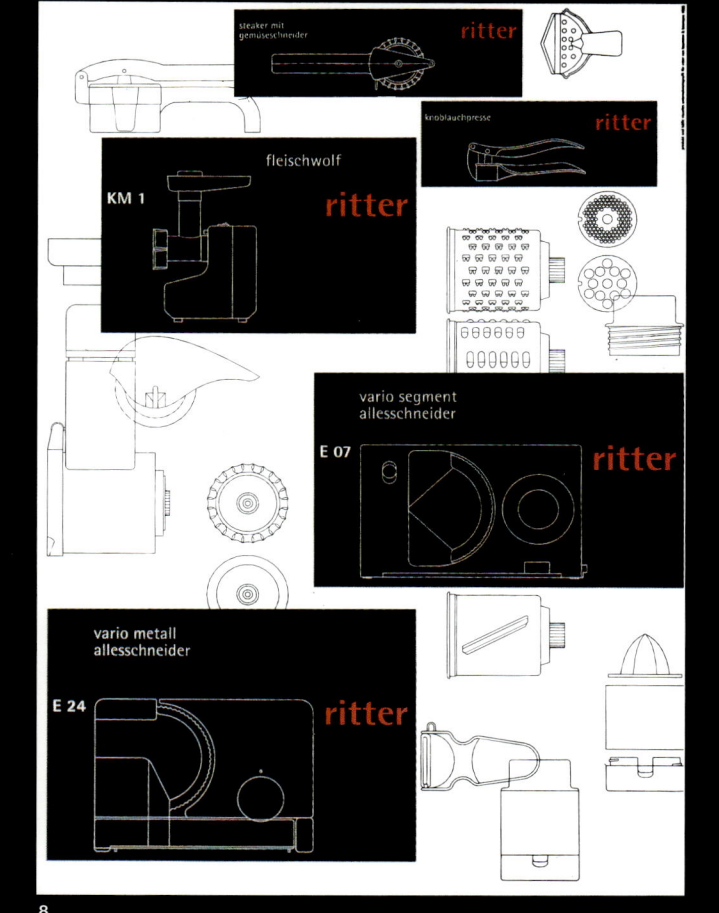

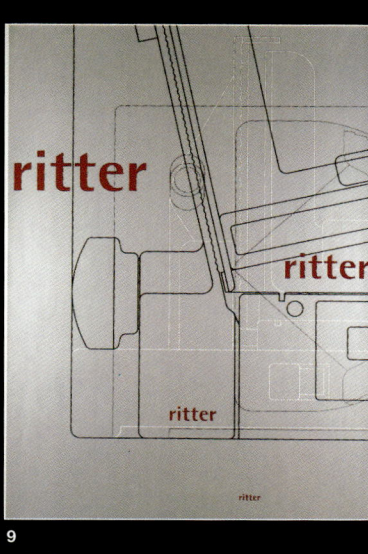

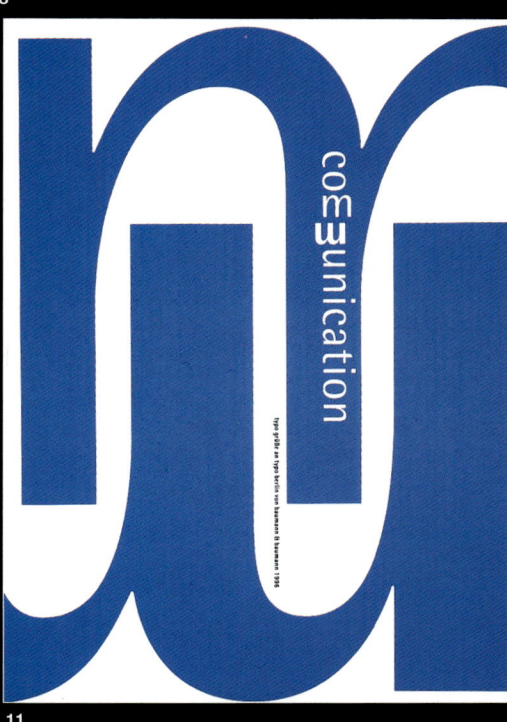

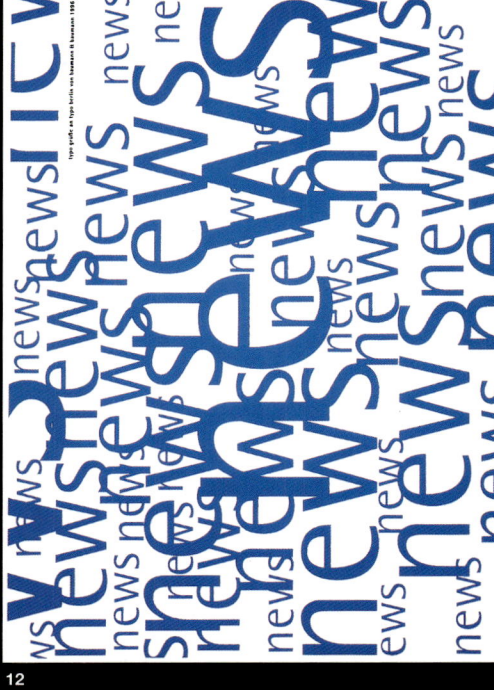

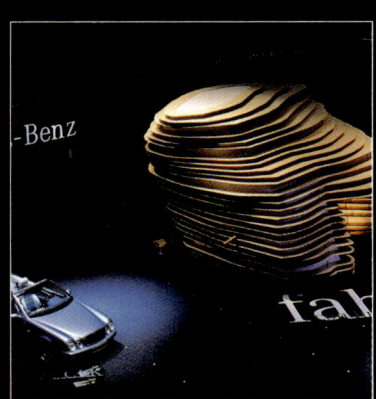

PAGE

THE LEADING DESIGN MAGAZINE IN GERMANY!

If you are a graphic designer, publisher, producer or media designer and want to stay on top, not only now but in the future, then PAGE is the magazine for you. PAGE is the ultimate cross-platform magazine for professionals. PAGE sniffs out trends in the digital creation of pictures, texts and layouts. PAGE presents new tools and materials. PAGE assesses new products and technologies. So that you are aware of what's happening and know which investments are advisable for you. PAGE is up-to-date, practical, competent and informative. PAGE provides ideas and impetus, input and inspiration – month by month.

subscribe — Interested in getting to know PAGE?

Test two issues free! Order hotline: **(00 49) 180-531 05 33** Or mail us at **page@interabo.de**

If you're satisfied with PAGE and do not cancel your order within 10 days of receiving the 2nd issue, your subscription (which you can cancel anytime) is valid for one year. You will receive a bi-annual invoice. Should you wish to cancel your subscription, you'll get your money back for the issues already paid for.

advertise — Interested in advertising in PAGE?

Belinda de Angelis or Samira Holtorf will be happy to provide you with information.
Telephone (Germany) **(00 49) 40-851 83-5 04** Telefax: **(00 49) 40-851 83-5 49**
Or via e-mail: **deangelis@page-online.de**

licence — Interested in a licence?

If you are a publisher or magazine editor and want to make sure that PAGE is published in your country, please contact Brigitte Pinske in Germany.
Telephone: **(00 49) 40-851 83-1 12** Telefax: **(00 49) 40-851 83-1 01**
Or via e-mail: **brigitte.pi@macup.com**

MoreAdvertising. Hamburg

zgraf

international
exhibition of
graphic design
and visual
communications
zagreb/croatia

14.03.-04.04.1999.

www.zgraf.hr

osam
eight

By Tim Rich

Europe's westernmost country is home to a fast-growing and extraordinary band of Web designers and entrepreneurs.

icelandic saga

Like a volcano out of the sea, Iceland emerged on the cultural scene in dramatic style. Written off by some as a freezing wasteland with a few hot springs and horribly sobering bar prices—the sort of place teetotal geologists might take their vacation—positive references to the country began to pop up across Europe in the early '90s. The music press lauded a band called The Sugarcubes and their seismically charged vocalist Björk. Then images of steaming rock pools and industrial-chic geothermal power stations started gracing pop promos, print ads, fashion shoots, and TV commercials. Both Iceland's music and its landscape were seen as starkly beautiful, and the image impresarios came trooping over in their designer anoraks.

Yes, of all places, Iceland—a rugged, inflammable island whose main industry is fishing—became and remains peculiarly fashionable. In truth, the country has played host to volcano- and geyser-fascinated tourists since the turn of the century. But the new visitor interest has centred on Iceland's cultural character. As more pop bands began to export their talent—most notably, Björk and dreamy dance band Gus Gus—other European musicians started to hang out in Reykjavík, the capital. Damon Albarn, lead singer of Brit popsters Blur, has even invested in a bar in the city (recognizable by its glowing London Underground sign outside). Why? Well, perhaps because Reykjavík—despite having just 140,000 inhabitants—is said to be one hell of a party town on weekends.

I planned to investigate the capital's Saturday night capabilities while I was there, purely for research purposes, of course. The real reason for my visit was to discover more about another phenomenon—the country's exploding Internet design scene.

Despite its remote location and a population of just 270,000, Iceland has grabbed at the opportunities presented by the Net. An Internet Industry Almanac survey analyzing Net usage worldwide placed Icelanders third (with 227.3 users per 1000 people), behind the Finns (244.5) and Norwegians (231.1) and some distance ahead of the U.S. (203.4). The Internet version of the Icelandic newspaper Morgunbladid (www.mbl.is) also carried a Gallup survey stating that 28 percent of the total population in Iceland uses the Internet on a regular basis.

Fast-increasing Net access has inspired Iceland's business, cultural, and governmental communities to invest in Web sites. Ask your search engine for listings (they usually have an ".is" ending) and you'll be given links to everything from the Icelandic Kayak Club to Reykjavík's cemeteries. Many politicians have their own site, too.

Almost all .is sites have been designed in Iceland. One reason is that the government insists they use the Icelandic language or, at the very least, offer an Icelandic version. Web site owners and designers seem delighted to comply, which suggests that the widely held apocalyptic vision of the Internet steamrolling national cultures is simplistic.

But then, Iceland isn't like anywhere else. I learn that as I arrive. Flying into Keflavík National Airport, which Iceland shares with NATO, my plane comes in low across black beaches and treeless lava fields. Next to the runway, angular fighter planes under camouflage canopies mirror the sharp lines of a distant mountain range. Steam from the nearby Black Lagoon geothermal power station floats upwards. It's like landing on a recently colonized planet.

Into Reykjavík in search of Web people. My first stop is x.net, Reykjavík's highest-profile Internet café. Ari Thor Johannesson greets me and, despite the blazing sun outside, looks with concern at my light attire. "It will be very wet shortly," he says enigmatically. Then I remember the Icelandic climate's reputation for mood swings.

Bearded, avuncular, and with the lilt and rolled rrr's characteristic of the Icelandic accent, Johannesson is something of a telecoms entrepreneur. He has had a few run-ins with his old employers and comes across as a bit of a bad boy of telecoms.

x.net (www.xnet.is) was established two years ago. A centre for Net activities, commercially it has yet to find its footing and it will shortly reopen as a Net café aimed at businesspeople and tourists. Johannesson has also had to reassess his involvement in Web design. "I was trying to sell home pages two years ago, and very few people listened to me. People simply said they weren't interested. But the Internet is everywhere now."

What changed? Five years ago, Telecom Iceland was the only company allowed to sell modems; now there's a modem in every new PC. Johannesson's complaint today, a gripe echoed throughout Iceland's Web businesses, is that it's difficult to discover and keep Web design talent. "I found a good designer and taught him how to make home pages. He did that, was successful, became very expensive, and then moved on to another company." His attention is diverted to the window and the thick rain now hurling itself at the ground. "Everyone is looking for people who know about the Internet. It is a big problem. I think we had three or four of them that we trained up and the same thing happened—it even happened when I trained up a friend of mine!"

With the language issue and a Mac-PC compatibility problem (there are relatively few Macs in Iceland), going abroad for Web design isn't feasible for Johannesson. However, he points out that in-demand designers can locate their studio anywhere within the country and people will remain delighted to use them.

The thick fiber-optic cabling that rings the island aids such flexibility.

Twenty-six-year-old Web designer Arnar Thor Oskarsson (www.vefur.is) has established a flourishing business outside the capital. Oskarsson, head of the Icelandic chapter of the International Webmasters' Association (IWA), lives about an hour's drive from Reykjavík in southern Iceland. He creates and maintains a number of excellent Web sites for local communities, organizations, and companies, including Árborg (www.selfoss.is), the Association of Local Authorities in Southern Iceland (www.sudurland.is), and the Agricultural Association of South Iceland (www.bssl.is).

Oskarsson started Web designing about three years ago. "I worked for a local computer shop for a year and I spent most of my free time studying HTML and graphic design," he says. "When I was asked to design the Web site for Selfoss, I quit my job and started my own business. Before I started working with computers, I spent five years as an auto refinisher."

A description of his life conjures up images of hippie Net designers living an idyllic existence far from urban pressure. Not so. "The Web business is pretty ruthless," declares Oskarsson. "There are a lot of Web design companies in this market. Also, most of the ISPs [Internet service providers] and advertising agencies offer Web design services, often as a part of a larger package, such as Internet access and solutions for companies, or complete corporate identity packages by the ad agencies. In some cases, the companies and organizations have an in-house Web or Intranet specialist. I run the only full-time Web design company in the region [Selfoss], but I receive a lot of competition from the companies in Reykjavík. But that's all right—I have some clients there, too."

Back in Reykjavík, I set off in search of the most intriguing of my intended interviewees, Clean Design. Linked closely with ISP Net Taekni (NT), their work is sharp, and the company C.V. includes odd phrases like "extreme marketing." They have attitude. They also appear to have an office in a light industrial unit on the edge of town. My elderly taxi driver (a sort of Blake Carrington look-alike) is bemused. We're at the right address, but the front door is guarded by an enormous crate of cabbages. We wander inside and, after quizzing several individuals wearing white hats and rubber gloves, discover we are in a food processing plant. A passerby comes to my rescue—yes, there is an Internet company somewhere in this building, but they're out. Hmm. I leave a message for them to be at my hotel the next day at 6 P.M.

Next stop: I arrive—with rain dripping from my hair— at the offices of one of the most important local newspapers, DV. The paper has had a site for several

---

1 Arnar Thor Oskarsson's personal Web site.

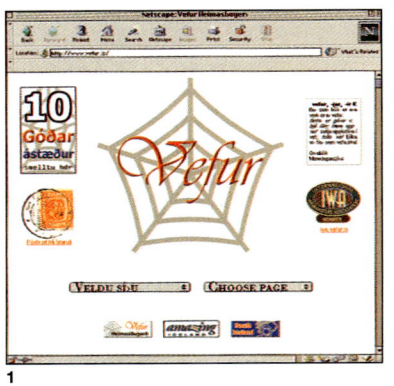

2 Frame from Web site for DV/ Independent Media Corp. Design firm: Visir; designer: Thorarinn Leifsson.

3 Web site for Gallery Kjöt Gourmet Shop. Design firm: Clean Design.

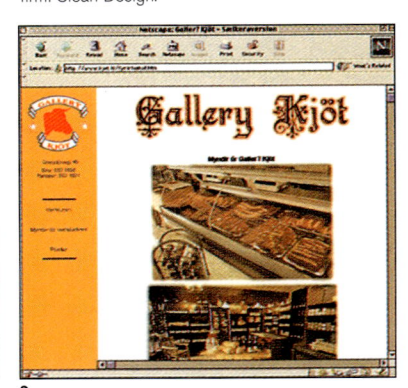

4 Web site for Siglo, a city in northern Iceland (www.siglo.is).

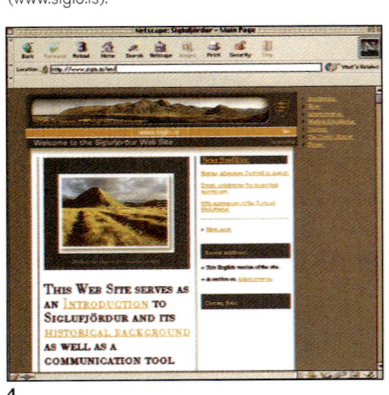

years but its new project, www.visir.is, is much more than an on-line news service. Set up in April 1998, it brings together news, features, guides, shopping, entertainment, on-line chat, and a host of other activities. DV director of new media Asgeir Fridgeirsson explains: "I define it as an electronic meeting point where news and information is the main reason people want to visit us. It is like a mall with various activities and interests, which is why we have designed the front page like it is."

The site contains around 70 news stories every day, with different divisions and publications within owner Independent Media Corporation contributing content. A designer works closely with writers and reports to Fridgeirsson, who before pursuing Web-based activities was the editor of the superbly art-directed and written travel and culture magazine Iceland Review. "The big difference in working with designers on this medium compared to magazines and newspapers is that with a magazine you know the format and you don't have that many alternatives when it comes to structure. With the Web, you have these vital considerations about the architecture. A good Web designer is definitely a rare combination: someone who has the qualities to sense and understand form and colour and typography, yet also knows how to operate the numerous software programs you really need to conduct the process."

Yes, Fridgeirsson has had to look hard for design talent of the calibre of Thorarinn Leifsson, the current Visir designer. "It requires enormous understanding of the content and the way we want people to 'travel,'" says Fridgeirsson. "Just across the road is the College of Art and Design. A professor friend of mine says they are expecting perhaps two people to graduate this year who are able to design for the Web. Last year there were none, and none the year before."

Visir is getting 11,000 to 15,000 visits each day. Fridgeirsson wants to make it the most visited Icelandic Web site and is positioning to compete with radio and TV. On a wider level, he sees enormous potential for the Web in Iceland, with traditional industries such as seafood benefiting from its export function. Travel and tourism will be another beneficiary, he says. Oskarsson agrees: "The Internet can be a very powerful tool for Icelandic businesses and for the travel industry, which is becoming more important each year. But I think it is essential that Iceland's Internet link to the outside world is both stable and able to carry a lot of bandwidth. This, sadly, has not been the case so far."

As I exit through DV's heavy swinging doors, I'm slapped in the face by the coldest wind this side of Ice Station Zebra. The sun is setting messily over the harbour, like a broken egg dripping yellows and whites down a pink sky and into the water. There is a strange feeling in the air.

Back at my hotel. 6 P.M. A knock. I open the door to see two fashionable young men. One is Hreinn Jonasson of Clean Design, the other Brynjar Hauksson of NT. We decide to talk in a local café-bar. Having scored three delicious hot chocolates, I ask them to describe their work. Hauksson explains, with crisp enunciation (and rolling rrr's), that NT was established in October 1997, has seven employees and connects around 1200 users to the Net. The company also creates computer networks for corporations and offers clients Web design services through third-party firms such as Clean Design. There are two owners, Hauksson and 23-year-old Birkir Jonsson. "He is the oldest person in the company," says Hauksson, who, it transpires, is 21, "and he is the only person in the company who is not gay. This is a bit unusual for companies in this sector."

Hauksson started writing software at the age of 9. Despite his youth, clients have no problems trusting his company, he says. "Yes, they trust me. For example, there are two schools connected through us, and it is because they knew us before; they knew what we could do. They are very satisfied." NT (www.nt.is) also counts a number of government organizations as clients.

I turn to Hreinn Jonasson (www.clean-design.com), a sort of Leonardo DiCaprio Jr. "I'm 18 and I started with the Web about four years ago by creating a site for my father, who owns a gourmet shop," he explains. I had already visited this site, www.kjot.is, and liked it. I ask about his clients. "Companies don't know much about the Internet, and they certainly don't know much about the design work you can do on it. You can now do really cool Web sites, but I don't think cool Web sites are the best for communicating the best information," he says, and outlines his "clean" philosophy. "Other Web designers don't understand why I want to do clean pages. They sometimes ask me why I'm not using Flash or more GIF animations. Well, it's slow and it doesn't really serve a purpose. It's just fancy."

Mature ideas he has, but getting client trust is a problem for Jonasson. "Yes, age is an issue, but young people have much more knowledge of computers and the Internet, and most of the design companies here in Iceland are people under 30." So what's his solution? "I have always tried to be very, very cheap. I charge about 20,000 kr [about $300] for a site when other people are charging around 80,000 kr just for a layout. It's cheap for a business reason. We are very, very young. We haven't done much for companies. We need experience, then we can sell. But I'm not designing Web pages for the money. I just want enough money to live. It gives me so much enjoyment to be creating something."

I imagine those words would probably strike fear into the hearts of many other Icelandic designers. Later, I ask Arnar Thor Oskarsson, who, as head of the IWA, is involved in defining commercial practices, what he thinks. "Good for them," he says. "You have to start somewhere, don't you?"

Jonasson and Hauksson tell me more about their business plans. They are wily and ambitious. Hauksson's commercial nous is particularly impressive. I suspect they're hyping up their activities for my tape recorder, but I like them anyway. This new breed of Web designers is learning the ways of the entrepreneur—yeah, good for them.

I leave them in the bar and head back to pack for my flight. Snow is falling, the first since last winter. People are carrying broad smiles around the softly lit streets. I can think of no better environment to create something unusual, exciting, and engaging for the Internet.

But, of course, more important than this saga of design and the Web: Is it true what they say about Reykjavík on a Saturday night? Oh yes. Oh yes.

A Virtual Tour
Some of Iceland's top sites

www.centrum.is/icerev Daily news and features from the *Iceland Review* site. Best Headline to date: "Housewife bites customs officer."
www.siglo.is Great site for information about the northernmost town in Iceland.
http://ff.halo.hi.is/fcst Graphically sophisticated weather forecasting site.
www.icelandair.is The national airline's site; includes an excellent tour and historical information.
www.norvol.hi.is One for volcano lovers and the geologically minded.
www.vefur.is Anar Oskarsson's excellent site has links to Web designers and sites for South Iceland. You can even send an Icelandic postcard.

Tim Rich thanks Arnar Thor Oskarsson and the IWA for assistance with research for this article. The Icelandic Chapter of the IWA can be found at www.iwa.vefur.is

spanish high By Chris Foges

Madrid-based Tau Diseño is an examplar of Spain's fast-growing graphic design profession.

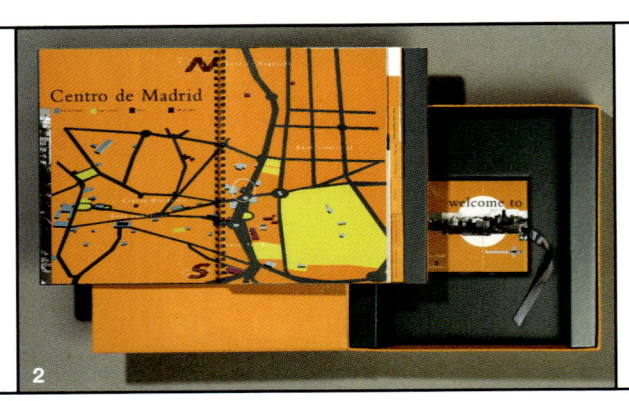

Spain is a place where cultures collide. It is the watershed between Europe and Africa, and has been populated, and fought over, by Africans and Europeans, Fascists and Communists, Christians and Muslims. It was Spain from which an Italian adventurer set off to find the New World, and Spain which is now working hard to make its mark on the world after half a century of political and cultural isolation. From the Civil War of 1936 until 1975 the country suffered under the repressive Fascist dictatorship of Francisco Franco, who shut Spain off from the rest of Europe. Today, Spain is determined to prove that it is a team player in a federated Europe, as well as a developed, forward-thinking country in its own right.

One side effect of the need to compete in an international marketplace has been the rapid growth of a graphic design profession that did not exist 25 years ago. The work of Spanish designers has been attracting attention on the international scene for some time now—designers such as Fernando Gutiérrez in Barcelona, whose strong art direction of Colours and Matador magazines has won numerous awards, and Enric Satué, also based in Barcelona, whose colourful posters provided a memorable identity for the 1992 Olympics in Barcelona.

One firm whose work regularly appears in magazines and awards annuals internationally is Tau Diseño. Now based in a converted private apartment in a smart section of Madrid close to the Museo del Prado and the verdant expanses of Retiro Park, Tau has been operating under the guidance of founder-partner Emilio Gil since 1980—roughly spanning the history of modern Spanish graphic design as a whole. With eight full-time designers working across a variety of disciplines including packaging, print, multimedia, and identity work, Tau is only slightly larger than the average Spanish design consultancy, but its influence on the rest of the industry, both in terms of working practices and creativity and ideas, is disproportionate to its size.

Along with the entire graphic design field, Tau has benefited from Spain's fast-track change to late-20th-century capitalism over the last quarter century, which, one or two recessions notwithstanding, has seen almost continuous economic growth. The removal of trade restrictions opened Spain up to foreign competition and forced Spanish businesses to respond aggressively. As Emilio Gil explains: "The arrival of foreign companies, products, franchises, brands, superstores, TV channels, and so on, has resulted in hard competition for everything related to the world of communication and image in general. Thus, Spanish businesses have had to react, and sometimes the results have been excellent."

When I first visited Tau Diseño in the spring of 1997, the company seemed relaxed about its success, the pace of work busy if not frantic (the workweek came to an early conclusion with a Friday afternoon visit to a local tapas bar). Harriet Miller, an English designer who has been at Tau for several years, stated that in the last year, it seems as though corporate Spain has "discovered" graphic design, and that Tau, like many design companies, is experiencing an unprecedented boom. Tau earned over half of its income last year from new business—a mixture of corporate and cultural clients in both state and private ownership.

As in many countries where design is a relative newcomer to the corporate scene, Spanish designers have trouble convincing business of the value and purpose of what they do. "The main problem in Spain," says Gil, "is that some designers have transmitted the idea that to design is just to superficially change the image of something. This frivolous approach still influences people's perception of design today." In Spain, graphic design is traditionally associated with other branches of the arts and cultural institutions, and while the values of attractive presentation in that context are widely appreciated, the role of design in business is not yet fully understood. There are strong links between those working in design and the arts: Many Spanish designers receive their training in fine art rather than graphic design, while clients commissioning design often have an arts background. According to Gil, the "art" preconception is fading: "The change has been fast and radical. Commissions from businesses in other sectors [than art] have become more frequent."

Gil graduated in architecture from the Universidad Politecnica de Madrid in 1975, the year of Franco's death. While at the university, he developed his interest in graphic design, inspired by the Swiss and American designers of the day. When he elected to do further study in the field, it was at the School of Visual Arts in New York. As he now observes: "During those years, there were no design schools in Madrid, so the training for professionals here was more a question of each one creating his own training, by means of studying the work of the leading designers, including the influential work of the Americans."

A mixture of influences—Swiss typography, American illustration, and Spanish cultural iconography—is much in evidence in the work of Tau

1, 2 Report for the sale of a retail property in Madrid. Art director/designer: Jorge García; photographer: Valerie de la Dehesa.
3, 4 Two CDs for Polygram: Great Guitarists and Flamenco Singers. Art director: Emilio Gil; designer: Harriet Miller; illustrator: Luis Mayo.
5, 6 Posters for the 22nd Festival of Film in Huesca. Art director/designer: Jorge García.
7–10 Covers of Pautas magazine. Art director: Emilio Gil; designers: Harriet Miller (Figs. 7, 8, 9), Jorge García (Fig. 10); illustrators: Nuria Díaz and Vicente Guallert (Fig. 7), Manolo Prieto (Fig. 8), Fernando Bellver (Fig. 9), Raúl (Fig. 10).
11, 12 Cover and contents page of Un Toro Negro y Enorme. Art director: Emilio Gil; designers: Emilio Gil, Jorge García.
13 Exhibition design for "Manolo Prieto y el Toro Osborne." Art director/designer: Jorge García.
14, 15 1997 annual report for Amper. Art director: Emilio Gil; designer: Harriet Miller.

continued

Chris Foges is editor of Graphics International magazine in London.

16, 17 Spreads from a special issue of Experimenta magazine, celebrating 25 years of graphic design in Spain. Art director: Emilio Gil; designer: Harriet Miller.
18, 19 Corporate identity manual for Indra. Art director: Emilio Gil; designers: Gloria Rodríguez, Esperanza de la Fuente; project coordinator: Esther Santos.
20, 21 Covers of Pautas magazine. Art director/designer: Emilio Gil.

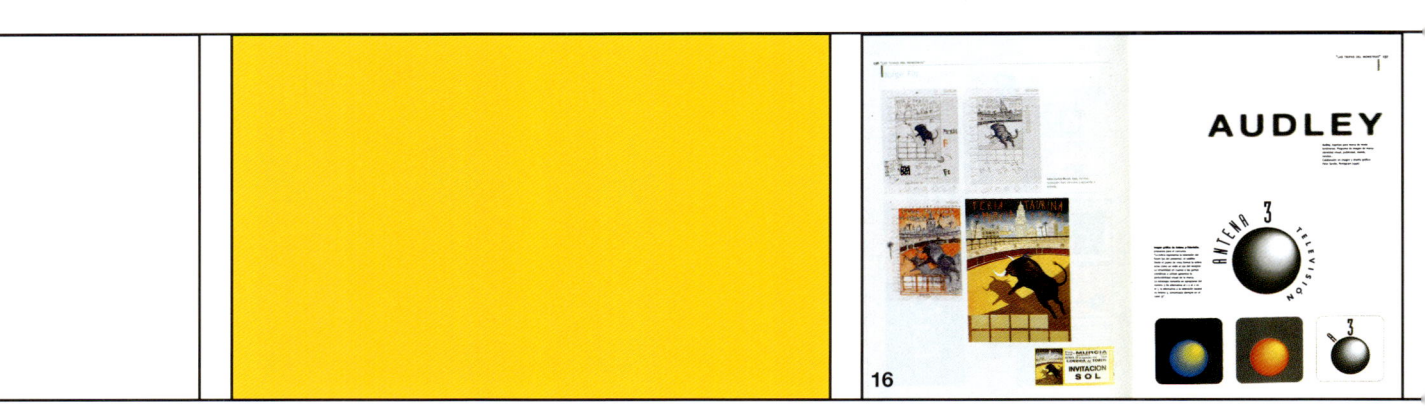

Diseño. Gil himself is anxious to stress that although any identifiable Spanish qualities in his studio's work are welcome, there is no deliberate intention to create or maintain a Spanish esthetic. It seems inevitable, however, that Spanish design will have a local accent as tradition and its visual manifestations (the image of the bull, for example) are more prevalent in Spain than in most other European, and indeed non-European, countries. Continuing the Spanish tradition of opposing cultures living cheek by jowl, Madrid's Moorish-influenced architecture stands next to modern glass-and-steel office blocks, while old wooden bullfighting rings —still in use—coexist with the state-of-the-art stadiums built for the '92 Barcelona Olympics. Many of the Spanish icons that appear in Tau's work, such as bulls and fans, owe as much to the nature of the brief or circumstances of a job as they do to a desire to put a Spanish spin on the work.

Indeed, several of the company's projects that have dealt specifically with traditional Spanish imagery have an international air about them that acts almost as a counterbalance to the content. One example is the book Un Toro Negro y Enorme, about the Osborne bull, a silhouetted cutout advertising a brand of sherry and a familiar sight on hillsides all over Spain. While the subject matter is uniquely Spanish, the typography, use of photography, and flat, matte colour owe as much to Swiss and Northern European influences as to any local esthetic.

Another characteristic of the consultancy's work is the use of hand-rendered illustration. This betrays an American influence, but it also stems from the fact that many of the designers employed by Tau were educated at Madrid's School of Fine Arts. One long-standing Tau member, Jorge García, is responsible for much of the group's illustration output, which in turn goes some way in accounting for the distinctive look of the work.

Its retention of the traditional skills and practices of design, such as in-house image-making and the use of pens and sketchbooks, might suggest to some that the studio is technologically backward in its approach. The opposite is true. Tau was one of the first companies in Spain to use the Apple Macintosh computer, more than a decade ago, and has recently been testing the waters of multimedia design with a CD-ROM for Sofres A.M., a client that assesses TV viewing numbers. It is an area of activity that Gil is keen to develop, although multimedia acceptance by Spanish clients in general has been disappointingly slow. Those multimedia jobs that do come up are often won by information technology companies rather than design consultancies, and Gil, who is widely recognized as an arbiter of standards in this field and is a familiar multimedia awards judge both at home and abroad, is uninspired by the quality of Spain's digital output. As a judge at the Premios Laus awards, he pondered whether it was advisable to make any awards at all, so poor was the quality of new-media work coming out of the traditional design-for-print studios. "There is a high demand but low expectations on the part of clients," says Gil. "Almost anything goes in this area, resulting in work with an inadequate level of design".

However, one gets the sense that Gil feels the new technologies have a significant role to play. When asked what the future holds for Spanish design as a whole, Gil says, "[That depends] on the new generation of designers in Spain. Also on how the Internet will influence the designer—will the number of printed jobs decrease, for example?" Similarly, when queried about his own plans, he says that he would like to collaborate with U.S.-based designers, and that this cooperation may be possible "in multimedia, where the technological aspect of the work permits great ease when developing stages of a project and exchanging ideas".

For all its rapid growth and international outlook, however, the Spanish graphic design industry is still finding its way. Many of the structures and institutions that underpin its counterparts in London or New York, creating a community and shaping the industry, are still relatively underdeveloped. Such factors as the fledgling design education system, limited movement between companies, a wide geographical dispersement, and few forums for criticism and debate mean, among other things, that the sense of community among designers is not nearly as strong as it is in other countries. The original old guard is still predominant. But Gil is optimistic. "The current generation of designers is one of continuity, because their work follows the work of the pioneers," he says. "The relationship [between generations] is an excellent one, friendly and respectful.

"If we approach each job not as something to get finished and out of the way, and if we resolve problems while remembering that the best way to help businesses see design as a sensible investment rather than simply as a cost is to provide design of quality—well, then, the future will be good".

EL PAIS
Libro de estilo

17

Indra
Manual
de Identidad
Visual
Corporativo

18

Logomarca
Configuración
Indra
Indra

19

PAVTAS
A
S
E
I
6
El Comic
en crisis

20

PAVTAS
A
S
E
I
Revistas
y diseño

21

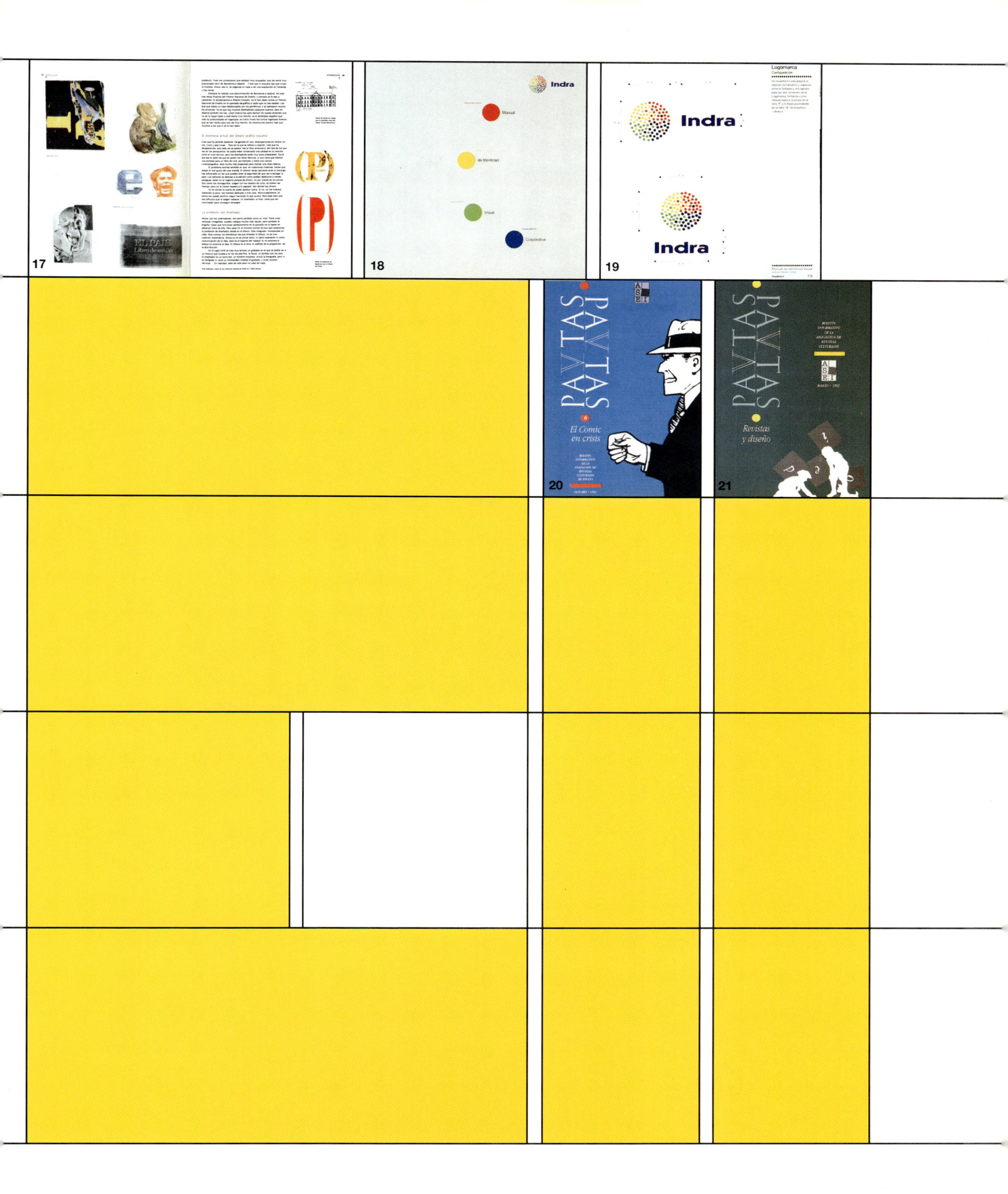

Get the finest every month *

ÉTAPES *graphiques*

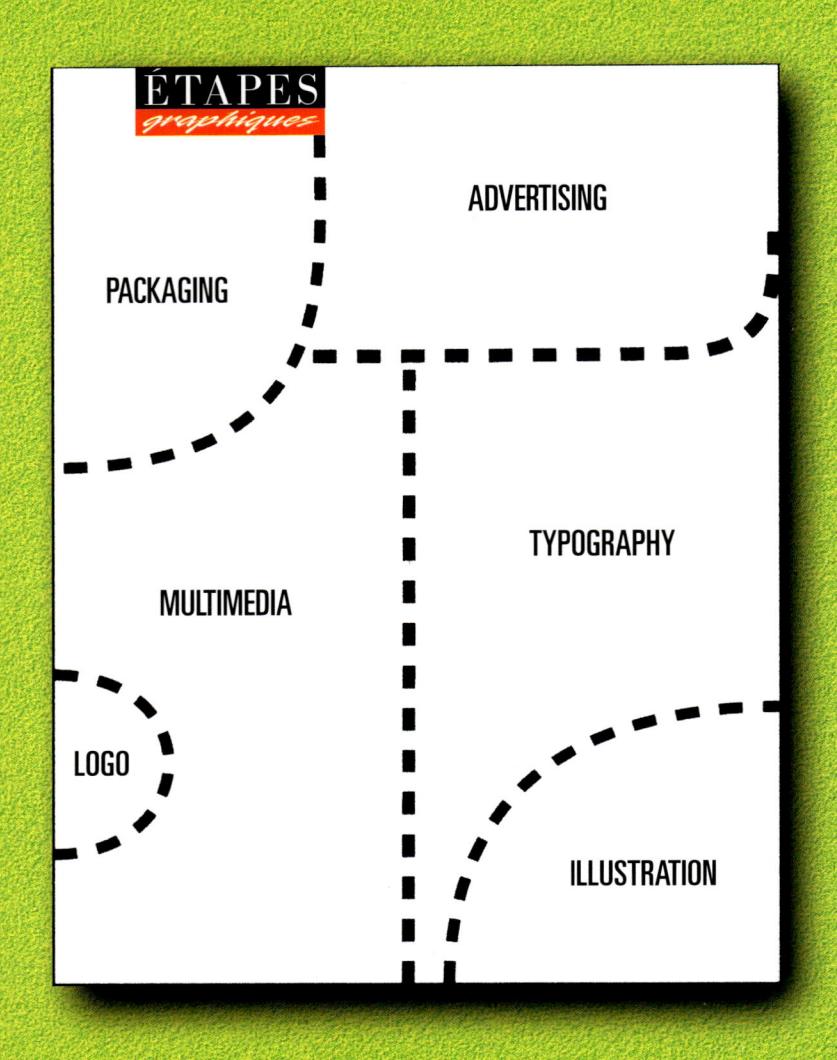

- PACKAGING
- ADVERTISING
- MULTIMEDIA
- TYPOGRAPHY
- LOGO
- ILLUSTRATION

* Get a free issue of Étapes Graphiques by filling in the insert *

*

Étapes Graphiques is the french professional magazine of graphic design and visual communication

15, rue de Turbigo 75002 Paris Tel : (33) 140 260 099 Fax : (33) 140 260 703 www.pyramyd.fr

Winners Directory 4

AUSTRIA

Art & Joy
Vienna
Telephone: +43 1 214 107800
Fax: +43 1 214 107850
e-mail: art.joy emporium.co.at
Fig.10 (p.13)

Bayer, Richard
Linz
Telephone: +43 732 7702 7755
Fax: +43 732 771 071
e-mail: r.bayer@sucdesign.co.at
Figs.3 , 5 (p.12)

Caldonazzi Grafik-Design
Frastanz-Amerlügen
Telephone: +43 5522 52100
Fax: +43 5522 52100 25
Fig.15 (p.13)0

Createam Werbeagentur
Linz
Telephone: +43 732 7702 770
Fax: +43 732 7710 71
e-mail: agentur@createam.co.at
Fig.1 (p.12)

Faschingbauer & Schaar
Graz
Telephone: +43 316 338930
Fax: +43 316 33893050
e-mail: faschingbauer_schaar@magnet.at
Fig.12 (p.13)

Gandl, Stefan
Vienna
Telephone: +43 1 985 6607
Telephone/Fax [Germany]:
+49 30 4411075
e-mail: stefan@onlineoffice.de
Fig.9 (p.13)

Göbl, Markus
Vienna
Telephone/Fax: +43 1 3192394
Fig.4 (p.12)

Heider & Klausner
Atelier für Corporate Design
Vienna
Telephone/fax: +43 1 587 6501 /
586 0575
e-mail: heider+klausner@magnet.at
Fig.2 (p.12)

Heinzle, Lothar Ämilian
Vienna
Telephone: +43 1 586 08524
Fax: +43 1 586 0852-14
e-mail: heinzle@treangeli.at
Fig.11 (p.13)

Inwirements
Vienna
Telephone: +43 1 817 14780
Fax: +43 1 81714788
e-mail: frank@frank.co.at
Fig.14 (p.13)

Kaitan, Robert
Vienna
Telephone: +43 1 405 9318
Fig.7, 8 (p.12)

Kopf, Elisabeth
Vienna
Telephone: +43 1 8897866
Fax: +43 1 812 0209-11
e-mail: echoraum@ping.at
Fig.6 (p.12)

Projektagentur
Linz
Telephone: +43 732 7702 7755
Fax: +43 732 771 071
e-mail: r.bayer@sucdesign.co.at
Fig.5 (p.12)

BELARUS

Belaya Karona
Minsk
Telephone: +375 172 174161
Fax: +375 172 174171
e-mail: karona@open.by
Fig.5 (p.87)

BELGIUM

Seven Productions
Wilrijk
Telephone: +32 3 449 6022
Fax: +32 3 449 5023
e-mail: sven.seven@skynet.be
Fig.2 (p.15)

Zizó!
Antwerp
Telephone: +32 3 281 3495
Fax: +32 3 239 5912
e-mail: ingrid@zizo.be
Fig.1 (p.15)

CROATIA

Croatia Airlines
Zagreb
Telephone: +385 1 616 0016
Fax: +385 1 617 6845
e-mail: marketing-ctn@ctn.tel.hr
Fig.2 (p.17)

Likovni Studio, D.O.O.
Sveta Nedelja
Telephone: +385 1 337 0593
Fax: +385 40 310 825
Figs.3,4,6-8 (p.17)

Sensus Design Factory
Zagreb
Telephone/fax: +385 1 388 6439
e-mail: nedjeljko.spoljar@zg.tel.hr
Figs.1,5 (p.17)

DENMARK

2 x Brix Design
Copenhagen
Telephone: +45 31 18 30 88
Fig.19 (p.21)

Datagraf Auning As
Auning
Telephone: +45 87 95 55 55
Fax: +45 87 95 55 544
e-mail: epost@datagraf.dk
Fig.4 (p.19)

Griffin Grafisk Design
Aalborg
Telephone: +45 98 12 26 59
Fax: +45 98 12 75 99
e-mail: griffin@post12.tele.dk
Figs.6,7 (p.19), 11-12 (p.20)

Hovedkvarteret APS
Copenhagen
Telephone: +45 33 14 16 66
Fax: +45 33 14 16 46
e-mail: hq@hovedkvarteret.dk
Figs.2 (p.19), 8,9,13 (p.20)

Kontrapunkt AS
Copenhagen
Telephone: +45 33 93 18 83
Fax: +45 33 93 18 54
e-mail: mail@kontrapunkt.dk
Figs.1, 3, 5 (p.19), 14-16 (p.20),

Kühnel Grafisk Design
Copenhagen
Telephone: +45 35 36 04 08
Fax: +45 35 36 04 32
e-mail: kuhnel@pip.dknet.dk
Figs.10 (p.20), 17, 18 (p.21)

Special Production
Copenhagen
Telephone: +45 35 43 33 68
Fax: +45 35 43 33 69
Figs.22, 23 (p.21)

Umwelt
Copenhagen
Telephone: +45 35 36 56 54
Fax: +45 35 36 56 64
e-mail: umwelt@umwelt.dk
Figs.20, 21 (p.21)

FINLAND

Suunnittelutoimisto Kirnauskis Oy
Helsinki
Telephone: +358 9 680 3420
Fax: +358 9 680 34224
e-mail: tuula.aula@kirnauskis.com
Fig.2 (p.23)

Taivas Oy
Helsinki
Telephone: +358 9 666 266
Fax: +358 9 666 064
e-mail: klaus@taivas.com
Figs.1, 3 (p.23)

FRANCE

Alyen
Marseille
Telephone: +33 4 91 85 46 34
Fax: +33 4 91 34 08 34
e-mail: alyen@aix.pacwan.net
Fig.9 (p.27)

Borgers Unlimited
Paris
Telephone: +33 1 43 57 07 21
Fax: +33 1 43 38 50 80
e-mail: mbunltd@imaginet.fr
Fig.7 (p.27)

Daedalus Design
Angoulême
Telephone: +33 5 45 95 37 70
Fax: +33 5 45 95 06 24
Fig.8 (p.27)

Demirel, Selçuk
Paris
Telephone: +33 1 45 31 76 66
Fax: +33 1 45 31 03 02
Fig.1 (p.26)

De-Vi-Zu
Paris
Telephone: +33 1 42 40 31 03
Fax: +33 1 42 40 30 81
Figs.6, 10, 11 (p.27)

Doctor Design
Paris
Fig.11 (p.27)
(see De-Vi-Zu for contact details)

O 'De Formes
Lyon
Telephone: +33 4 72 38 87 57
Fax: +33 4 72 38 87 58
Figs.2, 3 (p.26)

Porchez Typofonderie
Malakoff
Telephone/Fax: +33 1 46 54 26 92
e-mail: jfporchez@hol.fr
Fig.4 (p.26)

Saluces Design & Communication
Avignon
Telephone: +33 4 90 85 23 85
Fax: +33 4 90 27 08 98
Fig.5 (p.26)

Saunier, Claude-Henri
Sainville
Telephone: +33 2 37 24 65 48
Fax: +33 2 37 24 64 85
Fig.12 (p.27)

GERMANY

10eG Visual
Oberhausen
Telephone: +49 208 8246410
Fax: +49 208 8246420
e-mail: team@10eg.com
Fig.20 (p.33)

Adidas Salomon AG
Herzogenaurach
Telephone: +49 9132 84 2156
Fax: +49 9132 84 3401
e-mail: susanne.birkmann@adidas.com
Fig.87 (p.44)

akzent design
Mühltal
Telephone: +49 6151 91550
Fax: +49 6151 915555
e-mail: mail@akzent-design.de
Figs.31 (p.35), 104 (p.47)

Bach-Backhaus
Hamburg
Telephone: +49 40 2798355
Fax: +49 40 27800640
e-mail: typischc@aol.com
Fig.88 (p.45)

Backe/Meixner/Gross
Frankfurt
Telephone/fax: +49 69 95990037
e-mail: backe@stud.uni-frankfurt.de
Fig.50 (p.39)

Barten & Barten:
Die Agentur GmbH
Cologne
Telephone: +49 221 9218210
Fax: +49 221 9218218
e-mail: mail@barten.de
Figs.35, 36 (p.36)

Beyrow, Matthias
Berlin
Telephone: +49 30 264 84900
Fax: +49 30 264 84901
e-mail: beyrow@vossnet.de
Fig.94 (p.46)

Bruchmann, Schneider, Bruchmann
Cologne
Telephone: +49 221 121055
Fax: +49 221 135246
e-mail: f.bruchmann@bsb-koeln.de
Fig.54 (p.39)

Büroecco!
Kommunikationsdesign
Augsburg
Telephone: +49 821 527010
Fax: +49 821 527060
e-mail: bueroecco@newsfactory.net
Fig.82 (p.44)

Büro Hamburg
Hamburg
Telephone: +49 40 3747970
Fax: +49 40 371155
e-mail: mailbox@buero-hamburg.de
Fig.13 (p.32)

Büro Kottmann
Reutlingen
Telephone: +49 7121 491941
Fax: +49 7121 491943
Fig.103 (p.47)

Eikes Grafischer Hort
Frankfurt
Telephone: +49 69 944 19820
Fax: +49 69 944 19821
e-mail: hort@bigfoot.com
Figs.5-7 (p.31)

Englich + Wagner
Berlin
Fig.19 (p.33)
(see under "Wilkhahn" for contact details)

Factor Design
Hamburg
Telephone: +49 40 432 5710
Fax: +49 40 432 57199
e-mail: mail@factordesign.com
Figs.30, (p.35), 47, 49 (p.38), 73 (p.42), 77, 78 (p.43), 95(p.46),

Fantastic New Designment GmbH
Wiesbaden
Telephone: +49 611 910 0277
Fax: +49 611 910 0278
e-mail: mail@fantastic-net.de
Fig.10 (p.32), 80 (p.43)

Finkel, Prof.Gerd
Kreiensen
Telephone:+49 5563 8061
Fax: +49 5563 8091
Fig.21 (p.34)

Firma Ströer
Dresden
Telephone: +49 351 3119978
Fax: +49 351 3119956
Fig.39 (p.37)

Fleischmann & Kirsch
Stuttgart
Telephone: +49 711 2851620
Fax: +49 711 2851621
Figs.23 (p.34), 59 (p.40)

Fons M Hickman Design
Düsseldorf
Telephone: +49 211 494730
Fax: +49 211 494654
Fig.48 (p.38)

Gesine Grotrian-Steinweg
Düsseldorf
Telephone: +49 211 494730
Fax: +49 211 494654
Fig.15 (p.33)

Gräfe und Unzer Verlag GmbH
Munich
Telephone: +49 89 4198 101 29
Fax: +49 89 4198 810 260
Fig.92 (p.45)

Groothuis+Malsy
Bremen
Telephone: +49 421 347 8606
Fax: +49 221 347 8607
Fig.90 (p.45)

Heine/Lenz/Zizkk
Frankfurt
Telephone: +49 69 242 5250
Fax: +49 69 242 52599
Fig.17 (p.33)

Heye & Partner
Munich
Telephone: +49 89 665 32386
Fax: +49 89 665 32275
Figs.2 (p.30), 74 (p.42)

Imago 87 GmbH
Freising
Telephone: +49 8161 97870
Fax: +49 8161 978787
e-mail: info@imago87.de
Fig.91 (p.45)

Jetzt/M.Rindermann
Munich
Telephone: +49 89 21838416
Fax: +49 89 21838529
e-mail: markus.rindermann@jetzt.de
Figs.61, 62 (p.40), 68 . (p.41)

JvM Werbeagentur
Hamburg
Telephone: +49 40 431 3530
Fax: +49 40 431 353113
e-mail: mail@jvm.de
Figs.14 (p.32), 75 (p.42)

Klaus Lemke Team
Melsungen
Telephone: +49 5 661 2210
Fax: +49 5 661 2211
Figs.16 (p.32), 22 (p.34)

Knopp Werbeagentur
Göppingen
Telephone: +49 7161 911 600
Fax: +49 7161 911 6010
Fig.76 (p.43)

Kommunikationsdesign
Kalletal
Telephone: +49 5264 5265
e-mail: andrea.traeger@t-online.de
Fig.58 (p.40)

Macron Advertising
Munich
Telephone: +49 89 360 52520
Fax: +49 89 360 25244
e-mail: mgoerden@macron.de
Figs.8, 9 (p.31) 81 (p.43)

Maksimovic & Partners
Saarbrücken
Telephone: +49 681 31916
Fax: +49 681 31917
e-mail: maks@internett.de
Fig.45 (p.38)

Matthias Schäfer Design
Wiesbaden
Telephone/fax: +49 611 842 629
e-mail: mschdesign@hotmail.com
Figs.11 (p.32), 28 (p.35)

Meiré & Meiré
Königsdorf
Telephone: +49 2234 966 050
Fax: +49 2234 966 055
Figs.51, 53 (p.39), 85 (p.44)

Milch: Büro für Gestaltung
Munich
Telephone: +49 89 520 4660
Fax: +49 89 520 46621
e-mail: milch@compuserve.com
Fig.63 (p.41)

Moniteurs
Berlin
Fig.79 (p.43)
(see under "Xplicit ffm" for contact details)

Münkillus
Hamburg
Telephone/Fax: +49 40 319 1592
Figs.71, 72 (p.42), 83, 86 (p.44)

Neumann Design
Hamburg
Telephone: +49 40 450 39290
Fax: +49 40 45039413
Fig.37 (p.36)

Oktober Kommunikationsdesign
Bochum
Telephone: +49 2327 92855
Fax: +49 2327 92856
e-mail: post@oktober.de
Fig.25 (p.34)

Pencil Corporate Art
Braunschweig
Telephone: +49 531 72964
Fax: +49 531 76894
Figs.26, 27 (p.35)

Post, Mechthild
Heuchlingen
Tel: +49 7174 802 723
Fax: +49 7174 802 274
Figs.32 (p.35), 44 (p.37)

Rempen & Partner:
Das Design Büro
Düsseldorf
Telephone: +49 211 8395 247
Fax: +49 211 8395 111
e-mail: hinterwinkler@rempen.de
Fig.1 (p.30)

Winners Directory 165

Rong Design
Waiblingen
Telephone: +49 7151 21195
Fax: +49 7151 23807
e-mail: fngauss@aol.com
Fig.12 (p.32)

Sabine Bock Grafik
Ketsch
Telephone/Fax: +49 6202 63761
Fig.24 (p.34)

Scarabaeus Dialogwerbung
Rosenheim
Telephone: +49 8031 289394
Fax: +49 8031 289333
e-mail: scarabaeus.dialogwerbung
@t-online.de
Figs.38, (p.37), 99 (p.46)

Scheppe Böhm Associates
Munich
Telephone: +49 89 54403588
Fax: +49 89 54403589
e-mail: sba@dcdu.com
Figs.18 (p.33), 100 (p.47)

Scholz & Friends n.a.s.a.
Hamburg
Telephone/Fax: +49 40 37681277
e-mail: j.eberstein@scholz-and-
friends.de
Fig.84 (p.44)

**Schreiter's Ideeanarchiv
& Artwork**
Frankfurt
Telephone: +49 69 95520411
Fax: +49 69 95520412
e-mail: ideeart@aol.com
Figs.42, 43 (p.37)

Sibylle Schwartz
Weissach
Phone: +49 7152 52665
Fax: +49 7152 905632
Fig.89 (p.45)

Sign Kommunikation
Frankfurt
Telephone: +49 69 9443240
Fax: +49 69 94432450
e-mail: ahenschel@sign.de
Fig.34 (p.36)

**Simon & Goetz
Kommunikation GmbH**
Frankfurt
Telephone: +49 69 968 8550
Fax: +49 69 968 85544
e-mail: simongoetz@aol.com
Fig.102 (p.47)

**Sisa & Winkler Büro für
Gestaltung**
Schwäbisch Gmünd
Telephone/fax: +49 7171 66642
Fig.3 (p.30)

Springer & Jacoby GmbH
Hamburg
Telephone: +49 40 35603 693 or
486
Fax: +49 40 35603 111 or 261
e-mail: torsten_rieken@sj.com
Figs.4 (p.30), 55 (p.39), 97 (p.46)

Steinbeck, Carolyn
Berlin
Telephone/fax: +49 30 4268512
Fig.57 (p.40)

Taste!
Neu-Isenburg
Telephone: +49 6102 712526
Fax: +49 6102 25235
Figs.46 (p.38), 93 (p.45)

Trafodesign
Neuss
Telephone: +49 2131 541598
Fax: +49 2131 541508
e-mail: atelierhaus@online-club.de
Fig.60 (p.40)

Universität Essen
Essen
Telephone: +49 20 11833335
Fig.70 (p.42)

Vorwerk & Co.
Wuppertal
Telephone/Fax: +49 202 564 1221
e-mail: liv.kionka@vorwerk.de
Fig.107 (p.47)

**Wächter & Wächter
Werbeagentur München GmbH**
Munich
Telephone: +49 89 747 2420
Fax: +49 89 747 24240
e-mail: waechter@waechter-
waechter.de
Figs.40, 41 (p.37)

W.A.F Werbegesellschaft
Berlin
Telephone: +49 30 303 0050
Fax: +49 30 303 00530
e-mail: waf_werbegembh@
compuserve.com
Fig.29 (p.35)

Waidmann, Stefan
Heuchlingen
Telephone: +49 7174 802273
Fax: +49 7174 802274
Figs.32 (p.35), 44 (p.37), 64 (p.41)

Wagner, Marion
Berlin
Fig.94 (p.46)
(see under "Beyrow" for contact
details)

**Weigang Marketing
Partner GmbH**
Würzburg
Telephone: +49 931 355150
Fax: +49 931 3551515
e-mail: wmp@weigang-
marketing.de
Fig.98 (p.46)

Werbewelt GmbH
Ludwigsburg
Telephone: +49 7141 451260
Fax: +49 7141 4512610
Fig.33 (p.36)

Wilkhahn
Bad Münder
Telephone: +49 50 42999 867
Fax: +49 50 42999 230
e-mail: wilkhahn.marketing@t-
online.de
Fig.19 (p.33)

Wüschner und Rohwer
Munich
Telephone: +49 89 2900330
Fax: +49 89 29003313
e-mail: wueschner@wrb.de
Figs.56 (p.40), 65-67 (p.41), 96
(p.46)

xplicit Ffm
Frankfurt
Telephone: +49 69 9759230
Fax: +49 69 97592727
e-mail: xplicit@xplicit.de
Figs.69 (p.41), 79 (p.43)

Zink & Kraemer
Trier
Telephone: +49 651 978 920
Fax: +49 651 978 9219
e-mail: info@zuk.de
Figs.52 (p.39)

HUNGARY

Art-Core
Budapest
Telephone: +36 30 229101
Fax: +36 12128105
Fig.6 (p.49)

Art Force Studio
Budapest
Telephone/fax: +36 1 340 8114
e-mail: art-f@elender.hu
Fig.7 (p.49)

Kóbor, Mátyás
Székesfehérvár
Figs.2-5 (p.49)

Sárkány Graphics Design
Budapest
Telephone/fax: +36 1 379 3171
Fig.1 (p.49)

IRELAND

Averill Brophy Associates
Dublin
Telephone: +353 1 677 4888
Fax: +353 1 677 4254
e-mail: info@abadesign.ie
Fig.7 (p.51)

Creative Inputs
Dublin
Telephone: +353 1 497 2711
Fax: +353 1 497 2779
e-mail: cinputs@indigo.ie
Fig.9 (p.51)

Daly, Carla
Dublin
Telephone/fax: +353 1 283 7363
Fig.8 (p.51)

Index Creative Communications
Dublin
Telephone: +353 1 6614504
Fax: +353 1 6755456
e-mail: index@iol.ie
Fig.1 (p.51)

Webfactory
Dublin
Telephone: +353 1 678 9992
Fax: +353 1 662 5970
e-mail: info@webfactory.ie
Figs.2-6 (p.51)

ITALY

AReA Strategic Design
Rome
Telephone: +39 06 8413001
Fax: +39 06 8413699
e-mail: area.sd@flashnet.it
Figs.5-7 (p.54), 19 (p.56)

Cap Design
Potenza
Telephone: +39 0971 55073
Fax: +39 0971 470 515
Figs.10 (p.55)

Caproni, Chiara
Rome
Telephone/fax: +39 06 512 1056
e-mail: chiaracaproni@iol.it
Figs 39, 42, 43 (p.59)

Carmi e Ubertis Associati Srl
Casale Monferrato
Telephone: +39 0142 71686
Fax: +39 0142 76444
e-mail: carmieub@dialup.italnet.it
Fig.33 (p.58)

CDM Associati
Udine
Telephone/fax: +39 0432 507382
e-mail: cdm.associati@iol.it
Figs.13 (p.55), 35 (p.59)

**DSDS (Dudka Sala Design
Strategy)**
Milan
Telephone/fax: +39 02 33601194
e-mail: igrab@tin.it
Fig.30 (p.58)

Fausta Orecchio Design
Rome
Telephone: +39 06 583 6939
Fax: +39 06 583 31097
e-mail: f.orecchio@agora.stm.it
Figs.1-4, 8, 9 (p.54), 20 (p.56), 26-
28 (p.57), 31, 32 (p.58), 36 (p.59)

Hand Made Group
Stia (Arezzo)
Telephone: +39 0575 582 083
Fax: +39 0575 582 2198
e-mail: handmade@dada.it
Figs.12, 14, 16 (p.55), 17 (p.56),
23 (p.57)

IMDCR srl.
Vicenza
Telephone: +39 0444 924044
Fax: +39 0444 938056
e-mail: imdcr@tin.it
Fig.22 (p.56)

Maiarelli + Rathkopf
Bologna
Telephone: +39 051 266757
Fax: +39 051 266987
e-mail: pem6645@iperbole.bologna.it
Figs.12, 14, 16 (p.55), 17 (p.56),
23 (p.57)

McCann-Erickson Italiana Spa
Rome
Telephone: +39 06 500991
Fax: +39 06 5022438
e-mail:
antonietta_cordeschi@mccann.com
Figs.21 (p.56), 34 (p.58)

no.parking
Vicenza
Telephone: +39 0444 327861
Fax: +39 0444 231499
e-mail: inbox@noparking.it
Fig.18 (p.56)

**Pavese Toscano Studio
Associato**
Rome
Telephone: +39 06 6781074
Fax: +39 06 6795392
e-mail: mg.toscano@agora.stm.it
Figs.29 (p.58)

Ruggieri, Alberto
Rome
Telephone: +39 06 5781637
Fax: +39 06 5754854
e-mail: a.ruggieri@mclink.it
Fig.25 (p.57)

Studio Emo Risaliti
Agliana
Telephone/Fax: +39 0574 750256
e-mail: emoworks@mbox.match.it
Fig.40 (p.59)

Studio Gianni Bortolotti
Bologna
Telephone/Fax: +39 051 267049
e-mail: sa10075@iperbole.bologna.it
Fig.11 (p.55)

Studio GT & P
Foligno
Telephone/Fax: +39 0742 320372
e-mail: gt&p@cline.it
Figs.37, 38 (p.59)

Studio Karavil
Milan
Telephone/fax: +39 02 58112031
e-mail: bessikaravil@tin.it
Fig.24 (p.57)

Studio Tam
Venice
Telephone/fax: +39 41 5226974
e-mail: tamre@tin.it
Fig.41 (p.59)

Tipolito Maggioni srl
Milan
Telephone: +39 02 313 673
Fax: +39 02 33101994
e-mail: maggioni@tipolitomaggioni.it
Fig.15 (p.55)

LITHUANIA

RIC Ltd
Vilnius
Telephone: +370 2 220655
Fax: +370 2 220655
e-mail: ric@post.5ci.lt
Figs.1, 2 (p.61)

THE NETHERLANDS

Ad Broeders Graphic Design BV
Middelbeers
Telephone: +31 13 5141619
Fax: +31 13 5142915
e-mail: info@adbroeders.nl
Fig.23 (p.67)

Addition Advertising
Hilversum
Telephone: +31 35 6400646
Fax: +31 35 6216399
e-mail: addition@wxs.nl
Fig.4 (p.64)

Anker x Strybos
Utrecht
Telephone: +31 30 2318288
Fax: +31 30 2369159
e-mail: info@ankerxs.nl
Figs.8 (p.65), 18 (p.66)

BRS Premsela Vonk
Amsterdam
Telephone: +31 20 6262030
Fax: +31 20 6265079
e-mail: bpv@xs4all.nl
Figs.2 (p.64), 9 (p.65)

DC3 interaction
Amsterdam
Figs.2 (p.64), 9 (p.65)
(see under "BRS Premsela Vonk" for
contact details)

Gerard Unger Design
Bussum
Telephone: +39 3569 36621
Fax: +39 3569 39121
Fig.1 (p.64)

Heijnen, Jan
The Hague
Telephone/fax: +31 70 389 7791
e-mail: jheijnen@xs4all.nl
Fig.17 (p.66)

Kader
The Hague
Telephone: +31 70 3882087
Fax: +31 70 3881868
e-mail: kader@xs4all.nl
Figs.5 (p.64), 28 (p.68)

KesselsKramer
Amsterdam
Telephone: +31 20 5301060
Fax: +31 20 5301061
e-mail: church@euronet.nl
Figs.10 (p.65), 16 (p.66), 30 (p.68),
31 (p.69)

Langtry Associates
Hilversum
Telephone: +31 35 6248091
Fax: +31 35 6299088
e-mail: langtry@euronet.nl
Fig.24 (p.67)

Limage Dangereuse
Rotterdam
Telephone: –31 10 4764800
Fax: +31 10 4764880
e-mail: info@limage-dangereuse.nl
Fig.15 (p.66), 21 (p.67)

M + M Grafisch Ontwerpers
Arnhem
Telephone: +31 26 3518415
Fax: +31 26 3511184
e-mail: mplusm@worldonline.nl
Fig.14 (p.66)

Malmberg
Den Bosch
Telephone: +31 73 6288811
Fax: +31 73 6213669
e-mail: c.kuitenbrouwer@malmberg.nl
Fig.19 (p.67)

n/p/k industrial design
Leiden
Telephone: +31 715 141341
Fax: +31 715 130410
e-mail: npk@npk.nl
Fig.1 (p.64)

Ontwerpbureau 3005
The Hague
Telephone: +31 70 4279963
Fax: +31 70 3464003
e-mail: 3005@bart.nl
Fig.29 (p.68)

Ontwerpbureau FAH BV
Nuth
Telephone/fax: +31 45 5241869
Fig.6 (p.64)

Openbaar Gevoel
Amsterdam
Telephone: +31 20 447 3734
Fax: +31 20 447 3733
e-mail: vulkers@noord.bart.nl
Fig.7 (p.65)

Polka Design
Roermond
Telephone: +31 475 350659
Fax: +31 475 336526
e-mail: joep@fontana.nl
Figs.26, 27 (p.68)

**Proforma Grafisch Ontwerp
& Advies**
Rotterdam
Telephone: +31 10 2441442
Fax: +31 10 2441444
e-mail: lc@pro.nl
Figs.3 (p.64), 20 (p.67), 34 (p.69)

Shape BV
Amsterdam
Telephone: +31 20 6220606
Fax: +31 20 6225355
e-mail: shapebv@euronet.nl
Fig.25 (p.68)

**Studio Gonnissen en
Widdershoven**
Amsterdam
Telephone: +31 20 4683525
Fax: +31 20 4683524
e-mail: gonwid@xs4all.nl
Figs.32, 33 (p.79)

Studio Knegtmans
Amsterdam
Telephone: +31 20 4206255
Fax: +31 20 4208976
e-mail: marise@xs4all.nl
Fig.13 (p.66)

Tel Design
The Hague
Telephone: +31 70 3856305
Fax: +31 70 3836311
e-mail: gk@teldesign.nl
URL: http://www.teldesign.nl
Figs.11, 12 (p.65)

Total Design Amsterdam BV
Amsterdam
Telephone: +31 20 5789650
Fix: +31 20 5789621
e-mail: tm@totaldesign.com
Fig.22 (p.67)

NORWAY

Ashley Booth Design AS
Oslo
Telephone: +47 22 806980
Fax: +47- 22 382008
e-mail: abd@abd.no
Figs.1, 2, 8 (p.71)

Gazette AS
Oslo
Telephone: +47 22 33 4410
Fax: +47 22 33 4430
e-mail: gazette@gazette.no
Fig.3 (p.71)

Kutal Graphic Design AS
Oslo
Telephone/fax: +47 22 699097
e-mail: kutal@online.no
Figs.5, 6 (p.71)

Rose + Hopp Design
Oslo
Telephone: +47 22 562025
Fax: +47 22 562023
e-mail: rosehopp@rosehopp.no
Figs.4, 9 (p.71)

Trigger Design
Kristiansand
Telephone: +47 381 28080
Fax: +47 381 28090
e-mail: trigger@online.no
Fig.7 (p.71)

POLAND

Agencja Reklamowa Fart
Wroclaw
Telephone: +48 71 444693
Fax: +48 71 442542
e-mail: fart@fart.com.pl
Figs.9 (p.75)

Agencja-Vi
Torun
Telephone: +48 56 6544200
Fax: +48 56 6210200
e-mail: vi@man.torun.pl
Fig.20 (p.77)

Atelier Tadeusz Piechura
Lodz
Telephone/Fax: +48 42 654 4633
Figs.10 (p.76)

Corporate Profiles
Warsaw
Telephone: +48 22 6390150
Fax: +48 22 390183
e-mail: cpddb@it.com.pl
Figs.33-36, 38 (p.79)

Definition Design
Warsaw
Telephone: +48 22 63901850
Fax: 48 22 6390190
Figs.11 (p.76), 25, 26 (p.78)

Hestia Art Sp.z.o.o.
Sopot
Telephone: +48 58 550 2961
Fax: +48 58 551 2014
Fig.30 (p.79)

KOREK Studio
Warsaw
Telephone: +48 22 8180 128
Fax: +48 22 638 3875
e-mail: korek@atcom.net.pl
Figs.7, 8 (p.75), 15(p.76), 16, 21, 22 (p.77), 27, 28 (p.78), 31, 32 (p.79)

Moby Dick Group
Szczecin
Telephone: +48 91 423 1440
Fax: +48 91 423 3742
e-mail: mobydick@mobydick.com.pl
Figs.5 (p.75), 37 (p.79)

Rozycki, Mark
Warsaw
Telephone: +48 22 483 922
Fax: +48 22 497 808
e-mail: vfp@it.com.pl
Figs.2, 6 (p.74),17-19 (p.77), 23, 24 (p.78)

Studio DN Design Group
Warsaw
Telephone: +48 22 754 4545
Fax: +48 22 751 1830 ex. 23
e-mail: studiodn@top.pl
Figs.12, 13 (p.76)

Studio PK
Lodz
Telephone/fax: +48 42 630 4172
e-mail: studiopk@priv3.onet.pl
Fig.29 (p.78)

Studio Pro
Torun
Telephone: +48 56 6549229
Fax: +48 56 6549288
e-mail: studiopro@studiopro.com.pl
Figs.1, 3, 4 (p.74), 14 (p.76)

PORTUGAL

Atelier de Design e Comunicação
Lisbon
Telephone: +351 1 814 1576
Fax: +351 1 814 1579
e-mail: nuno.alves@ip.pt
Figs.28, 29 (p.85)

EURO RSCG
Oeiras
Tel : +351 1 440 885 00
Fax : +351 1 441 3013
e-mail: eugenio.chorao@euroscg.pt
Fig.25 (p.85)

João Machado Design LDA
Porto
Telephone: 351 2 610 3772
Fax: +351 2 610 3773
e-mail: jmachado.design@mail.telepac.pt
Figs.2, 4 (p.82), 11-14 (p.83), 18 (p.84)

Novodesign
Lisbon
Telephone: +351 1 392 3000
Fax: +351 1 395 3849
e-mail: jcandersen@novodesign.pt
Fig.17 (p.84)

PÃ Design
Porto
Telephone: +351 2 339 2190
Fax: +351 2 200 2306
E-mail: padesignprt@mail.telepac.pt
Figs.1, 3 (p.82), 10 (p.83), 20 (p.84), 24 (p.85)

Planet Design
Carnaxide
Telephone: +351 1 424 5781
Fax: +351 1 424 1015
Fig.8 (p.82)

Publicis Design
Lisbon
Telephone: +351 1 301 3261
E-mail: josedionisio@publicis.pt
Figs.15 (p.83), 22 (p.84)

R2 Design
Matosinhos
Telephone: +351 2 938 6865
Fax: +351 2 938 9482
e-mail: r2design@mail.telepac.pt
Fig.19 (p.84)

Reis, Carlos
Lisbon
Telephone: +351 1 390 8946
e-mail: reis@ip.pt
Figs.5, 6 (p.82), 21, 26 (p.84)

Ricardo Mealha–Atelier
Lisbon
Telephone: +351 1 382 5340
Fax: +351 1 385 6274
e-mail: centra@esoterica.pt
Figs.7 (p.82), 9, 16 (p.83), 23 (p.84), 30, 31 (p.85)

Setezeroum
Vila Nova de Gaia
Telephone: +351 2 550 9685
Fax: +351 2 550 9687
Fig.27 (p.85)

RUSSIA

Melnikova, Gelena & Kusnetzov, Denis
Moscow
Telephone/Fax: +7 95 2426625
e-mail: estampe@glasnet,ru
Figs.1-4 (p.87)

SLOVENIA

Kompas Design
Ljubljana
Telephone: +361 61 324 391
Fax: +361 61 318 197
Figs.1, 3, 5, 6 (p.90)

KROG
Ljubljana
Telephone/fax: +386 61 126 5092
Figs.2, 4 (p.90), 7, 8, 13 (p.91)

Medja & Karlson
Ljubljana
Telephone: +386 61 173 7403
Fax: +386 61 173 7407
Figs.9-12 (p.91)

Movera
Ljubljana
Telephone/fax: +386 61 165 3230
e-mail: movera@siol.net
Fig.14 (p.91)

SPAIN

ABM Serveis de Comunicació
Barcelona
Telephone: +34 93 2001315
Fax: +34 93 2000556
e-mail: abmsc@conexis.es
Fig.15 (p.95)

Artimaña, Disseny I Comunicació S.L.
Barcelona
Telephone: +34 93 207 5356
Fax: +34 93 207 5739
e-mail: artinet@artinet.net
Figs.18 (p.96), 36 (p.97)

Camper Communication Service
Madrid
Telephone: +34 91 531 2277
Fax: +34 91 522 2248
e-mail: pepcarrio@mx2.redestb.es
Figs.1-7 (p.94)

Design Workshop, The
Barcelona
Telephone: +34 93 418 1065
Fax: +34 93 418 6726
e-mail: crolando@ralles.com
Figs.19, 20, 23-25 (p.96), 34, 35 (p.97)

Estudio Forma
Oviedo
Telephone: +34 985 275 127
Fax: +34 985 275127
e-mail: forma.dg@arrakis.es
Figs.21 (p.96), 27 (p.97)

Hetcett
Barcelona
Telephone: +34 93 310 4400
Fax: +34 93 319 5544
e-mail: idep@idep.es
Fig.32 (p.97)

Impreso Estudio
Oviedo
Telephone: +34 98 523 6962
Fax: +34 98 527 3721
e-mail: impreso@arrakis.es
Fig.13 (p.95)

Osoxile S.L.
Barcelona
Telephone: +34 93 207 0684
Fax: +34 93 457 5875
e-mail: osoxile@seric.es
Figs.9, (p.95), 16, 17 (p.96), 28, 29 (p.97)

Pepe Gimeno, S.L.
Godella, Valencia
Telephone: +34 96 390 4074
Fax: +34 96 390 4076
e-mail: gimeno@ctv.es
Fig.33 (p.97)

Pepvalls, Estudi
Igualada
Telephone: +34 93 805 2464
Fax: +39 93 805 4901
Pep.valls@ceina.es
Fig.11 (p.95)

Puig Falco Associats
Barcelona
Telephone: +34 93 488 3036
Fax: +34 93 488 3083
e-mail: puigfalco@puigfalco.com
Figs.30, 31 (p.97)

Sonsoles Llorens Diseny Gráfic
Barcelona
Telephone: +34 93 412 4171
Fax: +34 93 412 4298
e-mail: sonsoles@ssc.es
Figs.8, 14 (p.95), 22, 26 (p.96)

Tau Diseño
Madrid
Telephone: +34 91 369 3234
Fax: +34 91 369 3486
e-mail: spain@taudesign.com
Figs.10, 12 (p.95)

SWEDEN

Agitator i Helsingborg AB
Helsingborg
Telephone : +46 42 133 595
Fax: +46 42 133 375
e-mail: jesper@agitator.se
Fig.47 (p.105)

Anders Lindholm Prod AB
Stockholm
Telephone: +46 8 651 1937
Fax: +46 8 650 5918
e-mail: anders.lindholm@stockholm.mail.telia.com
Fig.21 (p.102)

Bodebeck Grafisk Form AB
Gothenburg
Telephone:
Fax:
e-mail:
Fig.42 (p.105)

Brand Internet
Stockholm
Telephone : +46 8 506 12413
Fax: +46 8 506 12439
e-mail: frederik.lewander@bmn.se
Figs.33 (p.103), 37 (p.104),45 (p.105)

CEMK AB (Centrum för Målinriktad Kommunikation AB)
Gothenburg
Telephone : +46 31 179050
Fax:
e-mail: info@cemk.se
Figs.10 (p.100), 23 (p.102)

Dagnå Graisk Design
Stockholm
Telephone: +46 8 643 1055
Fax: +46 8 643 1065
e-mail: gunnar@dagna.se
Fig.40 (p.104)

Design X Stockholm
Stockholm
Telephone: +46 8 678 1810
Fax: +46 8 611 7550
e-mail: monica@designx.se
Figs.22 (p.102), 39 (p.104), 44 (p.105)

Fältman & Malmén AB
Stockholm
Telephone: +46 8 406 6500
Fax: +46 8 406 6505
e-mail: info@faltman-malmen.se
Fig.3 (p.100)

Glitter & Company
Stockholm
Telephone: +46 8 332 044
Fax: +46 8 328 810
e-mail: glitter@swipnet.se
Figs.20 (p.102), 36 (p104)

Göthberg & Co. Design
Gothenburg
Telephone: +46 31 409 040
Fax: +46 31 404 698
e-mail: design@gothberg.se
Fig.46 (p.105)

GRITS
Stockholm
Telephone: +46 8 653 2740
Fax: +34 93 654 3240
e-mail: bo.sundin@grits.se
Figs.13, 14 (p.101)

Jerlov & Co.
Gothenburg
Telephone: +46 31 774 0150
Fax: +46 31 774 1750
e-mail: we@jerlov-company.com
Figs.25, 26 (p.102)

Log Kommunikation
Stockholm
Telephone: +46 8 653 7777
Fax: +46 8 653 0737
e-mail: mail@log.se
Figs.31, 34 (p.103)

Neo Media AB
Stockholm
Telephone: +46 8 702 3020
Fax: +46 8 642 0840
e-mail: stefan@neo.se
Fig.11 (p.101), 28, 29 (p.103), 43 (p.105)

Nina Ulmaja Grafisk Form
Stockholm
Telephone: +46 8 566 14743
Fax: +46 8 566 14744
e-mail: ulmaja@algonet.se
Figs.9 (p.100), 32 (p.103), 38(p.104)

OCH-Herrmann, Liljendahl & Co. AB
Stockholm
Telephone: +46 8 644 5075
Fax: +46 8 640 7146
e-mail: och@och.se
Figs.12, 17(p.101)

Publicis Welinder
Stockholm
Telephone: +46 8 679 0200
Fax: +46 8 611 4775
e-mail: mari.stromquist@publicis.se
Fig.27 (p.103)

Skarbovik, Lasse
Stockholm
Telephone: +46 8 642 0646
e-mail: lasse.skarbovik@swipnet.se
Figs.1, 2, 4-7 (p100), 24 (p.102), 30 (p.103)

Sviestins, Ivar (fotograf)
Stockholm
Telephone: +46 8 332 599
Fax: +46 8 332 099
e-mail: ivar@mbox314.swipnet.se
Fig.35 (p.104)

SWEDEN

Stockholm
Telephone: +46 8 652 0066
Fax: +46 8 652 0033
e-mail: nille@swedengraphics.com
Figs.15, 16, 18, 19 (p.101)

Tennis, anyone?
Gothenburg
Telephone: +46 31 106 060
Fax: +46 31 106 070
e-mail: tennis@tennisanyone.se
Fig.8 (p.100)

Typisk Form designbyrå
Stockholm
Telephone: +46 8 668 0071/72
Fax: +46 8 669 5143
e-mail: post@typiskform.se
Fig.41 (p.105)

SWITZERLAND

Albert Gomm Atelier für Buchgestaltung
Basel
Telephone/Fax: +41 61 362 0620
Figs.8, 17 (p.108)

Bolt, Koch & Ko
Zürich
Telephone: +41 1 385 5858
Fax: +41 1 385 5859
e-mail: boko@boltkoch.ch
Figs.9, 11, 12 (p.108)

Communication Graphic Design
St. Gallen
Telephone/fax: +41 71 245 8404
e-mail: mario.romano@bluewin.ch
Fig.27 (p.109)

Eclat AG
Erlenbach
Telephone: +41 1 910 3940
Fax: +41 1 910 3950
e-mail: dzehntner@eclat.ch
Figs.7, 13-15 (p.108)

G/D/S Agenzia Publicitaria
Lugano
Telephone: +41 91 910 1000
Fax: +41 91 910 1009
e-mail: info@gdsswiss.ch
Fig.4 (p.107)

Ideart
Lucerne
Telephone: +41 370 5712
Fax: +41 370 2017
e-mail: martschini@ideart.ch
Figs.24, 25 (p.108)

Imboden, Melchior
Buochs
Telephone: +41 620 0914
Fig.5 (p.107)

LineUp
Bern
Telephone: +41 31 318 4141
Fax: +41 31 312 7066
e-mail: email@lineup.ch
Fig.16 (p.108)

Neeser & Müller
Basel
Telephone: +41 61 363 2482
Fax: +41 61 363 2481
e-mail: neesermueller@datacomm.ch
Fig.2 (p.107)

Niklaus Troxler Design
Willisau
Telephone: +41 41 970 2731
Fax: +41 41 970 3231
e-mail: troxler@centralnet.ch
Figs.18 (p.108), 19-21, 26 (p,109)

Odermatt & Tissi
Zürich
Telephone/fax: +44 1 211 9477
Figs.1, 3 (p.107), 10, 23 (p.108)

Winners Directory 167

Sandra Kunz Visuelle Gestaltung
Basel
Telephone: +41 61 261 2775
Fax: +41 61 261 2779
e-mail: sandrakunz@access.ch
Fig.22 (p.108)

Wild & Frey
Zürich
Telephone: +41 1 280 0898
Fax: +41 1 280 0899
e-mail: office@wildfrey.ch
Figs.6 (p.107)

TURKEY

G.C. Graphic Design Ltd
Istanbul
Telephone: +90 212 258 7501
Fax: +90 212 258 7502
e-mail: gulizarcep@superonline.com
Fig.1 (p.111)

UNITED KINGDOM

Addison
London
Telephone: +44 171 403 7444
Fax: +44 171 403 1243
e-mail: rebecca.le_mesurier@addison.co.uk
Fig.5, 7 (p.115), 24 (p.119)

Attik, The
Huddersfield
Telephone: +44 1484 537494
Fax: +44 148 434 4958
e-mail: rachael@attik.co.uk
Fig.20 (p.118)

Baber Smith
London
Telephone: +44 171 428 9008
Fax: +44 171 428 9009
info@babersmith.co.uk
Fig.22 (p.119)

Blackburn's Ltd.
London
Telephone: +44 171 734 7646
Fax: +44 171 437 0017
e-mail: sam@blackburns.ltd.uk
Figs.79 (p.127), 86 (p.128)

Bradbourne Publishing Ltd.
East Malling
Telephone: +44 1732 875200
Fax: +44 1732 875300
e-mail: type@baselinemagazine@.com
Fig.62-64 (p.125)

Brewer Riddiford
London
Telephone: +44 171 240 9351
Fax: +44 171 836 2897
e-mail: enquiries@brewer.ridd.co.uk
Figs.53 (p.123), 76 (p.127)

Chase Creative Consultants, The
Manchester
Telephone: +44 161 832 5575
Fax: +44 161 832 5576
e-mail: creative@thechase.demon.co.uk
Figs.12 (p.116), 91, 92 (p.129)

Cleaver et al
London
Telephone: +44 181 566 2807
Fax: +44 181 579 7334
Fig.74 (p.126)

D.design
London
Telephone: +44 171 266 0231
Fig.15 (p.117)

Dazeley, Peter
London
Telephone +44 171 736 3171
Fax: +44 171 371 8876
Figs.36-39 (p.121)

Device
London
Telephone: +44 171 221 9580
Fax: +44 171 221 9589
e-mail: rianhughes@aol.com
Fig 11 (p.116)

Dew Gibbons
London
Telephone: +44 171 388 3577
Fax: +44 171 388 1122
e-mail: itsgreat@dewgibbons.demon.co.uk
Figs.2 (p.114), 82 (p.128), 89, 90 (p.129)

Fitch
London
Telephone: +44 171 509 500
Fax: +44 171 509 0100
e-mail: zuilmah_wallis@fitch.co.uk
Figs.58, 59 (p.124)

Four IV
London
Telephone: +44 171 837 8659
Fax: +44 171 837 8679
e-mail: design@fouriv.com
Fig.51 (p.123)

Frost Design
London
Telephone: +44 171 490 7994
Fax: +44 171 490 7995
e-mail: info@frostdesign.demon.co.uk
Figs.32 (p.120), 41 (p.121), 88, 93 (p.129)

Graphic Partners
Edinburgh
Telephone: +44 131 557 3558
Fax: +44 131 558 1430
e-mail: creativethinking@graphicpartners.co.uk
Fig.72 (p.126)

Graphics Team, The
Aylesbury
Telephone +44 1296 382717
Fax: +44 1246 383392
e-mail: mgoodwin@buckscc.gov.uk
Fig.49 (p.122)

HGV
London
Telephone: +44 171 278 4419
Fax: 44 171 837 4666
e-mail: design@hgv.co.uk
Figs.45, 47 (p.122), 50, 56 (p.123), 69 (p.126), 94 (p.129)

Ideology
London
Telephone: +44 171 253 0439
Fax: 44 171 490 5764
Figs.3, 4 (p.114)

Image Bank, The
London
Telephone: +44 171 312 0300
Fax: +44 171 391 9111
e-mail: mcass@theimagebank.com
Fig.42 (p.121)

Imagination Ltd
London
Telephone +44 171 323 3300
Fax: +44 171 462 2841
e-mail: holly.browne@imagination.co.uk
Fig.78 (p.127)

Imagine
Manchester
Telephone: +44 161 272 8334
Fax: +44 161 272 8335
e-mail: imagine@thestables.unet.com
Fig.18 (p.118)

Jannuzzi Smith
London
Telephone: +44 171 234 0557
Fax: +44 171 234 0558
e-mail: richard@jannuzzismith.com
Fig.14 (p.117)

Jones & Co. Design
Farnham
Telephone: +44 1252 733311
Fax: +44 1252 733313
Fig.87 (p.128)

Lewis Moberly
London
Telephone: +44 171 580 9252
Fax: +44 171 255 1671
e-mail: lewismoberly@enterprise.net
Figs.10 (p.116), 35 (p.120), 52 (p.123)

Lippa Pearce Design
Twickenham
Telephone +44 181 744 2100
Fax: +44 181 744 2770
e-mail: mail@lippapearcedesign.com
Fax: +44-181-744-2770
Figs.13 (p.117), 43 (p.121), 46 (p.122), 67 (p.125), 71 (p.126)

Luxon Carrà
London
Telephone: +44 171 402 5402
Fax: +44 171 262 3410
e-mail: psmith@luxoncarra.co.uk
Figs.95, 96 (p.129)

Michael Nash Associates
London
Telephone: +44 171 631 3370
Fax: 44 171 637 9629
e-mail: mna.ndirect.co.uk
Figs.21 (p.118), 27 (p.119), 66 (p.125), 85 (p.128)

Minale Tattersfield+Partners
Richmond
Telephone +44 181 948 7999
Fax: +44 181 948 2435
e-mail: mtp@mintat.demon.co.uk
Figs.6 (p.115), 44 (p.122), 70 (p.126), 80 (p.127)

NE6 Design Consultants
Newcastle
Telephone +44 191 221 2606
Fax: +44 191 221 2607
e-mail: info@ne6design.demon.co.uk
Fig.84 (p.128)

Omnific Studios
London
Telephone:+44-171-359-1201
Figs.25 (p.119), 34 (p.120)

Paper White Ltd
London
Telephone: +44 171 401 8358
Fax: +44 171 401 8357
e-mail: anita@paperwhite.co.uk
Fig.54 (p.123)

Pearlfisher
London
Telephone: +44 171 603 8666
Fax: +44 171 603 1208
jonathan@pearlfisher.co.uk
Fig.26 (p.113)

Pure Design
Edinburgh
Telephone: +44 131 220 5522
Fax: +44 131 220 5533
e-mail: mick@puredesign.co.uk
Figs.65, 68 (p.125)

Roundel
London
Telephone: +44 171 221 1951
Fax: +44 171 221 1843
e-mail: info@roundel.com
Figs.1 (p.114), 8 (p.115), 48 (p.122), 60 (p.124)

Saatchi & Saatchi Design
London
Telephone: +44 171 307 5327
Fax: +44 171 307 5328
Fig.77 (p.127)

Stocks Austin Sice
London
Telephone: +44 171 243 3232
Fax: +44 171 243 3216
e-mail: dstocks@sasdesign.co.uk
Figs.33 (p.120), 75 (p.127)

Struktur Design
London
Telephone: +44 171 833 5626
Fax: +44 171 833 5636
e-mail: struktur@easynet.co.uk
Figs.16 (p.117)

TBWA GGT Simons Palmer
London
Telephone: +44 171 573 6666
Fax: +44 171 573 6667
e-mail: p.belford@btinternet.com
Figs.28-31 (p.120)

Team, The
London
Telephone: +44 181 877 0888
Fax: +44 181 874 6994
e-mail: info@theteam.co.uk
Figs.19 (p.118), 40 (p.121), 83 (p.128)

Thomas Manss & Company
London
Telephone: +44 171 722 3186
Fax: +44 171 722 5273
e-mail: manss@bogo.co.uk
Fig.81 (p.127)

Trickett & Webb
London
Telephone: +44 171 388 5832
Fax: 44 171 387 4287
Figs.17 (p.118), 23 (p.119)

Turner Duckworth
London
Telephone: +44 181 994 7190
Fax: +44 181 994 7192
Figs.9 (p.116), 55 (p.123), 57 (p.124)

WPA Pinfold
Leeds
Telephone: +44 113 244 8549
Fax: +44 113 244 8580
e-mail: design@wpa-pinfold.co.uk
Figs.61 (p.124), 73 (p.126)

YUGOSLAVIA

I & F McCann-Erickson Belgrade
Belgrade
Telehone: + 381 11 328 3255
Fax: +381 11 328 3257
e-mail: mccann@EUnet.yu
Fig.6 (p.131)

S Team Saatchi & Saatchi
Belgrade
Telephone: +381 11 322 9992
Fax: +381 11 620 560
e-mail: product@EUnet.yu
Figs.1-5, 7-9 (p.131)